T0256111

Blockchain for Business

Scrivener Publishing
100 Cummings Center, Suite 541J
Beverly, MA 01915-6106

Publishers at Scrivener
Martin Scrivener (martin@scrivenerpublishing.com)
Phillip Carmical (pcarmical@scrivenerpublishing.com)

Blockchain for Business

How It Works and Creates Value

Edited by
**S.S. Tyagi and
Shaveta Bhatia**

Scrivener
Publishing

WILEY

This edition first published 2021 by John Wiley & Sons, Inc., 111 River Street, Hoboken, NJ 07030, USA
and Scrivener Publishing LLC, 100 Cummings Center, Suite 541J, Beverly, MA 01915, USA
© 2021 Scrivener Publishing LLC
For more information about Scrivener publications please visit www.scrivenerpublishing.com.

Wiley Global Headquarters

111 River Street, Hoboken, NJ 07030, USA

For details of our global editorial offices, customer services, and more information about Wiley products visit us at www.wiley.com.

Limit of Liability/Disclaimer of Warranty

Library of Congress Cataloging-in-Publication Data

ISBN 978-1-119-71104-9

Cover image: Pixabay.Com
Cover design by: Russell Richardson

Set in size of 11pt and Minion Pro by Manila Typesetting Company, Makati, Philippines

Printed in the USA

10 9 8 7 6 5 4 3 2 1

Contents

7 Blockchain-Based Identity Management   141
Abhishek Bhattacharya

8 Blockchain & IoT: A Paradigm Shift for Supply Chain Management   159
Abhishek Bhattacharya

12 Deficiencies in Blockchain Technology and Potential Augmentation in Cyber Security

Eshan Bajal, Madhulika Bhatia, Lata Nautiyal
and Madhurima Hooda

Preface

The motivation behind this book was the desire to impart succinct knowledge in the field of blockchain technology—a technology that has been singled out as a pillar of the Fourth Industrial Revolution by World Bank. However, it was written not only to fulfill the desire of the editors and contributing authors but also to address the desire for such a book expressed by all the technical students, researchers, academicians, and professionals who we interact with on a daily basis. We understood the need for this book after observing numerous sessions and independent lectures on the subject of blockchain technology. It was evident that blockchain technology is currently one of the most important futuristic technologies, and that researchers and professionals all across the world are beginning to show tremendous interest in learning about this piece of technology.

The world essentially became aware of blockchain technology way back in 2008 with its first ever massive-scale implementation in the form of a digital currency called Bitcoin, introduced in Satoshi Nakamoto's whitepaper. However, a lesser known fact is that the first occurrence of blockchain technology and its associated concepts was observed in papers published from 1991 to 1997 titled "How to Time-Stamp a Digital Document," "Improving the Efficiency and Reliability of Digital Time-Stamping," and "Secure Names for Bit-Strings" authored by W. Scott Stornetta *et al.*—also known as the founding fathers of blockchain technology—the mention of which can be found in the "references" of Satoshi Nakamoto's bitcoin whitepaper.

When LinkedIn ranked blockchain technology as the number-one "hard skill" for 2020, we could sense the sudden influx of further interest in the technology, which cemented the idea of this book in our minds. This book has taken the shape of a reference as well as a textbook that can help academics, researchers, professionals, and experts alike. The approach followed in the book is that of a reference manual, starting with certain very important blockchain technology-related topics, including an introduction to the technology, a discussion of the ecosystem that people have started building around it and other topics (i.e., Ethereum, Wallets, Governance, Bitcoin), its challenges, and many more.

Furthermore, this book takes a deep dive into the inclusion of additional technologies, such as the Internet of Things, to discuss the changes rendered in the areas of supply chain management, identity management, etc. Blockchain applications are focused on in order to provide viable references to the readers and help them imagine real-world implementations across other sectors.

Another benefit of the book is the inclusion of business use cases that give a new dimension to the knowledge imparted. Practical concepts are discussed beyond the expected theory, which should help the readers obtain an added advantage as they go through the chapters discussed below.

In Chapter 1, "Introduction to Blockchain," after blockchain is defined, its importance is discussed in the current scenario. Here the author explains the concepts of de-anonymization, identity privacy preservation, and the future of blockchain regulation with business model challenges.

In Chapter 2, "The Scope of Blockchain Ecosystem," the delineation of the foundation of the blockchain ecosystem in businesses is dealt with, explaining how blockchain acts as a game changer and drilling down to a level of detail about the effect that energy production from business ecosystem has on the planet.

In Chapter 3, "Business Use Cases of Blockchain Technology," a detailed discussion is presented of bitcoin as a cryptocurrency that uses blockchain as its transactions medium. The author also discusses the double-spending problem, bitcoin mining, bitcoin ICO, and ICO token.

In Chapter 4, "Ethereum," the aim is to bring together the concepts of Ethereum and smart contractors along with the creation of virtual machine in easy steps. The chapter also explains Ethereum installation, its workings, the concept of Ethereum gas, ways to buy ETH, and the workings of Smart contracts and DApps along with their decentralized application areas.

In Chapter 5, "E-Wallet," an overview of wallet technology is presented, and the steps for creating and navigating an HD wallet are explained.

In Chapter 6, "Blockchain and Governance: Theory, Applications, and Challenges," the advantages reaped by using blockchain infrastructure are highlighted along with ventures wherein blockchains have been utilized to bring about improvements from the current centralized implementations, and finally the challenges that need to be addressed before moving to a decentralized model of governance.

In Chapter 7, "Blockchain-Based Identity Management," the instant verification of identities is discussed, which is very important for today's systems and processes to be functional. Blockchain-based identity mechanisms are presented that can help with identity verifications without the involvement of intermediaries.

In Chapter 8, "Blockchain and IoT: A Paradigm Shift for Supply Chain Management," blockchain- and IoT-based supply chain practices are delved into that can enable instant tracking even up to the level of a consumer. It provides a view of how blockchain can be useful in devising and facilitating a framework for path tracing and quality management in supply chains.

In Chapter 9, "Blockchain-Enabled Supply Chain Management," the application of blockchain and digital currencies for better outcomes in a supply chain is discussed. This chapter also focuses on the applicability of blockchains along with how smart contracts and ledgers can help in managing the overpriced gaps starting from procure-to-play.

In Chapter 10, "Security Concerns of Blockchain," the author discusses the security threats posed by blockchain, the different types of security attacks, and their prevention when developing advanced blockchain systems.

In Chapter 11, "Acceptance and Adoption of Blockchain Technology: An Examination of the Security and Privacy Challenges," the prevalent security and privacy challenges associated with blockchain are explored along with the negative implications of these challenges. The author also details certain blockchain applications that reflect the acceptance and adoption of blockchain technology.

In Chapter 12, "Deficiencies in Blockchain Technology and Potential Augmentation in Cyber Security," the major security concerns related to blockchain are discussed as well as issues and facts that reveal that blockchain invites new challenges or edging off risk of security. The author also discusses privacy as well as decentralization challenges related to blockchain technology.

In Chapter 13, "Internet of Things and Blockchain," the historical background of the IoT is discussed along with the IoT gadgets currently being used and those being proposed for the future, different kinds of sensors and actuators, and a mix of blockchain and IoT.

In Chapter 14, "Blockchain Applications," the author discusses the specific qualities every particular application possesses such as blockchain in big data predictive task automation along with digital identity verification, decentralized government services, and global public health.

In Chapter 15, "Advanced Concepts of Blockchain," the future applications of blockchain technology are discussed. The author also discusses community supercomputing, blockchain geonomics, blockchain learning, community coin, monetary and nonmonetary currencies, some prominent alternate coins, and demurrage currencies in detail.

In conclusion, we would like to thank all the authors for their contributions to this book.

The Editors
December 2020

Introduction to Blockchain

Akshay Mudgal

GD Goenka University, Sohna, Gurugram, India

Abstract

Since its origin, the blockchain innovation has demonstrated promising application possibilities. From the initial crypto-currency to the current shrewd agreement, blockchain has been applied to numerous fields. In spite of the fact that there are a few investigations on the security and protection issues of blockchain, there comes up short on an efficient assessment on the security of blockchain system. Blockchain, as a decentralized and distributed open record technology in distributed system, has gotten significant consideration recently. It applies a connected square structure to check and store information, and applies the believed agreement instrument to synchronize changes in information, which makes it conceivable to make a sealed advanced stage for putting and sharing information. It is accepted that blockchain can be applied to differing Internet intelligent frameworks (e.g., Internet of Things, flexibly chain frameworks, human identity management and so on). In any case, there are some security challenges that may obstruct the wide utilization of blockchain. For all such in this chapter the broader aspects of privacy issues, decentralisation and regulatory challenges will be parleyed, whereas business models in association with blockchain will also be taken care off with a keen focus on security and privacy aspects of the blockchain.

Keywords: Blockchain, security, privacy, de-centralized, crypto-currency, data theft

1.1 Introduction

Since the presentation of Bitcoin in 2009, its fundamental strategy, blockchain, has indicated promising application prospects and pulled in heaps of considerations from the scholarly community and industry [4]. Being

---

Email: toakshaymudgal@gmail.com

S.S. Tyagi and Shaveta Bhatia (eds.) *Blockchain for Business: How it Works and Creates Value*, (1–28) © 2021 Scrivener Publishing LLC

the first digital money, Bitcoin was appraised as the top performing cash in 2015 and the best performing product in 2016, also, has more than 300K affirmed exchanges day by day in May, 2017. Simultaneously, the blockchain system has been applied to numerous fields, including medication, financial matters, Web of things, programming designing, etc. [4]. The presentation of Turing-complete programming dialects to empower clients to create brilliant agreements running on the blockchain marks the beginning of blockchain 2.0 time. With the decentralized accord component of blockchain, keen agreements permit commonly doubted clients to finish information trade or exchange without the need of any outsider confided in power [4]. Ethereum is presently (May of 2017) the most broadly utilized blockchain supporting keen agreements, where there are now 317,506 savvy contracts and in excess of 75,000 exchanges happened day by day [4].

Security comes on the top priority or the at most concern for any piece of action that is needed to be done or auctioned, hence the blockchain comes in a role play (Figure 1.1). Blockchain was basically developed by a group of researchers in the year 1991 to impart or emboss a time stamp on the digital documents but that didn't work well and the experiment was the failure, due to which today's psychedelic technology was garbaged [2]. In the year 2004 a computer scientist named Hal Finuey again reintroduced the blockchain with an alteration which was RPOW (Reusable Proof of Work).

A blockchain is a collection of four major components which collectively forms a block [2]. A blockchain is a decentralized, distributed, public

Figure 1.1 Demonstrating the pictorial impression of blockchain [2].

ledger. It (blockchain) is a place to keep the record (transactional) which is decentralized as it can be created anywhere, whereas it is accessible anywhere, hence it is distributed, but what about the security aspect? as it can be accessed and created by anywhere and by anyone, which means there is a need to make the concept more feasible and secure.

When it is about privacy and security of any element/product/or a system, then it should have the basic working and the architectural knowledge of it. So, that the level of the security which are already existing can be updated or replaced for the better future [2].

In reference to the second chapter of this book, it explains to us about the working of the Blockchain. In this section of this chapter the basic architecture of the blockchain will be discussed, but moving ahead towards the architecture one should discuss few of the important terms which will be majorly used in the security and privacy aspects of the blockchain.

1. Immutable—Making the ledge secures with the digital signature or hash function.
2. POW—Proof of work, which is a protocol which has the main goal to deterring the cyber attacks.
3. Hash—It is unique value being assigned by the set of rules/algorithms/functions or the combination of all to make the ledger unique and separated from other blocks.
4. Digital Signature—It is another means of securing measure of the ledge, so that the data must be verified and treated as authentic.
5. Mining—Mining in general an activity to collect the useful out of whole.

These are the major terms which we may encounter in this chapter commonly. You will get to know more about these terms in the coming sections of this chapter, but before that the different types of blockchain architectures will be discussed below.

Logically, a blockchain is a chain of blocks which contain specific information (database), but in a secure and genuine way that is grouped together in a network (peer-to-peer) as shown in Figure 1.2. In other words, blockchain is a combination of computers linked to each other instead of a central server, meaning that the whole network is decentralized (Figure 1.3) [3].

Understanding it with the help of a relevant example like work on the Google docs and wait for others to make the necessary changes if required the same scenario is in the decentralized architecture of the blockchain.

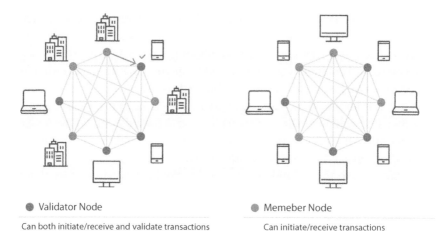

Validator Node
Can both initiate/receive and validate transactions

Memeber Node
Can initiate/receive transactions

Figure 1.2 The diagrammatic representation of the types of blockchain architecture [3].

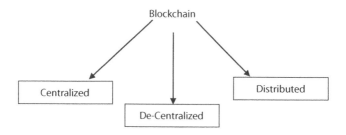

Figure 1.3 Figure states the types of blockchains in trend.

Blockchain allows and permit us to make the relevant docs shared rather copied [2, 3]. This distributed piece of information (ledger) provides the trust factor and the security of data.

Whereas the exact different case is there in the centralized architecture, the information or ledger which was shared is now kept private and shared with the authentic and with those who have required and necessary authority to access the data, which means now the data/ledger is kept private and not shared globally.

Now what left the distributed architecture, in this type a local copy of the ledger is given to all the parties/entities, so that the major alterations are done by the high officials or the major party whereas the information of the ledger is being distributed within the complete locality.

Table 1.1 will make the concept more clear and transparent to understand.

Table 1.1 A novel comparison among public, consortium, private blockchain.

Property	Public blockchain	Consortium blockchain	Private blockchain
Consensus determination	All miners	Selected set of nodes	Within one organization
Read permission	Public	Public or restricted	Public or restricted
Immutability level	Almost impossible to tamper	Could be tampered	Could be tampered
Efficiency (use of resources)	Low	High	High
Centralization	No	Partial	Yes
Consensus process	Permission less	Needs permission	Needs permission

1.1.1 Public Blockchain Architecture

A public blockchain architecture states that the data or the ledger and access to the system is available to anyone who is willing to participate for instance Bitcoin, Ethereum, and Litecoin blockchain systems are public and can be accessed by anyone globally [2, 3].

1.1.2 Private Blockchain Architecture

An opposite situation to the public blockchain architecture, the private system is highly controlled and managed only by users from a specific organization or institution or the company or authorized users who have an invitation for participation.

1.1.3 Consortium Blockchain Architecture

This blockchain structure can consist of a few organizations [3]. In a consortium, procedures are set up and controlled by the preliminary assigned users. It a system that is 'semi-private' and has a group which controls it, but works across different organizations. In simple terms it can be said as a distributed blockchain architecture.

The following table provides a detailed comparison among these three blockchain systems [3]:

1.2   The Privacy Challenges of Blockchain

In the previous section, the basic introductory part of blockchain is discussed. In this part the requirement of privacy including different tools and techniques are going to be discussed.

As shown in Figure 1.4 in this section, a blockchain is a highly secure mechanism or technology which allows the user to make secure and safe transactions [1, 3]. It is a statement said by many engineers, scientist and researchers but how......?

To know about this said statement in detail, one should back track a blockchain and need to collect the required information about how this technique is too strong and safe for transactions. Here we also need to know if this technology is too tremendous then why was it being garbaged in 1991 and then again re-launched in 2004 [1].

The working paradigm of a blockchain:

Let's have a closer and a deeper look at Figure 1.4 that illustrates what a block is in a blockchain.

Each block in a blockchain consists of:

- certain data
- the hash of the block
- the hash from the previous block (HOPB).

The data stored in each block completely depends on the type of blockchain. For instance, in the Bitcoin blockchain structure, the block maintains data about the receiver, sender, and the amount of coins.

A hash is a unique set of alphanumeric codes which is auto generated by the algorithms and the functions of the blockchain (in general terms it can be treated as the fingerprint, long record consisting of some digits and

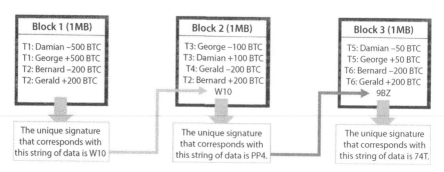

Figure 1.4 The figure states the internal working paradigm of a blockchain.

letters). Each block hash is generated with the help of a cryptographic hash algorithm (SHA 256) [1]. As a result, this helps to identify each and every block in a blockchain structure easily. The moment a block (of blockchain) is created, it automatically gets connected or attaches a hash, while any changes made in a block either in the ledger field or anywhere it straightened affects the change of a hash too which makes the technology precisely highly safe and secure. In simple terms, the hashes help to detect any changes in blocks of a blockchain.

The final element within the block is the hash which is from a previous block (refer to Figure 1.4). This creates a chain of blocks and is the main element behind blockchain architecture's security [4]. As an example, assume a bock range from 1 till 46; block 45 points to block 46. The very first block in a chain is a bit special—all confirmed and validated blocks are derived from the genesis/creator block.

Any corrupt attempt provokes/results the blocks to change [4, 5]. All the assumed block's hashes get changed resulting to the mismatch of hashes which then carry incorrect or invalid information and render the whole blockchain system invalid.

On the other hand, in theory, it could be possible enough to adjust or alter all the blocks with the help of strong computer processors (processors here means highly configured computers). However, there is a solution that eliminates this possibility called proof-of-work [1]. This allows a user to slow down the process of creation of new blocks. In the architecture of Bitcoin blockchain, it majorly takes around 10 min to determine or collects the necessary information of proof-of-work and adds a new block to the chain, but as it was discussed the block can only be added by the person which have the best computational system, here logical ability works rare rather than the system power, hence this work is done by miners—special nodes within the Bitcoin blockchain structure. The miners who win in the race get to keep the transaction fees from the block that they verified as a reward [1, 4].

Each new user (node) joining the peer-to-peer network (a network which have internet connection to share files and folders) of blockchain receives a full copy of the system. Once a new block is created, the detail of it is sent to each node within the blockchain system [4]. Then, each node verifies the information of the block and checks whether the information/data stated there in the block is correct. If everything is alright, the block is added to the local blockchain in each node.

All the nodes inside blockchain architecture create a consensus protocol. A consensus system is a set of network rules, and if everyone abides by them, they become self-enforced inside the blockchain.

To manage and protect the term privacy under blockchain technology, one must satisfy the subsequent requirements:

1. The links between the transactions must not be visible or discoverable.
2. The data of the transactions is merely and only known to their members.

The private or open blockchain must have an entrance control strategy or approval plan to fulfil the security prerequisites of blockchain, which fulfils the total straightforwardness of the blockchain information. Be that as it may, if the case is of an open setting, everybody can have an access to the blockchain with no limitations, the protection issues must be handled on the following factors:

1. Identity Privacy: Which alludes the intractability and unmanageability in the middle of the transaction contents and thus the original identities of their partakers stay sheltered, safe and secure about.
2. Transaction Privacy: In the following the transactional contents (e.g., amount or transacting patterns) can only be accessed and captured by the specified user(s), and kept secret, unknown and safe to the common or general public blockchain network [1, 4].

As it is referenced over, a transaction or a block of a blockchain contains the identity of the previous transaction, the addresses of its members or participants, values (trade), timestamp and unique mark of its sender. Due to its natural behavior or characteristic, it is possible to trace back and follow the flow of transactions to extract and collect the users' physical identities or other common and additional private information through the tools techniques and also of data mining. In this section, it is referred towards the Bitcoin system as a typical instance to analyze the privacy threats for the blockchain network.

1.3   De-Anonymization

Users majorly/always create an alias when they hook up with the Bitcoin system. However, thanks to the general public and openness of blockchain, it's possible to run a static analysis of the blockchain which allow us to track and unhide the masked users, that's what de-anonymization is. Here, we have list out many attacks which will work under to de-anonymize the users' real identities.

1.3.1 Analysis of Network

The blockchain majorly performs its work on the P2P network, which suggests that a node will share public its IP address when broadcasting the transactions. Researchers and scientist have identified three abnormal relay patterns for analyzing the network which could be mapped to Bitcoin addresses to IP addresses (i.e., multi-relayer & non-rerelayed transaction, single-relayer transactions and multi-relayer & rerelayed transactions).

1.3.2 Transaction Fingerprinting

Another major issue or threat that can cause problem to the data of transaction and for which the anonymity becomes problem is a transaction's user-related features. Androulaki *et al.* have explained six characteristics that may portray a few highlights of transaction conduct, i.e., Random time-interval (RTI), hour of day (HOD), time of hour (TOH), time of day (TOD), coin flow (CF) and input and output balance (IOB). Abundance consideration on these characteristics may expand the odds to de-anonymize an individual client [1].

1.3.3 DoS Attacks

A denial-of-service assault might be a cyber assault and the most known and basic issue, where the noxious assailant attempts to look for or hack a machine or system asset being inaccessible to its customers by disturbing or ending web/network services of the host associated with the web or neighborhood server. The most well-known way or method to deal and handle with, be covered up by IP addresses or to hide the IP in P2P network is utilizing anonymity network systems (e.g., TOR).

1.3.4 Sybil Attacks

A Sybil attack is another digital attack where the pernicious attacker and programmers destabilize the stature or notoriety system of a P2P network by making an outsized number of nom de plume or phony characters, utilizing them to understand a disadvantageous impact. Concerning the de-anonymization inside the blockchain, Bissias *et al.* broke down and judge that Sybil attacks could stop and break the decentralized anonymity protocol and can expand the likelihood to search out the clients' genuine identities.

1.4   Transaction Pattern Exposure

Except some personal information, majorly all transactional information goes to the public network which can be used to get the statistical distribution, which may help to get some guidelines and regulations for the blockchain applications.

1.4.1   Transaction Graph Analysis

Under this the major focus is on discovering and analyzing some overall transaction features (e.g., daily turnover, exchange rate or transaction pattern) over time.

1.4.2   AS-Level Deployment Analysis

This technique aims to get the bitcoin network by recursively connecting to clients, requesting and collecting their lists of other connected or peer IP addresses. In this flow, one can obtain concrete and correct information and data on size, structure and distribution of the bitcoin's core network.

1.5   Methodology: Identity Privacy Preservation

This part of the chapter presents a summarized overview of solutions that have been recently proposed by researchers aimed at maintaining and preserving privacy of the blockchain [1]. In a public blockchain, for example, in the digital currency or crypto currency Decreed, it is adviced and proposed that the clients' address should have been adjusted and altered by creating another key pair for every session. Except that, there are three frequently-used systems and methods for safety and security and protecting anonymity in the blockchain and they summarized by: mixing services, ring signature, and non-interactive zero-knowledge proof.

1.5.1   Mixing Services

As per the structure discussed in previous few sections the blockchains are linked with each other like sender or receiver of a transaction, therefore, by calculating and analyzing the public content (i.e., analytical attack), an

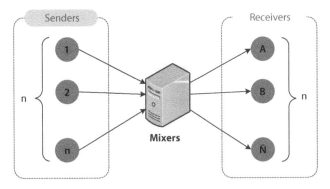

Figure 1.5 Basic architecture of mixing services [1].

individual can deduce some secret or privacy information or data to eliminate such attacks. One of the solutions is to confuse or blur the transaction's relationships with the help of *mixer* (aka *tumbler* or *laundry*) as shown in Figure 1.5. The first mixing service introduced by Chaum [1], allows the user to hide his content of communication as well as the participants of the communication. The same concept is shown below in pictorial manner.

Assume that one element prepares a message M for delivery to another substance at address R by encrypting it with the receiver's open key KR, appending and attaching the address R, and afterward encrypting the result with the intermediary's open key KI. The left-hand of the accompanying expression means the cipher content, which is transferred to an intermediary:

$$KI (r0, KR (r1, M), R) \rightarrow KR (r1, M), R [1].$$

The symbol indicates the transformation of the cipher message by the intermediary into another cipher content appeared on the right-hand side. These transformations perform a decryption on the original cipher message by the intermediary with its private key. At that point the intermediary delivers the sub-cipher content to R who at that point decrypts it with his/her own private key. It is important to take note that r1 and r0 are random numbers which ensure that no message is transferred more than once [1].

At the point when the intermediary gets much information on input and output, this mechanism will shroud the correspondences between each message's origin and destination. The order of arrival is covered up by yielding the uniformly estimated items in random patterns. Moreover, to minimize the danger of the single intermediary being the attacker, multiple intermediaries can be connected together thereby creating a mix cascade [1, 2].

Over the most recent couple of years, the services have been applied to the blockchain network to obfuscate the transaction history and reduce the risk of de-anonymization. These research efforts center around two main methods: (I) centralized mixing and (ii) decentralized mixing.

a. Centralized mixing is to mix transactions anonymously at the cost of some service fees. There are plenty of websites which work or behave like online mixers and swap the transactions among different users so as to shroud the relationship between their incoming and active transactions [1]. Likewise, most of them are reachable or contactable just through the TOR network which empowers anonymous communications through a free, worldwide, volunteer overlay network.

b. Decentralized mixing Decentralized mixing is to moderate the denial of services (DOS) danger caused or raised by the centralized services; a decentralized mixing design is proposed to empower a lot of commonly entrusted companions to distribute their messages at the same time and anonymously without the need of an outsider anonymity proxy [1, 4]. Another significant advantage of this methodology is the end of the requirement for mixing expenses. Moreover, it is nearer and progressively perfect to the decentralized structure of blockchain contrasted with the incorporated mixing design. Up until this point, there are for the most part two strategies to accomplish the decentralized mixing process, i.e., Coin Join and multi-party calculation (MPC).

1.5.2   Ring Signature

Although the decentralized mixing techniques gives an "excellent" mixing in the blockchain, but they still need a delay till the time participants discover or find their partners for their transactions to be mixed. The ring signature enables a user (also a member of a set) to sign a message on behalf of the "ring" of members but there is no way to say that which one is real and who have signed. The core idea and methodology of this technology is the choice of a set without any central manager, which will significantly improve privacy in blockchain [1].

Brief of mixing services in blockchain [1].

Protocol	Anonymity	Centralized Party	Mix Cost	Sybil Strength	Dos Strength	Mixing Scale	Theft Strength	Waiting Time
Mixing website	Linkable at mixer	Required	Yes	Good	Poor	L/A	High	Long
CoinSwap	Linkable at mixer	Required	Yes	Good	Poor	N/A	Safe	Long
Mixcoin	Linkable at mixer	Required	Yes	Good	Poor	N/A	Accountable	Long
Blindcoin	Unlinkable	Required	Yes	Good	Poor	N/A	Accountable	Long
Blindly Signed Contracts	Unlinkable	Required	Yes	Good	Poor	N/A	Safe	Long
TumbleBit	Unlinkable	Required	Yes	Good	Good	L/T	Safe	Long
Dash	Unlinkable	Required Many	Yes	Good	Good	Less	P/D	Normal
CoinJoin	Internal Unlinkable	Decentralized	No	Poor	Poor	Less	High	Long
CoinShuffle	Unlinkable	Decentralized	No	Good	Moderate	Less	High	Long
XIM	Unlinkable	Decentralized	No	Moderate with fees	Moderate with fees	Large	Low	Long

Abbreviations:
L/A—Limited to access
N/A—No Limitation
L/T—Limited by transaction
P/D—Prevented with deposit

1.6   Decentralization Challenges Exist in Blockchain

The very basic definition of Blockchain states and implies that, in relation to Figure 1.6, it is a decentralized ledger that can store information quite securely and immutably, utilizing cryptographic encryption and hashing techniques. But it seems in reality, that the word 'decentralized' is somehow stuck only to the definition [5]. A number of Blockchains out there in the market make use of centralized mechanisms.

But what exactly does this word "decentralization" means? Does it only refer to data being processed "not at the same place (distributed)?"

As explained by Vitalik Buterin in his blog, the decentralization can be categorized or viewed into three perspectives—first is "Architectural". This states the number of physical computers attached or is in the network? Second comes "Political"—How many entities control these computers? And the last "Logical"—that derives that does the data structure and interfaces of the computers or systems act like a single structure or a swarm [5]?

No one controls Blockchains and they don't have the infrastructural central or head point of failure. Hence, they are politically and architecturally decentralized. However, they are or can be said logically centralized since they act and behave like a single entity/computer.

But even if the above definition is correct and acceptable, then are blockchains as they are today decentralized?

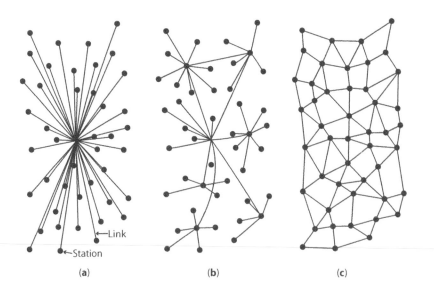

Figure 1.6 Different types of Networks in blockchain [5]. (a) Centralized. (b) Decentralized. (c) Distributed networks.

The answer majorly comes is NO, because of these possible reasons:

Having four computers instead of having one is always better. But what if all the computers get infected with same issue or defect?

All the nodes in a Blockchain run the same client software, and if they get some issues or turns out to be buggy, reason may be any or then the whole system can come to a pause/standstill. This can put a question mark on the architectural decentralization of the Blockchains [5, 6].

In a Blockchain which uses the proof-of-work consensus mechanism and majority of the miners are from the same country, the government of that country can choose or decide to seize and control or stop all the mining farms on the account of national security [7]. This scenario or case is a major threat to the political decentralization of Blockchain.

Similarly, in a proof of stake Blockchain, if more than 70% of the coins at stake are held at one exchange, can put the political decentralization of the Blockchain at risk.

Moreover, if the majority of mining hardware (infrastructure) is built by the same company, it can also compromise the political decentralization of the Blockchain [8].

So, that means centralized Blockchains are not that good or of no use?

Not majorly, and this is because Blockchains serve various purposes, and these may require them to be centralized.

According to the report of Crytpo asset Taxonomy, about 16% of crypto currencies are said to be fully decentralized. The other crypto currencies reviewed are either centralized, or only semi-decentralized. Only 9% of all utility tokens were found to be sufficiently decentralized and only 7% of financial assets such as those born from initial coin offerings are decentralized [9, 10]. Crypto currencies such as Bitcoin, Stellar, Litecoin that work primarily as a payment method are among the most decentralized types of crypto assets, as per the report.

While the original crypto currency—Bitcoin, was designed and developed to be decentralized and removing the control of governments or any central organization, some experts claim and suggest that even Bitcoin can't be termed as fully decentralized since a majority of the Bitcoin miners are from China.

1.7   Conclusion

Decentralization is a process that is beyond and above the computers and networks. It involves organizations and individuals in plural. Partial decentralization can be achieved at present [8]. However, the complete decentralization is very difficult to accomplish and it would take time for the Blockchains to become truly decentralized, if they intend to do so. It will not only involve Blockchain Technology but also artificial intelligence algorithms that would replace humans to eliminate biases.

1.8   Regulatory Challenges

A blockchain is a type of distributed ledger technology can be termed as DLT, consisting of a decentralised network of fixed or unchangeable databases, shared equally across the system. In the very beginning age of development of blockchain technology, blockchain has shown great potential in different areas from crypto currencies to smart contracts and so on [10, 11].

During the opening of the European Blockchain Partnership, Mariya Gabriel, EU Commissioner for Digital Economy and Society, clearly and boldly mentioned that "in the future, all public services will use blockchain technology". As this tending technology continues to develop and attract keen attention and consciousness, regulation of blockchain is becoming an important and needful discussion.

In the fourth section of our Blockchain series, the regulatory measures and challenges associated with blockchain management are going to be discussed.

1.9   Obstacles to Blockchain Regulation

Being a decentralized system of network, blockchains are treated as the most strenuous technology and that's the considerable reason to manacle it into strict regulations. Due to the innovative and dispensed nature, blockchains create numerous problems for regulators [12]. As it is already defined and know that Blockchains are distributed and decentralized. As a result, the nodes or sub systems within a network can be placed all around the world, without a definite 'home-base', making the question of legal jurisdiction complex.

The structure of blockchains creates issues concerning liability and accountability as un-authorized public blockchains have no form of a central authority or decision-maker that can be held responsible for the actions carried out within the network [12].

Apart from this, within a blockchain, data is shared across every node or participants of the network, each maintaining a full replica of the database. This case makes the situation more difficult as the real owner of the blockchain couldn't be determined or is quite difficult to be judge it for the already created blockchain [12–14]. This scenario presents a challenge where intellectual property is concerned, making it strenuous to determine the author or owner of the data.

Privacy is another great challenge for regulators of blockchain. Transactions are linked completely and solely to a network account address rather than a personal identification (PI number), apparently ensuring privacy. However, if a connection between the two node are made and on the same side it revealed, the protection of an individual(s) privacy is no longer exists [16].

1.10   The Current Regulatory Landscape

Blockchain regulation, like the technology itself, remains very much in its starting phase. Initiatives above the national level, such as the EU's Blockchain Observatory and Forum, the European Blockchain Partnership and the Mediterranean Seven, focus on supporting its use and development, largely avoiding regulatory issues. This is because of a lack of consensus and harmony on blockchain and its applications; while some nations have treated it with suspicious eye, including China, although other countries such as Malta and Estonia have passionately and embraced it. This has made a regulatory landscape which differs from nation to nation [17].

Italian and Swiss agencies are among those that have chosen it to observe and check, for the time being, rather than embarking on the time-consuming process of developing and managing new legislation and policies that may soon be outdated given the early stages of blockchain technology development. "Switzerland doesn't need new special regulations for blockchain", asserted Ueli Maurer, the country's Finance Minister [18]. The agencies of government have started opting to update and apply some new chances in their existing rules and laws to account for this novel technology.

Other nations have taken the some different kind of approach and have chosen to adopt and absorb some new national legislation, solely addressing and pointing sole aspects or specific applications of blockchain [17, 18]. Keen attention has been drawn up to the application of blockchain in the sector of finance and crypto tools and assets like Bitcoin. Countries such as Poland, France and Luxembourg have chosen to absorb some specific guidelines tailored to these issues.

Meanwhile, a few countries such as Liechtenstein have taken a more advanced and progressive and forward approach as the government has approved The 'Blockchain Act', which marks a milestone not just for Liechtenstein but for the international community which look at block-chain as a malicious and untrustworthy technology [19]. It provides the first holistic regulatory framework to govern the underlying concepts of blockchain.

1.11   The Future of Blockchain Regulation

Moving forward, regulators and policy makers will need to strike a fine balance when drafting blockchain legislation; overregulation will restrain development and also creates legal instability and uncertainty, which ulti-mately harms and affects the ultimate progress [19].

Blockchain must be regulated in such a way that accounts and support for the associated risks it produces while simultaneously encourages devel-opment of the technology. As such, legislation cannot simply consider cur-rent technologies but must seek and understand to be applicable to the generations of technology to follow.

Furthermore, while crypto and money explicit guideline is without a doubt fundamental, controllers should likewise embrace comprehensive structures equipped for directing the huge number of blockchain inno-vation applications, both now and to return. Non-money related appli-cations are probably going to accomplish more footing and impact over the moving toward years, in this way requiring more noteworthy core interest.

Gauges will assume a vital job inside the route forward for block-chain, controlling its improvement and moving take-up by guaranteeing that the innovation supposedly is secure and solid [19, 20]. This pat-tern is starting to show up the same number of standard-setting bodies are connecting with the issues identified with blockchain and DLT. The International Telecommunication Union (ITU) has made a spotlight Group on Application of Distributed Ledger Technology devoted to the occasion of DLT principles [21]. The Institute of Electrical and Electronics Engineers (IEEE) has built up a Blockchain Initiative to work together with its Standards Association on blockchain institutionalization endeavours. The alliance for Standards (ISO) includes a devoted Blockchain and DLTs Technical Committee as of now performing on a progression of block-chain and DLT rules, covering everything from wording to security to keen agreements, on account of be discharged in 2021 [22].

While organizations and organizations working with blockchain pres-ently work in a moderately guideline free space, this can probably adjust inside the not so distant future. It's significant that they follow of improvements and effectively look for cooperation inside the administrative procedure, to shape strategy results and guarantee an administrative structure that keeps on supporting development.

1.12   Business Model Challenges

Since the time Satoshi Nakamoto discharged the Bitcoin whitepaper and acquainted everybody with the blockchain innovation, the blockchain innovation appears to have increased its very own existence and has gotten a subject of enthusiasm over a wide assortment of organizations. A few organizations have begun working with another plan of action that is based around the blockchain. Right now, they are discussing fruitful usage of blockchain plans of action.

1.12.1   Traditional Business Models

A plan of action is an extravagant term used to clarify the arrangement/procedure that the organization needs to create benefit by selling an item or administration. The plan of action gives a diagram of the plans of the organization to create an item or administration and to showcase it. Various organizations will utilize a plan of action which best suits their necessities. There are four conventional plans of action:

- Manufacturer
- Distributor
- Retailer
- Franchise.

1.12.2   Manufacturer

This plan of action rotates around the formation of the item. The item could either be made without any preparation from normal assets or the maker can collect pre-assembled segments to make another item, for example, vehicles. An assembling business can follow two sub-models. It could either be "business-to-shopper" where they can sell their items straightforwardly to the buyers. Another choice includes re-appropriating the business part of the procedure to another organization, which is known as the business-to-business or B2B model. Right now, makers offer their item to the retailers who deal with the deals.

1.12.3   Distributor

The Distributor plan of action purchases the item from the maker and afterward they either offer it to the end clients or a retailer. In a common inventory network, makers are the purpose of root while wholesalers are the go betweens who associate the producers to their end-clients or the retail location.

1.12.4   Retailer

Retailers are physical shops or web based business sites which collect items from maker either straight forwardly or by means of a wholesaler. Retailers may be across the nation chains, or they could be free shops worked by a solitary substance. Retailers make it amazingly simple and clear for clients to purchase whatever items they need.

1.12.5   Franchise

An establishment plan of action may include any of the previously mentioned plans of action, i.e., producing, circulating, or retailing. Anybody can buy an establishment which can have the two focal points and disservices. The primary bit of leeway is that an establishment as of now has all the business procedures and conventions coordinated inside it. On the other side, the principle impediment is the absence of adaptability. This should give you a thought of the conventional plans of action that have existed up until now. Be that as it may, since the time the approach of blockchain innovation, it has seen a large group of new plans of action. Thus, before going further, let us comprehend what blockchain models are.

1.13   Utility Token Model

What is the meaning of Utility? Utility methods are the absolute fulfilment that is gotten by the utilization of the products or administrations. The utility token model drives the usefulness in their business by means of the utilization of the tokens. Wave and Stellar are incredible instances of these sorts of models. The banks that are a piece of their system can encourage support movement through the utilization of the XRP or XLM tokens. According to William Mougayar, token utility has three significant properties (Figure 1.7):

- Role
- Features
- Purpose

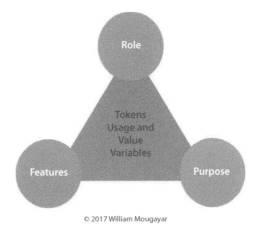

© 2017 William Mougayar

Figure 1.7 Demonstrating the properties of the model [23].

1.13.1 Right

By claiming a specific token, the holder gets a specific measure of rights inside the biological system e.g. by having DAO coins in your ownership, you could have casting a ballot rights inside the DAO to choose which activities get subsidizing and which don't.

1.13.2 Value Exchange

The tokens make an inward monetary framework inside the limits of the venture itself. The tokens can support the purchasers and merchants exchange incentive inside the biological system. This permits clients to pick up endless supply of specific assignments. This creation and upkeep of individual, interior economies is one of the most basic elements of tokens.

1.13.3 Toll

It can likewise go about as a cost passage for you to utilize explicit functionalities of a specific framework e.g. In Golem, you have to have GNT (golem tokens) to access the advantages of the Golem supercomputer.

1.13.4 Function

The token can likewise empower the holders to advance the client experience inside the bounds of the specific condition. e.g. In Brave (an internet browser), holders of BAT (tokens utilized in Brave) will get the rights to advance client experience by utilizing their tokens to include ads or other consideration put together administrations with respect to the Brave stage.

1.13.5   Currency

Can be utilized as a store of significant worth which can be utilized to direct exchanges both inside and outside the given environment.

1.13.6   Earning

Helps in a fair dispersion of benefits or other related monetary advantages among financial specialists in a specific task. Consider staking pools in Cardano.

For this model to viably the work, the local token must take up whatever number jobs as could be allowed. The more properties the token can tick off, the greater utility and worth it will bring into the biological system.

1.14   Blockchain as a Service

The blockchain and the decentralized biological system, when all is said in done, can be unbelievably scary for a newcomer. The Blockchain-as-a-Service (BaaS) model offers assistance where a business' customers can re-appropriate all the alarming backend stuff while focussing just on the frontend. BaaS sellers offer types of assistance like client validation, database the board, remote refreshing, and pop-up messages (for portable applications), distributed storage, and facilitating [23, 24].

Assume you have an online business and have made a splendid site which will undoubtedly get a ton of hits. On the off chance that you decide to have it from your PC or server, at that point you will either need to do all the support work yourself (which can be tedious) or contract a staff to take of it for you (which can be costly).

Rather than taking such a lot of pressure, you can just acquire the administrations of an outer web facilitating supplier like Amazon Web Services or HostGator. In return for an expense, they will deal with all the foundation and upkeep issues [23, 25].

BaaS works like the subsequent choice and permits you to concentrate on your center site usefulness. Their administration incorporates bolster exercises like data transmission the board, appropriate designation of assets, facilitating prerequisites, and security highlights like the anticipation of hacking endeavors.

It won't be a stretch to consider BaaS an essential impetus that will prompt more extensive and more profound infiltration of blockchain innovation across different industry divisions and organizations. Consider it, a business person, whose business requires blockchain coordination, had just the accompanying choices before BaaS [23]:

Contract blockchain specialists. Who are uncommon and costly?

Train your current staff on blockchain innovation, which is going to take a great deal of time and cash.

You can simply stop. Well that is not so much going to support anybody.

Regardless of whether you some way or another despite everything figures out how to get your blockchain up, you will need to manage all the upkeep. All in all, why not just agent it to the specialists?

Some enormous scope dependable firms have just begun offering their BaaS administrations:

Microsoft has a BaaS module on its Azure stage.

IBM has its own BaaS which is centered on private consortium blockchains.

Amazon offers BaaS administrations.

Prophet offers blockchain cloud facilitating also.

1.15 Securities

This is a plan of action that is a nearly late one. As of late, numerous organizations have taken up the protections or "security token contribution" plan of action. A token is named security when there is a desire for benefit from the exertion of others [25, 26]. On the off chance that the ICO doesn't follow explicit guidelines, at that point they could be dependent upon punishments. Be that as it may, in the event that all the standards are appropriately met, at that point these tokens have tremendously incredible use-cases [23, 25].

Since it has just secured utility tokens previously, how about to investigate the contrasts among utility and security tokens.

Utility Tokens versus Security Tokens

Okay, so how about if the token gets perceived, how these two tokens do straight on?

Security Token = Investment Contract

At its very embodiment, a security token is a venture contract which speaks to legitimate responsibility for physical or computerized resource like land, ETFs, and so forth. This proprietorship must be confirmed inside the blockchain [23].

After the proprietorship is checked, security token holders can:

- Exchange away their tokens for different resources
- Use them as guarantee for a credit
- Store them in various wallets.

Having said that, the genuine incentive in security tokens lies by the way they can totally rethink the significance of "proprietorship." They can democratize resources and disperse them among individuals everywhere throughout the world. To give an unrefined model, rather than owning a gold coin, which might be out of many individuals spending plan, it is currently feasible for 100 individuals to hold divisions of that gold coin [23, 25].

1.16   Development Platforms

The blockchain environment is still in its earliest stages, and the main way it can develop is assuming an ever increasing number of engineers enter the space [23]. A great deal of advancement and research goes into blockchain as new companies are attempting to take care of issues particularly. A greater part of these new businesses are making Dapps (decentralized applications) on improvement stages. Along these lines, this makes one wonder.

For what reason should designers' trouble fiddling with the blockchain innovation?

- Improves security through decentralization and cryptographic capacities.
- Expels unchanging nature by means of cryptographic hash capacities.
- Improves documentation, detect ability, and audit ability.
- Encourages you assemble a proficient and discernible database.
- Builds trust through straightforwardness.

Metcalfe's Law?

Metcalfe's Law is a hypothesis of system impact. As per Wikipedia, "Metcalfe's law expresses the impact of a broadcast communications organize is relative to the square of the quantity of associated clients of the framework (n^2)" [23].

The Systemic Value of Compatibly
Communicating Devices Grows as the
Square of Their Number:

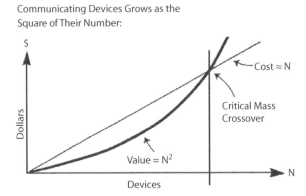

Devices

It was formulated by Bob Metcalfe, the inventor of Ethernet and co-founder of 3Com [23].

1.17   Scandals and Public Perceptions

Without a doubt Blockchain is an inescapable Technology which has tremendous potential. The manner in which it is displaying its utilization cases and fining applications in all the business specialties, it turns into a superb innovation for what's to come. Blockchain got recognizable after Bitcoin appeared. It is the fundamental innovation of Bitcoin at the same time, from 2009 to date, Blockchain has experienced an enormous change, it has become an innovation which has more uses when contrasted with. The designers are attempting to discover use instances of Blockchain innovation with the goal that it can turn into a piece of standard life. It have been heard a ton about Blockchain and its utilization, how it can decidedly impact the world, however at the equivalent, it can't disregard the way that it is at an exceptionally beginning stage and to make it impeccable there is a requirement for some act of spontaneities. In spite of countless supporters supporting this innovation, in despite everything have the disadvantages that should be tended to. There are a few territories of worry on which the designers need to work with the goal that they can make a full-confirmation innovation which can deal with a huge volume of information and simultaneously it likewise guarantees wellbeing and security. Numerous individuals accept that Blockchain is air pockets that will before long empty, however for most, it is a promising innovation.

Right now, will feature what the main 5 difficulties that Blockchain innovation is looking in its way of development are.

1.17.1   Privacy Limitations

Pseudonymity is one of the basic highlights of Blockchain Technology, and when it discusses namelessness, at that point it implies that the exchanges or exchanging is going on from somewhere; however there's no genuine personality joined to the equivalent. It raises the worry, imagine a scenario where there is a fake, and by what means will the system track the individual, whom to get if there should arise an occurrence of extortion or hacking. If there should arise an occurrence of the public Blockchain, the subtleties of brilliant agreements entered by the clients in the Ethereum arrange become open to the public. Under such conditions, uploading information like well-being records, individual data, clinical archives and character confirmation, money related reports become defenceless against programmers assault.

1.17.2   Lack of Regulations and Governance

The basic component of Blockchain Technology is that it lacks guideline. It permits distributed exchange which implies there is no delegate. In addition, there it likewise requires governance from approved bodies. You can't consider anybody liable for keeping up the system standard along these lines making the whole framework unpredictable and distrustful.

1.17.3   Cost to Set Up

The cost to setup-the designers may be lecturing a great deal about Blockchain Technology, yet it can't disregard the way that to set up the whole arrangement of Blockchain Technology is costly particularly on the off chance that you wish to set up the entire activity in-house. Additionally, you may likewise need to purchase particular equipment for utilize this software. Aside from the software and equipment cost discover an individual to take a shot at this framework effectively is one more zone of cost as far as time. Since the innovation is completely new and there are visit changes in the equivalent, the associations need to go through a great deal of cash in preparing, setting up the framework and different zones of cost, accordingly making it a costly issue.

1.17.4   Huge Consumption of Energy

One of the significant zones of concerns while utilizing Blockchain Technology for crypto currency trade is the energy it expends. Regardless of whether it is Bitcoin or Ethereum arrange, to approve the exchanges they follow Proof-Of-Work component which expends a great deal of energy while taking care of complex numerical issues. According to the white-paper distributed in June 2017, the energy customers in Bitcoin system can be utilized by 700 normal American houses. With such an enormous consumption of energy, it gets mandatory to think of an elective accord component that could expend less force.

1.17.5 Public Perception

The greatest disadvantage in the method for the accomplishment of Blockchain is the perception it holds according to individuals. Right off the bat, individuals don't see it be a piece of standard working. Besides, the greater part of the individuals accepts that this innovation won't keep going long. The component like the lack of governance, simple access to turn into an individual from public Blockchain and lack of guideline further falls apart the picture of Blockchain according to individuals. Every one of these factors contributes as difficulties for the development of this Technology.

For Blockchain to rise as a victor and a piece of the standard, it is significant that the engineers need to split the ice and think of a framework which is more secure and make sure about.

References

1. Feng, Q., He, D., Zeadally, S., Khan, M.K., Kumar, N., A survey on privacy protection in blockchain system. *J. Netw. Comput. Appl.*, 126, 45–58, 2018.
2. Ressi, A., Di Iorio, A., What the Future of Blockchain Means for Entrepreneurs available at https://fi.co/insight/what-the-future-of-blockchain-means-for-entrepreneurs-according-to-the-co-founder-of-ethereum/, 2018.
3. MLSDEV, Blockchain Architecture Basics: Components, Structure, Benefits & Creation, [URL] https://mlsdev.com/blog/156-how-to-build-your-own-block-chain-architecture, 2019.
4. Li, X., Jiang, P., Chen, T., Luo, X., Wen, Q., A survey on the security of block-chain systems. *Future Gener. Comput. Syst.*, 107, 841–853, 2017.
5. Buterin, V., Meaning of decentralization, https://medium.com/@VitalikButerin/the-meaning-of-decentralization-a0c92b76a274", 2017.
6. Henry, R., Herzberg, A., Kate, A., Blockchain security and privacy. *IEEE J.*, 16, 11–12, 2018.
7. Ajao, L.A., Agajo, J., Adedokun, E.A., Karngon, L., Crypto Hash Algorithm-Based Blockch ain Technology for Managing Decentralized Ledger Database in Oil and Gas Industry. *Multidiscip. Sci. J.*, 2(3), 300–325, 2019.
8. Swanson, T., deloitte.com, available at https://www2.deloitte.com/content/dam/Deloitte/uk/Documents/Innovation/deloitte-uk-blockchain-key-challenges.pdf, 2018.

9. deloitte.com, Blockchain gets down to business, [URL]https://www2. deloitte.com/content/dam/Deloitte/se/Documents/risk/DI_2019-global-blockchain-survey.pdf, 2019.

10. Salmon, J. and Myers, G., Blockchain and Associated Legal Issues for Emerging Markets. *Int. Finance Coop.*, 2019.

11. Fulmer, N., Exploring the Legal Issues of Blockchain Applications. *Akron Law J.*, Akron University, 52, 161–193, 2019.

12. Yeoh, P., Regulatory Issues in Blockchain Technology. *J. Financial Regul. Compliance*, 25, 196–208, 2017.

13. Maxwell, Coinjoin: Bitcoin privacy for the real world, in Post on Bitcoin Forum, *European Symposium on Research in Computer Security*, Springer, pp. 345–364, 2013.

14. Greenberg, Dark wallet is about to make bitcoin money laundering easier than ever, URL http://www. wired. com/2014/04/darkwallet, 2014.

15. Joinmarket—coinjoin that people will actually use. *Bitcoin Talk*, https://bitcointalk.org/index.php?topic=919116.msg10096563, 126, 45–58, 2015.

16. Ruffing, T., Moreno-Sanchez, P., Kate, A., Coinshuffle: Practical decentralized coin mixing for bitcoin, in: *European Symposium on Research in Computer Security*, 2014.

17. Barber, S., Boyen, X., Shi, E., Uzun, E., Bitter to betterhow to make bitcoin a better currency, in: *International Conference on Financial Cryptography and Data Security*, Springer, pp. 399–414, 2012.

18. Ziegeldorf, J.H., Grossmann, F., Henze, M., Inden, N., Wehrle, K., Coinparty: Secure multi-party mixing of bitcoins, in: *Proceedings of the 5th ACM Conference on Data and Application Security and Privacy*, ACM, pp. 75–86, 2015.

19. Rivest, R., Shamir, A., Tauman, Y., How to leak a secret. *Advances in CryptologyASIACRYPT 2001*, pp. 552–565, 2001.

20. Fujisaki, E. and Suzuki, K., Traceable ring signature, in: *Public Key Cryptography*, pp. 181–200, Springer, https://link.springer.com/chapter/10.1007/978-3-540-71677-8_13, 2007.

21. Bartoletti, M. and Pompianu, L., An empirical analysis of smart contracts: Platforms,applications, and design patterns, in: *1st Workshop on Trusted Smart Contracts*, 2017.

22. BlockGeeks, Smart contracts: The blockchain technology that will replace lawyers, URL https://blockgeeks.com/guides/smart-contracts/, 2016.

23. Hajdarbegovic, N., Bitcoin miners ditch ghash.io pool over fears of 51% attack, URL http://www.coindesk.com/bitcoin-miners-ditch-ghash-iopool-51-attack/, 2014.

24. Mayer, H., Ecdsa security in bitcoin and ethereum: a research survey, URL http://blog.coinfabrik.com/wp- content/uploads/2016/06/ECDSA-Security-in-Bitcoin-and-Ethereum-a-Research-Survey.pdf, 2016.

25. Ekblaw, A., Azaria, A., Halamka, J.D., Lippman, A., A case study for blockchain in healthcare: Medrec prototype for electronic health records and medical research data, URL https://www.media.mit.edu/publications/medrecwhitepaper/, 2016.

26. Sharma, T.K., https://www.blockchain-council.org/blockchain/top-5-challenges-with-pubilc-blockchain/, 2018.

2

The Scope for Blockchain Ecosystem

Manisha Suri

K.L. Mehta Dayanand College for Women, Faridabad, India

Abstract

As the up gradation in modern technologies has not only resulted in an eruption of huge data sets being captured and recorded in various fields, but also turn up to the security of records to avoid forge during depository, transportation, processing, updating and accessing. Transactions can be a commutation of an asset, the execution of the terms of a self-executing script-smart contract, or an updation into anecdote. Vital exposure of blockchain ecosystem and its comprehensive danger are entrenched in its ecosystem – the hub of miners, developers, suppliers, consumers, shareholders or stakeholders, and actors. Latterly blockchain technology is not limited to crypto currency but operating on financial and business applications. Decentralization, non changeable and clarity are the base on which blockchain technology working. This ecosystem is propagating with involvement from both sectors actors-public & private. This chapter deals with delineation of the foundation of the blockchain ecosystem in businesses, starting with the definition then blockchain act as a game changer and drilling down to a level of detail about effect of energy production from business ecosystem on the planet. In order to explicate the components of the blockchain ecosystem, this chapter provides examples of companies currently operating in different areas. However, blockchain companies (Bloq, Factom, Symbiont, Blockstream, PayStand, tZERO, Skuchain.) may function in more than one zone as they do not easily accommodate into one area of ecosystem, develop in capabilities and transition between areas over period of time.

Keywords: App-decentralized application, BCD-blockchain development, Baas-blockchain as a service, KYC—know your customers, actors—users

Email: manishasuri81@gmail.com

S.S. Tyagi and Shaveta Bhatia (eds.) Blockchain for Business: How it Works and Creates Value, (29–58) © 2021 Scrivener Publishing LLC

2.1   Introduction

Blockchain is a type of database that is shared across a network of computers, by allowing the transparency of transaction. Records containing information are added to the database, bundled together into what called as blocks. These blocks are then linked together to form a chain—hence blockchain. When we talk about blockchain ecosystems (a group of organisms interacting with one another within their surroundings), there are the groups of actors (users, miners, developers & researchers, etc.) interacting with each other within the world of blockchain and with the encompassing off-chain world. The core interactions between these actors take place in the form of transactions, but these transactions are almost entirely limited to the blockchain itself. In lay man language to understand blockchain-at present some of the countries already adopted an online ballot voting system which includes a voting registration database, electronic devices and software. For voting, firstly individual has to register himself which includes his identity number, name, phone number and personal information then it is stored in the software. From the cyber security perspective it is easy to disrupt the software by just attacking on the voter's registration database. Each part in the election process whether it is hardware or software is at major risk of hacking. When the software system is manipulated it can lead to the inappropriate election result. Not limited to that, after hacking the database of voters they can easily access their social media accounts. So, the sufferers at the end are the common people. To solve this issue the new technology blockchain can be used to provide security during voting time.

With its transparency, immutability and accountability properties this can be attained up to some exact level. It ensures that digital data must come from the trusted source by using cryptography.

Blockchain's property once data is entered can never be destroyed enables it to store individual's identity records such as biometrics, iris scanning and many more for authentication voters and to record their records in the tabulation format. Blockchain technology is like having public key—visible to anyone, can help each individual voters and election conducting officials in counting number of votes without any malfunctioning in the system and which tends to a fair election outcome. Basically, this new technology has completely eradicated the third party i.e. electronic devices (Hardware), hence does not involve disturbance in the entire system. Moreover it enhances the security level of the entire system by providing copy of data to other nodes existing in the network. If hacker tries to modify the record of one node then it has to manipulate the data on the other nodes too on which same information exists which is quite complicated. Thus blockchain acts as a shield for preventing the system against cyber-attacks. Fraudulency can be minimized as the data has been copied to more than one place.

Like in Crypto currency, its ecosystem is based on Blockchain and has four parts or elements: the users who use crypto currencies to receive and send currency, crypto currency miners who produce the crypto currency, investors who buy crypto currency and the developers who write programs related to this system and network and develop it. No part of this system can continue working each without the other.

An ecosystem comprises entities that collaborate along perpetuity of consumer's needs to deliver greater value and bolster the addressable retail market. An ecosystem is defined by constructing a ring around organizations, individuals, and things that share or complement a set of interests. This circle will be defined by the mindsets of the stakeholders and whether they would want to create efficiencies, curate new markets, and improve collaboration.

The collaborator-stakeholders defined ecosystem as a scope from creating economically broad and sustainable markets aligning with emerging customer preferences and leveraging open source development for complex problems. These interests can include intercommunications within and cross wide organizations, different sectors of the economy, and industries. A blockchain ecosystem is said to be developed if it allows the interconnectedness not only with producers or sellers but also with the consumers. Its aforementioned correlativity permits to build systems that can selectively take profit of the blockchain—in its trustworthiness, clarity, and decentralization. The Blockchain ecosystem is helpful to maintain the environmental sustainability as it is having potential to verify the transparency of the transaction records—data which has to be transferred and the person having the data at present can both be verified by blockchain technology. This can be implemented by the decentralization and digitalization of the conclusion. Blockchain ecosystem also promises to improve the existing governance environmental models which are progressing at steady rate and intermediaries associated with the models taking sweat equities charging high by empowering broader people of stakeholders. Moreover, Blockchain are public—records are visible to everyone but none have permission to delete those records or destroy them. Basically Blockchain are of three types: public-like decentralized organization, private-degree of openness is limited to specific users like in Audit companies, Consortium—refers to an agreement between the organization and actors. In nature, ecosystems tend to arise naturally. To ensure the ecosystems fulfill their purpose, they're often controlled by the creation of applications, integration with external systems, added on by the creator also. There are Self-fulfilling agreements, the smart contracts which can manage the system automatically, by the members of the ecosystem just in case.

2.2   Blockchain as Game Changer for Environment

Transformation in the existing environment ecosystem can be imported by the blockchain technology by adapting decentralized, efficient energy resources and water systems. Data like—how much water used at household level, how much energy required per area, etc. Eradication of the species from earth seems like becoming the trend, as the lessening of biodiversity at its peak. The ocean is becoming more acidic day by day as its plants are consuming greenhouse gases. As predicted by scientists by 2050 we will be having fall of 30–35% water as the water's demand is increasing by 1% every year. Along with that, the Earth's atmosphere circular system and climatic changes, deforestation rates, are also calculated that approx 7.5–8.5 million tons of plastic are present in the sea water which is effecting the food chain.

All these records can be maintained on the blockchain environment system with the help of smart sensors. The data which can't be collected manually if collated contains partial information base on which decision makers of centralized organization and retailers make their conclusions. This inadequacy has been improved by blockchain technology by providing more informed decision making and transforming the centralized into the decentralized one. With the help of blockchain ecosystem we can easily trace and verify the renewable energy resources, P2P transaction, make value as dynamic plus to that balance of the demand side economy. This technology can be used as a base to make people aware of the natural calamities—it prepared the communities in advance for upcoming disasters. Through smart contracts it ensures the transmission of important information among the large range of users at the time of natural mishap. The role of the blockchain resembles that of a wild card for the already existing ecosystems which does not disturb and is effective for climate change and other environmental challenges, known to be as game changers can be stated as follows:

1)Supply Chain Management: see through chains-

2)Incentivizing circular economies via Recycling:

3)Energy:

4). Environmental Agreement:

5). Profitless contribution :

6) Carbon Tax

7). Earth management platforms

1. Supply Chain Management: See Through Chains
    Whenever the customer buys the product a trust factor is associated with that brand like Johnson's, Maggi, or Lakme. The information that consumer keenly is looking for is that the manufacturing of that product should be fair which is not available and sometimes it becomes difficult for them to verify whether the product is genuine or fake. For the product to reach the store it has to travel through many intermediaries—producers, suppliers, retailers, in-between reconstruction or remodeling can be done with the product's brand—chemicals can be added, basic materials can be changed or replica of the product can also be made with low quality constituents. At the end it is the customer who will be suffering. Here comes the savior for consumers i.e. blockchain. Blockchain enables tracking of the path of product beginning with manufacturing, traveling till its destination

like a GPS of product's route. Customer can get all the answers of the four questions:

a. Where the products are produced?
b. How efficiently is it produced?
c. Where they dispose their waste?
d. How much biasness is involved?

Blockchain has the potential to make the supply chain transparent which can help the buyers buy more environment-friendly products. To track the path of food also seems to be benefitted in cutting down the carbon emission as the consumer will avoid traveling long distances. It brings all the stakeholders-investors, developers, workers, producers, suppliers, retailers, the consumer under one roof by interconnecting all of them which makes this platform a unique one. Blockchain technology also assures that the sea food must be coming from the sustainable fisherman. For food tracking Dapp has developed Foodtrax; Provenance is one of blockchain's project helping actors to see through supply chains.

2. Incentivizing Circular Economies via Recycling
   Various efforts have been made to carry out the recycling programs in separate cities which often led to failure and sometimes not being able to track & compare the impact of the recycling plans .These reusing program give rewards for submitting plastic containers or bottles in the form of a token. With the help of blockchain technology we can easily track the location where this recycling program is implementing. It is also helpful in increasing incentives as for depositing each plastic article participants are getting in return crypto currency which overall is good for the circular economy. Blockchain keeps the record of the volume of the material that has been deposited which is value and profit for evaluation. In coming years we will be using plastic money as plastic bank is a project which aims to convert plastic into currency in exchange of plastic materials by setting up collection centers at different locations. Dapp Recycle to coin also enables communities to receive tokens in return of plastic bottles.

3. Energy
   It's a common problem faced by all the commoners' or businesses covering the world and not an issue for some

particular human beings. During the breakdown of natural calamities, poverty or extreme climate changes, interruption of electricity is a very common problem encountered by every citizen not accessing to power which ultimately leads to blackouts. Blockchain environmental ecosystem prepares for this kind of situation if it ever takes place. To decrease the requirement to transmit the electricity to far places it has P2P blockchain which is based on blockchain energy system. This can help in transmission of the electricity from local areas where it's originally generated to the areas where it is required. This also supports in reducing the energy storage. A platform which can solve this problem working on the blockchain is a Trans active Grid which is a combined legal agreement between two blockchain companies, ConsenSys and LO3 Energy. If someone wants to get return or want to gain profit there is a way provided by the blockchain environment ecosystem. You can simply invest in the renewable energy installation through blockchain platform and get returns as a token seeking how to invest where to invest which can be done by dapp-EcoChain. For solar energy–renewable energy, sun contract is a blockchain which bases on P2P trading platform. Solar coin app aims to maximize solar installations is based on an electric chain i.e. a blockchain platform.

4. Environmental Agreement

If we talk about the promises made by the leaders sometimes left incomplete as we are able to judge by itself or the agreement between two companies had been cancelled due to not completing the task assign to it .But what about the environmental agreement is that visible to all of us or are we going to observe itself only? Are we going to measure the impact of these agreements how much completed—how much left out? It is not possible for an individual to do all these things. For tracing the real impacts of environmental treaties there's a blockchain platform. In the long run the government and authorities are also not interested in keeping their promises. If data is presented it presents two main concerns: one is scamming, other is molding. To eradicate this problem, a centralized system-blockchain makes the whole system crystal clear by allowing the tracking of environmental data and peeking at every instance of all the commitments that were fulfilled or not. Not only does it do transparent tracking its job but also in reporting the progress made at what location and by what quantity Blockchain could dampen associations, business companies and governments from taking u-turns from promises related to environment. Blockchain has the potential to remove the fraud and manipulation by storing legalized records. Approximately 980 million per annum has been spent to administrate the blockchain system which is under scheme of global carbon credits.

5. Profitless Contribution

In India if we say the south region, it's common to have typhoon or flood. In 2007, there were terrible series of floods that occurred called as south Asian floods in which 30 million people suffered so that all citizens gathered to provide monetary help of which they donated very huge amounts. But have you ever thought that the amount we do donate for charity whether online or offline is reaching the proper recipients. Many people have donated money for Covid-19 (a viral disease)—though they have been provided IFSC codes. But one question that remains in our mind is will the amount really reach the affected people. If not, then how will it be spent. Looking at today's scenario, corruption has been inserted deeply into the roots or as they say to the tip of the roots where osmosis begins. Blockchain technology assures that the money which is intended for this purpose will help the affected people or for specific programs and will not be filling unintended pockets. The money can undoubtedly target its correct audience if it is based on blockchain platform (crypto currencies). Some rural areas are still lacking banking infrastructure and when there will be a natural hazard, in going to the bank or ATM for withdrawing, Blockchain technology has the potential to transfer the amount directly without making interruptions from the centralized system or any middleman. Two charities working with crypto currencies are Bit give and Bit hope.

6. Carbon Tax

The factors which have adverse impacts on the environment initiates from the automobiles, household items and so forth. Nowadays, sources include those that have to do with a lavish lifestyle whiuch directly or indirectly affects the environment, but by how much? Can you determine how much every product is making an effect on the environment? It can be calculated if we are aware of the carbon imprints. When planning to buy a four-wheeler petrol, diesel or CNG vehicle, which one would you prefer apart from monetization point of view? Obviously, that one which has less carbon emission so that global warming will not go beyond its alarming rate. Carbon tax is the tax which is applied at the time of extraction of fuel which is an indirect strategy to control emission of greenhouse gases produced when burning hydrocarbon (carbon compounds). The private sector imposed tax on the carbon with aim of lessening the emission of Co2 in the environment which results to degradation of forests. When these taxes are collected they should be used in the afforestation program but due to the many political winds the funds collected are used somewhere else. Blockchain technology has driven towards afforestation and degradation. It directly transfers the funds to the environmental ecosystem not in the pockets of intermediaries. In this context, the blockchain keeps the transparency between all the participants so that the funds obtain by depositing carbon will be applied in forest conservation program only. Considering the effect of CO_2, manufacturers and producers also join hands by giving incentives to those companies who are selling products with low carbon footprints and a little piece of cake to the consumers also who are following this trend. Blockchain acts as a game changer as it is provides the tracking of carbon imprints of every product. However some companies are producing products which have high carbon footprints so that Blockchain technology will compel them to change their supply chain as well as customers to buy products that have less adverse effect on the environment. The score based on the carbon footprints of the products sold by each company is determined by the blockchain-based system. Thus by adapting blockchain, there will be more transparency and termination of practices which are harmful to environment. The main Interest of this technology is to construct a global market of carbon trading for communities and businesses.

7. Earth Management Platforms

Telecom companies (such as Voda, Airtel or Jio) have to face new problems each day in order to increase the customer satisfaction and revenue. The perspective of the organization is the expansion of the network which involves the choice of location which requires a geo platform—a platform which conveys information about the location. Similarly Earth's natural system also needs attention which are under unknown stress due to the boundation of the planet. The New Blockchain Geospatial platform interprets geographic data and helps to understand the new patterns not only on the surface of the earth but deeper in the sea as well, i.e., it traces the data of the ocean. This platform analyzes, visualizes and manages the data of the earth in a ledger of geospatial platform. After the scaling the data blockchain technology ensures transaction across the globe and environmental domains are verifiable and trustful. This technology helps in protecting life not only on land but also the live of sea animals by improve their health. By removing the unbiasness and providing proper visualization to the water resources, blockchain enables to secure fishing rights whereas on land it strengthens the property rights of the participants and all the actors. The Geospatial Blockchain environmental ecosystem has the potential to observe the weather conditions and monitor the performance of the forecast required with the help of Internet of Things.

The above-mentioned game changers provide the power to structure the sustainable future with the collaboration of upgrading technologies. The blockchain environment ecosystem should target the right problem in order to empower the communities.

2.3   Blockchain in Business Ecosystem

By 2025, global investment in blockchain technology in energy markets is set to reach $34.7 billion. Although $35 billion seems high, it's exceeding by the net worth of $1.85 trillion for the energy market as a whole. Key actors using blockchain and DLT in the field include Accenture, AWS, Bigchain db, Deloitte, IBM, Infosys, Microsoft, Nodal block, Oracle, SAP, Enosi, and Electron.

Blockchain is used within energy markets for data management, financial tracking and interactions. Drivers for adoption include reducing operational costs and capital expenditure. Increasing automation will see blockchain employed for data security and integrity. On top of the list are banking and financial applications whereas the Medicare businesses, regulators and retailers are progressively speeding up in this blockchain market. Interest in this technology is increasing rapidly which drives its route towards the business ecosystem. New entrepreneurs have started to look for the business solution within the blockchain business ecosystem.

2.3.1 Business Ecosystem

A business ecosystem comprises of a huge number of participants, which can either be business organization or actors. They are linked in such a manner that they can affect each other. Interrelation enables assorted interaction among the members. Interaction can be competitive or cooperative. Together with interconnectedness they proportioned consequences between the organizations. The members are reliant on each other—the downfall of one organization result in failure of other firms.

2.3.1.1 What Is Business Model?

A model which provides an overview of how the organization is going to make maximum profit in which field, whether in selling services or producing products or selling businesses without any intermediate to the right choice of consumers. It can be online or offline mode. This model includes a plan of all the expenditures arising initially on the manufacturer side, marketing and finally reaching to the customers.

2.3.1.2 Business Model—Traditional

In this type of model the consumers are physically present for purchasing the goods from the market. It is just like buying products from the local store. This model is a purely centralized one which is controlled by some regulators. Different businesses exist which are centralized by different regulators, controlled and managed by the authorities which includes:

    a. The organization,
    b. The stakeholder or owners,
    c. The workers, and
    d. The consumers.

Traditional business model are divided into the following types:

1. Manufacturer
2. Distributor

3. Need of customers fulfilled
4. Franchise.

1. Manufacturers
   They are the ones who make products from the raw materials; they can also assemble the components to make the products. Common examples are computer & automobiles. This model can directly sell products to the customers, i.e., B2C or they can outsource to other businesses, i.e., B2B also. For example, dye manufacturers sell to the retailers which then sell them to the customers.
2. Distributors
   The organization with the distributor model purchases the products directly from the manufacturers and they supply to the wholesalers then to retailers or to the customers. The main responsibility of this model is to set the value which in return provides profit to the company. Adding on to that, it makes marketing strategies which can bring more sales of the products. In general, its role is an inter-mediator between the manufacturer and the local users.
3. Need of Customers Fulfilled
   The companies which are having retailer business model have the function to sell products directly from distributors to the customers. Retailers can supply products both via online and offline mode. Online retailers like those selling products on e-commerce website include Amazon, Flipkart, Myntra & Shopclues. Offline retailers are similar to those departmental stores, local shops which exit physically.
4. Franchise
   This model comprises of other business models which are mentioned above. The purchaser of franchise is called franchisee for e.g. Pizza Hut.
   A traditional business model provides services or products and gains profit from them. Consumers purchase the product or service at the recommended rate. This price is set correspondingly and it also has the description about the earnings and other expenditures aroused by the business while providing the goods or services.

2.3.2   Are Blockchain Business Models Really Needed?

The Blockchain business models provide an opportunity to the centralized platform to upgrade their businesses into decentralization. It turns the individual elements, transactions, profits, and also assures growth. This technology has the potential to give benefit to both—actors and centralized employees. Before switching to the Blockchain models certain points should be memorized about it:

- Entrepreneur or startups or already established organization can implement the blockchain in their businesses.
- Not easy to delete records which are already on Blockchain.
- Blockchain's main uniqueness is its transparency which helps in uplifting of the functioning of supply chain.

An application of this technology can be seen in the fourth industrial revolution where many firms have developed their own decentralization of Artificial intelligence model.

2.3.2.1   *Blockchain Business Model*

2.3.2.2   *Model 1: Utility Token Model*

A token can be regarded as a value, stake or representation of anything functioning in a particular ecosystem. Unlike crypto currencies, they are not dependent on some platform but tokens (golem) are used for a specific platform within the ecosystem called as native token. The utility token provides products and services to the users. The tokens have the potential to promote more functionality in the business. Examples of these kinds of models are Ripple and Stellar. The utility tokens power the network and expedite the network activities. A part of the utility tokens is held by businesses and the rest is liberated for the functioning of the network. The stake of utility token changes because it works according to the supply–demand criteria; if the demand of the product increases, its supply decreases which tends to increase in value. This way, this model provides benefit to the businesses. It involves properties such as:

a. Role
b. Features
c. Purpose.

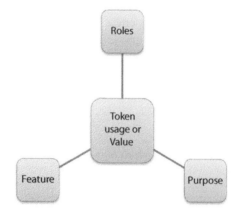

Crypto Token Usage and Value

Roles	Purpose	Features
1. Right	Bootstapping Engagement	Using Products—voting Authentication—Product access Contribution—Ownership
2. Value Exchange	Economy Creation	Rewards for Work-Selling some product Purchasing—Active/Passive work Expenses-Manufacturing product
3. Toll	Skin In the game	Running smart contracts Security Deposits Usage Charges

(Continued)

(*Continued*)

Roles	Purpose	Features
4. Function	Enriching User experience	Network joining Users Connectivity Usage's Incentives
5. Currency	Frictionless transaction	Payment unit Transaction unit
6. Earnings	Distributing profits	Profit sharing Benefit Sharing

To make the work more effective the token can take many roles as possible.

2.3.2.3   Model 2: BaaS

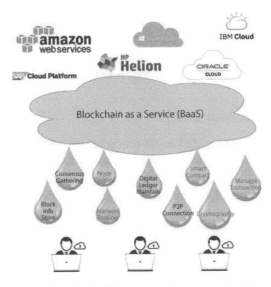

This model provides the link between the organization and the companies with blockchain platform. For example when a singer records a song, all the backend materials need consideration by the music director including mike, lyrics, recording room and bass volume, maintenance of software records, etc. which tend to be time-consuming and expensive. BaaS works as similar type handles, all the backend things so that the music director gets only focused on song without concerning himself about the infrastructure, costing and maintenance. It enables the client to focus only on the frontend instead of backend stuff. An agreement has been made between the organizations in which BaaS agrees to be responsible for all the blockchain technology including monitoring of the system, management of bandwidth and providing security of system against hacking attacks. By making contract with the BaaS partners the startups/entrepreneurs transfer the load of infrastructure and system performance allowing them to focus on their main business and competitive strategies. BaaS enables customers to develop their own blockchain applications by using cloud-based services, ensuring its functioning, hosting and usage which resemble that with the web hosting providers.

Apart from this if entrepreneur manages to get blockchain up, then he/she has to deal with all the maintenance. The can be overcome by making smart contract with the organizations with blockchain technology platforms.

In the market there are some famous existing BaaS providers such as: Oracle, IBM-blue mix, Google Firebase Microsoft-Azure module and Amazon-AWS. It includes providing businesses with an ecosystem to help manage their blockchain system. The costing varies while using Baas services. It depends on multiple factors like how much transaction has been done, how many simultaneous transaction made at what rate. It implies pay according to the units of the services that are in use.

2.3.2.4   Model 3: Securities

The security which is provided on the blockchain is called as securities. Many of the convenient businesses have moved towards new technology including finance and stock market. Another name for security tokens are equity tokens, which are regulated by the government in comparison to the utility one. They provide more speed and soothe blockchain to the traditional businesses by ensuring security against any bug or fraudulent activities.

Security Token is Equal to Investment Contract
Assets like four-wheeler, real estate or stocks of organizations—which contain some value. For these assets, security tokens are the bonds (smart contracts) containing fragment of amount. This token ensures the freehold of any strong suit that is stored and secures on the new technology platform. After verification of the proprietorship the people who hold security token can:

- Be beneficial for other investment.
- Be used as an assurance for sanctioning of loan.
- Can be put in distinct pocketbook.

2.3.2.5 Model 4: Development Platforms

The blockchain is a space where many entrepreneurs and startups are landing with the agenda of solving their problems in a different manner. Most of them are developing decentralize applications.

As stated by Metcalfe's Law, the more networks in use, the more will be its value. Like with two telephones, you are only able to make a single connection, if there's single phone it is useless, by using the formula

$$n(n-1)/2$$

$$2*1/2 = 1.$$

However, when there are 5 phones, you can make 10 connections. Involvement of enormous people makes the network more in use. That's why most fortunate networks can enjoy severe aggressive hike.

There are three models which are specific:

- Charging Fees for using network.
- Recruiting Auditors.
- Other Services.

a. Charging Fees for Using Network
Ethereum requires gas for producing fuel which is helpful in running of blockchain 24 days and 7 nights. Anyone who develops dapps on this platform pays an amount similar to toll tax payable in the form of gas fees. The charges depend on the completion of the transaction, how much complex it is varies accordingly. Gas tokens are used in NEO for creating dapps. The tokens which can be purchased and sold are Golem Network Tokens. GNT is a method of payment for computation of the resource providers. One pays what for the service is measured by GNT.

b. Recruiting Auditors
If in case it was found that transaction record on blockchain is illegal or not authorized or classification is not done correctly then this led to the need of an auditor to carry out its procedure on management's estimates. Even if we say blockchain does not require a third party but when it comes to check whether the product was solely delivered and does

not require an auditor to go through the transactions process. When the organizations make business with other parties, they prefer auditors to verify smart contract as these contracts are for automation of the process of business. Decentralized applications consume a very big amount for the working of the code appropriately. If there is a minor bug it will lean towards the failure of the entire system. A recent example of this is a DAO smart contract which led to the split of Ethereum community into Ethereum and Ethereum Classic.

This model can work in two ways:

- The smart contract needed to be checked—developers need to hire the auditing company.
- Independently auditors and developers check the code and look for defects if they found any in the code. Also, the developers put up a premium on their contract.

c. Other Services

A blockchain startup needs lots of work. The startup first requires a website with good content and frameworks. These startups either recruit freelancers or agencies to save both time and money including taking care of these services for them.

2.3.2.6   Model 5: Blockchain-Based Software Products

This includes small scale businesses which sell to the higher scale businesses in return for reasonable amount for the applications based on the technology. Apart from getting a reasonable payment upfront, exposure of blockchain technology to the organizations is beneficial to them. They will also need to provide support post-implementation. Media Chain blockchain being sold to Spotify. To resolve royalty issues prevalent in the music industry. As companies don't want to bear the load of tedious procedure—acquiring talent is another reason for acquiring this business model.

2.3.2.7   Model 6: Blockchain Professional Services

This model offers services to the entrepreneur, corporate or startup businesses to make their hands on practice on this new technology. Some companies like Deloitte and IBM are already making projects on blockchain technology that can be contacted for completion of project by other businesses. There is no need to put money in the h/w or s/w—connecting directly to the services offered by these companies.

2.3.2.8   Model 7: Business Model—P2P

P2P model ensures direct interaction between end-users. It allows the end users to use the technology (blockchain) for building software that makes the whole internet as non-authorized. Casting of this can be done by BaaS, tokens, and charging from network. Tools which based on this model are File coin, Sia, Etheria and IPFS. Like Wikipedia, is open to everyone—anyone can make changes in the contents or can revise the contents. Its serve as a medium for true P2P exchange.

1. IPFS
   This system works as a replacement of http—it is developed in such a manner that it can hold the transaction in outer space even i.e. the pending issues of http are solved by this web applications.
2. File Coin
   This is a monetary based system developed for storage of information and having its own crypto currency. In exchange of user's not used storage space they provide them some value.
3. Sia
   This tool uses the new technology for transaction aim towards replacing of Dropbox, Google Drive.
4. Etheria
   This protocol focused on the blockchain gaming properties by building blocks in the upgrading ecosystem. Some games like Beyond the Void and Spells of Genesis are built on blockchain gaming platform.

What makes blockchain business model different from the traditional one is that it assures P2P interactions, removing all the middle man. By creating a trustless system, vanishing mediator for verification of records and fasten the faith. In Pvt Ltd companies, in this platform board of director and owners are absent. However they are present in the blockchain model theoretically and their interactions methods are changed dramatically.

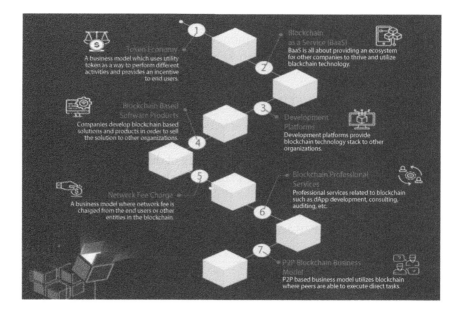

2.4   Is Blockchain Business Ecosystem Profitable?

As for blockchain entrepreneurs and developers to make profit is a straight path—in the hope that their project will work out and value of their assets will increase by keeping some parts of the token as equity share combined with liquidity of their tokens as return of their reward. It's not simple to understand though how they cover the costs. At the initial stage, the investors get the crypto assets at low prices. Many of the crypto assets developers and entrepreneurs hold an Initial coin offering to crowd fund their project. In this way, developer gets sufficient amount to cover the costs.

Revenue can be earned by any one of the following:-

1. By charging network fee for using network or gas fee.
2. Value of dapp increases with the increase in the number of users implies token may up in price. A utility token can be traded within the network. For example, in video games digital currency which help in accessing the game is taken to be as utility token which helps in buying game materials, and can be traded.
3. By selling technology to a higher business like previously mentioned media chain blockchain acquired by Spotify.

2.5 How Do You "Design" a Business Ecosystem?

Where Traditional business model is related to planning and planting a flower, designing an ecosystem is far like growing a whole forest: more complicated, with extra players to interact & unexpected coming results. Certain challenges also exist resembling that of a consumption–outcome problem or like chicken–egg problem.

However, business ecosystems, analogous to construction of forest, can't be entirely planned and designed—they also come up. For ecosystem designing the following steps should be kept in mind which are interconnected:

1	• Knowing about the problem to be solved.
2	• What are the components of the ecosystem?
3	• Know about the starting governance model of ecosystem?
4	• How to grab the cost of ecosystem?
5	• Can you determine the consumption-outcome problem at the time of beginning?
6	• Assuring the reliability of ecosystem?

1. Knowing about the problem to be solved.
2. What are the components of the ecosystem?
3. Know about the starting governance model of ecosystem?
4. How to grab the cost of ecosystem?
5. Can you determine the consumption–outcome problem at the time of beginning?
6. Assuring the reliability of ecosystem?

Step 1: Knowing about the problem to be solved?
Initially, problem should be defined clearly which the ecosystem is going to solve so that it can convince the high business investors and right actors for participation. If someone has ever thought 20 years ago that businesses like YouTube and Instagram could be built on taking selfies, then posting photos of your meals, and animals clips.

- Is ecosystem the best choice?
  Ecosystem–blockchain business includes everything that a physical ecosystem (servers, clients, h/w, s/w) contains. The following are key points in what scenario ecosystem might be preferred:

> ➢ Need for decentralization, transparency and immutability of records.
> ➢ When Gateways are more expensive and time consuming like Expedia or Airnb.
> ➢ Need for more security among users and developers.
> ➢ When the speed of the new data is increasing anonymously as well as previous record is also mandatory to be stored.

What type of ecosystem you required?
Since all business ecosystem functionalities are not same, some business ecosystems work on the project completion—as small level players in the market and then handing over the project to the higher players. Some work on the transaction ecosystem by linking the providers and the requestors. Some work on the solution ecosystem which combines all the elements of the solution of the problem. As a startup business in this technology, one needs to know about the type of ecosystem, as they all differ in their construction, purpose, monetary mechanism and most importantly, success factors.

Step 2: What are the components of ecosystem?
Different participants get roles on the basis of the value prototype. A solution ecosystem can be understood by the examples of chorus having many mentors, suppliers and middleman.

In transaction ecosystems, the band director guide's (who teaches chorus) role is played by the owner of the business ecosystem whose role is to tie a bond between manufacturers, suppliers and customers. The director guide constructs the ecosystem, inspires to join the system, describes about regulations, standards and rules. The success of the ecosystem depends on the responsibility completed by the assigned role. Also equating investment needed for the longevity of ecosystem is sustained. The failure of the ecosystem or we can say dissociation of the system is because of the Band director guide not being able to fulfill the duty assigned to him.

Step 3: Know about the starting governance/authority model of ecosystem?
Determining Degree of Openness
    Authority required balancing two requirements for the business ecosystem to get success: amount creating & sharing.
    Main governance query for business ecosystem which is emerging-what is the degree of its openness. Queries in 3 areas having solution:

- Admittance: In the business ecosystem that are going to be as partners? In order to get entry to the ecosystem and its resources what conditions do they have to fulfill?

- Partners: To structure the business ecosystem at what extent are participants invited? What are the capacity, fine points, and severity of the rules allowing this? Who's going to decide the distribution of the value among the various participants?
- Assurance: Are the participants permitted to opt for multi-mode in competing with other businesses? In few sectors, they battle for their own degree of openness. If we have a look Android broke the superiority of Apple iOS by providing connectivity of openness, Facebook conquers the fragility of MySpace's open model by providing the icon of accepting request or deleting i.e. providing property in friend's feature. From the monetary point of view open ecosystem grows faster as compared to the others at the time of execution. It also encourages decentralization and allows variety of developers and partners.

However, to authorize the open ecosystem is not easy though, therefore it iswell adapted for goods and services with finite drawback and less cost of deterioration. Growth v/s quality, decentralized v/s interconnectedness, and speed v/s flexibility are various individual factors on which the exact degree of openness for business ecosystem will rely on.

Step 4: How to grab the cost of ecosystem?
For what charges are applicable?
The main question of the ecosystem "chorus" is the value i.e. money should be distributed equally among the participants and keep share of profit for its own. Also, the amount should be enough to be assigned among the participants. Apple takes itself 30% from the app that it sold from its application store. Similarly the businesses create ecosystem that can be sold as a service to higher businesses in order to capture value.

Step 5: Can you determine the consumption-outcome problem at the time of beginning?
What conditions led to its failure?
The failure of the ecosystem at the time of execution is because the authority was not able to calculate the size of the participants—how many buyers will be there? How many sellers will be there? Due to this, they are not able to protect the network which results in crash of the ecosystem. Sometimes they overestimate the profit and is negligent towards the importance of network effects. This race is not coming at first position but first with complete solution. For example, Apple iPod was not first in the

digital market but it was first with a combination of software iTunes with hardware. Another very important factor is to get to know about the number of transactions by the number of participants. Being aware of network density is an important driver of amount for the actors.

Lastly, the selection of participant is important. It doesn't matter how many participants are there but their quality matters. For example in Uber, there are equal numbers of riders and drivers so it is a balanced one.

Step 6: How can you assure the reliability of ecosystem?
Is scaling can be possible?

Yahoo search engine initially started as a hierarchical database edited by employees and WebPages are classified based on tree structure. Yahoo gained popularity for a very small time with the advent growth in internet—at that time it was not scalable and ultimately taken over by Google with the scaling page rank algorithm. So, if you desire to have long term viability of the ecosystem, it is important to get best knowledge of the scalability position, design and strategy of the developing business ecosystem. Among the three, scalability is the main step for the availability.

How expansion of the ecosystem takes place?

Expansion. Let's have a look on some examples—Instant change in technologies and customers preferences Microsoft still manages to defend Windows as an operating system over the three decades. Uber initially started its ride services but extended to the food delivery and bike riders services. When LinkedIn started, its aim was to establish a link with the professionals but at present it serves as an online recruiting and publishing contents. Therefore, for the expansion of ecosystem, it should be having two features: stability and flexibility so that new functionalities can be added to the system accordingly. In reference to this, we can say expansion of ecosystem takes places by:

1. New products can be added in to an existing system.
2. Expanding the services in the same market (Uber).
3. Creating advantage after the success of one ecosystem (Apple iPods).

How can you protect against adverse reaction?

Large business ecosystem has experienced adverse reaction from the customers and managers. On the top of list is Amazon who was recently criticized for not collecting sales tax in order to come first in the race of competitors similarly with eBay. Also, Uber was blamed for security, violation of the rules of transportation, insurance and rights of the drivers and worker's rights that are applicable to taxis. Last on the list is Facebook which was criticized for not securing the data of the users. Hence, the ecosystem should be designed in such a manner that it should not only verified legally but also socially for its longevity. Business ecosystem can only thrive in future if it tries to persistently adhere to concrete value for their consumers and disseminate equal value to all its contributors.

To design an ecosystem is a main attempt so the above-mentioned six interconnected steps are helpful in designing a business ecosystem. Any entrepreneur or start up can be structured if the design is followed wisely or it can bring transition in the existing organization. It is also important to understand that any business ecosystem cannot be completely designed as well as planned like in the case of a forest they also emerge.

Those ecosystems that want to gain profit in the future will have to be flexible, ready for the up gradation in technologies—both hardware/software, unwanted happenstance and also working according to customer preferences.

2.6   Redesigning Future With Blockchain

To sum up, for someone to excel in new technology is not enough for Blockchain business ecosystem, but what is required is to reconsider the market role, existing industries ecosystem and their financial worth. Many elements have to be (re)designed in this composite system.

2.6.1   Is Earth Prepared for Blockchain?

Blockchain technology adaption whether in the environment ecosystem or in business ecosystem are having bundle of advantages but with the adoption of new technology there are many unintended outcomes also in the coming years—the blockchain can really become a burden that planet earth has to bear with. The technology require energy to keeps its longevity so in the blockchain technology the energy released by using the crypto currency are of very high intensity. Crypto currencies are bitcoin, litecoin, doge coin, bat, Ethereum, neo, ripplexrp, cardano and many more. Whenever in use, it require a significant amount of energy, although not all of them. Some operate on less amount of energy. Transaction of crypto currencies—Ehereum, Neo and Cardano—require 13 times lesser than the energy needed to transact bitcoin. This is an additional feature that blockchain solution is adding to the next gen computers to be as energy efficient directed with the increase in power and computational speed but keeping the low usage of energy. Many organizations are constructing energy bare blockchain framework which will be operating on PoA. In order to make earth a better planet, Building Blockchains so that the blockchain energy usage can be applied in the appropriate direction i.e. the incentives arising from the uptake of renewable resources and de-carbonization must be used for the reforestation. If the transaction of single Bitcoin can consume power almost one fifth of the country's houses per day then it can be predicted how much there is a need for blockchain solution as an energy savior. Moreover to that, for every 11 min a new Bitcoin transaction takes place. This is the need of an hour for the Blockchain technology which is at its beginning state that will be beneficial for many sectors if used appropriately in both technology protocols and its applications parts.

To develop Effective Blockchain solution:

1. Tackle blockchain for environmental value
    Construction of international bank shared between two countries and multiagency blockchain initiative led to a number of profits that can be seen in different fields such as ocean health, plastic articles, electronic machines and management of the natural resources. If the actors want that blockchain will meet the expectations of the global environment then again interconnections are necessary for the international organizations in order to receive the reward of this technology.
2. Combine blockchain with AI & IoT
    The traditional method that we were using for sharing information whose privacy is not confirmed has transformed into the new blockchain technology which has given a transparency factor in sending or receiving data. Combining with

IoT, this technology has completely converted the central-ized regulatory into the decentralized one due to the envi-ronmental problems of the natural system of the third planet which can be monitored, analyzed deeply adding that cli-mate changes can be well-observed and how much energy usage per crypto currency is making adverse effect on the environment. To date, cloud computing and big data have been profitable by IoT and now it's blockchain's.

3. Collaborate for interdisciplinary solutions
   It is clear now that blockchain builds the system as crystal clear providing transparency of data, but this technology can meet the expectations of the planet if there exists coop-eration between all the participants. Different sectors can collaborate and interconnect in order to enable blockchain's applications to run smoothly. Shareholders, miners, domain specialist and actors are required to interact with each other for optimizing the services provided by this new blockchain technology.

   To make earth a better planet, interconnectedness among NGO, non-profit sectors, private and public are needed. A successful digital infrastructure has been developed by var-ious efforts by the energy companies and the finance orga-nization which is openly helping towards decentralization and de-carbonization the energy system. To implement the interdisciplinary approach—combining data scientists with environment and industry practitioner—is possible by working together in a research institution. Thereby, how can this blockchain technology can be of use? What are its impacts if used excessively? And what are risks that the envi-ronment has to face?

   The answers to the above-mentioned three queries can be possible if all the experienced technology scientists are researching together to ensure the sustainability of block-chain technology.

4. Prediction of challenges and unintended consequences-political economy
   New technology has the power to change the existing system-industries into the authorized one. The regulators must be concerned about if these changes take place how will it affect the economy rate and the participants of the

existing systems. Stakeholders worry more about handling of trust factor of data privacy and security.

5. Deliver "responsible blockchain"

While focusing on the reduction of energy consumption and increasing revenues for the developers and the participants, if the strategy becomes out of plan then the blockchain technology looks in to privacy rights and clarifications of the accountability. GDF organization works together with other companies for governance, so that stakeholders involve themselves directly within blockchain ecosystem in a systematic manner.

Making important arrangements required by governance.

6. Development of rapid approach to governance and regulation

In present scenario we are having the centralized system—having management to control the system if any harm occurs in the technology where the regulators play an important role in monitoring the developments and taking action if they found any malfunction in the technology. If the differences occur between the authorities is at the greatest level then it will become a major challenge within the distributed system.

7. Frame more globally coordinated solution

The global interconnected architecture can be structured by the blockchain technology as it has spread its roots in all the fields. Following are the points on how the blockchain ecosystem is governed:

a. Making organization to be self-regulated

Without worrying for the formal regulations proceedings—blockchain provides new choices to this system; financial freedom and self-sovereignty are underpinnings of self-regulation. A global code which is a supplement for regulations can be identified by global good practice. Some of the self-regulating processes already running in a few countries—U.S.(EQWITY), Japan(Last roots), Philippines (startups), and Singapore(TBD). To make relations with the environment, the self-regulators can be compromised and central regulation can develop the set of requirements.

b. Government policies which makes nations to be regulated

Recently, this is the best method to command blockchain with local managers who are responsible to maintain area of authority in order to battle if any recognized fault arises.

Greener protocol can be adopted by the blockchain communities. The funds which are received by government can be used for blockchain research which looks for scaling public-private projects.

c. Regulations comprehensible globally

To run blockchain technology at an international level— The international authorities and global managers are facing challenges in to order to understand the regulations globally. If small firms are having difficulty with blockchain, global organization will look into it, will establish a relation with environment along with harmony crosswise jurisdiction.

2.7   Challenges and Opportunities

In this chapter we discuss about the blockchain as a game changer, technology in both environment and business ecosystems. No doubt, this technology is better in every field for providing the transparency, saving energy usage and is far better as compared to the traditional models. But whenever some technology comes in the market it brings some challenges along with it. The technical issue that blockchain technology address is limited with is scalability because of foreordain in terms of the size of blocks and energy used by the crypto currencies. Though blockchain technology is decentralized, distributed and based on cryptographic techniques, it is not totally exempted from security issues as rising of cloud computing and quantum computing combined with the physical, digital and biological areas with the increase in speed and intelligence can prove dangerous to the blockchain ecosystem.

The challenges can't be avoided—they also concur with the 4th industrial revolution i.e., AI, IoT, where an autonomous vehicle is able to generate opportunities for global development and creation of value. These technologies also have the power to speed up the environment's degradation.

No doubt that these challenges need attention as the technology is upgrading day-by-day. Soon there will 6G technology, though China has already launched 6G phones, Japan announce the startup of 7G technology. As the advancement of revolutions is at its peak, blockchain developers have to cope-up with these technologies. Nevertheless, the opportunity window not be open forever.

The opportunities offered by the responsible blockchain ecosystem need to be authorized sincerely and regulators should be ready for not expected outcomes and failures. Just in case things go wrong, a variety of rules are required assuring an agreement with privacy rights to improvising security issues. Shareholders willingly share all these duties. The demand of the present time has compelled all the actors, miners, developers, producers, suppliers and retailers to use the blockchain technology for solving everything. For this requirement, a structured approach can help the practitioners on how to use this technology.

In the end, the future of blockchain is ready for time being, aware of the commitments and going through the facts and data. There are far more companies and people with data and views on the immediate and future of blockchain. Covering everything is not possible so creating a list of more forecasts on the future of blockchain in the real world versus the virtual one need focus on the practical—the real instead of the promises, the applications and the industries.

References

1. Schlapkohl, K., *Blockchain Pulse : IBM Blog*, IBM, United States, 2019, January 3, Retrieved from https://www.ibm.com/blogs/blockchain/2019/01/whats-the-difference-between-a-blockchain-and-a-database/#:~:text=-Blockchains%20versus%20traditional%20databases,the%20provenance%20of%20the%20data

2. AlMuhairi, O., Mariam, 2020, May 8, Retrieved from https://www.weforum.org/agenda/2020/05/why-covid-19-makes-a-compelling-case-for-wider-integration-of-blockchain/.

3. Meunier, S., *When do you need blockchain? Decision models*, San Francisco, California, 2019, August, Retrieved from Medium Blockchain: https://medium.com/@sbmeunier/when-do-you-need-blockchain-decision-models-a5c40e7c9ba1

3

Business Use Cases of Blockchain Technology

Vasudha Arora[1]*, Shweta Mongia[2], Sugandha Sharma[2] and Shaveta Malik[3]

[1]GD Goenka University, Gurugram, India
[2]UPES, Dehradun, India
[3]Terna Engineering College, Navi Mumbai, India

Abstract

Exchange of cryptocurrencies using digital coins such as bitcoin has changed the model for transactions and lead us to enter an entirely new world of businesses. Bitcoins can be thought of as a digital currency through a digital wallet which does not requires any trusted third party such as a bank or any other centralized authority for making transactions. In fact this digital transaction model uses a blockchain technology and is based on the concept of 'proof of work' where users execute their transactions by signing their transactions using digital signatures. As there is no concept for trusted third party hence implementations also provide a solution for double spending problems. This chapter presents the detailed discussions about the bitcoin as a cryptocurrency which uses blockchain as its medium of transactions. The transaction using bitcoins before entering into a blockchain must be validated by miners using blockchain mining. The miners, for validating a transaction, are awarded incentives that make the business of bitcoins based on blockchain alive. A Bitcoin Initial Coin Offering (ICO) can be broadly explained in terms of mechanism of crowd raising funds for entrepreneurial firms for their innovative and promising ideas where they are able to sell their tokens to investors in exchange funds for capital just like shares in Initial Public Offering (IPO). Studies have shown that bitcoins have been largely accepted by merchants for their businesses.

Keywords: Bitcoin, cryptocurrency, bitcoin transactions, bitcoin mining, ICO

---

*Corresponding author: vasudharora6@gmail.com

S.S. Tyagi and Shaveta Bhatia (eds.) Blockchain for Business: How it Works and Creates Value,
(59–76) © 2021 Scrivener Publishing LLC

3.1   Introduction to Cryptocurrency

A cryptocurrency can be defined as a modern digital or Internet-based currency, which, with the help of cryptographic functions is able to perform financial transactions without the intervention of a trusted third party such as a bank or some other financial institution. Instead of creating a Trust-based model it uses a peer-to-peer network terminology creating a blockchain. This method of performing financial transactions is a transparent method which decentralizes the control of any governing body or trusted third party.

Transactions once executed and entered into the blockchain become immutable as a part of open ledger that is shared by every peer entry in the network. The transaction can be done between any two parties on the same network using cryptographic keys. As no third party is involved in between hence the transactions are very fast and parties need not to pay any fee for the transactions.

The concept of cryptocurrency was born in 2009 while implementing a concept of Bitcoin given by Satoshi Nakamoto. Earlier to this concept, a number of attempts have been made to create the successful flow of digital currency but unfortunately all the attempts were failures. One of the most important reasons behind the success of cryptocurrencies was its ability to deal with double spending problem.

Since its conception, Bitcoin as a cryptocurrency is gaining popularity in the digital world for doing online transactions. Bitcoin is nothing but a sequence of cryptographically encrypted bits which has some monetary value. Digital signatures using hash functions are used for authenticating the peer-to-peer network addresses. Hence, Bitcoins can also be thought of as chain of digital signatures required for execution of transaction between two entities.

Although cryptocurrencies are gaining wide interest due to transparency in their transactions and also for their resistance to inflation, sometimes, they are criticized for their vulnerabilities in the infrastructure they are using.

This chapter details about the concept of bitcoin, Double spending problem Digital signatures, Working of bitcoin, ICO, and Merchant acceptance of Bitcoin.

3.2   What is a Bitcoin?

Shavers *et al.* in 2013 [2] defined a digital currency as:

"A medium of exchange that operates like a currency in some environments but does not have all the attributes of real currency."

The first ever implementation of cryptocurrency that came into existence in the world is Bitcoin. It's a form of digital money that uses the concept of cryptography and facilitates a new payment system. Money flows over decentralized peer-to-peer network where there is no central authority to monitor. It is completely driven by the users. Cryptography is used to control the creation and transactions and that is how Cash is flowing over the internet.

Satoshi Nakamoto in 2009 published the first article as a proof of concept and specification on Bitcoin. Bitcoin is driven by an open source community and is growing exponentially through developers. Its codes, technical requirements are available freely over the internet and hence any developer can contribute and can develop its modified version.

Bitcoin is not controlled by any trusted third party such as a financial institution. It is for the users and is driven by the users who can connect over the same peer to peer network. Even the developers cannot control bitcoin and force a particular change in the protocols for the following reasons: one, if developers have full control over how the transactions are being executed then the motive of not depending on a trust based model would be defeated; second, there is a need to have a compatibility in all versions of the software, otherwise different users may opt for different versions and transactions may fail due to incompatibility issues.

A bitcoin can be viewed from two different angles. One, from User perspective, it is nothing more than an application software program using which, users can send and receive digital money over the network and maintain a digital wallet. It allows its users to have online payments between a seller and the corresponding buyer. On the other hand, unlike the currency that we use today, a Bitcoin is created using an address. It is traded using blockchain technology that maintains a distributed and decentralized open ledger for all its users making an entry for all financial transactions. These transactions are cryptographically encrypted and digitally signed for authentication and validated by number of different users before the completion of execution of transactions.

Satoshi Nakamoto in their whitepaper in 2009 defined the bitcoin as chain or sequence of digital signatures. Whenever a transaction is initiated, the owner of the bitcoin creates a digital signature using the hash of his previous transaction combined with the public key of another participant (next owner) in the transaction. This hash value is appended at the end of bitcoin under transaction. This complete value i.e. bitcoin address and appended hash are encrypted by user's private key that act as a digital signature of the current owner.

3.2.1 Bitcoin Transactions and Their Processing

Transactions are the instances of buying and selling between two or more parties or owners. Digital cash such as a Bitcoin allows for the online transactions between the buyers and sellers having a bitcoin digital wallet. A digital ledger is maintained for such transactions in order to keep track of the transactions and account balances.

The exchange of Bitcoin is done by using cryptographically assisted cryptocurrency protocols which define the entire procedure from the creation of bitcoins through their validations to final confirmations. To understand the entire process of exchanges lets us first understand what a transaction actually is and how the information is processed using these transactions?

    a. Bitcoin Transaction
       A transaction using bitcoin can be visualized as follows:

       A transaction involving bitcoins must contain:

- A unique transaction identifier that is a hash value generated using SHA256 hash algorit hm (here in Figure 3.1 we represented this hash value as x and y. Generally it is of the form e.g. 8907a34ef56b70d43789fe9876af54d3f670f8a999f6f18).

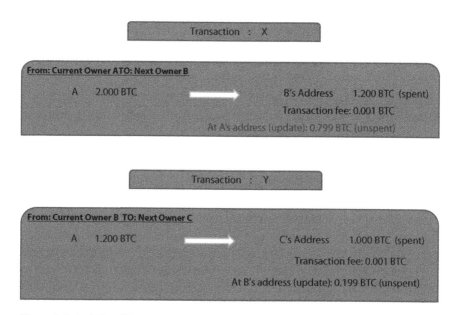

Figure 3.1 A chain of bitcoin transactions.

- The bitcoin addresses of the current owner which is used to identify the bitcoins that need to be transferred in the current transaction. These are generally the output of the previous transaction which can be used to identify the current owner of the bitcoin and is able to check his available balance.
- The transaction must contain the details about the amount i.e. the number of bitcoins to be transferred.
- The transaction must contain the bitcoin addresses of receiver i.e. the next owner. If there are unspent bitcoins of the sender the output of the transaction should also include an entry for the current owner's address to send it back and an entry for "Transaction Fee" and an entry for bitcoins to be sent to another receiver if any.

The output of one transaction is used as an input for the next transaction in order to create a chain of ownership as and when a bitcoin is transferred from one address to another.

b. Validating a Bitcoin Transaction
As there is no centralized authority in the entire transaction process, every user node in the peer-to-peer network is authorized to verify and validate each and every transaction in the network for its authenticity, duplicity and availability of bitcoins.

A bitcoin address is used to identify the bitcoin wallet account that initiates the transaction. Each address has its pair of public and private keys. A hash value using previous transaction of the sender and his public key is calculated using SHA256 algorithm. This calculated hash value is appended to the bitcoin address and then it is digitally signed by the owner's private key.

In order to verify the identity of the sender, the transactions are signed using his private key. As shown in Figure 3.2 these digital signatures from the sender can be verified by using his corresponding public key which can be made publicly available to all the nodes in the network.

Once the transaction is initiated the bitcoin system arranges these transactions into lists known as *blocks*. These different blocks are then linked together to create a

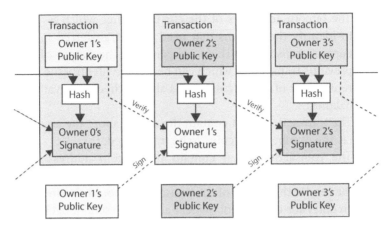

Figure 3.2 Validating transactions [1].

blockchain, which is distributed open ledger containing all confirmed transactions. The transactions that are not yet included in the blockchain ledger are considered unconfirmed and are reversible.

c. Final Confirmation of a Bitcoin Transaction

A process of verifying a transaction and processing them for final confirmation is known as mining. A group of people, known as miners, in the same network confirm the transactions and add them to a blockchain open ledger. The major problems with this kind of transactions is that the next owner, i.e. payee, in no way is able to identify that payer did not double spend bitcoins during the transaction. In order to deal with a double spending problem, a transaction is considered as confirmed only if it receives a certain number of confirmations.

A bitcoin transaction is said to be confirmed only if it gets minimum of 6 confirmations. Here, confirmation means addition of block including the transaction under consideration added to the pool of ledger. So, it simply means the owner has to wait for at least 6 such blocks. As a protocol a block is added after every 10 min in the blockchain.

A distributed copy of blockchain is sent to every node in the network and is updated whenever a new confirmed transaction enters the blockchain after final confirmation by miners.

Hence, a bitcoin transaction process flow from creating a transaction to its validation process can be summarized as follows:

- When two parties, i.e., a buyer and the seller agree upon exchange of bitcoins, a transaction is created.
- The transaction is then broadcast to all the nodes that are participating in a peer to peer network.
- Each new transaction is listed inside a block.
- These new as well as previous transactions are validated by different nodes, acting as miners, in the same network by finding a suitable hash as a proof of work for this block.
- The miner node which is able to validate the transactions broadcasts the confirmation for validation to the entire network.
- After specific number of confirmations, the block is validated and accepted to be entered into the blockchain.

3.2.2   Double Spending Problem

In general, the problem of double spending can be defined as a potential flaw in the flow of any digital currency or cryptocurrency where the owner can have the possibility of spending the same digital coin more than once, i.e. payee, in no way is able to identify that payer did not double spend bitcoins during the transaction. As a solution there can be a centralized node which can check each and every transaction for double spending. But this solution will change the entire concept of bitcoin wallets as there can be no centralized authority.

Therefore, the only solution to the double spend problem that justifies its concept also may be that each participating node in the network must be aware of each and every transaction. In a system based on centralized authority model, the centralized authority is aware of all transactions and the authority decides which transaction arrived first. Only that transaction is validated and other is not considered a valid transaction.

Hence, to validate one of two transactions under consideration without a trusted central authority, each transaction has to be broadcast [3] to all the nodes in the network. A system must be implemented that maintains an order of transactions in which they are received. This system must be able to provide a proof of the time at which a particular transaction was received so that majority of nodes may agree upon which transaction was received first.

As a solution to this required proof Satoshi Nakamoto [1] proposed the requirement of a timestamp server. Timestamping is basically a medium that can prove the existence of a digital document at a particular time. Massias *et al.* in Ref. [5] define a digital timestamp as follows:

"A digital certificate intended to assure the existence of a generic document at a certain time."

In order to maintain the privacy of the transactions and for authentication purposes, instead of timestamping a block of transactions, the timestamp is given to the hash of the block. The purpose of timestamping a block is to prove the existence of data at that time. The hash of previous timestamp and the block is calculated and this hash is timestamped by the participants in the network. The previous timestamps are reinforced with each additional timestamp.

Timestamp
Having a timestamp server in a centralized system requires that whenever a client has some digital document to be timestamped it sends the document to a timestamp server where it is timestamped and a copy of the document with timestamp is retained on the server. But in case of peer-to-peer network where there is no centralized authority, to implement a timestamp server a proof-of-work [1] system is used publicly announce the hash with timestamp. This system is similar to the Hash cash [6] proposed by Adam Back.

A PoW (Proof-of-work) can be thought as a small sized data, such as hash code, which is very difficult to calculate but it is very easy for others to verify it. In order to generate a valid PoW using a random hit and trial methods requires a lot of efforts. A hash cashPoW system as shown in Figure 3.3 is used by bitcoin transaction protocols.

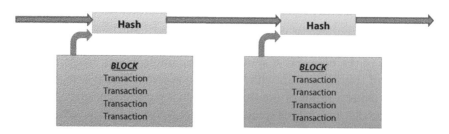

Figure 3.3 Timestamping block of transactions using hash.

Hashes can be thought of as large strings that are used to serve as PoW. When a hash function is applied to a given set of data it will always generate the same hash. But even a minor change is applied even to a single bit of the same data, and then due to avalanche effect it results in an entirely new hash code. Hash algorithms also exhibit a property that whatever be the size of dataset under consideration, the hash generated by a given algorithm always provides the hash of same length. Generally, one-way hash functions are used to calculate hash values, i.e., hash functions cannot be used to get back the original data from the generated hash rather it can be used to verify that the hash values generated match the hash values of original data or not.

A PoW for bitcoin transactions is based on finding a value that when hashed, produces a value that matches a given condition. In order to generate a hash containing specified result requires an average of exponential work but can be verified easily. This can be implemented by using a nonce (number used only once) in the block of transactions to be validated. This *nonce* when combined with the data provided in the block and passed through a hash function, such as SHA256, must provide a result that matches the given condition, for example the corresponding hash must begin with a specified number of zero bits. If a matching result is found the other nodes in the network verify the validity of the result.

Therefore, it is impossible to add a block in the blockchain without first finding a valid nonce which in turn generates a solution of the specific block called 'BlockHash'. Each validated block contains a 'block hash' that represents the work done by the miner. This is why it is termed as proof-of-work.

Proof-of-work prevents the network against number of different attacks. In order for an attack to be successful in the network requires lot of computing power and lot of time for computations. If an attacker wishes to modify a previous block that has been already added into the blockchain, the attacker has to recomputed the 'block hash' of the block and for all the blocks that have been added after that block in the chain before any other could calculate the block hash for current block being added. If the blocks are being generated too fast, the difficulty for redoing increases exponentially.

3.2.3   Bitcoin Mining

Bitcoins were created as an alternative to the centralized banking system. This means that the bitcoin transaction system transfers the amount from one account to another without any centralized authority. But how this is possible in a system having decentralized ledger? How someone is able to update the decentralized ledger without giving him so much of power that he can't corrupt anything?

In fact anyone can participate in the process of updating the distributed ledger in the blockchain. These participants are termed as miners, who mine the transactions to generate a nonce that could finally lead to the hash correct hash of the block as required. One using his computing power and a brute force attack method for guessing the right hash is able to append the current block of transaction to the end of the blockchain.

Mining as a step by step approach can be seen as follows:

- In order to have a transaction between a buyer and seller the transaction must be recorded in a block.
- The transactions and blocks are securely encrypted and all the contributing miners on the network can receive these encrypted blocks.
- In order to encrypt this block, miners need to crack cryptographic functions using powerful hardware and processing techniques to find the hash for the block. With a huge reliable application specific hardware there is a decent chance of being first to solve the given proof of work puzzle.
- Once the miner is able to do so, other miners must verify and validate it. Only then the block is added by the miner, who solved the PoW problem, in the blockchain. The miner who does so is suitably rewarded with newly created coins.

A new block is added every 10 min in the blockchain by the miners by generating a valid hash. The puzzles given to the miners for calculating hash are accomplished by establishing some "target". Various difficulty levels are set according the transactions for generating the target hash. For example, if the puzzle says the hash starts with four zeros and the actual hash for the block is say

00000129639082239efd54dd3426129639082239efd583b5273b1bd-75e8d78ff2e8d.

Let the block contains 1,000 transactions which involves 1,200 bitcoin, as well as the header of the previous block. Now if a user changes even one transaction amount by 0.0001 bitcoin, the resultant hash would be unrecognizable, and the network would reject the fraud.

3.3   Bitcoin ICO

Start-ups and budding Entrepreneurs usually face many hurdles in terms of insufficient funds or capital despite having a brilliant innovative idea to sell. A certain capital amount is required for growth and sustenance by a firm. Nobody will easily finance these new firms because of lack of trust as compared to already established businesses. Besides trust issues, distorted and insufficient information, accountability issues, agency conflicts, and exorbitant transaction costs for funding agencies or financial backers such as banks, stock exchange, venture capitalist or public are a few major reasons for a lack of financing for these new firms [7].

Hence, a new approach of financing Entrepreneurs and start-ups called Initial Coin Offering (ICO) came into existence. ICOs are primarily used by start-ups for raising funds in order to offer the products and services. ICO is based on the Blockchain technology, which was introduced in 2008 by Satoshi Nakamoto in his white paper about "*Bitcoin*".

Although there is no universal definition of ICO, but it can be broadly explained in terms of mechanism of crowd raising funds for entrepreneurial firms for their innovative and promising ideas where they are able to sell their tokens to investors in exchange for funds for capital just like shares in Initial Public Offering (IPO) [2]. ICOs are more or less similar to the stocks but they are utilized for services or products offered. But while using ICO for business one has to be careful as they can output huge returns for investors or they can be fraud or total failure to the businesses.

3.3.1   ICO Token

A token represents a contract and not a cryptocurrency like Bitcoin, Ethereum, etc. which is built on blockchain technology. A Bitcoin is a money equivalent; it has some value associated with it. You can buy a token with a coin but not a coin with a token. The value of cryptocurrency Bitcoin depends upon blockchain miners but the value of a token is independent of mining. If it is a Laptop manufacturing start-up, one token can be equal to one laptop or in an IT start-up firm, a token can be an annual license offer of software. Any service can be tokenized [8].

Working of a Token Contract
Let us have a look at the full contract cycle of bitcoin as an example

1. Token creation: Startups and budding Entrepreneurs give details about their idea in whitepaper where they provide

    description of token (information like token's name, token price, number of tokens, rules and conditions, uses of tokens, start and end dates of the ICO sale, offer price of token during ICO sale).

2. Token Acquisition: Token acquisition means acquiring a token for example consider a scenario if 'A' wants to buy a 'X' product in a vending machine. 'A' puts in the coin in the vending machine and selects 'X' product (the token that you want to buy in our case). Now the machine checks whether 'X' product is in stock and checks the eligibility of 'A' to buy 'X' is qualified. If everything goes well 'A' gets to have 'X' and the inventory stock information of 'X' gets updated (in our case number of tokens).

3. Token Transaction: Continuing with example in token acquisition, either 'A' can have 'X' for himself or he can pass it to his friend 'B' for some amount of money or for free. For transaction, both the parties ('A' and 'B') should have the token wallet that is supported by the same platform of the party that issued the token (vending machine in our example).

All the transactions are verified, monitored, recorded and updated by virtual notary which is driven by a standard secure contract. This contract ensures that the transactions are governed by the rules.

When a token transaction (buying or selling) happens, some operation-processing fee called 'gas' is also charged.

3.3.2 How to Participate in ICO

Figure 3.4 shows the entire transaction process for buying and selling ICOs. In order to buy or sell cryptocurrency, one must register with the cryptocurrency exchange as it is not possible deal in fiat currency and carefully read the ICO agreement and must understand what is the price per coin, how the token sale works, what is the timeline for that, general terms and token purchase agreement, etc. Once you go through the agreement, you must download the wallet as per recommendations by the ICO team. These agreements contains systematic guide for the token sale participation. Before the token transaction some operation fee called gas amount is decided. When the token sales start, there can be three possible scenarios. Firstly, you may receive the token right away, or you may need to wait for some time for collection of the token or lastly you may redeem your token manually. ICOs are unregulated and hence while using them one must be extra cautious and diligent in order to research, trade or invest in ICOs.

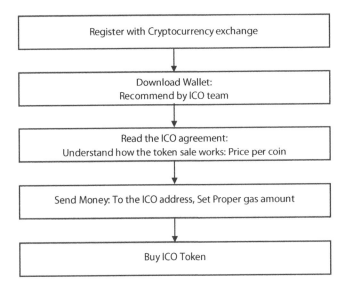

Figure 3.4 ICO process.

3.3.3 Types of Tokens

Typically, almost all currency falls under one of the three types of tokens: Payment token, Utility token and security token. Following is the explanation of these three tokens.

Cryptocurrency or Payment tokens: It is used as a medium of digital exchange for investors or a means of payment for goods and services and also known as coins. For example, Bitcoin is a cryptocurrency used to purchase goods or services from online retailers, merchants.

Utility Token: It is an incentive-based crowdfunding cryptocurrency. Investors finance the development of ICO project and become entitled for availing the specific services or products in the future by the start-ups who released the ICO.

Security Token: Security tokens are the most promising tokens and are also known as equity tokens just like shares of a company. The Investors become the stakeholder of the start-ups who issued the ICO and are able to take part in decision making process of the company. In order to verify whether a transaction qualifies as "token contract" or not a Howey test is conducted that is why Security tokens fall under the scope of U.S. Securities and Exchange Commission (SEC). SEC provides information about companies and investment professionals in order to help investors in taking decisions regarding investments.

3.4 Advantages and Disadvantages of ICO

Company Perspective

Advantages	Disadvantages
No Geographic restriction and Global publicity Scope	Huge amount of effort has to be made in managing the communication with the investor community worldwide
You can raise funds fast and money is quickly available	The funds raised in the initial phase are inherently exceptionally volatile
No extensive disclosure for fund raiser (company)	The company might get into trouble it comes under scanner of the regulator like (SEC)
The company can raise huge amount of fund at the initial establishing stage.	Due to highly speculative nature of ICO, investors become impatient. They pressurize the company to make quick progress.

Investors Perspective

Advantages	Disadvantages
High risk, High reward asset	If the money gets lost there is no way to get it back. If the hackers steal your token or you lose your private keys, nothing can be done.
Due to utility tokens, investors can avail the goods and services of companies.	ICO investors are highly prone to Pump and dump schemes (which artificially inflate the price of an ICO through false and misleading positive statements in order to sell the cheaply purchased stock at higher price).
The investors can use an escrow services (monitor the activities of the ICO projects to make sure that they are adhering to their contract) to verify how the funds are being used by the ICO company.	Lack of transparency, the escrow agents are third party companies. That refers to ICO ratings to provide their services to the investors. There is no enforceable obligation for an ICO company to disclose the progress made by it.

(Continued)

(*Continued*)

Advantages	Disadvantages
Early fund contributors can access and have more liquidity at the early stage of companies	Products and projects are very immature, that highly increases the risk of making an investment.

3.5   Merchant Acceptance of Bitcoin

Although, bitcoin came into existence in 2009 but due to the high risk in investing in ICO's the adoption of this cryptocurrency still remains one of the biggest obstacles. To solve this, various payment providers have come into the market that allows the cryptocurrency holders to make and accept payments.

Few of the payment providers are Flexa: Spedn app, Monero: DogeCoinapp, Dash app: Bitcoincash app, online stores:

1. Living Room of Satoshi is an online store which sells house goods accepts Monero, Bitcoin, Bitcoin cash, Litecoin, Ethereum.
2. Bitroadmarket.com is an online store sells a range of products and accepts Litcoin, Bitcoin, Dashcoin, Dogecoin
3. Bitify.com is an online store to buy and sell items and accepts Bitcoin and Litecoin
4. Btctrip is an online travel booking service which accept Litecoin, Bitcoin, Dogecoin
5. Cryptopet.com is an online petstore which accepts Darkcoin, Litecoin, Bitcoin, DogecoinFew merchants which accepts bitcoin are Microsoft, Reeds Jewelers, More stamps global, PizzaForCoins, Newegg, CheapAir, Shopify, Expedia, eGifter, Planet Express, Overstock.

Although acceptance of bitcoin as a medium of transactions for payment is still an open issue. Although cryptocurrency is the future considering today's scenario accepting Bitcoin as a payment medium poses a big problem. Any merchant doing business must have a profit margin, say 5% or 10% or 30%. If someone is paying in bitcoins, the value of bitcoins may go up to say 5% or 10% or so and may also possibly go down to say 5% or 10% or so within a day. Hence, if one's business is cash rich and doesn't require money to continue this business, bitcoin transactions must be chosen as in long run say after a period of 5–10 years its value probably might increase and returns profit.

Otherwise bitcoin payment may not be a good option. Despite all these facts, bitcoins are being accepted at various levels. It even emerged as the best performing currency of 2015 as shown in Figure 3.5. Authors in Ref. [9] have shown that based on data collected from December 2014 to December 2015 Bitcoins outperformed all the currencies including the US dollar.

Even after 2015, year after year bitcoins are getting popular for online transactions. When comparing with most of the cryptocurrencies available bitcoin has shown its dominance in market capitalization among all. It captures more than 67% of the market capital, in comparison to Ethereum which ranks second after bitcoin but captures about 9% market capital. Current value for one BTC is more than $8,863 and bitcoin transactions include a total market capital of more than $162,972,287,227. On the other hand Ethereum has a value more than $204 and includes a total market capital of $22,692,982,978.

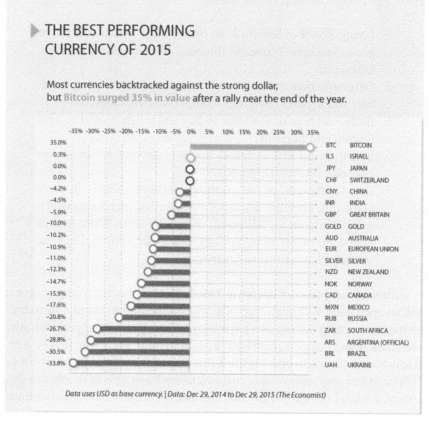

▶ THE BEST PERFORMING
CURRENCY OF 2015

Most currencies backtracked against the strong dollar,
but Bitcoin surged 35% in value after a rally near the end of the year.

35.0%	BTC	BITCOIN
0.3%	ILS	ISRAEL
0.0%	JPY	JAPAN
0.0%	CHF	SWITZERLAND
−4.2%	CNY	CHINA
−4.5%	INR	INDIA
−5.9%	GBP	GREAT BRITAIN
−10.0%	GOLD	GOLD
−10.2%	AUD	AUSTRALIA
−10.9%	EUR	EUROPEAN UNION
−11.0%	SILVER	SILVER
−12.3%	NZD	NEW ZEALAND
−14.7%	NOK	NORWAY
−15.9%	CAD	CANADA
−17.6%	MXN	MEXICO
−20.8%	RUB	RUSSIA
−26.7%	ZAR	SOUTH AFRICA
−28.8%	ARS	ARGENTINA (OFFICIAL)
−30.5%	BRL	BRAZIL
−33.8%	UAH	UKRAINE

Data uses USD as base currency. | Data: Dec 29, 2014 to Dec 29, 2015 (The Economist)

Figure 3.5 Best performing currency of 2015 [9].

Bitcoin are designed in such a way that it has become a viable currency that has raised it in status over so many years, but by virtue of its design only a fixed number of bitcoins can exist. Bitcoins are being mined with never ending returns thereby generating new bitcoins until the maximum limit is reached. A maximum of twenty one million bitcoins [10] can be created. As the value of bitcoins is limited, no inflation will be there due to excess availability of bitcoins. Also these cryptocurrencies will be protected from inflation due to any changes in government or any restrictions [11]. Hence, they are safe for investors who want to invest their wealth into bitcoins. Besides not responding to inflation, the price of bitcoins can fluctuate due to some of the external factors. All these factors helped bitcoin to be the best performing currency for the year 2015 [9] and are the highest value currency in the entire world.

References

1. Nakamoto, S., *Bitcoin: A Peer-to-Peer Electronic Cash System*, 2008, https://bitcoin.org/bitcoin.pdf.
2. Shavers, S., *Application of fincen's is regulations to persons administering, exchanging or using virtual currencies*, Department of the Treasury Finance, 2013.
3. Dai, W., b-money, http://www.weidai.com/bmoney.txt, 1998.
4. Haber, S. and Stornetta, W.S., How to time-stamp a digital document. *J. Cryptol.*, 3, 2, 99–111, 1991.
5. Massias, H., Avila, X.S., Quisquater, J.-J., Design of a secure timestamping service with minimal trust requirements, in: *20th Symposium on Information Theory in the Benelux*, May 1999.
6. Back, A., Hashcash—A denial of service counter-measure, http://www.hashcash.org/papers/hashcash.pdf, 2002.
7. Burns, L. and Moro, A., What Makes an ICO Successful? An Investigation of the Role of ICO Characteristics, Team Quality and Market Sentiment. *SSRN Electron. J.*, 2018.
8. Masiak, C., Block, J.H., Masiak, T., Neuenkirch, M., Pielen, K.N., The triangle of ICOs, Bitcoin and Ethereum: A time series analysis, *J. Res. Papers Econ.* 4, 18, 2018.
9. Desjardins, J., It's Official: Bitcoin was the Top Performing Currency of 2015, Retrieved from The Money Project Website: http://money.visualcapitalist.com/its-official-bitcoin-was-the-topperforming-currency-of-2015.
10. King, R.S., By reading this article, you're mining bitcoins, Retrieved from Quartz.com Website: http://qz.com/154877/by-reading-this-page-you-are-mining-bitcoins 2013.
11. Magro, P., What Greece can learn from bitcoin adoption in Latin America. Retrieved July 2016, from International Business Times, Website: http://www.ibtimes.co.uk/what-greece-can-learn-bitcoinadoption-latin-america-1511183

4

Ethereum

Shaveta Bhatia[1]* and S.S Tyagi[2]

[1]Faculty of Computer Applications, Manav Rachna International Institute of Research & Studies, Faridabad, India
[2]Faculty of Engineering and Technology, Manav Rachna International Institute of Research & Studies, Faridabad, India

Abstract

Ethereum is a significant blockchain-based platform for keen agreements—Turing complete programs that are executed in a decentralized system and generally control advanced units of significant values. A shared or p-to-p system of mutually distrusting node keeps up a typical perspective on the worldwide state and executes code upo n demand. The expressed (code) is put away in a blockchain made sure about by a proof-of-work agreement component like that in Bitcoin. The fundamental belief of Ethereum is completely reliable interpolate programming language reasonable for executing complex business rationale. Decentralized applications without a trust of third party are engaging in different sectors like crowd funding, budgetary administrations, identity management and gambling. Shrewd agreements are a difficult examination theme that ranges over zones extending from cryptography, consensus algorithm, and programming dialects to administration, fund, and law.

This chapter discusses about the Ethereum installation, working, Gas, ETH, ways to buy ETH, working of Smart contracts and DApps along with their decentralized application areas.

Keywords: Ethereum, GAS, BITCOIN, ethereum virtual machine, ETH, smart contractors

Corresponding author: Shaveta26@gmail.com; shyamtyagi@hotmail.com

S.S. Tyagi and Shaveta Bhatia (eds.) Blockchain for Business: How it Works and Creates Value, (77–96) © 2021 Scrivener Publishing LLC

4.1 Introduction

Ethereum is a new age of internet to make money and payments, user can own their data and your application, everyone can access to open financial system, open access infrastructure, no company or person have control. It is a programmable blockchain which means the developer can be used to build a new application. Bitcoin blockchain is the mother of all blockchains. It was intended for peer-to-peer transfer of values. The framework of code execution was introduced by Ethereum forums. The center place and thrust of the Ethereum blockchain is smart contractors. Ethereum has a decentralized application which has benefit of cryptocurrency and blockchain. The Ethereum set of rules are simple and practical, even at the amount of some data storage or time efficient. A common programmer needs to preferably be capable to follow and implement the specification, in that way to entirely understand the unequal democratizing ability that cryptocurrency brings and further the imaginative and prescient of Ethereum has a protocol that is accessible to ever user. Any development which provides complexity should not be blanketed unless that development leads to great benefit.

Ethereum was firstly reported by Vitalik Buterin in "white paper". He was a programmer and co-founder of Bitcoin Magazine and in the year 2013 he set an aim of building decentralized application. Buterin had stated that Bitcoin needed a scripting language for application development. He suggested to develop a new platform with a more general scripting language. Joseph Lubin, Gavin Wood, & Jeffrey Wilke were jointed as founders in the year 2014. Ethereum was finally launched in 2015.

The chunk of the Ethereum must be created as it can exchanged and divisible to be feasible. Their intention is to develop a program that gives facility to a single user to make a small protocol change in one location; the utility stack might not stop to feature without similarly change. Development consisting of Ethash, Patricia Bushes and RLP libraries. Ethereum does not require special features, its main intention is to provide the entire cryptocurrency environment. Every user must have an account on Ethereum known as Extremely Owned Accounts (EOA).

4.2 Basic Features of Ethereum

1. The capacity of resolving the problems correctly makes Ethereum blockchain the pleasant community to assist any

business or program. It is true that there's no different coin inside the crypto sphere which has potential of doing it extra correctly than Ethereum.

2. Ethereum records transaction details in just 12 s.

3. Ethereum has a natural boom and it seems to be stable. Even after the presence of DDoS and forking, to date Ethereum blockchain is in call for. The Increasing demand of Ethereum serves as a hallmark of its potential.

4. The potential of Ethereum to behave as a good platform for DApps is widely attracting businesses. Ethereum has been adopted by many companies and start-ups as a manner to transact. In February 2017, there were multiple fundamental businesses like Intel, Microsoft, JPMorgan, BP, and Thomson Reuters who collaborated at the Ethereum community technology for incorporating Ethereum into their groups. It is sponsored by Bank of America that is the primary economic institution to work with the Ethereum blockchain.

4.3 Difference between Bitcoin and Ethereum

1. Bitcoin and Ethereum are cryptocurrency. Bitcoins are only for digital currency whereas Ethereum is a well-known implementation of blockchain technology.

2. Bitcoin's common block time is round 10 min while Ethereum takes simply 12 s.

3. More than 65 percentage of bitcoin has already been extracted whereas not more than 50 percentage of Ethereum has been extracted to date.

4. Ethereum uses Gas to measure fees required to execute the program while Bitcoin cost of transaction depends upon the block-size.

5. Bitcoin and Ethereum vary in reason: Bitcoin is pitched as a change currency, or digital foreign money, Ethereum facilitates peer-to-peer contracts and packages via its own forex automobile. That's why bitcoin has emerged as greater solid digital foreign money, while Ethereum is more approximately clever contract applications.

6. Bitcoin blockchain has a limit of 1 MB for a block. A new bitcoin blockchain takes about 10 min to mine or create new

block. Bitcoin network can handle 3–4 transaction per second. Whereas Ethereum does not have any block limit. The number of transaction for block is decided by the miner. Each block takes 12–14 s to be mined and there are around 15 transactions per second.

7. Bitcoin and Ethereum have different methods of transaction like:

Bitcoin—"Ram sends 10BTC to Shyam."

Ethereum—"Send 10 ETH from Ram to Shyam if Ram balance is 15 ETH and date is 10.01.2020."

The table below shows a detailed difference between Ethereum and Blockchain:

BASIS	BITCOIN	ETHEREUM
CURRENCY ISSUE	It creates 12.5 bitcoin in every 10 min	It creates 3 new ETH in every 15 s
CURRENCY CAP	It has a limit of 21 million bit coins, of which 17million have been created so far.	Ethereum has no cap currently, but there are plans to decrease or not to issue in a year or two. There are 100 million Ethers issued.
New blocks addition	It creates a block every 10 min.	It creates a new block every 15 s.
Language support	It has limited built in scripting languages functionality with only a few dozen operations.	It has all required language to build programs and are called as "smart contracts".
Costing	The amount is decided on the basis of size.	It fixes a cost, called as Gas, to each for reposit in the blockchain.

(Continued)

(*Continued*)

BASIS	BITCOIN	ETHEREUM
Processing Time	Every slabin BTC is restricted to 1 MB in size (or 8BM in the case of Bitcoin Cash). Bitcoin can process 4 transactions per second	In this slap are limited with the gas-limit, the total overhead of all the operations in the block. It process approximately 15 transactions per second.
Ease of Mining	Bitcoin's hashing algorithm (SHA-256) can be performed efficiently with special purpose hardware, known as ASICs (application-specific integrated circuit).	The Ethereum "hashing algorithm "(KECCAK-256) is storage consuming which makes difficult to make an "economical Special-purpose chip". This permits Ethereum to mine decentralization.
Future strategy	Bitcoin currently has no such plans.	It has schemes to move far from extracting inside and out by altering the computation from "Proof-of-Work (Pow) to Proof-of-Stake (PoS)". Postakes squares dependent on the token property of the hubs instead of computational force. Likewise, it has schemes to handle versatility by actualizing "sharding" separates the blockchain into various interconnected sub-blockchains.

4.4   EVM (Ethereum Virtual Machine)

EVM aims on delivering security and executing unreliable code by computer. EVM make sure that programs do not have approach to others code and it also make sure that communication can be built without any prospective intrusion. EVM are created to provide a "Runtime Environment" to create smart contracts". Almost all cryptocurrency uses smart contracts. EVM method can be used to robotically conduct transaction.

This virtual machine is executable in various programming languages like: C++, Java, JavaScript, Python, Ruby, and many others.

The EVM is needed in the Ethereum guided and is influential to the concert mechanism of this virtual machine.

The programming language for this virtual machine is known as 'Ethereum Bytecode'. If source-code is inscribed it is esteemed for programming languages with Ethereum settlement-targeted language. This source-code is compiled to bytecode so that virtual machine can recognize the code.

This virtual machine achieve "Turing Complete" uses a marketplace that charges software steering done in preference to according to economic transaction executed as other cryptocurrency like "Bitcoin". In place of a transaction fee, you got a form of cost for coping with applications.

Programming language is exactly same as the structures that run and modify information. If those regulations may be used to imitate Turing's computing system, these regulations are seemed to be 'Turing entire'. This system may be numerically established to have ability to perform a viable computation. In various phrases, a Turing whole device is numerically capable of remedy any hassle which you provide. Virtual Machine is best "Quasi-Turing complete" because execution via the system are limited by way of gasoline, which act as a hindrance to the variety of computing that can be executed.

One can create its own virtual machine by installing Virtual Box on your system. After installing Virtual Box, The screenshots shown below gives step by step creation of virtual machine in order to run ethereumubuntu. Ova file to create nodes and transact them in blockchain. For Creating the Virtual Machine, Click on settings of Virtual Box and set the parameters as follows:

    Set memory Size of Virtual Machine: 2,048 MB
    Set operating system: Linux
    Set Network to NAT
    Set Advance features to Bidirectional
    Install EtherumUbantu.OVA file and Run by clicking Start.

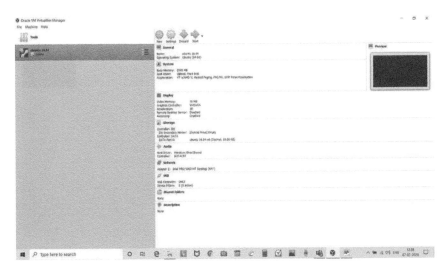

Screenshot 1 Creating virtual machine after installing virtual box on Windows 10.

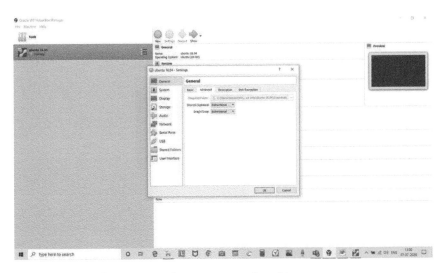

Screenshot 2 Set the parameters for creating virtual machine.

Virtual Machine is an application which one can use for different operating systems virtually on the host operating system. Here, as shown in above screenshots, Ubuntu 16.04 runs virtually on Windows as host operating system.

All the transactions are executed through Ethereum after running Etherum.Ova file. All the transactions are executed through this file. Ethereum actually took a significant step for transforming the blockchain

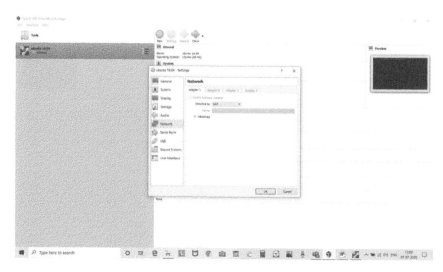

Screenshot 3 Set the network connection to NAT.

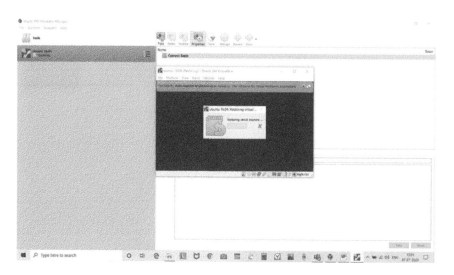

Screenshot 4 Virtual machine is created.

into computational framework that opened up a whole world of opportunities into decentralizing them. Ethereum supports smart contractors and virtual machine on which smart contractors execute. Smart contractors in turn enable decentralized applications that accomplish more than a transfer of values with an efficient automation of decentralized applications.

4.5   Gas

Gas is a mechanism to evaluate the fees that will be acquired for a program to be executed. Each transaction that is executed on the Ethereum wants cost to be attached to it, paid in the form of Gas. Gas price is the measure of "ETH" that an individual is interested to invest on each Gas. Wei is the smallest unit of Ether.

1 Ether = 10^{18} Wei

Ether = Tx fees = Gas price $*$ Gas Limit

Actual Tx Cost Fee: The amount fees which the user will pay for transactions in Ether.

4.5.1   Gas Price Chart

Unit	Wei
Wei	1
Kwei/ada/femtotether	1,000
Mwei/babbage/picoether	1,000,000
Gwei/Shannon/nano	1,000,000,000
Szabo/microether/micro	1,000,000,000,000
Finney/Milliether/milli	1,000,000,000,000,000
Ether	1,000,000,000,000,000,000

Ether smallest unit is Wei. Gwei hold billions of Wei. Before Buying Ether the user must check the current price.

Before executing the sender has to set gas price and limit fixed to transaction. "Run-out or invalid" is possible when the sender does not fixes the "Limit or amount" of Gas.

Miner decides the price of Gas. If transaction does not meet the process it can be reduced.

It is crucial to note that the gas limit can be (and is typically) greater than the real fuel used inside the transaction. In instances of an ICO, the common gas fee will tend to be exponentially better as human beings might be speeding to participate within the ICO. This could result in extra people

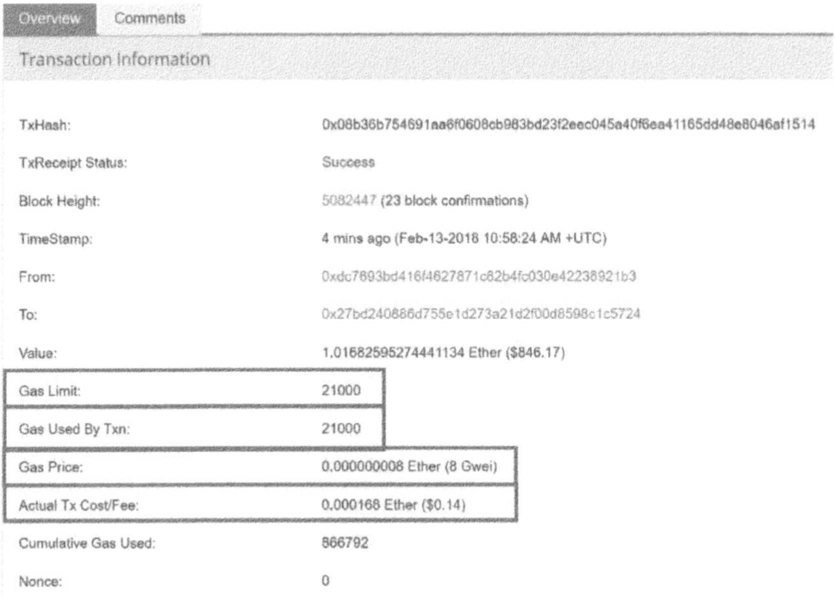

Overview	Comments

Transaction Information

TxHash:	0x08b36b754691aa6f0608cb983bd23f2eec045a40f6ea41165dd48e8046af1514
TxReceipt Status:	Success
Block Height:	5082447 (23 block confirmations)
TimeStamp:	4 mins ago (Feb-13-2018 10:58:24 AM +UTC)
From:	0xdc7693bd416f4627871c82b4fc030e42238921b3
To:	0x27bd240886d755e1d273a21d2f00d8598c1c5724
Value:	1.01682595274441134 Ether ($846.17)
Gas Limit:	21000
Gas Used By Txn:	21000
Gas Price:	0.000000008 Ether (8 Gwei)
Actual Tx Cost/Fee:	0.000168 Ether ($0.14)
Cumulative Gas Used:	866792
Nonce:	0

Figure 4.1 Transaction of block [Ref:https://masterthecrypto.com].

increasing their gas prices to have a better hazard of confirming their ICO transaction.

Figure 4.1 shows an example of transaction of Block.

The transactions can be speed up. One can virtually pick out the priority level of its own transaction. Miners will "paintings on" and execute transactions that provide a better gasoline price, as they'll get to keep the expenses which they pay. Therefore, they'll be incentivized to prioritize transactions which have a better Gwei.

If the transaction is required to finish at a faster pace, then you have to be inclined to pay a higher fuel rate. You have to pay 8 Gwei if you need your transaction to be finalized inside 2 min. It all relies upon for your urgency.

4.6   Applications Built on the Basis of Ethereum

1. Open Finance: This points out to a number of decentralized protocols developing open monetary infrastructure. These protocols are treasured because they're creating the vital exploration to permit everyone within the international

borders with an internet connection to get entry to self-sovereign, censorship resistant economic offerings.

2. Marketplace: It is built on Ethereum that allows for the buying and selling of ERC-721 tokens together with crypto collectibles.

3. Oracles: Oracles refers to an offering to connect Ethereum to off-chain records. They may be implemented for querying statistics from the net, information about one of a kind chains (e.g. BTC transactions), or even as dispute decision mechanisms regarding different assets.

4. Gaming: Digital ledger games are the games that encompass digital ledger era in its hind or mechanics in widespread.

4.7 ETH

Ethereum has native cryptocurrency called ETH. It is a digital money. It has same features like Bitcoin. It can be sent or receive everywhere in the world. It is used to store values, make payments or as security for re-payments.

The user has to buy ETH to use Ethereum network. The user can buy ETH only from the person who is already to own it. ETH which the user owns has to be stored in hardware wallet. There are some cryptocurrency exchanges from where one can acquire ETH with fiat or cryptocurrency: Binance, Coinbase, Gemini, Kraken, Dether, and Localcryptos.

4.7.1 Why Users Want to Buy ETH?

Ethereum is currently having number of the maximum famous and widely used cryptocurrencies all around the globe. This crypto coin is of high ROI for the user that would really like to change ETH to USD and vice versa for anyone to use it on the Ethereum blockchain. It is also of specific interest for those expert buyers who are agree with the ETH rate for large-extent exchange transactions. Thus, Ethereum is said to be a proper desire for all who are interested and want to perceive it as a software asset as well as those who really would really like to exchange it.

In addition to the application cost of Ethereum, its fee is greater attractive while compared to the one of Bitcoin. While ETH is numerous times cheaper than BTC, it could draw the attention of the people who are interested in gaining some cryptocurrency but aren't limited to a particular crypto coin. Some people are also interested in making any funding through the blockchain technology and following the concept of cash decentralization. Thus, Ethereum is one of the currencies that are broadly traded by the people at the internet and frequently used option for crypto-currency exchanges.

4.7.2   How to Buy ETH?

ETH can be bought through an online exchange like GDAX, Coinbase, Bitpanda and others through credit or Debit Cards.

To buy ETH, you need to follow the following steps:

1. Create an account on Binance, Coinbase, Gemini, and Kraken. To confirm the account you're required to feature files to reveal yourself. Once uploaded documents, verification takes place which takes about a day or two days.
2. Follow the guidance at the trade to deposit USD. These rely upon your financial group and twine switch. This may take three-5 corporative days.
3. Now you have got USD in you change account so now you are capable to buy ETH.
4. When you get all the ETH that you need, withdraw ETH into wallet you manipulate. Exchanges are widely diagnosed to be hacked and you need fund to be in the area which have non-public key.
5. You can deploy My-crypto pc app until the time you're expecting verification and switch.
6. During the execution, create new wallet and create fresh pockets. Use the password which you'll by no means forget about and create the account. Then it's going to offer you address starts like 0x. This is what you may use to move ETH from their account in your account.
7. For safety of your account set Address (04x234), password and private key. You must have backup of system where My crypto application is present.

4.7.3   Alternate Way to Buy ETH

Shape Shift is used to covert Bitcoin to ETH. Start a BTC<-ETH and it's going to tell you where to send BTC.

Then, create an Ethereum account and lower back it up. From where you have stored your BTC, send it to BTC deal with supplied via Space-Shift. The ETH will be available within 20 min in ETH wallet.

4.7.4   Conversion of ETH to US Dollar

The Markets Insider money calculator offers a forex conversion from Ethereum to USD in a few seconds. Vacationers in Krypto can make conversions at the contemporary change rate. The money calculator presents a great tool for traders making an investment in global stock exchanges by selecting one kind of currency.

QUICK STATS	
Ethereum Price	$153.64
Ethereum ROI Beta	2948.3%↑
Market Cap	$16,987,545,314
Market Cap Dominance	8.79%
Trading Volume	$12,696,580,059
Volume / Market Cap	0.7512
24h Low / 24h High	$152.05 / $164.94
7d Low / 7d High	$157.74 / $172.80
Market Cap Rank	#2
All-Time High	$1,448.18 -89.4% Jan 13, 2018 (about 2 years)
All-Time Low	$0.432979 35396.3% Oct 20, 2015 (over 4 years)
Ethereum/Bitcoin Ratio	1 BTC = 43.86 ETH

Figure 4.2 Transaction for buying Ethernet [Ref:https://www.coingecko.com/en/coins/ethereum].

Conversion from Ethereum to USD can be performed at day of exchange charges as well as rate at which it was allotted to do that, select the alternate fee date. Current date is ready via default. The money calculator gives the remaining price of the day prior to this in addition to the highest and lowest prices of the converting from Ethereum to USD. The consequences are displayed in a definitely organized desk. The Ethereum–USD price, the Markets Insider forex calculator additionally gives different change quotes in about a hundred and sixty worldwide currencies. User needs to first check the current price of cryptocurrency before buying and selling. Figure 4.2 shows the transaction of buying Ethernet.

4.8   Smart Contracts

EVM is a platform which is used to execute packages of "Smart contracts". It can be referred to as a "decentralized-worldwide-computer" where the computing of the system can be done through the nodes of Ethereum where any node can offer the computing of system and are paid for their work done in the forms of Ether tokens.

These are specially known as the "Smart-Contracts" because it works on the basis of the written contracts which are to be performed whenever the requirements are successfully matched.

For instance, consider developing a "Kickstarter"—like the practice of funding a venture by raising money from a large number of people where each one of them contributes a relatively small provider with Ethereum. Someone should install an Ethereum smart agreement that could pool coins to be despatched to someone else. The clever settlement is supposed to be a written contract that describes the terms-and-conditions, e.g. after $100.000 of forex is brought for the pool, it'll all be directly sent to the recipient. Suppose, if in any case, the threshold of $1,000,000 is not matched like we imagined inside a month, all the currencies can be sent back to the unique holders of the currency. Of course, this will use Ether tokens in desire to US greenbacks.

Contracts may be built on any blockchain platform. Smart Contracts can be used in lots of Economical Services and clinical Insurance.

4.8.1   Government

Insiders vouch that it is extraordinarily hard for our vote casting machine to be improvise, however, smart contracts may relieve all issues via offering an infinitely greater 'Secure' machine. Ledger-protected votes might want to be encrypted and require excessive computing power to get access. No one has that a whole lot computing capacity that is why it want protagonist to hack the system! Another smart contracts need to hike low voter turnout. Much of the inertia comes from a mismanaged device that includes lining up, displaying your identity, and finishing bureaucracy. With clever contracts, volunteers can switch balloting online and voter will turn out all collectively to vote for his or her applicant's management

4.8.2   Management

Properties like accuracy, transparency and automated system, the block-chain avoids mis-communication and discrepancies on workflow while providing a trust worthy single ledger. Ordinarily, enterprise operations ought to undergo a two & fro, even as watching for consent and for inner or outside issues to type themselves out. This is served by crypto-ledger. It removes disparities that normally occur with impartial processing and that may reason steeply-priced proceedings and agreement slow down.

4.8.3   Benefits of Smart Contracts

- Autonomy—One must not rely upon brokers, legal professional or other agents to confirm. It removes the risk of manipulation through another party, on the grounds that execution is managed by predefined algorithms, in preference to via one or more, probably biased, organization that may fail to adhere to the proper or accepted standards.
- Trust—Your files are encoded on a crypto ledger. Misplacement of these files is highly unlikely.
- Backup—Encrypted files are shared all over the networks. Creating multiple copies for every user on the blockchain to have your back.
- Safety—Encryption makes document safe which makes hacking impossible.
- Speed—Processing of documents requires time and paperwork.
- Saving—Ethereum removes intermediary which saves money of users. For example, user should pay an official to prove his or transactions.

- Accuracy—Automatic contracts aren't quicker and inexpensive; it removes the errors that may be possible from manually filling out thousands of forms.

4.8.4   Problems With Smart Contracts

Smart contracts are some distance away from accuracy. Bugs in program result in alteration of contracts. How government can receive tax on this smart contract?

4.8.5   Solution to Overcome This Problem

The Information technology resource centre, Search Compliance indicates that smart contracts can clash changes in sure organization (companies), which includes regulation. Legal professionals will transfer from writing standard contracts to produce standard smart settlement contracts, much like the standardized traditional contracts which you'll find on LegalZoom. Other organization together with service provider acquirers, credit businesses, and accountants may hire smart contracts for responsibilities, along with real-time auditing and risk checks. Actually, the website Blockchain Technologies sees smart contracts merging into a hybrid of paper and digital content where contracts are validated through blockchain and substantiated by physical copy.

4.8.6   Languages to Build Smart Contracts

Smart Contracts are basically built through various programming languages as follows:

1. JavaScript
2. C++
3. Golang
4. Java
5. Sql
6. Solodity.

FLETA is an upcoming blockchain platform creating a sustainable smart contract DApp environment, as we're operating toward ensuring that the proper languages are supported in our ecosystem, our beta testnetsmart contract is constructed primarily based on Solidity. And we are able to guide Golang, Javascript, Java, C++ and SQP for smart agreement development on the main net inside the destiny.

4.9   DApp (Decentralized Application or Smart Contract)

DApp
Bitcoin laid the primary stone with its cryptographically saved ledger, scarce-asset model, and peer-to-peer technology that brings a brand new version to assist constructing massively scalable and worthwhile packages. A new type of software program referred to as decentralized applications, or DApps, require those vital functions to be built. The time period application is usually used to relate to a software program that it defines a particular aim. Most of the applications that we use observe a centralized server–consumer version; a few are allotted and now increasingly have become decentralized.

4.9.1   DApp in Ethereum

Ethereum Platform created a protocol for building decentralized programs. It is an open-source public, blockchain-primarily based dispensed computing platform which features clever contracts capability, additionally referred to as scripting. It provides a decentralized Turing-complete virtual system, the Ethereum Virtual Machine (EVM), which executes scripts the usage of an international network of public nodes. DApps are greatly flexible, transparent, dispensed, and resilient and have a higher incentivized shape software model.

Developers are sharing exceptional reviews as what defines exactly DApp. Few developers say that there has no significant factor of failure which is its most vital characteristic and others say that there are greater necessities to it. The Ethereum Platform can allow anyone to write smart contracts and decentralized packages where you may pick out your personal 'policies' for possession, transactions formats and transitions capabilities. Multiple sorts are being created, along with economic, governance, community, felony, health, training. They allow a greater direct interplay among parties.

4.9.2   Applications of DApps

Various applications of DApps are as follows:

1. Maker DAO: The Maker DAO Collateralized Debt Position (CDP) is a smart settlement which execute at the Ethereum blockchain. It is a basic element of the Dai Stablecoin System

whose motive is to create Dai in change for collateral which it then holds in written agreement till the borrowed Dai is lower back.

2. Chainlock: Chainlock connects clever contracts to actual-international information, events and bills. The Chainlink community offers dependable tamper-proof inputs and outputs for complicated clever contracts on any block-chain. Smart contracts are unable to connect to key outside sources along with off-chain records and APIs on their own. Chainlink allows this connection securely and reliably thru a comfortable decentralized oracle network.

3. Status: Status combines a peer-to-peer messenger, crypto wallet, and web3 browser into a private and comfort-able communiqué device. Chat with pals, save crypto and explore the destiny of the net without being exploited in your records.

4. My Crypto Heros: If you ever dreamed of walking your own digital employment enterprise for ancient heroes, My Crypto Heros is the blockchain based totally casual RPG for you! Available for each cellular and on-line PC's, My Crypto Heroes lets you acquire and educate heroes from history. Equip your heroes with special and legendary items to shape the ultimate, unbeatable crew. Take your team into epic struggle and triumph over the crypto international.

5. Uniswap: A simple smart settlement surface for interchange of ERC20 tokens. A formalized simulation for pooling liquidity reserves. An open supply frontend interface for buyers and liquidity vendors. A determination to decentral-ized asset change.

6. Axie Infinity: Axie Infinity is a digital puppy universe where players struggle, raise, and change delusion creatures called Axies. Axie is the first blockchain sport to introduce: a mobile software. The potential to earn cash with the aid of certainly gambling the game.

7. Synthetix: Synthetix (formerly Havven) is a decentralized artificial asset platform. These assets—synths—are crypto-subsidized artificial property that music the fee of under-lying property and permit publicity to an asset without the requirement of really holding it.

4.10   Conclusion

Ethereum is not only decentralized cryptocurrency to make payments but it can also be used to create real world application. Applications are created in the same way smart contracts are created. In this cryptocurrency there is no need of middle person. The person who buys Ethereum can circulate directly to new participants in the form of smart contract.

Ethereum provides transparency to all of its users, which means user can open own their data, application, and can access to open financial system. Ethereum can be used to develop build application. Ethereum has its own virtual machine called as EVM. EVM is accessible to every user to create their new application and smart contracts. To measure value of each application and smart contracts GAS tool is used.

Benefit of creating as smart contracts is to store contracts and user information in encrypted format and store in different servers all over the world which gives some extra feature like: safety, backup, speed.

Both Bitcoin and Ethereum have the same purpose of circulating digital money. Both uses the same technology called "Blockchain" to circulate money. Bitcoin is only used to make and receive payments all over the world whereas Ethereum is not only used to make and receive payments, it is also used to make new application. Bitcoin and Ethereum have different fuel by their native-coin called BTC and ETH. Ethereum has better model than Bitcoin. Ethereum can be used for multitasking and an Ethereum transaction fee is less expensive than Bitcoin.

References

1. Norvill, R. *et al.*, Visual emulation for Ethereum's virtual machine. *Proceedings of IEEE Conference on Network Operations and Management Symposium*, April,2018.
2. Vujicic, D. *et al.*, Blockchain technology, Bitcoin, and Ethereum: A brief overview. *Proceedings of 17th International Symposium INFOTEH-JAHORINA (INFOTEH)*, March,2018.
3. Buntinx, J.B., What is the Ethereum Virtual Machine?, available at https://themerkle.com/what-is-the-ethereum-virtual-machine, 96, 2017.
4. Wu, Y. *et al.*, A Study of Smart Construction and Information Management Models of AEC projects in China. *Smart Constr. Res.*, 17, 24P, 2018.
5. Wood, G., *ETHEREUM: A Secure Decentralised Generalised Transaction Ledger*, Petersburg, USA, Yellow Paper, 2019.

6. Oliva, G.A. *et al.*, *An exploratory study of smart contracts in the Ethereum blockchain platform*, Springer, USA, 2020.
7. di Angelo, M. *et al.*, A Survey of Tools for Analyzing Ethereum Smart Contracts. *Proceedings of IEEE International Conference on Decentralized Applications and Infrastructures (DAPPCON)*, 2019.
8. Wikipedia, Ethereum, available at https://en.wikipedia.org/wiki/Ethereum retrieved on 3rd March,2020.
9. Alharby, M. *et al.*, A Systematic Mapping Study on Current Research Topics in Smart Contracts. *Int. J. Comput. Sci. Inf. Technol. (IJCSIT)*, 9, 5, 151–164, 2017.
10. Solaiman, E. *et al.*, *Implementation and evaluation of smart contracts using a hybrid on- and off-blockchain architecture*, Special issue, Wiley, NJ, USA, 2020.
11. Perez, D., Broken Metre: Attacking Resource Metering in EVM. *Network and Distributed Systems Security (NDSS) Symposium, 2020*, San Diego, CA, USA, 23–26 February 2020.

5

E-Wallet

Ms. Vishawjyoti

ManavRachna International Institute of Research and Studies, Faridabad, India

Abstract

Bitcoin wallets are cryptocurrency wallets that allows user to manage distinct kind of crypto currencies, for example Bitcoin, Ethereum, etc. Bitcoin wallets is very beneficial in exchanging of a sort funds very easily, transactions are secured as they are Digitally(cryptographically) signed and the wallets can be accessed from the web or mobile devices. Along with this privacy and identity of users is definitely secured and maintained. Therefore a bitcoin wallet provides every feature, which may be important for having a safe-secure transfer and trade of assets amongst different parties. A bitcoin wallet is a cryptocurrency wallet that permits usersto manage crypto currencies, it is extremely comparable to the process of receiving/sending money across any e-wallet or several other gateway which you are using nowadays but now you can practice cryptocurrency in its place, similar to PayPal which you're using for making transactions with your Fiat currency. The ecosystem of Bitcoin wallets like electrum, Bitcoin .info, Jaxx, myceliium, Samurai and Bitcoin-paper wallet. These are the names of few Bitcoinwallet which are existing in the market but there exist many further can becreated on the necessity you entertain, based on the safety you require, and based on the kind of wallet which suffices your need.

Keywords: Bitcoin wallet, cryptocurrency, cryptographical transactions, bitcoin paper wallet

5.1 Introduction to Wallet Technology

Bitcoins or BTC are the new age invested currency. They don't exist in the physical plain or form; therefore, this digital currency cannot be stored

---

Email: vishaw.fca@mriu.edu.in

S.S. Tyagi and Shaveta Bhatia (eds.) *Blockchain for Business: How it Works and Creates Value*, (97–112) © 2021 Scrivener Publishing LLC

anywhere, i.e., bitcoins are just mere records of numbers and transactions, done entirely over digital networks. Instead, they are maintained through private keys—which are used to access public addresses and transaction logs—that need to be protected and stored securely. A combination of the recipient's public address and an account (wallet) bearer's private key are the crucial and the only backbone which makes a Bitcoin transaction possible. Thus, there develops a need for wallets, as they provide backup and security for these keys and related transactional logs.

There are different forms of bitcoin wallets and they are divided on different requirements and also dependent on the terms of security, accessibility, convenience, and so on.

5.2   Types of Wallet

5.2.1   Paper

Paper wallets, as the name suggests, are physical wallets or are wallets which show output of some kind for transactions to be processed. These are typically documenting for the purpose of storing public addresses and private keys for receiving and spending bitcoins. Paper wallets are usually printouts in the form of QR codes, which makes it easier for the user to scan these codes and store the keys in their wallets for transactional purposes. There are several services available for the generation of the paper wallets like, BitAddress or Bitcoinpaperwallet. These services allow users to create complex, secure and completely random addresses for bitcoins with their own private keys, which can further be printed, provided no security temperament or resistance, in the forms of readable (scan) codes.

Since, the printouts are done offline, the safety of the keys is offline too, which means keys are safe from hackers and malware attacks. However, there is the reason of safety for the keys being offline too, the user must be precautious and take necessary needs for the protection of their private keys. User must make sure that no one is watching them, or they are in the vicinity of trusted people only, before generating a private key. And to prevent from any spyware watching you and your activities, users are recommended with a clean operating system like, Ubuntu, operating from a remote, offline device, or using output devices which are not connected to any network.

Moreover, the printout must be promptly and properly safeguarded after its purpose is completed, as it contains valuable, important and private piece of information. People use unbreakable lockers, or safety deposit boxes under authorized third-party protection.

5.2.2   Physical Bitcoins

Physical bitcoin is an unusual way of transaction processing of the bitcoins, with the intention of not allowing to spend bitcoins till the private keys are hidden. It works as the same as a warranty seal works, a tamper-evident seal is used in it, once opened the bitcoin loses all its worth. The initial idea was to generate a credit card like structure to access these spending, but then it was converted into a circular card having private keys hidden under a peel-able hologram. This hologram, when removed, leaves a tamper mark, indicating the redeem done over the related bitcoins.

Physical bitcoin is the most convenient and extremely useful way of storing and trading funds offline. The biggest disadvantage, however extremely rare, is that of the company generating these cards getting sealed or closed up, that way these cards and their related funds may lose all value and worth, because Bitcoins are still illegally in the gray area for many countries and can be countered by money-related authorities.

5.2.3   Mobile

A mobile wallet is an essential tool for the daily basis users, who pay for goods in shops, trading bitcoins face-to-face. It runs on mobile applications over the smartphones, allowing users to pay directly from their phones by safely storing their private keys under the user's personal mobile lock. These mobile locks are also of varieties from which the user can choose. With the increasing technology and next generation features in smartphones these days, there comes the advantage of tap-and-pay, and near-field communication, helping the users with the ease of payment without providing any information at all.

Mobile wallets also have advantage over accessing the blockchain ledger, as they access only the subsets of the blockchain, the trusted nodes on the bitcoin network to ensure that they have verified information. Other full bitcoin clients require to access a full and constantly growing blockchain ledger, and also require GBs to store, mobile wallets dial down the range of these ledgers and only target specific and trusted addresses.

Despite being convenient, mobile wallets have their own typical disadvantages. They are prone to hacker attacks very easily, they are insecure when someone simply gains access to them without the user's consent, or gets in hands of a naïve user who may or may not know what they are doing.

Some common examples of mobile wallets are:

FreeWallet, Edge, Atomic Wallet, Lumi Wallet, Blockchain Wallet, Copay, Jaxx, Mycelium, etc.

5.2.4   Web

Web wallets, also known as e-wallets, are used to store private keys on a constantly online server which is controlled and maintained by an under-agreement third-party. Web wallets are versatile in nature as they can be linked with other types of wallets as well, like mobile-web wallets, desktop-web wallets. They replicate the addresses on the devices a user owns.

Since they can be linked to the devices having internet connection, similar to mobile wallets, e-wallets also provide the ease and convenience of on-the-go transactions and the transfer of funds.

Parallel to the ease, the disadvantages run head-to-head for these e-wallets. Hacker attacks, cross-site scripting, phishing websites, are the most common vulnerabilities. Also, these e-wallets work on exchanges too, which may get cut-off in between the transfer process, completely shutting down a user's instances of all their funds, giving complete currency loss.

Some common examples of e-wallets are:

Coinbase, Lumi Wallet, Circle, Blockchain, Strongcoin, Xapo, etc.

5.2.5   Desktop

Desktop wallets are downloadable softwares which are installed on the desktop for storing private keys and generating public addresses. Compared to e-wallets and mobile wallets, desktop wallets are more secure as they store and backup offline and they don't depend upon any kind of third-party or related agreements. Their vulnerability arises with the operating systems they are working on. The operating system must be connected to internet for transactions to be processed, so riskier the OS is, more vulnerabilities the desktop wallet might endure. Alternatively, desktop wallets provide better solutions for the small amount traders of bitcoins.

Some common examples of desktop wallets are:

Electrum, Exodus, Atomic Wallet, Bitcoin Core, Copay, Armory, etc.

5.2.6   Hardware

Hardware wallets are a unique kind of wallet, used in an offline manner, stores private keys in a secure hardware device. Hardware wallet is the most secure method to store and backup private keys and funds of bitcoin. There are approximately zero chances of this type of wallets being hacked. Immune to computer viruses, these wallets don't need any software imports to be handled, they can easily be transferred out in plain text into open source softwares.

There are multiple types of hardware wallets, some even having their own screen like that of a pager, displaying important information related to their wallet. Some manufacturers also authenticate their devices over physical damage, and may charge their customers higher than the others but, definitely give them an assured, strong and trustworthy hardware wallet for securing the funds.

Some common examples of hardware wallets are:

Ledger Nano S, TREZOR, KeepKey, etc.

5.2.7   Bank

Not that much popular among the other wallet methods for storing bitcoins, bank wallet is just like a trusted party system, where the users trust a certain bank to secure their private keys and bitcoin funds for them. Unethical to the cause, banks usually don't accept bitcoins as their measure for investment, so a union of bitcoin agencies came up with a Bitcoin Crypto Bank. This Bitcoin Crypto Bank works just like a normal bank, it manages bitcoin deposits, tracks their transactions, and also keeps the up to date and deep understanding of the bitcoin market.

5.3   Security of Bitcoin Wallets

Malwares or malicious software can wipe out all bitcoins. It's not even the main problem, tracking these malwares is the most difficult task. A major issue of copying keys is also a problem. The decryption of a valid key may be at risk if the system scans 2 keys of same code. Also, there is the problem of Trojan horse, having even 1 file effected, the Trojan can then easily detect the number of bitcoins in the wallet.

Advice from experts of bitcoin says that, any user must avoid wallets that can directly be accessed from the internet. Third-Party storage feature should always be the last option. Be aware of frauds like, phishing and spam.

5.4   Workings of Wallet Technology

To understand the working of bitcoin wallets, we must understand the need and importance of these wallets. We must answer 2 questions:

1. What does these bitcoin wallets store?
2. Why is it important what they store?

Bitcoin wallets store a very important piece of information that enables a user to access their bitcoins in the blockchain. Each coin always remains in an address over the blockchain, which mean that NO coins are in these wallets. Instead, information to access and control these bitcoins reside in these wallets, which in technical term, is the most important information. A user cannot determine the location of the coins in the blockchain because of the security algorithms that prevent these coins to stay in one address.

So, a wallet does the work of accessing these blockchain coins in a manner that the private keys in the wallet line up with the blockchain addresses of the coins and then further again, the algorithm triggers itself, randomly addressing the coins in the blockchain subset.

A crypto currency wallet, compared with bank account, is a storage facility which safeguards a pair of encrypted public and private keys. Public keys are responsible for providing address for the wallet to receive bitcoins, and the private key is responsible for spending those wallet bitcoins.

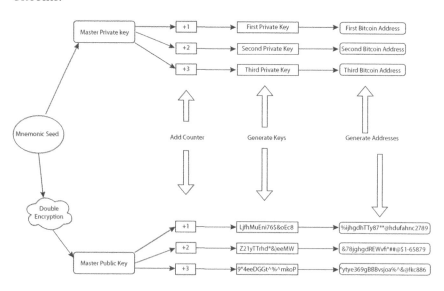

5.5   Create HD Wallet From Seed

An HD wallet, or Hierarchical Deterministic wallet, is an autonomous, digital wallet of the new age of cryptocurrency, which automatically generates a tree of private and public keys, unique to each bitcoin (cryptocurrency). These keys thus reduce the complications for the user to generate them by themselves. These keys are very complex in nature, difficult to understand by any other such system of Hashing Keys. Creating an HD wallet from seeds in a three-way process including the following steps:

- Initiation: Creating the wallet using tools like particl-qt, or ledger nano S, etc.
- Safeguard: Protecting our Wallet is essential for security purposes.
- Utilization: Address generation allows our wallet to provide transactional functionalities.

5.5.1   Initiation

Wallet creation tools are the software applications used to create seeds from the predefined Bitcoin Improvement Proposal(s) or BIPs. BIPs are dictionaries of random and easy to remember words. Each dictionary has no 2 similar words in it, and each dictionary is of different language. BIP39, is the most commonly used BIP as it uses word list of the English Language, typically the English used in the US. BIP39 serves as a backup for the Wallet, transactions, coins, the events of the wallet transactional logs, and the wallet security, compromised, lost, or destroyed.

BIP39 is used to create seeds in the form of 12-word list or 24-word list. These generated seeds are also known as mnemonic seeds (phrase), recovery seeds (phrase), wallet back up, master seed, etc. These seeds are the basis of generating private and public keys for the wallet security and transactional functionalities. The BIP39 has 208 lists of words, and the seeds are pulled from these 2,048 random words, to generate the phrase. For example, if someone wants to generate an HD wallet from 12-word seeds, then the number of possible combinations will be,

$$2,048^{12} = 2^{132}$$

hence, the phrase having a 132-bit security.

An example of a 12-word seed phrase:

collapse feed open chair terrace late creek fire full storm again far

5.5.2   Steps for Creating an HD Wallet From a 24-Word Seed Phrase Through Particl-qt Tool

1. After opening the particl-qt app, select 'Create'.

2. Then click on generate to generate a seed or 24-word seed phrase.

3. As soon as the phrase is generated, we see a note mnemonic symbol, indicating that a BIP dictionary is active. In this case, the dictionary is BIP39, and the words generated are in English.

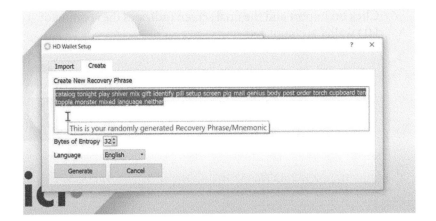

4. Import the generated mnemonic phrase to process a passphrase.

5. Finally, secure this mnemonic phrase by generating a user defined passphrase, which is not to be lost as it is your passphrase for your private key.

6. Click on import and the final screen indicates the creation of HD wallet is completed.

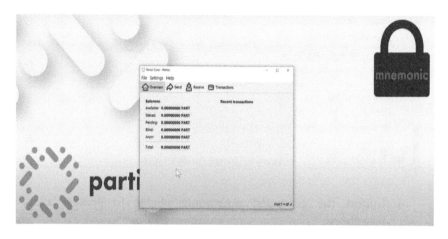

7. Safeguard
The process of protecting your wallet is very, very crucial. It involves encryption of the passphrase created by the user, which then encrypts the mnemonic code and thus protecting the private keys.

5.5.3 Steps for Encrypting the HD Wallet

1. Go to settings and select 'Encrypt Wallet'.

2. Add new passphrase or your choice and re-confirm it.

3. The next steps are important messages & warnings flashes for the user to understand and agree to them.

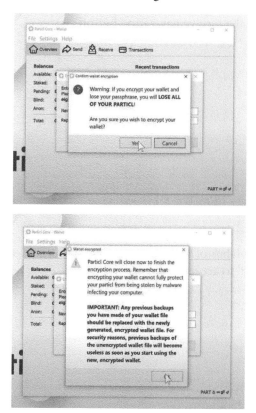

5.5.4   Utilization

After the creation and encryption of an HD wallet is concluded, it is then ready to be used for cryptocurrency transactions. Each transaction is unique because the address generated through the wallets are new for each & different transaction. Thus, making the address secure under the user's functionality, as the user may decide to whether make it a public address, to be registered by public keys as well as private keys, or to make it a private address for personal transactions, registered through private keys only.

5.5.5   Steps for Generating Address to Access Transactions on the HD Wallet

1. Re-open the particl-qt tool, and under a whole new window, click on the receive navigation button.

2. Enter a label of your own choice, and click on 'Request Payment' to accept a transfer

3. Finally, your address will be generated with a QR code. The payer may scan the code or copy the address to complete the transactional payment.

5.6   Navigating HD Wallet

HD (hierarchical deterministic) wallets, as the name suggests, is a tree-like hierarchical structure for the cryptocurrency wallet, which generates keys, public private, and their corresponding addresses, all from a single seed. This seed is a phrase of 12/24 randomly selected words from the BIP dictionaries. The pattern these dictionaries use for selecting these random words is very complex, and the algorithm is of the manner that it changes for each and every seed, preventing other users from guessing or inferencing any details or information about the combination of these words in the phrase and their respected passphrases.

The ability of HD wallet to create infinite number of combinations for the production of seeds, makes this new age digital wallet a very useful asset for the security of cryptocurrency and its owners, and also to improve the security in the blockchain system to overlook the transactions.

A cryptocurrency wallet owner has tokens stored in their wallets, and for these tokens to be useful, the owner must do transactions through these. A public address is generated for the receiving of these tokens, and a private key is generated for the spending of them. Recognizing the complex combinations of the keys generated, HD wallet thus offers and ensures the safety of the tokens and the privacy of all the transactions.

However, the only setback for normal crypto-wallets is that of the storage. As the number of complex combinations increases with every transaction, the backup for the latter becomes hefty and complex in itself, increasing the load on user to take care of every log and its backup too. But HD wallet overcomes this problem as well. HD wallets use a tree splitting algorithm for the addresses and their related child nodes. SHA-256 hash algorithm produces the key tree in such a manner that the addresses stored in the child nodes are easily manageable, without any errors, through continuous backup and generation of new addresses for new transactions, making it transparent for the users to just store the backups and not the logs of the transactions.

The ability of infinite combinations also provides anonymity for these HD wallets. Every time a transaction is done over cryptocurrency, user can use a different address to store the transaction logs and history secret, thus, making all the wallet activities anonymous.

Some of the most popular HD wallets are—Trezor, KeepKey, Ledger Nano S, Mycellium, Jaxx, and Elektrum. HD wallet gives users more control over cryptocurrency transactions than the other normal crypto-wallets.

5.7   Conclusion

In the world of business, trading, and transactions, a currency is the medium that binds all entities. And, in the world of bleeding edge technologies, bitcoin is that medium for commerce. But, with every currency/asset, there must be a system to store and secure these prospects of business. And thus, the need for banks, security houses, storage facilities, or fields for investment. For bitcoin, the security of hiding the transactions is done in blockchain, and the secure storage is done through wallets. These wallets are banks for the bitcoins.

Wallets are just like lockers in a bank, they need to be locked and secured for the risk of theft, and in the case of bitcoin wallets, keeping them safe is as essential as keeping yourself safe. These bitcoin wallets are targeted by hackers as they represent high value for them.

There are many ways to safeguard bitcoin wallets. Some of the common ones are—strong & complex encryption, and cold storages, i.e., offline storages. Backups are a major advantage, as software and hardware problems might erase your assets and holdings.

References

1. Bitcoin for Beginners, https://cointelegraph.com/bitcoin-for-beginners/what-is-bitcoin-wallets, 2018.
2. Bitcoin Wallet,https://www.investopedia.com/terms/b/bitcoin-wallet.asp, 2020.

3. Types of Bitcoins, https://www.coindesk.com/learn/bitcoin-101/what-is-bitcoin, 2020.
4. Creation of HD wallets, https://www.youtube.com/watch?v=GSTiKjnBaes, 2019.
5. Encryption of HD wallets, https://www.youtube.com/watch?v=wWCIQFNf_8g, 2020.
6. Transaction handling in HD Wallets, https://www.youtube.com/watch?v=zTHtK1ctgp0, 2018.

6

Blockchain and Governance: Theory, Applications and Challenges

Bhavya Ahuja Grover[1], Bhawna Chaudhary[2], Nikhil Kumar Rajput[1]*
and Om Dukiya[3]

[1]*Department of Computer Science, Ramanujan College (University of Delhi),*
New Delhi, India
[2]*School of Computer Systems and Sciences, Jawaharlal Nehru University,*
New Delhi, India
[3]*PTC India Pvt Ltd, Gurugram, India*

Abstract

Every systematic organization abides by laws, even the universe. There needs to be an authority, a Governor, who can frame rules, implement them and monitor each system. The present scenario has been dictated by a centralized scheme of governance. The scheme has its own flaws. There is a lack of trust and transparency, delayed processing, and complexity involved in the whole system. Hence, the wave is transitioning towards decentralized governance and it may become the modus operandi in the near future. A decentralized control structure makes the system more versatile and trustworthy by eliminating several unwanted middle authorities as well as removing the single locus of control. Blockchain has emerged as a powerful tool and can serve as a building block for realizing the implementation and benefits of decentralized governance. In this piece of work, we attempt to highlight the advantages that the blockchain infrastructure can reap in, ventures wherein blockchains have been utilized to bring about improvements from the current centralized implementations and finally the challenges that need to be catered to before we can fully switch to a decentralized model of governance.

Keywords: Blockchain, decentralized governance, blockchain governance

---

*Corresponding author: n.rajput@ramanujan.du.ac.in

S.S. Tyagi and Shaveta Bhatia (eds.) Blockchain for Business: How it Works and Creates Value,
(113–140) © 2021 Scrivener Publishing LLC

6.1 Introduction

Governance using blockchain indicates the process of governing something utilizing the power of blockchain technology. Governance may be undertaken by distinct entities: a central government, a market or, a network. It is the way rules, norms or guidelines are designed, implemented, maintained, regulated, and held accountable [1, 2]. Through governance, one can bring a proper system into the way the society transacts, to establish the methodology of interaction, and to build a cohesive institutional framework. Informally, governance relates to the political processes executing within an organization and between organizations. Generally, governance is implemented in a centralized manner in which there is a single entity, say governing body that is endowed with the complete responsibility of maintaining order through formulated laws. Its decisions are binding and need to be strictly adhered to [3].

There are undoubtedly some issues with this centralized model of governance. The structure involves hierarchy and top-down coordination. Often there is a lag in this which results in slowing down the basic processes. This results in incompetency to imbibe innovations, speedily cope with challenges and to evolve with the changing requirements of the society. The majority of the power lies with few individuals and if this central locus of power fails, the entire system drowns. There is an inevitable need for complete trust on the entities higher up and this backbone is split into pieces if there is evidence of corruption [4].

Blockchain has been one of the most promising technologies in recent times. It has paved the way for finding new managerial methods for the systems where trust is involved. The blockchain technology has been well utilized in building a financial transit system with cryptocurrencies like bitcoin and Ethereum. It has paved the way for a decentralized system that can actually be trusted and in which the power lies with each participating member. Every entity is held accountable for its actions and governed by strict laws in the surveillance of every other participant [5]. Blockchain develops on four important features: a distributed architecture, trust, immutability, and transparency. Trust is the most important attribute sought for in a government and blockchains are a perfect way to provide seamless trust through the several cryptographic primitives deployed, digital signatures, and through mining. With decentralization, the power is no longer in the hands of few but is distributed. This could help the entities involved to achieve political equality and transparency. The norms are established and monitored by each member reducing the scope for corruption or forgery. With immutability and authorization, the chances of disagreements are reduced [1, 5].

There have been recurring debates on the mode of governance being centralized or decentralized. The people supporting complete decentralization consider the State as unnecessary and an obsolete monopoly. They feel the society should progress towards liberality with no single authoritative power, no hierarchical structures and a distributed consensus mode run by majority. The concept of cryptonations that is self-governed public services on the blockchain like Bitnation has already emerged. There are other views that support decentralization of services but with supervision by one central authority. Which architecture is finally adopted, time will tell. Not to forget, blockchain is still in its nascent stages with several technical and legal issues and its widespread adoption would need deliberation and time.

The organization of this chapter is as follows. Section 6.2 presents an analytical comparison of the centralized and decentralized modes of governance and the role that blockchain can play in realizing the benefits of decentralization. In Section 6.3, the key features that empower blockchain and make it suitable for completely developing a decentralized system have been explained. Section 6.4 outlines research proposals and projects directed towards a decentralized implementation utilizing blockchain to tackle the problems surfacing with current centralized governance systems in different areas like public service and corporate. Finally, we discuss the scopes and challenges involved in developing a fully fledged decentralized governance system through blockchain.

6.2 Governance: Centralized vs Decentralized

Most of the existing governance systems are centralized in nature. Blockchain technology provides the potential to overcome the flaws of centralized governance and if lucidly implemented, it can be proven as a significant solution to all the problems of centralized governance. This section highlights the advancements that can be achieved after embedding blockchain into governance.

- Transparency and Issue of Trust: Centralized governance is the main governance model functioning in our society, because we did not have any substitute for a long period. This model demands involvement of humans at every step and consensus of various people to make a decision. There is no transparency in decision making and trust has always been a hassle for all the participating entities in decision making. For the first time, this problem can be overcome by using blockchain technology. To reach consensus, this does not demand human interaction and coordination at global level can be achieved. This property inculcates the trust factor and provides complete transparency in decision making [7].

- Effect on Corruption: Blockchain technology was introduced to be virtually fraud-proof, containing a unique combination of cryptographic and security mechanisms. Blockchain is fully digital and managed by an application layer protocol that verifies and validates each transaction between point-to-point networks. Its operations and governance are completely distributed, open and self-executed (due to presence of smart contracts). There is no need to follow regulations framed by any third party or central, state or private organization. Hence, there is no chance of corruption, overfilling and exerting frauds. On the other hand, centralized governance is managed and controlled by human entities and corruption can only be mitigated by the state laws. However, no assurance can be guaranteed by any government and there are cases of wrong utilization of power when it is not distributed evenly [4, 8].

- Cost of deployment: Blockchain is proving its ability in various areas like financial services. As mentioned in Ref. [9], distributed ledger techniques can reduce the infrastructure cost by 15 to 20 billion dollars per annum. Insurance management can be handled by using smart contract technology and claim management can be benefitted by detecting frauds like multiple claims for a single event [5].

- Processing Time and Complexity: Another flaw of centralized governance model is delay in processing time and higher level of complexity in data management, accessing and sharing. Additionally, these platforms are not compatible in such structures where active participation of the stakeholders is required. This can be resolved in distributed governance, which enables the queries to be distributed among the nodes and encrypted data bases permit each participating entity or data collector to manage data access controls. Each member in blockchain stores an identical copy and provides the collective process of corroboration and verification of digital transactions of the network. Thus, reduces the complexity of the network and delay in processing time [18].

- Security and Privacy: The security and privacy in centralized system is not certain, because information flows through various unfiltered channels, hence bypassing any measures to control or remove it [8]. This concern can be efficiently handled in a decentralized model, as blockchain technology contains confidentiality, integrity and availability (to the authorized users). It uses public private key cryptography to determine the authenticity of the modifications occurring in transactions. Also, cryptographic hash functions are used to preserve the privacy of data and to secure the data from external attacks [31].

6.3   Blockchain's Features Supportive of Decentralization

Recently, we have witnessed that blockchain technology has validated a new form of global currency known as cryptocurrency or BitCoin. This currency has gained abundant attention due to its advantages such as decentralization, disintermediation, anonymity, data security, data integrity, and availability [1]. After the success of BitCoin, Blockchain applications are not only applicable to the mere execution of a transaction, but are useful in computation of network, banking, healthcare, crowd funding, and many others (each field has its own blockchain architecture demands) [5]. The fundamental key to the implementation of Blockchain in the respective area is smart contract technology. These smart contracts eliminate the need for human interaction and lower the risk of manipulation in documents. In simple terms, a smart contract is a piece of code that can be written into the blockchain to aid the validation or negotiation between two parties. It operates beneath a set of predefined conditions that both parties agree to and the conditions of the agreement are automatically carried out. There are various platforms available that provide smart contracts. The most popular is known as Ethereum, which enables a decentralized platform to operate smart contracts. The users who opted for ethereum can create their own set of rules and be able to run the applications as written by them in the coding [1, 3].

Blockchain facilitates new business models that involve the contemporary organization forms, new standards of work, and production where "access" is over ownership and "sharing" takes over the property. Blockchain moves the edges between the hierarchical organizations and spontaneously formed self-organizing economies. Decentralized organization and decentralized autonomous organizations models will provide new direction towards non-hierarchical governance and decision making will be spread equally on each peer of the network rather than being taken from the center. The implementation of these models will also lower the rate of corruption [2, 4].

Another important factor in the human functioning system is trust while dealing with monetary matters and resource management. When we implement a system using blockchain technology, it does not demand any trustworthy third party and removes the barriers of dependency on human interaction in its data transactions and does not leave the chance of manipulation from an eavesdropper [6]. If someone tries to tamper the blocks of data, the hash value and proof-of-work are efficient methods to handle the disparity. The Economist termed blockchain as 'the trust machine', pointing that blockchain manages the trust issues between any type of transaction. An additional cost of the intermediate party is fully eliminated. Also, privacy of data is always a concern if a third party is involved, however, it remains preserved [7, 8]. Hence to summarize, the management and technological advantages brought in by blockchain include:

1. Smart Contracts: A reliable smart digitized contract can be implemented between parties without any personal or institutional third party interruption. Smart contracts help in monitoring, verification, and also improve the performance of the contract between users.

2. Privacy Protection: Even though the transactions are public there are no chances to link and get the identity information from transactions. There can be certain defined protocols for log management and manipulation by the public which can help protect the privacy of blockchain governance.

3. Network Security: The blockchain in governance helps the system to become more immune to security attacks. As the database storage maintains shared copies in the blocks which help the system to stop unauthorized access and malicious attacks. Blockchain makes the governance system less vulnerable to attacks [16].

6.4   Noteworthy Application Areas for Blockchain-Based Governance

Blockchain based governance has been envisaged in several domain areas. There are several real world services and activities that have been conducted through a centralized mode of control since ages. With emerging issues and no other viable alternatives, there was dissatisfaction among the involved entities and no sign of improvement. Some of these areas have been discussed in the following subsections wherein the current mode of operation is described along with the prevailing issues. Proposition to switch to a decentralized framework utilizing the fruits of blockchain emerge as the key theme in these application areas.

6.4.1   Public Service Governance

The role of blockchains in the implementation of decentralized government services was emphasized upon taking the use case of the Republic of Moldova. The land faces the issue of the opacity of information and growing cases of corruption. It was proposed that blockchains could be efficiently used to deliver e-governance to the citizens who would empower the individuals. They could transact using smart contracts that would clearly lay down the rules to be followed. It would facilitate land registries, e-voting, licensing, and several other government services. Everything would be time-stamped and signed digitally to retain its authenticity. This would help devise a democratic governance framework and constitute the model of liquid democracy. This could bring about socio-economic development in the state and drastically improve the conditions of the impoverished citizens [9].

The concept of open governance was taken up as governance without bias and provision of the necessary information as per citizen's request abiding by the Right to Information. It is a tedious task to avail of some information from the governing bodies due to the long complex process involved as well as the time, money, and expertise required. Blockchain along with e-governance can provide a simplistic interface that allows the citizen's real-time access to authentic data. Every transaction would be accountable and would involve no additional costs. The government tendering process has been taken as a use case. A smart contract-based tendering architecture has been designed in which a tender is created as a smart contract and stored on the blockchain. The bidders can access the tender, review it, and generate a bid, pushed to the blockchain signed digitally.

The tendering agency can decrypt all bids, evaluate them using a code, and then push the result to the blockchain. Each citizen can download the tender contract and validate using the bidder's key whether the result of the evaluation. Hence, the entire process can be executed in a transparent manner, easily audited, and verified [10]. Georgia implements a property ownership e-governance solution empowered by blockchain. The system is entirely transparent, reliable, and trustworthy, induces protection of basic human proprietary rights, cost-effective and has a simple registration procedure. The major steps involved are as follows:

- An applicant files a registration or renewal request
- A property title document is automatically generated in the records maintained by the National Agency of Public Registry (NAPR).
- The document is digitally signed and timestamped
- Hash of the document is used to complete the transaction
- All the status information is easily accessible anywhere at NAPR's website.

Hence, the information is completely secure and auditable.

It is estimated that the project would reduce the cost by 95%, speed up the process 400 times and property disputes would reduce by 20%. The Georgian government is planning to use blockchain to implement other registration processes and public services. This would result in sustainable growth [11].

Several blockchain solutions have been proposed for public services like licensing, and academic records. This can significantly help in the reduction of the complex communication processes, bringing trust, and safe record keeping. Nine pilot projects were studied belonging to different domains, countries, and government sectors for a cost-benefit analysis [12].

Public services have largely been centrally administered. But this also leads to the monopolization of power and profits. With blockchains, the assurance between the governor and the governed is strengthened. Laws to be followed can be programmed on a blockchain and any violations would be notified. Blockchains allow for more people to propose rules and help tackle the problem of agenda-setting and vested interests in governing processes.

The vulnerabilities in the system include security attacks on the blockchain, high computational requirements for mining, and identifying malicious nodes [13].

New Public Governance (NPG) is the strategic organization of public administration in order to build collaboration with non-governmental stakeholders. The core elements of NPG are voluntary co-producing networks, inter-organizational governance, and trust-based management. With the key characteristics of data integrity, decentralization, consensus, and transparency, blockchains are aptly suited for the implementation of NPG. The characteristics of blockchain governance include decision rights, accountability, and incentives. The blockchain allows coordination of strategy processes by providing for negotiations between stakeholders. It also inculcates smart contracts to offer customized services. They can be used to assure the rights and responsibilities of citizens, businesses, organizations, and government. Data is easily accessible and monitored by public service agents to ensure that the process outcomes are satisfactory [14].

Effective governance requires people-centric policies, policies to prevent corruptive practices and fraud, complete transparency, and societal control. Blockchains empowered with smart contracts can be integrated to aim at a corruption-free organization. One of the major problems while writing contracts is the asymmetry in information. Smart contracts have the ability to provide symmetry in information disbursement. They execute automatically and cannot be changed. This brings transparency to the system. Transfer of funds, bidding, auctions; all can be done through automated smart contracts in a speedy, simple, and reliable manner.

There are issues with the adoption of blockchain for public governance. There is a whole new concept of state, democracy, and citizenship with the flattened structure brought in by the blockchain built on the principles of cryptography which is again a topic of serious discussion. It is yet to be seen how blockchains can work as hyper-political tools managing social interactions and overlaying established political hierarchy [15].

6.4.2   Knowledge and Shared Governance

An important area where blockchain can be effectively deployed is Dynamic Alliance (DA) which is a collation of some entities for mutual gain and market opportunity. DA has five important characteristics: mutual trust and benefit to all, dynamic, interactive, works as per demands, and systematic and requires proper coordination. DAs encompass quick response to consumer needs that involves proper and speedy communication of information, security and synchronization between members. Hence, it requires a strongly built system that provides shareability and trustworthiness. Governance of knowledge in DA has five key aspects: knowledge-seeking, sharing, integrating, innovating, and finally assessing.

Blockchain can adhere to all these requirements bearing attributes like shareability, trust, and security. Using blockchains, the governments can promptly share information in a speedy manner due to a lack of hierarchy. This would also help in mitigating any risks involved and coordinating capital. In the market scenario, the blockchains can introduce transparency and reliability as the information is univocally available to all. DAs can assure optimization of the profits earned by each member of the alliance. Smart contracts help the organizations raise their core competencies and encourage them to innovate. Also, blockchains help reduce the transaction costs as information is available at each node.

With a distributed ledger, all knowledge is public and traceable, hence reducing cases of cheating. The customers can directly be benefitted by removing any agents or middlemen. Smart contracts can help assure the implementation of all Service Level Agreements and provide sanctity in transactions [16].

The research fraternity faces a lot of challenges related to the quality of peer review, the rise of predatory journals, and plagiarism. With the immense growth in research initiatives and increasing manuscripts, it has become difficult to manage these challenges and carry out the publication process in an effective and speedy manner.

Blockchain may provide an architecture that can help govern the entire scientific publishing workflow. Author submission, manuscript handling, peer review, editorial assessment, revision and re-review, and finally production and post review and publication can all be mapped onto a Democratic Autonomous Organization (DAO) blockchain represented by transaction events that are timestamped. The participants include authors, editors, reviewers, and publishers. All the information can be securely and transparently stored and managed without any hassles. There would be a complete footprint of the life cycle of a manuscript and the publication process can be democratized. Bad actors or predatory journals can be identified by tracking their activities and removed from the system. The framework surely requires acceptance from the publishing and academic fraternity and can ensure research integrity [17].

Genomic data sharing is another field where blockchains can be of immense use. The major issues prevalent with genomic data sharing include legal, consensual, privacy, and interoperability of bioinformatics pipelines.

With centralized storage of data, the huge responsibility of data privacy and access is on one single entity. With permission blockchains this responsibility is shared among some trusted entities. There is transparency and efficiency in access management that can be controlled by the producer of the genomic data. Blockchain also provides the benefit of the immutability of data and complete authorization. Access control can be implemented through a smart contract that lays the conditions for the sharing of data. Also, reward systems could be set up for sharing personal genomic data. Hence with blockchains, data can be easily shared in a privacy controlled environment complying with legal and ethical standards [18].

Blockchains can help record each action of the government making them more answerable to the citizens. Since every record is stored as a distributed ledger, there is more transparency in the flow of data within governmental organizations. The decision making power can be well distributed to some key players who can make a decision only when there is consensus. The scope of scams and corruption hence reduces in such a decentralized framework wherein everybody has direct access to all the information. Energy and resource management can be done in an efficient manner, e-voting schemes can be implemented to inculcate more transparency and secrecy in the system, digital records for each individual's identification can be maintained securely and with easy access. Hence, blockchains can readily contribute to efficiently governing Smart Cities [19].

6.4.3   Governance in Supply Chain

A very useful application scenario for blockchain technology is the prevention of environmental degradation by governing the usage of natural resources to prevent them from depletion. A classic example is the use of blockchain to manage the supply chain of sand. Sand is widely used for construction activities of buildings, roads, glass, etc. Considering high demand, Sand has been extensively extracted and graded. There have also been instances of illegal mining and hence, it has become even more necessary to formulate a proper governance system for managing the supply of sand across the globe. The main problem in the supply chain management of sand is that the information related to the cost and other factors is not adequately available. This has had detrimental effects on the landscape, marine, wildlife, and the ecosystem as a whole.

Blockchain-based governance of the supply chain of sand can be especially effective in the prevention of smuggling and illegal trade of sand. All the information related to the management of the supply chain would be stored on the blockchain and would be securely accessible anywhere. The key participants in the blockchain would be government agents, mining agents, industry agents, and sand agents. The framework would help regulate the request from the industry to the mining agent who after cost–benefit analysis would forward the request for the approval of the government body. Only if the approval is granted is the mining operation allowed by the Sand agent. Hence, all the sand trades are monitored and the supply chain can be easily managed. This could really help the prevention of depletion of this resource [20].

In the medical field too, blockchains can be deployed successfully. The drug supply chain is an extremely important chain that needs to regularly governed and monitored. After the drugs are declared to be ready to be marketed and released, they enter the supply chain. These drugs may include vaccinations and plasma derivatives. It is essential that the utilization of each drug is tracked and traced. It is also imperative to track and remove counterfeit drugs to ensure the health and safety of the consumers. If the supply chain is not well managed, such drugs may become a part and due to the complexity of the inefficiency of the chain, it would become difficult to recall these drugs. This is a major cause of concern. Though there are technologies like RFID and barcodes that can be used for tracing, still counterfeit drugs are a part of the system.

Blockchains can provide a key solution to this problem by introducing transparency and monitoring the transactions associated with each drug provisioning complete tracing. GCoin blockchain has been used to manage the supply chain of drugs where G refers to Global governance. A Consortium Proof-of-Work approach has been used to prevent double-spending. The blockchain would involve government agencies, manufacturers, pharmacies and wholesaler hospitals, and patients. The complete information flow from manufacturer to distributor to the hospital or pharmacy and finally to the patient administered with the drug would be maintained on the blockchain. All transactions would be done through GCoin wallets and UTXO records would be saved. The governance model would hence be more of surveillance net over every participant involved in the supply chain [21].

6.4.4   Governance of Foreign Aid

Foreign aids are official development assistance provided in the form of funds by developed countries to developing countries. This aid is used by developing countries to implement poverty eradication, infrastructural development, sustainable growth or educational programs. But there are several problems that hinder the effective utilization of these funds. These include lack of commitment among states, vested strategic interests in the donor agencies, and limited transparency due to information asymmetry. The receiving countries often fail to spend the funds in the designated area. Hence, the principal-agent problem is again witnessed in which the principal delegates the work of disbursement of aid to an agent who can carry out the task effectively but in reality, due to communication gaps or hidden selfish motives, the recipient procurement is affected.

Blockchain provides the opportunity to circumvent this problem by introducing the important "trust" factor when the system involves several participants namely governments, international organizations, and NGOs. Mostly the aids are conditional i.e. the recipient organizations have to fulfill some necessary obligations before their aid is released. With blockchain smart contract implementation, the commitment issues can be easily resolved and there is less possibility of any cheating. As soon as all the conditions are met, the grant release can be automatically initiated. Also, blockchain based prediction markets can help provide authentic real world information related to aid relations managed by smart contracts. Hence, there is no information asymmetry. Due to the presence of several intermediaries, the transaction costs are high in the current system. But with blockchain, the transaction costs can be reduced, owing to less dependency on intermediaries. All the transactions are traceable, and hence there is no problem of accountability. Also, the accuracy and success of the project can be effectively evaluated because there will be input from both the donor and the beneficiaries reporting results. But of course, such a DAO can only be realized with the support and approval of the governments.

6.4.5   Environmental Governance

Several organizations across the world are liberally moving towards blockchain implementations catering to the need of the hour. Undoubtedly, organizations like the United Nations that play an important role in global environmental governance have begun to understand the hype of blockchain and consider it as an alternative model for governing environment related pacts and treaties. The main reason behind this transition is the power of blockchain to provide authentic data that is readily accessible; and data is of utmost importance before any strategies in the environmental hemisphere can be thought of. There is a generally a lack of open data as expressed by environmental activists. But with blockchain, facilitation of data and communication is simplified. Several projects have already been initiated and one such noteworthy project is Integrated Program for Climate Initiatives (DAO IPCI). The project was an initiative of Russian Carbon Fund and implemented by connecting to a nongovernmental Carbon registry due to dissatisfaction with governmental registry. An ethereum based system was developed with the participants being ones dealing with greenhouse-gas credit based and quota-based emissions. Smart contracts were used to simplify the trading process, reduce the cost of transactions and undertake processing of mitigation units in a transparent manner. The project was in line with the business processes devised by Eurasian Economic Union (EAEU) keeping in mind environmental concerns as well as the international climate regime coming from the Paris Agreement. In 2017, the first carbon credit transaction was carried out pioneered by DAO IPCI and Aera Group using blockchain.

Several eco cryptocurrencies also evolved. These include SolarCoin launched in 2014 and used in solar energy based projects like Solar Change and SolCrypto [26]. Blockchain powered marketplaces for renewable energy are also gaining popularity. There are several blockchains in the energy sector just to reduce the energy requirements of an organization, for instance, UK based Electron. Then there are blockchain systems like BitHope and BitGive that monitor the utilization of donations and charity funds. There are also projects like ClimateCoop—The Climate Consortium Blockchain aimed at developing a platform for global environmental governance to decentralize climate actions based on matrix governance approach.

However, there are several issues that need to be resolved before blockchain technology can truly be adopted in this area. The energy consumption of some blockchain solutions like one designed for Bitcoins is extremely high. This raises concerns of the environmentalists.

6.4.6   Corporate Governance

Corporate Governance is another important area where blockchain can play a significant role. Corporates are often affected by the agency problem to which there is no well-defined solution. The agency problem arises due to a lack of trust between a principal and an agent who the principal hires to represent him/her. The agent is authorized with the decision making abilities on behalf of the principal. Whenever there is a lag in communication between the two entities or the agent makes decisions to fulfill his own selfish motives, a conflict situation prevails. Due to the nonalignment of trust between the two parties, a residual loss is incurred. Hence, the agency costs which include monitoring costs, bonding costs, and residual loss actually increase the expenditure for the principal. Blockchain offers a highly reliable and secure decentralized network to overcome agency costs. To prevent this, the principals have to resort to costly mechanisms to improve information flow and to continuously monitor the activities of the agent. Existing universal governance solutions are inadequate as the nature of agency conflicts varies across firms. There is no such solution that could have a wider reach.

Blockchain can serve as the savior in such a scenario. The monitoring activity can easily be delegated to a decentralized system freeing principals off this time consuming and expensive activity. The agency costs can be reduced and a proper channel of communication can be established through smart contracts. Blockchains guarantee that each transaction is executed as per the rules outlined and in a secure manner, hence assuring the integrity of the governance framework. All information is validated by the principal and agent and its authenticity is guaranteed by digital signatures without compromising privacy. This results in building a zero agency cost coordination relationship between the principal and the agent.

An agent-less system is also proposed on the lines of the decentralized autonomous organizations (DAO). This would help establish peer to peer connectivity and collaboration without the traditional hierarchical corporate layers. Optimization routines would then run at each node to improve the performance of the DAO and implementation of value to effort workflows by rewarding the entities bringing in profits. Hence, if the required infrastructural resources are made available, then a networked decentralized environment can be created without any internal or external monitoring mechanisms created for resolving agency problems [22].

A blockchain model for the Annual General Meeting (AGM) was proposed with a motive to strengthen the decision-making function of the AGM. Due to limited information and time, the decisions made in an AGM are generally flawed. Specifically, small share-holders do not get to play a vital role in the decision-making process. This is attributed to the higher transaction costs of voting. The main problems include the chain of intermediaries involved in buying shares and the immense costs of cross border participation of shareholders. These problems can be easily catered to by deploying a private blockchain facilitated by smart contracts. All information is available to all shareholders. As soon as a proposal is added to a blockchain, each stakeholder is notified and can exercise his voting power to participate in the decision-making process. The entire process would be transparent and complete authenticity and representation is guaranteed [23].

Blockchains have removed costs like agency costs but they have added three new costs incurred while transacting via smart contracts. Inflexibility costs occur due to problems while devising the rules to be encoded as smart contracts. Oracle costs are a result of inaccurate information provided by agents that lead to inappropriate execution of smart contracts. Security costs needed to ensure the security of the blockchain framework. But blockchains can definitely impact the costs related to monitoring agent interests and other firm operations and lead to unrealized indirect profits [24].

A virtual corporation designed using ethereum blockchain was simulated. The role of smart contracts in trading goods and services was highlighted. However, it is very important to create smart contracts with the utmost caution to prevent any conflict of interests and losses.

But a proper regulatory framework for such virtual corporations needs to be designed for its effective implementation [25].

6.4.7   Economic Governance

There are certain platforms that work on the sharing economy, and utilize blockchains technology for resources and product tracing. The other platform is related to fundraising issues. For example, BitHope [27] and BitGive [28] provide transparency in spending donations and also reduce the frauds related to charity. Blockchain Management technologies, such as Backfeed [29], can be used by large groups for equity sharing schemes. It helps to achieve crowd sourcing mechanisms and provide indirect coordination to groups [26].

Several research projects are being undertaken throughout the world developing blockchain solutions for managing governance. Some of them are presented in Table 16.1. The source of the information is Blockchain in Government Tracker [35] and a comprehensive list can be found there.

6.5   Scopes and Challenges

There have been several propositions of including blockchains in e-governance initiatives. Blockchain has been readily prescribed for use in the

Table 6.1 Some Blockchain solutions for managing governance.

Government entity	Project name	Project type	Project description	Current progress	Related industry	Project link
Australia Post	Digital Identity	Identity (Credentials/Licenses/Attestations)	A new mobile digital identity platform based on blockchain technology is proposed. The services offered would be identity verification using biometrics, application for passport, mortgages and licensing.	Under Development	Government Services	https://auspostenterprise.com.au/digital-identity-white-paper
Australia Post	Blockchain-Based Voting	Voting/Elections	This project is aimed at conducting voting for elections through blockchain using cryptographic protection. It is envisaged to be conducted for corporate and communal elections may be extended to parliamentary elections	Project Incubation	Government Services	http://www.parliament.vic.gov.au/images/stories/committees/emc/Inquiry_into_Electronic_Voting/Submissions/No_19_Australia_Post.pdf

(Continued)

Table 6.1 Some Blockchain solutions for managing governance. (*Continued*)

Government entity	Project name	Project type	Project description	Current progress	Related industry	Project link
University of Melbourne	Academic Credentials	Personal Records (Health, Financial, etc.),Identity (Credentials/ Licenses/ Attestations)	The University of Melbourne would deploy blockchain technology for access to students, administration and companies. It would be one of the pioneers in using the technology for this purpose.	Early Research, Project Incubation	Government Services, Education	http://newsroom. melbourne.edu/ news/melbourne-university-pilot-distributed-database-micro-credentials-0
DIACC & Province of British Columbia	Blockchain-based Corporate Registries	Public Records, Business Formation/ Licensing	IBM Canada and the Province of British Columbia, under the neutral governance of the DIACC, proposed a framework for secure and corporate registrations applicable for both within a single province and multiple jurisdictions.	Proof-of-Concept	Government Services	https://diacc. ca/2017/06/ is-blockchain-the-answer-to-corporate-registries-in-canada/

(Continued)

Table 6.1 Some Blockchain solutions for managing governance. (*Continued*)

Government entity	Project name	Project type	Project description	Current progress	Related industry	Project link
Human Environment and Transport Inspectorate	Toxic Waste Transport	Compliance/ Reporting, Regulatory	Transportation of toxic waste from the Netherlands to another EU State for disposal is a paper-intensive process and complicated due to multiple participants: the Human Environment and Transport Inspectorate (HETI), its foreign counterpart, the company willing to dispose waste, logistics involved and company undertaking the disposal. It was thought to make the logistics and approval process automated using smart contracts.	Early Research, Project Incubation, Proof-of-Concept	Government Services, Energy	https://media. wix.com/ugd/ df1122_3de6d e424d3b4f618af9e7 68e12d0ca0.pdf

(*Continued*)

Table 6.1 Some Blockchain solutions for managing governance. (*Continued*)

Government entity	Project name	Project type	Project description	Current progress	Related industry	Project link
Norwegian Centre for E-Health Research	Healthcare DLT Research & Innovation Network	Personal Records (Health, Financial, etc.),Identity (Credentials/ Licenses/ Attestations)	As a joint venture with Oslo Medtech, Oslo Cancer Cluster, NTNU CCIS, The Norwegian Centre for E-Health Research and Alpha Venturi (network manager), the project intends to create a knowledge sharing network of researchers and experts involved with DLT research and innovation.	Early Research	Healthcare	http://alpha-venturi. com/docs/DLT_ ResearchInnovation Network_Press Release_19062017. pdf

(*Continued*)

Table 6.1 Some Blockchain solutions for managing governance. (*Continued*)

Government entity	Project name	Project type	Project description	Current progress	Related industry	Project link
Thailand Post, State Railway of Thailand	Blockchain and IoT for Railway Logistics	Public Transportation, Supply Chain Management/ Trade	The State Railway of Thailand (SRT) and Thailand Post are planning to use the Internet of Things (IoT) and blockchain technology to improve logistics services. Blockchain would be used to keep record of high-value parcels.	Early Research, Project Incubation	Transportation, Supply Chain	http://www. bangkokpost. com/business/ telecom/1307071/ rail-and-post-to-use-IoT-blockchain
Cook County Recorder of Deeds	Land Title Registry	Land Title Registry	Cook County Recorder of Deeds would be the first land titling office in the US to record property transfer on the blockchain.	Early Research, Project Incubation	Real Estate, Government Services, Financial Services	https:// illinoisblockchain. tech/

(*Continued*)

Table 6.1 Some Blockchain solutions for managing governance. (*Continued*)

Government entity	Project name	Project type	Project description	Current progress	Related industry	Project link
State of Delaware	Blockchain-based Public Archives	General Infrastructure, Public Records	The project aims at using blockchain technology at the Delaware Public Archives, for retention and destruction of archival documents and several other features.	Project Incubation, Proof-of-Concept, Project in Development	Government Services	https://corpgov. law.harvard. edu/2017/03/16/ delaware-blockchain-initiative-transforming-the-foundational-infrastructure-of-corporate-finance/
Queensland Treasury Corporation	Government Bonds	Financial Services/ Market Infrastructure	Commonwealth Bank of Australia (Commonwealth Bank) has issued a crypto bond for Queensland Treasury Corporation using blockchain for bond issuance by a government entity both in Australia and in the world.	Proof-of-Concept, Project Incubation	Government Services, Financial Services	https://www. commbank.com. au/guidance/ newsroom/CBA-and-QTC-create-first-government-bond-using-blockchain-201701. html

health care sector to securely store and transmit the patient's records. Their use has been shown in educational institutions to properly manage information related to students, examinations, and results. Blockchain adoption in creating smart cities, for governing business supply chains, maintaining user identity records in Estonia, implementation of a secure e-voting mechanism and the taxation system are well pronounced. A digital tracking method for timber products to simplify governance of business supply chains was also proposed. A plan for the e-governance system in China was also proposed. But there are several challenges involved.

The most important of these are technological challenges like security, scalability, and flexibility. There are also concerns related to interoperability, computational efficiency, and storage size. An organizational transformation is needed to make the new decentralized system acceptable for use in e-governance systems. Also, there is a digital divide between developed and developing nations. Hence proper infrastructural facilities need to be developed and made available to ensure widespread adoption [30]. Organizational transformation steer various unexpected reactions inside the organization and can become a new challenge in accepting the new technology. The acceptability challenge may invoke from the users of the specific application. The fundamental reason is due to the lack of trust in blockchain technology because it is comparatively new and its efficacy is still not demonstrated yet [33].

There is immense investment required in the establishment of the hashing infrastructure which small organizations cannot afford to make. Also, there are concerns related to the scalability of the system. The control would still lie in the hands of some participants who have the ability to develop high computing power to perform the mathematical verification procedure. With the incentive mechanism of Bitcoin, it has been shown that due to a colluding group of selfish miners, 1/3 of the miners in the network would be able to control the entire network defying the goal of decentralization. In addition, the participants have to be constantly connected to the network, failing which they would lose their record due to unavailability of any paper-based backup [34].

From the present understanding, it can be inferred that blockchain definitely provides a viable solution to conceptualize a real world model of decentralized governance that is foolproof. The technological backbone of the system needs to be strengthened before it can be widely accepted. Services, supply chains, knowledge networks etc can then be readily governed through blockchain based infrastructure. What is exciting and intriguing is to see whether blockchain can lead to stateless governance i.e. a fully fledged decentralized model. This is bound to have repercussions. To be able to stand out as a hyper-political tool, all political interactions and policy making procedures would have to boil down to social contracts, which is totally debatable. Algorithms cannot bring in the human conscience while drafting policies and making decisions; though they can provide assistance in these endeavors. As of now, it seems they can definitely help decentralize some areas but the concept of a society without any central authority and totally based on decentralized platforms and distributed consensus needs to be deliberated upon [28].

6.6 Conclusion

The term governance has always been symbolic of a single authoritative power, an administrator that controls the management of events, entities, services, trades, etc. Centralized mode of governance has been the norm since centuries and any effort towards shifting to decentralization or distribution of power in multiple hands has been thwarted with the lack of a supportive plan of effective implementation. In this work, a brief discussion on the usage of the new generation blockchain technology for governance has been presented. The decentralization property of blockchain offers a new approach for governance where centralized control is distributed to multiple entities. This offers several advantages over the conventional centralized system. The chapter begins with a comprehensive account of the issues in the centralized mode and how a decentralized architecture can help overcome them. The principles and properties incumbent of blockchain that make it a feasible technology for conceiving the fruits of decentralization have also been detailed. Next, a number of use cases where blockchain has been used for governance have been explored. The areas where blockchain technology can play a vital role in making the governance more robust has been presented from the research projects undertaken. These include deployment of blockchain for managing public services, sharing and communicating knowledge via blockchain, an evenly regulated supply chain system, proper utilization of foreign aid, maintaining environmental values through environmental governance, resolving issues like the agency problem in corporate governance and finally economic governance. Finally, the advantages, challenges and scope of this marvel technology have been discussed for it to be fully utilized in building a completely decentralized model for governance.

References

1. Böhme, R., Christin, N., Edelman, B., Moore, T., Bitcoin: Economics, technology, and governance. *J. Econ. Perspect.*, 29, 2, 213, 2015.
2. Markusheuski, D., Rabava, N., Kukharchyk, V., Blockchain technology for e-governance. *The Conference of Innovation Governance in the Public Sector*, Kazan, Russia, 2017.
3. Aste, T., Tasca, P., Di Matteo, T., Blockchain technologies: The foreseeable impact on society and industry. *Computer*, 50, 9, 2017.
4. Al-Saqaf, W. and Seidler, N., Blockchain technology for social impact: opportunities and challenges ahead. *J. Cyber Policy*, 2, 3, 2017. 2. Peters, G.W. and Panayi, E., Understanding modern banking ledgers through blockchain technologies: Future of transaction processing and smart contracts on the internet of money, in: *Banking beyond banks and money*, Springer, 2016.
5. Peters, G.W. and Panayi, E., Understanding modern banking ledgers through blockchain technologies: Future of transaction processing and smart contracts on the internet of money, in: *Banking Beyond Banks and Money*, Springer, Cham, Switzerland, 2016.
6. Hardwick, F.S., Gioulis, A., Akram, R.N., Markantonakis, K., E-voting with blockchain: An e-voting protocol with decentralisation and voter privacy, in: *2018 IEEE International Conference on Internet of Things (iThings) and IEEE Green Computing and Communications (GreenCom) and IEEE Cyber, Physical and Social Computing (CPSCom) and IEEE Smart Data (SmartData)*, IEEE, p. 1561, 2018.
7. Glaser, F., *Pervasive decentralisation of digital infrastructures: A framework for blockchain enabled system and use case analysis*, In Proceedings of the 50th Hawaii international conference on system sciences. Hawaii, USA 2017.
8. De Filippi, P. and Loveluck, B., The invisible politics of bitcoin: Governance crisis of a decentralized infrastructure. *Internet Policy Rev.*, 5, 4, 2016.
9. Pilkington, M., Crudu, R., Grant, L.G., Blockchain and bitcoin as a way to lift a country out of poverty-tourism 2.0 and e-governance in the Republic of Moldova. *Int. J. Internet Technol. Secur. Trans.*, 7, 2, 115, 2017.
10. Hardwick, F.S., Akram, R.N., Markantonakis, K., Fair and Transparent Blockchain-based Tendering Framework-A Step towards Open Governance, in: *2018 17th IEEE International Conference on Trust, Security and Privacy In Computing And Communications/12th IEEE International Conference On Big Data Science And Engineering (TrustCom/BigDataSE)*, p. 1342, 2018.
11. Goderdzishvili, N., Gordadze, E., Gagnidze, N., Georgia's Blockchain-powered Property Registration: Never blocked, Always Secured: Ownership Data Kept Best!, in: *Proceedings of the 11th International Conference on Theory and Practice of Electronic Governance*, p. 673, 2018.
12. Allessie, D., Sobolewski, M., Vaccari, L., Identifying the true drivers of costs and benefits of blockchain implementation for public services. *Proceedings*

of the 19th Annual International Conference on Digital Government Research: Governance in the Data Age, p. 1, 2018.

13. Cowen, N., Markets for rules: The promise and peril of blockchain distributed governance. *J. Entrepreneurship Public Policy*, 9, 2, 213–226, 2019.

14. Brinkmann, M. and Heine, M., Can Blockchain Leverage for New Public Governance? A Conceptual Analysis on Process Level, in: *Proceedings of the 12th International Conference on Theory and Practice of Electronic Governance*, p. 338, 2019.

15. de Souza, R.C., Luciano, E.M., Wiedenhöft, G.C., The uses of the Blockchain Smart Contracts to reduce the levels of corruption: Some preliminary thoughts, in: *Proceedings of the 19th Annual International Conference on Digital Government Research: Governance in the Data Age*, 2018.

16. Zhang, Y., Sun, W., Xie, C., Blockchain in smart city development—The knowledge governance framework in dynamic alliance, in: *International Conference on Smart City and Intelligent Building*, Springer, p. 137, 2018.

17. Mackey, T.K., Shah, N., Miyachi, K., Short, J., Clauson, K.A., A., Framework Proposal for Blockchain-based Scientific Publishing using Shared Governance. *Front. Blockchain*, 2, 19, 2019.

18. Shabani, M., Blockchain-based platforms for genomic data sharing: a de-centralized approach in response to the governance problems? *J. Am. Med. Inform. Assoc.*, 26, 1, 76, 2019.

19. Patel, V.N. and Patel, C.N., Blockchain Technology: An Aid to the Governance of Smart Cities, in: *Information and Communication Technology for Sustainable Development*, Springer, p. 373, 2020.

20. Georgescu, A., Gheorghe, A.V., Piso, M.I., Katina, P.F., Governance by Emerging Technologies—The Case for Sand and Blockchain Technology, in: *Critical Space Infrastructures*, pp. 237–247, Springer, Cham, 2019.

21. Tseng, J.H., Liao, Y.C., Chong, B., Liao, S.W., Governance on the drug supply chain *via* gcoin blockchain. *Int. J. Environ. Res. Public Health*, 15, 6, 1055, 2018.

22. Kaal, W.A., Blockchain solutions for agency problems in corporate governance, in: *Economic Information To Facilitate Decision Making*, K.R. Balachandran (Ed.), World Scientific Publishers, Singapore, 2019.

23. Lafarre, A. and Van der Elst, C., Blockchain technology for corporate governance and shareholder activism. *European Corporate Governance Institute (ECGI)—Law Working Paper*, 2018.

24. Murray, A., Kuban, S., Josefy, M., Anderson, J., Contracting in the Smart Era: The Implications of Blockchain and Decentralized Autonomous Organizations for Contracting and Corporate Governance. *Academy of Management Perspectives*, (ja), 2019.

25. Leonhard, R., Corporate Governance on Ethereum's Blockchain. https://papers.ssrn.com/sol3/papers.cfm?abstract_id=2977522, 2017.

26. Vladimirova, A.V., Blockchain Revolution in Global Environmental Governance: Too Good to Be True?, in: *International Conference on Internet Science*, Springer, 2018.

27. Bitcoin Crowdfunding for Charity, https://bithope.org, 2018.

28. Bitgive—Vastly Improving Philanthropic Impact with Blockchain Technology, BitGive Foundation—1st Bitcoin and Blockchain Nonprofit, 2020.

29. Backfeed|Spreading Consensus. http://backfeed.cc/, 2019.

30. Batubara, F.R., Ubacht, J., Janssen, M., Challenges of blockchain technology adoption for e-government: a systematic literature review, in: *Proceedings of the 19th Annual International Conference on Digital Government Research: Governance in the Data Age*, 2018.

31. Sun, J., Yan, J., Zhang, K.Z., Blockchain-based sharing services: What blockchain technology can contribute to smart cities. *Financial Innov.*, 2, 1, 2016.

32. García-Bañuelos, L., Ponomarev, A., Dumas, M., Weber, I., Optimized execution of business processes on blockchain, in: *International Conference on Business Process Management*, Springer, 2017.

33. Sharples, M. and Domingue, J., The blockchain and kudos: A distributed system for educational record, reputation and reward, in: *European Conference on Technology Enhanced Learning*, Springer, Cham, 2016.

34. Atzori, M., Blockchain technology and decentralized governance: Is the state still necessary? Available at SSRN 2709713, 2015.

35. Blockchain in Government Tracker, https://airtable.com/universe/exps QEGKoZO2lExKK/blockchain-in-government-tracker, 2020.

7

Blockchain-Based Identity Management

Abhishek Bhattacharya

Whrrl, Thane, Maharashtra, India

Abstract

Identity Management comes at the crux of usability of systems and processes by eliminating the chances of fraudulent behavior. This can range from online voting and accessing government systems to as simple as logging into websites. This chapter takes a look at the potential of blockchain-based technology implementation in the use cases of identity management.

The chapter starts by taking a look at the currently existing identity management systems and the challenges associated with their usage. Next is the information about decentralized identifiers which set up the base for discussion around blockchain-based identification mechanisms and the kind of data security these systems are capable of providing—hence giving us the added advantage over stopping potential fraudulent behavior. With a global pandemic underway, it has become all the more important to explore more systems to verify identities—especially with the supposedly reducing role of contact in verification.

Keywords: Decentralized indentifiers, blockchain identity, hyperledger, nuggets, revocation

7.1 Introduction

Identity management has become one of the critical necessities in the present world. An effective identity management system is the one that provides access to data only for authorized and authenticated personnel. The greater the efficiency of the system, the better will be security. The demand for such a robust but easy-to-use identity management scheme is growing day-by-day owing to the increase in the number of cyberattacks.

Email: abhib.work@gmail.com

S.S. Tyagi and Shaveta Bhatia (eds.) Blockchain for Business: How it Works and Creates Value, (141–158) © 2021 Scrivener Publishing LLC

One of the recent developments in this arena is to make use of blockchain technology to deal with personal identification and legality. The prime reason behind the choice is the foolproof nature associated with the blockchain systems.

This chapter throws more light over the topic of using blockchain in identity management systems. First, we will review a few of the existing identity management protocols and try to figure out their challenges. Next, we will see how the blockchain-enabled systems provide potential solutions to these loopholes. Further, we will dive a little more into the topic and understand its prime concepts like Digital Identity Relationships, Decentralized Identifiers (DIDs), the process of authorization, know-hows of revocation, and others. Lastly, we covnclude by presenting a few points to ponder over and with a table summarizing the important differences between traditional and blockchain-based identity solutions.

7.2   Existing Identity Management Systems and Their Challenges

Most of the present identity systems are paper-based. Authorized agencies issue them after verifying the background of the personnel thoroughly. The percentage of trust and the validity of the issued certificate are bound with the confidence level associated with the issuing department. The only way to get authenticated would be to produce the original copies of the certificates when demanded. The process of verification usually demands an in-person visit and is time-consuming. Furthermore, paper-based identity certificates are highly vulnerable to undesired activities like theft, loss, duplication, and scam. In these cases, the person will not be able to recover them easily and would fail to establish his identity. This will lead to undesirable repercussions like denial of essential services, the inability to obtain government grants, and failure to remain accountable (Figure 7.1).

The growing use of online platforms has resulted in another popular means to establish one's identity. This is known as digital identity and is a result of actions like registering on a website, commenting on a social network, searching for an item, or online shopping. Each such action, performed on the world-wide-web, results in a digital footprint that can be used to verify a person's identity. Such a process considerably speeds up the process of authentication and most often eliminates the need for personal presence. However, currently, there is no dedicated, reliable system to accomplish this. Most of the time, the information submitted to

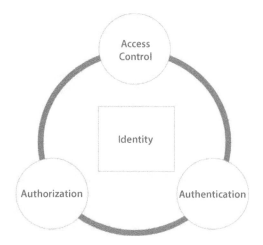

Figure 7.1 Identity controlling factors, authentication, and authorization, directly impact accessibility.

a particular website remains confined within it, making it usually non-usable on other platforms.

As a result, the user will be forced to re-enter all his data on every single website he uses. This repetitive task is time-taking and trivial in nature. One more issue with the existing systems is their centralized nature. That is, the majority of the prevalent systems store the user data on a centralized server. Once the data gets stock-piled, none can control it; leave alone the user, not even the database owner can know where it is stored and who all has accessed it. This puts user privacy at its greatest stake as his data can be accessed by any third party at any point of time without leaving even a single scar. Furthermore, it is well known that the centralized servers are vulnerable to issues like single-point failure and hacking [1], the number of which is increasing at an alarming rate during recent times.

Owing to the factors mentioned above, we can conclude that the existing identity management systems are weak and obsolete. There exist quite a lot of loopholes that need to be patched-up to increase their efficiency to the desired level. The truth associated with the statement is upheld, especially when it comes to factors like portability, time spent on verification, and, most importantly, privacy. This indicates that there is a critical need to develop a robust system wherein the user can store and manage his identity information securely while having complete control over its flow. That is, in such a system, an individual should have complete control over his data and must be able to decide on factors like 'what,' 'how much,' 'with whom' and 'when' while dealing with its sharing.

7.3   Concept of Decentralized Identifiers

From the previous section, it is evident that storing user information on a central database increases the risk of being hacked. This directly implies that there is a need to decentralize the process by increasing the number of nodes. A potential solution to this would be to store the data at one's personal device, say, mobile phone. Result? There will be as many data-laden nodes as the number of phones—greatly distributed network (Figure 7.2)! Undoubtedly, this creates a robust barrier for acts like data breaches. The associated idea of handling and controlling the identity by one's self is known as Self-Sovereign Identity (SSID) management [2] and is based on blockchain technology.

The starting point for SSID would be to generate a decentralized identity (DID) by signing up on a self-sovereign identity data platform [3]. This would generate a set of user-specific private and public keys. Public keys are the ones that will be rotated on the chain for maintenance reasons while the private keys play the magic of securing the data. The only feasible way to access the stored information would be to use the private keys (Figure 7.3), known only to the user. It's a 'no-key, no-data' kind of arrangement where the DIDs act as an incorruptible digital watermark defining a person's identity [4]. There is no way to access or corrupt the information except for the use of private keys.

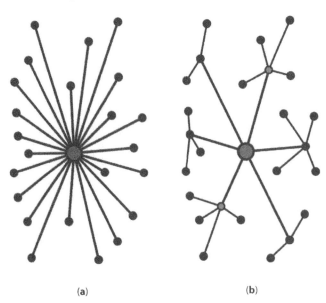

(a)   (b)

Figure 7.2 Pictorial representation of centralized, decentralized and distributed networks.

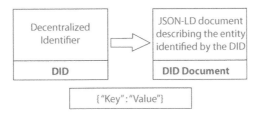

Figure 7.3 Pictorial presentation of 'key-data' concept.

7.4   The Workflow of Blockchain Identity Management Systems

Blockchain-enabled identity management systems revolve around three sets of people: Issuers, Owners, and Verifiers [5] (Figure 7.4). Each of them has a definite set of responsibilities and will have to function in a specific way to ensure the success of blockchain-enabled management systems.

Initially, a person who wishes to establish his identity would have to approach an identity issuer with all necessary proofs. This issuing agency can be any trusted party like government or bank, very similar to that in the existing system. On verifying the data produced, if found valid and legitimate, the issuer will deliver a set of credentials to that particular person. These documents will bear the cryptographic signature of the issuing authority as proof of attestation. Once handed over, these credentials will then fall under the possession of the applicant. From then on, the person becomes their sole 'owner', and the issuing party will not be having any monopoly over them.

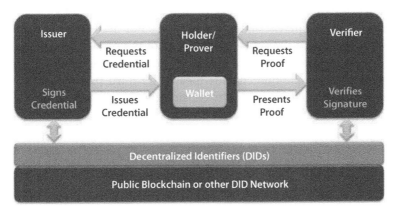

Figure 7.4 Analytical view of blockchain identity management system. Ref: Self-Sovereign Identity Livebook by Manning.

The identity owner can now store this information, in an encrypted form, within a personal digital wallet obtained from DID issuing platforms [6]. This data will not be available at any other database, unlike in the case of traditional systems. Besides, as previously explained, this data will be completely under the control of the owner and cannot be accessed by any other agency without his permission. So, when a third party wishes to verify the identity of the owner, it will have to request him to provide access to his credentials stored on the blockchain. The owner can then decide whether to share his key with the verifier or to discard the request. Moreover, he need not share his full information. Instead, he can share only the essential bits of data while preserving other sensitive material.

In blockchain systems, the actual information that gets stored on the blocks in the chain is only the references and attestations supplied by the issuers. This is very contradictory to the existing systems that store the exact data of the personnel over their databases. For instance, in case of a passport, the data that goes on the blockchain would be just its formal description and the cryptographic signature of the passport issuing agency, and not the actual passport information like full name, passport number, etc. As a result, the third-party verifier supplied with the owner's private key would be able to view only attestation information but not the exact passport details.

This means the owner's sensitive information remains undisclosed even for the verifier. Nonetheless, the process of authentication would be accomplished successfully (Figure 7.5).

The process is very different from that in the case of a traditional identity management system. Primely, because, in the latter systems, if any information is hidden from the verifier, then the owner will be declared as unauthenticated. However, as stated, in blockchain-enabled systems, the scenario is very different as the verifier does not decide on the authorization by validating the actual information of the owner. Instead, he will make a conclusion based on the credibility factor of the issuer. Concerning the passport example quoted, this means the third party (verifier) will declare the owner's authenticity by considering the trustworthiness of the passport granting agency.

Figure 7.5 Process of authorization in blockchain systems.

To ensure satisfactory implementation of all aforementioned features, blockchain-enabled systems employ powerful algorithms at their back-end. These programs are expected to be platform-independent to ensure maximum interoperability. And most importantly, they must protect the rights of their users and must function on legal grounds. Blockchain systems deployed by paying attention to these factors are likely to transform the way we view an 'identity'. Mainly because, then, we will have a user-centered working mode that is very different in comparison to the existing centralized one. The probable model that will then be functional would be laden with the following features (Figure 7.6).

- Security
  Blockchain-powered systems would offer the highest level of security and are expected to offer a tough-time for hackers.
- Minimalistic
  Novel systems working on blockchain technology would disclose only the minimum necessary amount of information to the verifier.

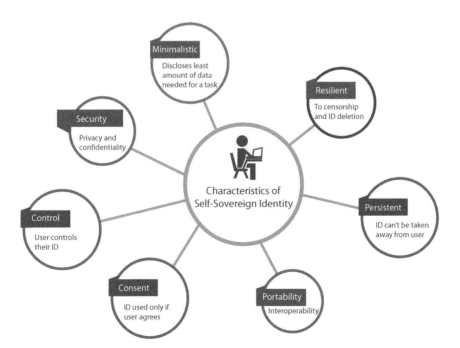

Figure 7.6 Features of self-sovereign systems. Ref: consensys.net.

- Resilient
  Blockchain identity management systems are highly resilient. They offer flexibility for every issue concerned with one's identity.
- Persistent
  Digital IDs, once created, cannot be retrieved or exchanged. They always remain associated with the same person.
- Portability
  Blockchain systems do not demand the user to carry bulky documents. Instead, it would just suffice to have his personal device that is connected to the chain.
- Consent
  In these blockchain-enabled systems, the verifier will have to get consent from the owner to verify his identity credentials.
- Control
  Complete power to grant or deny the access will remain solely with the owner, while no other third party can influence his decision.

7.5 How Does it Contribute to Data Security?

- DIDs are unique to a person and permanent as they are non-reassignable. As a result, even its keys, both private as well as public; remain undisclosed to third parties except the owner himself. Thus, in blockchain systems, only the owner will be able to successfully claim his wallet credentials. This makes blockchain identities robust to theft and impersonation like issues that are quite frequent in the prevailing identity management systems.
- Data, once stored in the blockchain, cannot be changed retroactively without being noticed by its nodes. In particular, the alteration of network data dem the consent from at least 51% of its connection points and requires huge computational power [7]. The process is trivial in nature and is neither commonly supported nor encouraged. As a result, all the stored information on the blockchain systems will be tamper-proof, making it's registered transaction fraud-proof. This and more reasons to use blockchain technology across various use cases are depicted in Figure 7.7.
- As mentioned earlier, in blockchain identity management systems, the actual user information will never be stored on

Figure 7.7 Advantages of using blockchain systems. Ref: Blockchain Council.

the network. Instead, they will be well-contained within the owner's personal device like a mobile or laptop. As a result, even if the network gets hacked, personal data of the user will not get into the hands of unauthorized people. This reduces the risk associated with sensitive data, which otherwise might be subjected to misuse.

- Blockchain management systems supply everyone with the 'same source of truth,' unlike in the case of current identity management solutions. Meaning, a single person cannot put forth two different sets of documents at any stage. For instance, he cannot claim to be owning the two assets that bear slightly different owner names, say, expanded version of initials. This constraint will put a serious bar over the probable fraudulent cases, unlike in the case of traditional systems.
- The owner can use his blockchain-stored data to claim his authentication over multiple platforms. This avoids repetitive signing up and verification activities when starting to use new boards as the user's authentication can readily be referred to from his pre-historic activities recorded on the blocks in the network. The result would be a well-established digital identity that keeps the person accounted for all his online activities, ranging from simple ones to most complicate.
- Sharing of data by the user at times of necessity in terms of soft copy highly speeds-up the verification process. Also, it eliminates the need for personal presence at the place of the

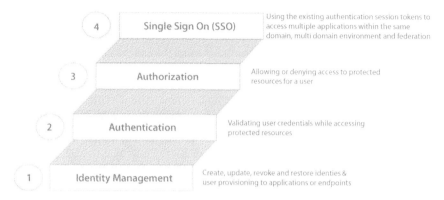

Figure 7.8 Process flow of blockchain identity management systems.

verifier. This means blockchain-enabled systems do possess the potential to act as a single metasystem that accomplishes faster, real-time authentication across multiple platforms. As a result, the speed associated with blockchain-enabled verification systems has posed a serious challenge for the traditional mode of verification. The entire process flow to support this mechanism has been shown in Figure 7.8.

7.6   Trending Blockchain Identity Management Projects

There are many organizations [9, 10] that are all set to design a fully functional, robust blockchain identity system. They are consistently striving to provide a better system for humanity that can add more value while addressing the present defects. A few of the trending projects dealing with blockchain-enabled identity systems and their salient features are mentioned here below.

- Hyperledger Indy
  This is an open-source community that aims at developing a stable framework, tools, and libraries that help in deploying blockchain systems. In terms of identity management, this Linux-founded project aims at developing smart contracts and data monetization.
- Civic
  Civic is a San Francisco based company that aims at developing a mobile app to store the user's information in encrypted

form. The impetus is to develop a platform-enabled verification system that would act as a serious threat to identity theft.

- Sovrin
  This is a non-profit organization working on developing self-sovereign identity systems. However, in these systems, not all users will be allowed to enter information into the blockchains. Instead, only the trusted parties will be authorized to do so.
- Bloom
  Bloom is a fully decentralized blockchain identity management system where the user has full control over his data. Besides maintaining global identity, it also allows the user to earn stars to raise his level of the trust factor.
- SelfKey
  This self-sovereign digital identity management system uses utility tokens called 'keys' to provide access to the platform. Using SelfKey, the user can develop his digital identity and then use it to claim for citizenship or online notarization.
- Every
  Evernym is a Utah-based private company that develops Plenum code to facilitate the creation and maintenance of self-sovereign IDs. This open-source code is exploited in a pilot project at Illinois to digitize the registration data concerned with birth details.
- KYC Chain
  This digital company aims at developing a platform that would help in easing the KYC process. The system is completely user-centric as it offers the owner full control over sharing his data through the use of his private keys.
- Nuggets
  Nuggets is a company mainly concentrating on offering a biometric-based decentralized system that facilitates identity verification. It is a token-based platform that provides an option to use its 'nuggets' to develop and maintain smart contracts.
- Austria
  This is a Spain-funded blockchain identity management system that is semi-public in operation. It works based on Quorum protocol and aims at benefitting the people of Alastria in developing smart contracts by requesting access to the system.

- Jolocom
  Jolocom concentrates on developing digital identities that can operate hassle-free across multiple platforms. This company develops open-source code to aid in the development of 100% self-sovereign systems eliminating the need for third parties.
- uPort
  This is a Brooklyn-based company that has developed an app to maintain identities in the digital sense. It is an Ethereum-based system put to trial run in Zug, Switzerland, to aid in the creation of credentials that can be used as an address proof.

7.7   Why and How of Revocation

Blockchain, by inheritance, is resistant to change, meaning whatever is put on it remains intact. This is the basic property that makes the blockchain-enabled identity management systems secure and foolproof. However, in some cases, the identity credentials need to be updated at regular intervals. One such example would be the number of family members that are likely to be changed based on births and/or deaths. So, in this case, how can we update the data already residing on the blockchain?

The solution to this problem manifests in the form of a revocation registry maintained on the blockchain network. This ledger will store the information regarding the validity of the owner's credentials. That is, it says whether the proof submitted is still valid or expired or updated. As a result, the verifying agency can know the current status of the owner's credentials by having a look into this registry. This revocation facility (Figure 7.9) imbibed into the blockchain-enabled system helps it preserve and respect the dynamic nature associated with one's identity.

Yet another case where the revocation registry becomes a critical necessity for blockchain identity management systems is when the owner's device storing his personal information gets lost or stolen. Such cases might put his data in the wrong hands, posing a serious threat to his identity. However, by the use of revocation registry, the owner can prevent this from happening by following two simple steps:

1. As a first step, the owner is expected to cancel the permission given to the device—that is now stolen or lost (say, mobile phone)—to use his credentials. For this, he can use his other

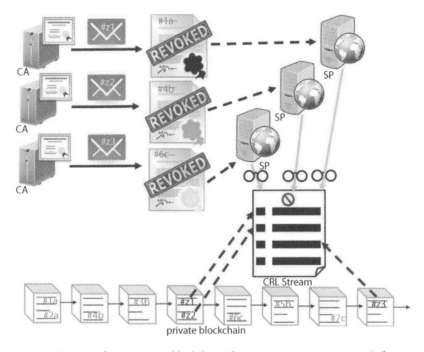

Figure 7.9 Process of revocation in blockchain identity management systems. Ref: ceur-ws.org.

authorized device (say, laptop) to write on the revocation registry the act of recalling the authorization from his stolen device.

Right from that moment, all the digital identity residing on the stolen device would become invalid. This prevents the possible impersonation that might occur if the device lands up with fraudulent people.

2. The next step would be to callback the authorization from the digital keys. That is, the owner must make them invalid by declaring them outdated. This will prevent the undesired person, now owning the phone, from exploring the existing connections between the owner and other devices/organizations. Also, he can no more use the owner's keys to build new relationships with any other third parties. As a result, the owner's data would remain intact and will not get hacked into. Nonetheless, this does not prevent the owner from using his credentials across his trusted network nodes, of course, through his non-stolen device, which, in this case, is a laptop.

7.8   Points to Ponder

This section briefs about the possible outcomes that might result due to the use of blockchain technology in managing identities.

- Data Monetization
  Self-sovereignty established by blockchain-enabled systems makes a person's identity surpass the limit established by the borders [11]. This is a contrasting strategy to the existing identities as they are usually bound to the nationalities within which they remain valid. Blockchain systems can efficiently develop one's digital identity by exploiting the data of his tamper-resistant browsing history. The resulting digital footprint can be easily tangled to the user's DID, helping him claim ownership, for example, and thus can facilitate the monetization of one's personal data.
- Growth in the Economy
  At present, around 1.1 billion people are estimated to be living without an ID [12] (Figure 7.10). The reason may be attributed to their inaccessibility to identity-issuing agencies, mere negligence towards possessing one, deteriorated economic condition, lower educational background, lack of information, or geographic isolation. Whatsoever the reason might be, the result would be the inability to gain access to the benefits

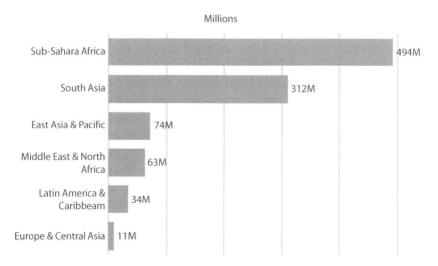

Figure 7.10 Statistics of people lacking ID by region. Ref: ourworldindata.org.

offered while being deprived of essential facilities. Blockchain management systems may hopefully solve this issue as most of this population is already using devices like mobile phones, which can be used to establish their digital identity. This would, in turn, lead to a substantial rise in the economic sector.

- Peer-to-Peer Communication
  Blockchain-enabled systems are bringing into reality the actual thought with which the internet emerged, peer-to-peer communication. Internet providers envisaged the internet as a platform that would facilitate data sharing on a one-to-one basis. However, as time passed, third parties, say the service providers, took over the control of data transferring between the users. As a result, the basic principle of peer-to-peer communication seemed to vanish into eternity. Nevertheless, with the emergence of blockchain, the principle is promisingly seen to revive [13]. The prime reason is, blockchain identity management systems do not demand the presence of a third party. The user will be the sole responsible person for his data and can share it with only the party whom he wants to.

- Factor of Concern
  In blockchain identity management systems, the verifier authenticates the user credentials by relying on the attestation provided by the issuer. On verification, the new verifier also attests his cryptographic signature to the document provided. Next, when some other third-party desires for checking the user's credentials, it takes the decision based on the previous testimonies. The chain continues, and the number of cryptographic signatures verifying the credentials keeps on increasing. However, in case, if one of these verifying parties lose their trust, then the authenticity of the entire chain may become questionable, posing a potential threat to the authenticity of the owner's credentials. A summation of the benefits that SSID can provide in our everyday use cases has been shown in Figure 7.11.

Self-Sovereign Identity Allows Users To

| Control their identities | Access and update information | Choose the information they wish to keep private | Transport the data to other organizations or jurisdictions | Aggregate their own data for enriching their own life |

Figure 7.11 Advantages of blockchain identity management systems. Ref: nec.com.

7.8.1   Comparison Between Traditional and Blockchain-Based Identity Management Systems

Summarizing, we can tabulate the differences between traditional and blockchain systems as follows; and, a clearer demarcation of how a blockchain-based identity mechanism can streamline processes and systems in a supply chain has been shown in Figure 7.12.

Traditional Systems	Blockchain Systems
Paper-based system	Digital oriented system
Data will be stored on a central database	Data will be stored on the user's personal device
User will have no control over his data	User will have full control over his data
Relatively complex to obtain an identity and hectic in terms of maintenance	Much easier to obtain and maintain
Creation of duplicate identity is relatively easier	Duplication of identity is almost impossible as the system is tamper-resistant
Validation will require the user to present the actual data	Validation does not demand actual data as it is a zero-knowledge proof system [14]
The verification process is tedious and often demands for in-person presence	Verification is relatively easier and does not depend on in-person presence
Third parties can access the data without the user consent	No one can access the data without the consent of the user
Does not support cross-platform functionality	Highly facilitates multi-platform activities
May get prone to single-point failure	Concept of single-point failure does not make sense
Ties the identity usually with the nationality of the person	Raises the concept of identity over the geographic boundaries
Highly vulnerable to data breaching activities	Resistant to data hacking and other mal-practices

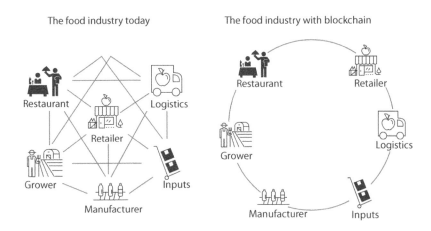

Figure 7.12 Traditional versus blockchain identity management systems. Ref: foodtruckoperator.com.

7.9 Conclusion

Encroachment of blockchain technology into identity management systems is expected to revolutionize the concept of identity handling. These systems operate on more agile algorithms and are more sophisticated when compared to currently deploy operating mechanisms. Such systems would operate on the basic concept of decentralization, leading to increased privacy and decreased possibility of data breaching—Bl—blockchain entity systems hand-over the responsibility of maintaining one's identity to himself. User, being the supreme authority can, then have complete control over his data and can decide sovereignly about all the factors related to its sharing. All blockchain-enabled systems operate on zero-knowledge, wherein a verifier validates a person's credentials by relying on the reputation of the attestor rather than the actual data itself.

Blockchain identity systems offer many potential benefits by patching-up the loopholes of similar systems that exist today. Increased data privacy, minimized time of verification, reducing the number of fraudulent activities, providing better user control, elimination of central authority and dismissal of the need for multiple signing and verification processes are just a few to mention. Speaking macroscopically, blockchain-enabled systems facilitate peer-to-peer communication resulting in data portability, data monetization, and economic growth. Owing to these factors, blockchain identity management systems are much likely to replace the existing traditional systems in trustworthy mode. Nevertheless, to reap all these benefits, it is essential to deploy the blockchain systems at a large scale while consistently keeping-an-eye over their behavior.

References

1. https://internetofbusiness.com/blockchain-IoT-security-2/.
2. Pakkath, R., Self-Sovereign Identity: A Distant Dream or an Immediate Possibility?, https://www.idaptive.com/blog/self-sovereign-identity-distant-dream-immediate-possibility/, on November 14, 2019.
3. Blockchain in Deigital Identity, https://consensys.net/blockchain-use-cases/digital-identity/.
4. Introduction to Blockchain Identity Management, https://selfkey.org/introduction-to-blockchain-identity-management/, 6 Dec 2018.
5. Identity Management with Blockchain: The Definitive Guide (2020 Update), https://tykn.tech/identity-management-blockchain/, March 13, 2019.
6. Mearian, L., How Blockchain May Kill the Password, https://www.computerworld.com/article/3329962/how-blockchain-may-kill-the-password.html, 2 January 2019.
7. Miles, C., Blockchain security: What keeps your transaction data safe?, https://www.ibm.com/blogs/blockchain/2017/12/blockchain-security-what-keeps-your-transaction-data-safe/, December 12, 2017.
8. How Blockchain revolutionizes identity management, https://www.accenture.com/nl-en/blogs/insights/how-blockchain-will-revolutionize-identity-management, May 28 2018.
9. Anwar, H., Blockchain for Digital Identity: The Decentralized and Self-Sovereign Identity (SSI), on October 2, 2019.
10. Kirk, J., Blockchain for Identity: 6 Hot Projects, on February 5, 2018.
11. Pina, G., Self-sovereign identity—Giving control back to passengers, https://www.sita.aero/resources/blog/self-sovereign-identity-giving-control-back-to-passengers, 20 June 2019.
12. ID4D Data: Global Identification Challenge by the Numbers, 2020.
13. Iansiti, M. et al., The Truth About Blockchain, https://hbr.org/2017/01/the-truth-about-blockchain, on January-February 2017.
14. Kasireddy, P., Fundamental Challenges with Public Blockchains, https://www.preethikasireddy.com/post/fundamental-challenges-with-public-blockchains, December 13, 2017.

8

Blockchain & IoT: A Paradigm Shift for Supply Chain Management

Abhishek Bhattacharya

Whrrl, Thane, Maharashtra, India

Abstract

In this chapter, we shall be taking a varied look at how blockchain can be useful in devising and facilitating a framework for path tracing and quality management in supply chains. Supply Chain Management (SCM) has always been in a need for transparency to make the process much robust, hence a framework based on blockchain could be an answer.

Efforts have been taken across the globe for a long time to shape the global supply chains. This perhaps is most important when it comes to consumer behavior and trust—quality parameters of what they consume. Blockchain technology has proven itself to be worthy of bringing about changes in the global supply chains, starting with food. This chapter takes a look into how blockchain can help with sustainable supply chain management.

Keywords: IoT, supply chain management, consensus, shared ledger, World Trade Organization

8.1 Introduction

Effective Supply Chain Management has now become of importance in organizations worldwide as it is a key element in achieving a competitive advantage. For this reason, supply chains are migrating towards digitalization, and central to this digitalization is blockchain and the Internet-of-Things (IoT). The use of these is relatively new and is still being explored. In this chapter

Email: abhib.work@gmail.com

S.S. Tyagi and Shaveta Bhatia (eds.) Blockchain for Business: How it Works and Creates Value, (159–178) © 2021 Scrivener Publishing LLC

we will delve into Blockchain and IoT with focus on their application in supply chain management and the opportunities they bring about.

8.2   Supply Chain Management

The Council of Supply Chain Management Professionals (CSCMP) defines Supply Chain Management as the management and planning of the activities involved in sourcing and procurement, conversion, and all other logistics management tasks[1]. According to Stock [23], supply chain management is the management of a network of relationships within a firm and between the organizations or business units it depends on. These business units consist of material suppliers, purchasing, production facilities, logistics, marketing, and related systems that facilitate the forward and reverse logistics, finances and information from the original producer to final customer, with the benefits of value addition, achievement of customer satisfaction, and profit maximisation through efficiencies[2].

Today's supply chains are becoming more complex and the visibility of key information, events and collaboration across organizational boundaries is increasingly viewed as an essential criterion for the long-term competitiveness of a supply chain network. The problem with most present-day supply chain models is that the relationships between members of the supply chain are not transparent and there is lack of information about the origin of the products. Organizations are therefore trying to better manage supply chains by putting together roadmaps for the digitalizing of supply chains[3]. Digitalization has the potential to overcome these barriers and transform supply chains into completely integrated ecosystems that are fully transparent to all the players. Among the numerous tools proposed for digitalization in supply chain management is Blockchain and IoT[4].

---

[1] A systematic literature review of blockchain-based applications. https://www.science direct.com/science/article/pii/S0736585318306324, Accessed 22 May, 2020.

[2] A research view of supply chain management: Developments, 25 Feb, 2016, https://www.researchgate.net/publication/272776867_A_research_view_of_supply_chain_management_Developments_and_topics_for_exploration, Accessed 22 May, 2020.

[3] Ensuring performance measurement integrity in logistics using .... https://www.semanticscholar.org/paper/Ensuring-performance-measurement-integrity-in-using-Kuhi-Kaare/874649dc188e83b4e1cb0d9c132d72343eb989f2/figure/0, Accessed 22 May, 2020.

[4] Industry 4.0: How digitization makes the supply ...—Strategy, https://www.strategyand.pwc.com/gx/en/insights/2016/digitization-more-efficient.html, Accessed 22 May, 2020.

8.2.1 The Aspects of a Supply Chain

Fundamentally, a supply chain can be formed with only three parties, which are suppliers, producers and customers. However, in any given supply chain, there is a set of companies having various functions. There might be suppliers of suppliers or customers of customers or in case of business-to-business operations, the final customer. It is worth mentioning that there are a lot of companies which are service providers at any of the steps in supply chain activities[5]. The various parties and how they may interact are shown in Figure 8.1.

Supply chain management covers a very wide range of business processes and activities. These activities are divided into five basic areas (as shown in Figure 8.2) and are called the five drivers of a supply chain, which are production, inventory, location, transportation and information[6].

Each of the drivers answers specific questions and relates to a particular element of the business process. Production covers most of the issues regarding the product itself. The typical questions in this area include questions about the product itself and the quantities to be produced. Inventory describes how much of a product should be stocked at each stage and how much of the products should be held fully assembled or as raw materials. Location answers the question "Where?".

In more detail, it refers to the geo-location of supply chain facilities. Transportation is the delivery of inventory during each stage of the supply chain. The most important decision to make at this stage is the kind of transport. Information addresses issues to do with determining the data that is essential and how much of it must be collected. The main targets of information flow are to coordinate daily activities and forecasting. In order to build a successful supply chain strategy, all these drivers are to be integrated with each other to achieve the strategic goals of the supply chain[7].

---

[5] Textbook of Supply Chain Management—Ashish Bhatnagar ...., https://books.google.com/books/about/Textbook_of_Supply_Chain_Management.html?id=rBO1AQAACAAJ, Accessed 22 May, 2020.

[6] Supply chain modelling, A practical approach—Theseus, 11 Sep. 2016, https://www.theseus.fi/bitstream/10024/118284/1/Koksharov_Vladislav.pdf, Accessed 22 May, 2020.

[7] Supply chain modelling. A practical approach—Theseus, 11 Sep. 2016, https://www.theseus.fi/bitstream/10024/118284/1/Koksharov_Vladislav.pdf, Accessed 22 May, 2020.

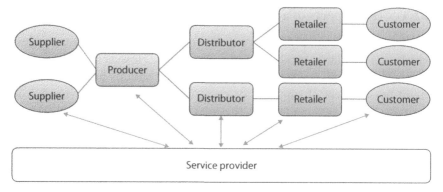

Figure 8.1 The parties in a Supply Chain.

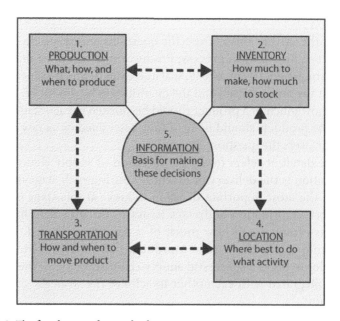

Figure 8.2 The five drivers of a supply chain.

8.2.2   Supply Chain Performance Dimensions

As a crucial component of an organisation the supply chain ought to have strategic objectives that the organisation consistently aims at improving. Supply chain performance has never been as important as it is today. In today's business environment, how a supply chain performs determines who will achieve more. Many companies however are unaware of how their supply chains are performing[8]. Operational performance is a construct which involves the effective translation of competitive priorities into strategic capabilities of a firm. It can be evaluated by shorter-term measures including efficiency, quality, cost, delivery and flexibility[9]. Competitive advantage known as the extent to which an organization is able to create a strong position over its competitors. Chang *et al.*[10], have highlighted that operational performance involves the improvement of supply chain related organisational measures such as logistics cost reduction, on-time delivery, inventory turnover, and cycle time reduction. Performance measurement is of importance when it comes to the evaluation of systems[11].

Operational performance comprises capabilities that allow an organization to differentiate itself from its competitors. The strategic objectives of a supply chain include cost, quality, speed, dependability, risk reduction, sustainability and flexibility. It is these objectives that necessitate the need for continuous improvement within the supply chain of an organization.

8.2.3   Supply Chain Migration Towards Digitalization

Digitalization is about organizations orienting themselves to the clients through online business, digital marketing, social media, and the client experience. Eventually, every part of business will be changed through the vertical incorporation of research and development, production, advertising and marketing, and other internal activities, and new plans of action will be founded on these advances[12]. In actuality, there is development toward a total digital environment. The up and coming age of performance management systems provides real-time, end-to-end transparency throughout the supply chain, for example, the specific position of trucks in the network at a given time during transportation. The digitization of the supply chains empowers organizations to address the requirements of the

---

[8] Operational Performance through Supply Chain Management ...., https://pdfs.semantic-scholar.org/f90b/2e3b523689e5f19caf257baade0273824a35.pdf, Accessed 22 May, 2020.

[9] The effect of supply chain quality management practices and ...., https://ideas.repec.org/a/eee/proeco/v212y2019icp227-235.html, Accessed 22 May, 2020.

[10] Supply chain integration and firm financial performance: A ...., https://www.science direct.com/science/article/pii/S0263237315001231, Accessed 22 May, 2020.

[11] Supplier integration and company performance: A ...., https://ideas.repec.org/a/eee/jomega/v41y2013i6p1029-1041.html, Accessed 22 May, 2020.

[12] Industry 4.0: How digitization makes the supply chain more ...., https://www.strategyand.pwc.com/gx/en/insights/2016/digitization-more-efficient.html, Accessed 3 Jul, 2020.

clients immediately, address the difficulties on the supply side and improve productivity[13].

As per Alicke *et al.* [1], digitalization is believed to realize Supply Chain 4.0 which will bring about the following advantages in supply chains:

- More adaptability
- More granular frameworks
- More precise frameworks
- More effective and straightforward frameworks.

8.3   Blockchain and IoT

Blockchain Technology (BT) comes under Industry 4.0 or all the more explicitly under Supply chain 4.0, which targets getting new advances as a means of increasing the efficiency of systems, while maintaining sensible or meaningful expenses. Blockchain is along these lines being investigated on the grounds that it fits into the worldwide focus and can be associated with supply chain development and speeding up. Blockchain innovation is presently gaining the enthusiasm of a wide assortment of industries, from finance, healthcare, utilities and even the government sector among many other sectors. The explanation behind this developing enthusiasm for the intrinsic qualities of blockchain architecture and configuration is that it is believed to provide properties like transparency, robustness, auditability, and security[14].

A blockchain is viewed as a distributed database that is organised as a list of ordered blocks and these blocks are both unchanging and cannot be changed[15]. A blockchain is a shared and disseminated (distributed) record that enables the process of recording transactions and tracking assets inside a business arrangement. An asset in this context can be tangible (for instance a house, a vehicle, money, land) or immaterial (intangible) like protected innovation, for example, licenses, copyrights, or branding. For all intents and purposes anything of significant worth or value can be tracked and traded

---

[13] Supply Chain 4.0—The next-generation digital ...—McKinsey, 27 Oct, 2016, https://www.mckinsey.com/business-functions/operations/our-insights/supply-chain-40--the-next-generation-digital-supply-chain, Accessed 3 Jul, 2020.

[14] How blockchain improves the supply chain: Case study ...., https://www.sciencedirect.com/science/article/pii/S187705091831158X, Accessed 3 Jul, 2020.

[15] Blockchain technology for enhancing supply chain resilience, https://ideas.repec.org/a/eee/bushor/v62y2019i1p35-45.html, Accessed 3 Jul, 2020.

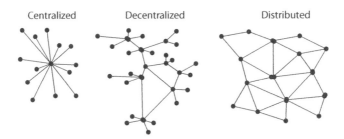

Figure 8.3 Different network structures.

on a blockchain system, hence decreasing risk and reducing expenses for all involved[16,17]. It can permit various degrees of access; private, open or consortium and be laid out in various types of distribution architectures such as centralized, decentralized or distributed as visualized in Figure 8.3[18].

A generally acknowledged meaning of the Internet of Things (IoT) is that it is a world-wide network of connected objects uniquely addressable, based on standard correspondence techniques. Beyond being connected, IoT gadgets play out a wide scope of refined calculations which may incorporate sensing and automation. Basically, IoT may likewise be alluded to as the interconnection and interoperability among devices, for example, PCs, watches, telephones and different gadgets[19].

IoT uses equipment, (for example, sensors) to gather data from the environment and connectivity is needed in order for this transmission and gathering of information to and from a server or cloud to be possible[20]. A connected gadget equipped with sensors or actuators detects its surrounding environment, comprehends what's going on and chooses keenly and autonomously or communicates with different nodes or clients to settle on the best choices. In short, IoT intends to add computer based rationale to a great deal of items (things), which thus can be checked or constrained by analytics. The

---

[16] Blockchain For Dummies® IBM Limited Edition—CSInvesting, http://csinvesting.org/wp-content/uploads/2018/06/Blockchain-for-Dummies.pdf, Accessed 3 Jul, 2020.

[17] A systematic literature review of blockchain ...., https://www.sciencedirect.com/science/article/pii/S0736585318306324, Accessed 3 Jul, 2020.

[18] Blockchain technology in food supply chains: A case ...., https://www.semanticscholar.org/paper/Blockchain-technology-in-food-supply-chains-%3A-A-of-Holmberg-%C3%85quist/9fec814ef3c09683ab5949e8bdf2d79c811dc871, Accessed 3 Jul, 2020.

[19] Perspectives on emerging directions in using IoT devices in ...., https://www.semanticscholar.org/paper/Perspectives-on-emerging-directions-in-using-IoT-in-Rao-Clarke/f9906910716eeaf401693728aaf9991a0dbf9ac1, Accessed 3 Jul, 2020.

[20] Blockchain-based IoT: A Survey—ScienceDirect, https://www.sciencedirect.com/science/article/pii/S1877050919310178, Accessed 3 Jul, 2020.

development of the IoT is increasingly suited to the ever-evolving needs of both firms and consumers. The IoT might be communicated as a straightforward equation which may be; 'IoT = Services + Data + Networks + Sensors'. In this manner, IoT is a mix of information from sensors and systems that likewise offer diverse shrewd types of assistance[21].

IoT allows for an individual to get to information regardless of their location, consequently achieving convenience. When correspondences are not fluent and straightforward, inefficiencies result, however with IoT gadgets, better correspondence is conceivable, and the transferring of information over a connected network saves both money and time. These interconnected devices also help achieve automation, which is one of the most important aspects in today's systems, where high quality tasks can be achieved without human intervention.

8.3.1   What Makes Blockchain Suitable for SCM?

Blockchain possesses various desirable properties, such as decentralization, auditability, persistency and anonymity. These properties have led to the consideration of the technology for a number of other applications beyond finance, such as Supply Chain Management (SCM). Countless partners take part in supply chains these days, and this is accompanied by massive flow of newly created and time sensitive information. This information is dealt with ineffectively by supply chain management systems since a shared database is not being used. As per Litke *et al.* [15], blockchain can essentially manage this by providing a networked and decentralized database for all supply chain parties to use. Along these lines, supply chain information is logged on a ledger which is shared among all network participants[22]. The different activities and procedures that happen during a product's journey are frequently inclined to human blunders, misrepresentation or even failure, which in turn decrease system performance. The benefit of blockchain is that most tasks are represented as electronic transactions and are submitted on the ledger record. In that case, they execute faster and without mistakes, henceforth, increasing system performance.

---

[21] IoT network types, data flow in IoT, data flow in IoT with ...., https://www.researchgate.net/figure/IoT-network-types-data-flow-in-IoT-data-flow-in-IoT-with-blockchain-technology_fig2_325661355, Accessed 3 Jul, 2020.

[22] (PDF) Blockchains for Supply Chain Management ...., 16 Jan, 2019, https://www.research gate.net/publication/330484023_Blockchains_for_Supply_Chain_Management_Architectural_Elements_and_Challenges_Towards_a_Global_Scale_Deployment, Accessed 3 Jul, 2020.

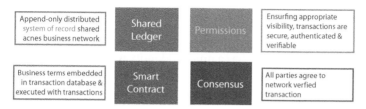

Figure 8.4 The four key concepts of blockchain.

To additionally understand how a blockchain for SCM functions, and to realise its potential for transforming that field, the key concepts of blockchain for business (as appeared on Figure 8.4) must be comprehended[23].

8.3.1.1   Shared Ledger

Ledgers have been utilized in double entry accounting since the thirteenth century. In any case, the idea of a common, appropriated record which is an unchanging record of all transactions on the supply chain system and a record that all system members can access is new[24]. In a common ledger, transactions are recorded once and consequently the duplication of effort is avoided. As per Gupta [7], the mutual ledger has the following qualities:

- Records all exchanges over a business ecosystem since the distributed ledger is the system of the record.
- Is shared among all system members.
- Is permissioned meaning members see just those transactions they are approved to see.

It is essential to note that blockchain offers every one of its functionalities and traits whilst disregarding the geo-location of its clients. Since it is a mutual ledger, the decentralized system can in this manner be shared over the web and any legitimate member of the supply chain can participate regardless of location. Supply chain systems coupled with blockchain technology would then find it simpler to work internationally. This adaptability of location can achieve time proficiency in supply chains[25].

---

[23] Blockchain For Dummies® IBM Limited Edition—CSInvesting, http://csinvesting.org/wp-content/uploads/2018/06/Blockchain-for-Dummies.pdf, Accessed 3 Jul, 2020.

[24] A review on blockchain applications in the agri-food sector ...., 5 Jul, 2019, https://onlinelibrary.wiley.com/doi/full/10.1002/jsfa.9912, Accessed 3 Jul, 2020.

[25] Blockchains for Supply Chain Management: Architectural ...., https://www.mdpi.com/2305-6290/3/1/5, Accessed 3 Jul, 2020.

8.3.1.2   Permissions

Blockchains can either be permissioned or permissionless. In a permissioned blockchain, every member has a unique identity which allows the utilization of policies to control network participation and access to transaction data. With the capacity to control network participation, companies can all the more effectively follow data security guidelines. Permissioned blockchains are powerful at controlling the consistency of the information that gets attached to the blockchain in a given system. More transaction data can be stored in the blockchain because of the ability to limit access to transaction data and members can determine the transaction details they are willing to permit others to see. Another perspective is that a few members might be approved to only see certain transactions, while others (like auditors) might be offered access to a more extensive scope of transactions[26].

In contrast to the modern day supply chains where a wide range of information is accessible and can be tempered with, blockchains contribute hugely with regards to data protection. The blockchain records contain unchanging data as well as the protection of users' data. Public, permissioned and private blockchains are all able to provide absolute anonymity within the system.

8.3.1.3   Consensus

As indicated by Mao *et al.* [16], in a business ecosystem where members are known and believed, transactions can be confirmed and committed to the ledger through different methods of agreement (consensus), including the ensuing:

- Proof of stake: Validators must hold a specific percentage of the system's value to approve transactions.
- Multi-signature: A greater part of validators in the system must concur that an exchange is substantial (for instance, seven out of nine)
- Practical Byzantine Fault Tolerance (PBFT): Is an algorithm intended to settle debates among system members when one member in a set of members creates diverse output from the others[27].

---

[26] Do you Need a Blockchain?, *Semantic Scholar*, https://www.semanticscholar.org/paper/Do-you-Need-a-Blockchain-W%C3%BCst-Gervais/ad9760ea1568263d4f670ed-c52e8d91875c95e42, Accessed 3 Jul, 2020.

[27] Innovative Blockchain-Based Approach for Sustainable and ...., https://www.mdpi.com/2071-1050/10/9/3149, Accessed 3 Jul, 2020.

The idea of consensus is to keep a general understanding between the nodes of the system about all submitted transaction data. The transaction data can be a timestamp subsequently showing the order transaction followed the addresses of both sender and beneficiary, the labels or electronic seal that go with the items, in addition to other things. Blockchain platforms bolster various sorts of agreement apparatuses reliant on the ledger level of access. A ledger can either be open (public) or private and the most widely recognized consensus algorithms are proof-of-stake, practical byzantine fault tolerance, proof-of-work and proof of elapsed time. The non-existence of a typical tool in current supply chains that sorts out and safeguards each step of the product in a bid to eliminate errors, fraud, and ware failure is the reason blockchain proves advantageous.

8.3.1.4 Smart Contracts

A smart contract is a set of rules or an understanding that administers a business's exchanges. A smart agreement is kept on the blockchain and is routinely executed as a part of an exchange. They may have numerous authoritative prerequisites that could be somewhat or completely self-executing, self-implementing, or both relying upon the members' inclinations. The reason for a smart contract is to give security that is superior to customary agreement law while diminishing the expenses and postponements related with the conventional agreements or exchanges[28]. For instance, a smart contract may define contractual conditions under which a bond move happens, or it might capture the terms and conditions of travel protection (insurance), which might be automatically executed when, for instance, a flight is delayed by over eight hours.

For instance, a malevolent individual in the supply chain could mess with receipt data and change paid values misguidedly. In such situations it is in this way critical to have a system that improves immutability and guarantees transaction confidentiality in supply chains. Blockchain gives an acceptable solution for the security issues introduced along supply chains and ensures integrity and transparency[29].

---

[28] How blockchain improves the supply chain: case study ...., https://www.sciencedirect.com/science/article/pii/S187705091831158X, Accessed 3 Jul, 2020.

[29] Blockchains for Supply Chain Management: Architectural ....,https://www.mdpi.com/2305-6290/3/1/5, Accessed 3 Jul, 2020.

8.3.2   The Role of Blockchain in Achieving the SCM Performance Dimensions

Kshetri [11], recognizes the different vital SCM goals and afterward shows the position of blockchain technology in accomplishing them. An innovation must be able to accomplish the key SC goals before its use is considered. Firms do not venture into innovative investments that do not profit their systems' fundamental goals. These goals (objectives) include risk reduction, cost, speed, flexibility and dependability.

The cost perspective in the adoption of blockchain technology might be seen in two different ways, initially the cost faced by companies through adoption and also, the costs that are cut or disposed of as a result of the adoption. In the businesses where traceability matters, issues involving flawed products can be effortlessly recognized at the source and vital decisions made. Kshetri likewise suggests that the allocation of the perfect measure of resources to perform transportation and different activities is one of the cost-cutting measures realized by blockchain in supply chain management. Paper records can be eliminated as digitally signed documents are used and these can securely store data and the identities of individuals and assets can be validated. Regulatory compliance expenses can be decreased as auditable information can be given to fulfil regulators' requests.

Speed can be improved by digitalizing physical procedures and decreasing associations and interchanges. Speed may likewise be improved through the disposal of excess procedures at each progression of the SC as parties trust each other. The digitally signed records' protected storage and sharing can validate the identities of people and resources and henceforth limit the requirements of physical interactions and correspondences.

Blockchain technology will apply pressure on supply chain members to be progressively mindful and responsible for their actions consequently encouraging trustworthiness. Blockchain will be advantageous to smaller companies that are new in the business as these are rarely contracted in light of the fact that the validation of their certifications is burdensome to organizations. Blockchain-based digital certification is thus a method for expanding reliability for all parties and will predominantly be of help to the smaller and newer companies. These supply chain certification procedures may likewise check provenance. Blockchain's excellent audit trail can address difficulties related with self-announced information that is given by supply chain accomplices. One of the interesting characteristics that accompany blockchain technology is its capacity to validate identities as this quality can confirm the provenance of things, for example, fine wines or rough cut diamonds. In the blockchain systems, only the commonly acknowledged individuals can take part in transitions within the system in particular touchpoints and in such cases the foolproof strategy for confirmed identity can lessen digital security related dangers[30].

Confirmation of an organization's stand with regards to sustainability is made conceivable by blockchain as it makes it possible to make measures identified with sustainability increasingly quantifiable and progressively important. Most companies are moving towards engaging with supply chain members that monitor the earth and their impact on it. Be that as it may, most companies are not ready to part with the assets and effort expected to monitor how sustainable their partner is and blockchain will realize this aspect to a business. Blockchain adoption will achieve supply chains which have an incredible adaptability to adjust to changing client requests with shorter lead times. The visibility inside the SC framework would then make it simpler to see any changes that should be made inside the supply chain networks.

8.3.3   The Role of IoT in the Implementation of Blockchain Technology

Blockchain technology may be used to track sensor data and prevent duplication with other malicious data. Sensors can in this manner trade information through a blockchain as opposed to using a third party for building up trust. The combination of blockchain and IoT helps enable autonomy and the combination would remove technical inefficiencies and bottlenecks. The expense of deployment of IoT will be decreased altogether on account of the absence of any other mediator. As per Thakore *et al.* [24], IoT can maximise on blockchain in four different ways, in particular; cost decrease, trust building, quickened information trade and scaled security. They proceed to highlight that the blend of IoT and blockchain will prompt the making of new value business models, improved ecosystems, diminished risk, freed up capital, lower exchange costs, speed processing, security, structure integrity and against imitation[31].

Moura and Santos[32] discuss that IoT gadgets are an empowering agent in blockchain use. The use of blockchain means a company must be willing to

---

[30] 1 Blockchain's roles in meeting key supply chain management ...., http://iranarze.ir/wp-content/uploads/2018/02/E6050-IranArze.pdf, Accessed 3 Jul, 2020.

[31] Blockchain-based IoT: A Survey—*ScienceDirect*, https://www.sciencedirect.com/science/article/pii/S1877050919310178, Accessed 3 Jul, 2020.

[32] Hands-On IoT Solutions with Blockchain—*ScholarVox* ...., https://international.scholarvox.com/catalog/book/88865966?_locale=en, Accessed 3 Jul, 2020.

embrace the IoT as it is a basic part of blockchain implementation. Before the implementation of blockchain, a company must analyse whether they have the important devices all through the supply chain in order to guarantee the advantages that come with blockchain are completely embraced. Since blockchain harps on the build system integration and digitality, IoT gadgets are a chief empowering agent in the effective utilization of blockchain technology. In the event that the SCM network doesn't have the fundamental IoT gadgets, an organization should in this manner be eager to invest into the necessary IoT gadgets as they are critical for the performance of blockchain in SCM. Blockchain additionally requires great connectivity and with the advanced world ceaselessly investigating systems with better speeds, blockchain will undoubtedly have the much needed network support. Ongoing steps in the fifth era of portable telecommunication (5G) shows how connection and network speed are persistently advancing the positive way. A company that is thinking about the adoption of this innovation should consequently analyze its SCM system when it comes to the utilization of IoT gadgets in the system as they are essential for the effective use of blockchain technology.

8.4   Blockchain Technology and IoT Use Cases in Supply Chain Management

ConsenSys is a market driving blockchain innovation organization that as of late introduced and gave some use cases of blockchain technology in SCM. The association is at present demonstrating the authenticity of lavish things to fight fraud and duplicating. The lavish products industry is managing the developing difficulties like intellectual property (IP) and imitations with regards to ensuring brand esteem and genuine relations among clients and brands. ConsenSys, in association with LVMH and Microsoft, as of late declared AURA, a platform that makes it workable for buyers to get to the item history and evidence of credibility of lavish merchandise. AURA follows from raw materials to the retail location, right to recycled markets[33].

Treum is a blockchain put together trust platform centered with respect to transparency, tradability and traceability in supply chains. Treum has a traceability highlight which flawlessly records an asset's start to finish source data. It is its transparency ability that permits makers to confirm

---

[33] Blockchain for Global Trade and Commerce—ConsenSys, https://consensys.net/blockchain-use-cases/global-trade-and-commerce/, Accessed 3 Jul, 2020.

that their SC meets item targets. Inside and out, Treum can give the two organizations and purchasers the full item story. Treum collaborated with GlaxoSmithKline to utilize blockchain to follow protected innovation (IP) licenses utilized by researchers just as guarantee that items are delivered, shipped, and put away in appropriate conditions.

Provenance led a starter venture in Indonesia to help traceability in the fishing business. Using blockchain, cell phones and smart labeling, Provenance followed fish caught by anglers. This undertaking adequately followed fish in Indonesia for half of the year in 2016. The fish tracing frameworks are basically founded on papers and reports and fish exchanges source from many pontoons, which makes the full quality control a difficult assignment. Nations in the locale, for example, Indonesia face issues, for example, overfishing, extortion, just as unlawful, unreported, unregulated fish and furthermore human rights mishandles. In light of this pilot venture it was presumed that blockchain can assist shoppers with following the wellspring of their food and address the key difficulties noted previously. Indonesia being one of the biggest fish providers around the world, gives a fruitful ground to testing the innovation so as to radically expand transparency in fish supply chains[34].

8.5   Benefits and Challenges in Blockchain-Based Supply Chain Management

Blockchain gives secure information trade and a temper evidence store for archives and different SCM information. Blockchain innovation may realize a huge decrease in postponements and fraud subsequently sparing companies gigantic sums of income. As per the World Trade Organization (WTO), the lessening of boundaries in international supply chains could increment overall GDP by nearly 5% and the all-out volume by 15%[35]. In corporate networks, the additions and motivating forces are common to all members. Impetuses in the blockchain business systems may not really be money related, however they may rather be perceivability, access, share, and trade rights. As per Stanton [22] data sharing in advanced supply chains is

---

[34] 1 Blockchain's roles in meeting key supply chain management ...., https://www.research gate.net/publication/324139564_1_Blockchain's_roles_in_meeting_key_supply_chain_management_objectives, Accessed 3 Jul, 2020.

[35] Trust in trade: Announcing a new blockchain partner—IBM, 9 Mar, 2017, https://www.ibm.com/blogs/blockchain/2017/03/trust-trade-announcing-new-blockchain-partner/, Accessed 3 Jul, 2020.

regularly limited as a result of three issues. The issues being, systems incomparability, information dependability and trust in members, notwithstanding, blockchain may fill in as an apparatus for expelling these limitations[36].

The distributed nature of blockchains is helpful for SCM in light of the fact that it takes into consideration the sharing of data in a manner that is hard to alter (permanent) or hack. Blockchain usage ordinarily shows auditability qualities. This attribute of the blockchain improves traceability and transparency of the information kept in the blockchain by guaranteeing that data once recorded is never altered or misplaced[37].

In responding to an inquiry concerning whether there is a requirement for an innovation like blockchain in SCM, Petersen [19] expressed it would doubtlessly seem so. He advocated his answer by expressing that the present systems cannot yet convey the best resolution, since fraudulent conduct or defilement/altering of items in supply chains is still occurring. He expressed that blockchain may be seen as the innovation that holds fairly semi mystical forces, in this interest to impact or fortify trust, reinforce data quality and automate documentation streams in inter-organizational connections.

The costs in a supply chain system are reduced significantly when blockchain technology is used. Fundamentally because of enormous distance transactions being more slow through banks, blockchain gives a monetary answer for the worldwide supply chain. Since most tasks can be represented as exchanges, the work process of the supply chain can be quicker than the antiquated ones. Blockchain can limit blunders and increment trust through the reconciliation of every exchange with a provider. Blockchain can likewise execute business rules using smart contracts. As expressed before, this implies exchanges possibly happen if at least two members approve them[38].

Litke *et al.* [15] summed up the points of interest as appeared in Table 8.1[39]. They gave an overview of the current limitations supply chain actors face and the positive impact brought by blockchain.

---

[36] Supply Chain Management For Dummies (For ...—Amazon.com), https://www.amazon.com/Management-Dummies-Business-Personal-Finance/dp/1119410193, Accessed 3 Jul, 2020.

[37] Applications, limitations, costs, and benefits related to the use ...., 5 Feb, 2019, https://nofimaas.sharepoint.com/:b:/s/public/EYKcUY4fS3NFk7s6T7XDI3gBd-MY6oYxD2qXpBdxocIYZw, Accessed 3 Jul, 2020.

[38] Blockchain Technology in Supply Chain Management: An ...., https://scholarspace.manoa.hawaii.edu/bitstream/10125/60124/0684.pdf, Accessed 3 Jul, 2020.

[39] Blockchains for Supply Chain Management: Architectural....16 Jan. 2019, https://www.researchgate.net/publication/330484023_Blockchains_for_Supply_Chain_Management_Architectural_Elements_and_Challenges_Towards_a_Global_Scale_Deployment. Accessed 23 May. 2020.

Table 8.1 Supply Chain actors, current limitations faced and blockchain impact.

Supply chain actor	Current limitations	Blockchain impact
Raw material/ Producer	Ability to prove in a global and transparent way the origin and quality metrics of products.	Benefits from increased trust of keep track of the production raw material and value chain from the raw material to the end consumer.
Manufacturer	Limited ability to monitor the product to the final destination. Limited capabilities of checking quality measured from raw material.	Added value from shared information system with raw material suppliers and distribution networks.
Distributor	Custom tracking systems with poor collaboration capabilities. Limited certification ability and trust issues.	Ability to have proof-of-location and conditions certifications registered in the ledger.
Wholesaler	Lack of trust and certification of the products' path.	Ability to check the origin of the goods and the transformation/ transportation condition.
Retailer	Lack of trust and certification of the products' path.	Track of each individual product between the end consumer and the wholesaler. Ability to handle effectively return of multifunctioning products.
End user/ Consumer	Lack of trust regarding the compliance of the product with respect to origin, quality and compliance of the product to the specified standards and origin.	Full and transparent view on the product origin and its whole journey from raw material to final, purchased product.

Regardless of the points of interest noted above, blockchain innovation has various significant difficulties to survive. The worldwide supply chain works in a perplexing situation that requires different partners to conform to various laws and guidelines. Since worldwide organizations work against the setting of these built up laws and customs, implementing blockchain-based arrangements the whole way across a worldwide supply chain can be a difficult mission. Usage of blockchain likewise comprises bringing all the significant parties together, which can be a troublesome endeavor much of the time as parties, may not completely fathom the requirement for the innovation. Due to the prerequisite of a high utilization of IoT, not all nations are prepared to take an interest in blockchain-based SCMs. Many supply chain members situated in developing and least developed nations are a long way from prepared with regards to the appropriation of blockchain and without their cooperation it might demonstrate hard to realize the fullest capability of blockchain in supply chain management[40].

8.6 Conclusion

Blockchain and IoT are great technological disruptions and their combination in supply chain management has a positive impact on the performance of supply chains. This chapter presented a brief discussion about these two technologies, their integration, and their application in supply chain management. The IoT and Blockchain were described individually and their relationship and the motive behind their use in supply chain management investigated. Some use cases of the technologies were discussed, and further, both the advantages and challenges of Blockchain and IoT use in Supply Chain Management were discussed.

References

1. Alicke, K., Rachor, J., Seyfert, A., *Supply Chain 4.0—The next-generation digital supply chain*, McKinsey, Available at: https://www.mckinsey.com/business-func tions/operations/our-insights/supply-chain-40–the-next-generation-digital-supply-chain, 2016.
2. Arun, J., Gaur, N., Cuomo, J., *Blockchain for Business*, Addison-Wesley Professional, Pearson, 2019.

---

[40] Blockchain's Roles in Meeting Key Supply Chain ...—Uncg., https://libres.uncg.edu/ir/uncg/f/N_Kshetri_Blockchains_Roles_2018.pdf, Accessed 3 Jul, 2020.

3. Casado-Vara, R. *et al.*, How blockchain improves the supply chain: Case study alimentary supply chain. *Procedia Comput. Sci.*, Elsevier B.V., 134, 393–398.

4. Casino, F., A systematic literature review of blockchain-based applications: Current status, classification and open issues. *Telemat. Inform.*, Elsevier, 36(November 2018), Volume 36, pp. 55–81.

5. Consensys, Blockchain and International Trade, Trade Finance, and Supply Chain, Available at: https://cdn2.hubspot.net/hubfs/4795067/BLOCKCHAIN AND INTERNATIONAL TRADE, TRADE FINANCE, AND SUPPLY CHAIN (1).pdf?utm_campaign=EnterpriseEthereum&utm_source=email&utm_medum=InternalEmail&utm_term=WebinarDeck&utm_content=TradeFinance Webinar Follow (Accessed: 23 August 2019).

6. Danese, P., Supplier integration and company performance: A configurational view. *Omega*, Elsevier, 41, 6, 1029–1041, 2013.

7. Gupta, M., *Blockchain for Dummies*, C.A. Burchfield *et al.* (Ed.), John Wiley & Sons, Inc., 2019.

8. Gyaneshwar, P. and Kushwaha, S., Operational Performance through Supply Chain Management Practices *Int. J. Business Social Science*, Volume 3, no. 2, 2012.

9. Hong, J., Liao, Y., Zhang, Y., Yu, Z. The effect of supply chain quality management practices and capabilities on operational and innovation performance: Evidence from Chinese manufacturers. *Int. J. Production Economics*, 2019.

10. Koksharov, V., *Supply Chain Modelling. A Practical*, Hämeen, University of Appied Sciences, 2016.

11. Kshetri, Blockchain's roles in meeting key supply chain management objectives. *Int. J. Inf. Manage.*, *Elsevier*, 39, 80–89, 2017.

12. Kuhi, K., Kaare, K., Koppel, O., Ensuring performance measurement integrity in logistics using blockchain. *Proceedings of the 2018 IEEE International Conference on Service Operations and Logistics, and Informatics, SOLI*, IEEE, pp. 256–261, 2018.

13. Leng, K., Bi, Y., Jing, L., Fu, H., & Nieuwenhuyse, I. (2018). Research on agricultural supply chain system with double chain architecture based on blockchain technology. *Future Gener. Comput. Syst.*, 86, 641–649.

14. Lieber, A., Trust in Trade: Announcing a new blockchain partner, Available at: https://www.ibm.com/blogs/blockchain/2017/03/.

15. Litke, A., Anagnostopoulos, D., Varvarigou, T., Blockchains for Supply Chain Management: Architectural Elements and Challenges Towards a Global Scale Deployment. *Logistics*, 3, 1, 5, 2019.

16. Mao, D., Hao, Z., Wang, F., Li, H. Innovative Blockchain-Based Approach for Sustainable and Credible Environment in Food Trade: A Case Study in Shandong Province, China. *Sustainability*. 10, 3149, 2018

17. Min, H. Blockchain technology for enhancing supply chain resilience, *Bus. Horiz.*, Elsevier, vol. 62(1), pages 35–45, 2019.

18. Olsen, P., Borit, M., Syed, S., Applications, limitations, costs, and benefits related to the use of blockchain technology in the food industry, 2019.

19. Petersen, K.J., Blockchain in Supply Chain, Cio, (June), 0–13, 2020, Available at: https://blockchain-technology.cioreviewindia.com/cioviewpoint/blockchain-in-supply-chain-nid-4275-cid-1.html.

20. Rao, A.R., & Clarke, D.J. (2020). Perspectives on emerging directions in using IoT devices in blockchain applications. Internet Things, 10, 100079.

21. Schrauf, S. and Berttram, P., Industry 4.0: *How digitization makes the supply chain more efficient, agile, and customer-focuse*d, https://www.strategyand.pwc.com/gx/en/insights/2016/digitization-more-efficient.html, 2016.

22. Stanton, D., *Supply chain management for Dummies, Production Planning & Control For Dummie*s, https://www.dummies.com/business/management/supply.

23. Stock, J., A research view of supply chain management: Developments and topics for exploration. *ORiON*, 25, 2, 147–160.

24. Thakore, R. *et al.*, Blockchain-based IoT: A survey. *Procedia Comput. Sci.*, Elsevier B.V., 155, 704–709, 2019.

25. Wang, Q., Zhu, X., Ni, Y., Gu, L., Zhu, H. (2019). Blockchain for the IoT and Industrial IoT: A Review. *Internet of Things*. 10. 100081.

9

Blockchain-Enabled Supply Chain Management System

Sonal Pathak

Faculty of Computer Applications, Manav Rachna International Institute of Research and Studies, Faridabad, India

Abstract

In the value of Organizational assets - Blockchain technology is found valuable these days. Any trading is possible and successful whenevery information and database is factual, reliable and with the consent of all participants. It can be converted in to transparent across groups, safe and easy to use format with the help of Network management. Any market data needs to be protected and validated along with the technological advancement. A reliable distributed ledger helps in connecting suppliers, market, organizations, and consumers byresolving the issues of defining separate and multiple ledgers. Digital currencies are associated with blockchain. In supply chain management, blockchain and digital currencies has various applications types. Many participants are required to be managed in a Supply chain network. In the supply chain networks of smart organizations, a digital ledger can be developed to manage real time transactions and movements through blockchains for all the participants. In this chapter author has discussed the application of blockchain and digital currencies for better outcomes in a supply chain. The aim of this chapter is to assess the applicability of blockchains and to provide a foundation for researchers and practitioners to direct their future projects towards improving the applications and technology. This chapter also describes how smart contracts and ledgers can help in managing the overpriced gaps from procure – to- pay.

Keywords: Blockchain, smart organizations, digital currency, digital ledger, transactional information, financial security, digital contracts, supply chain management

Email: pathak25@gmail.com

S.S. Tyagi and Shaveta Bhatia (eds.) Blockchain for Business: How it Works and Creates Value, (179–200) © 2021 Scrivener Publishing LLC

9.1   Introduction

New avenues for social and economic systems can be created through Blockchain technology. The blockchain can perceived as a game changer in bringing big transformation in the existing logistic, manufacturing and supply chain industry which seems to be transparent but complex. The supply chain solutions which are blockchain-enabled have drastically proven to minimize cost and improve efficiency in the supply chain industry. The complexity to create and distribute good makes a supply chain sequence a bit complex. Numerous stages and long-time duration in a supply chain involves large number of payments and invoices, geographical locations, people and entities depending upon the product involved.

But the transformational information should not disturb the simplicity of the tools. Decentralization of power and unbiases can be generated with the help of blockchain in the management of supply chain. All movement will be part of ledger and each participant will have a copy of digital ledger [8]. Benefits can be gained, and business can be restructured by optimal utilization of money, time, and efforts on several fronts. If there will be any fraud or perpetrate game in the system of company, it will be out of synchronization with rest of the ecosystem. In the procurement process as well more savings and visibility can be achieved through Blockchain, the digital payments and contracts can also be enhancing financial security.

9.1.1   Supply Chain Management

In the late 1980s, the term 'supply chain management' came into existence and applicability has arisen in the 1990s. The 'operations Management' and 'Logistics' were the terms used by businessman instead prior to that time. A few definitions of a supply chain are proposed below:

A supply chain is the alignment of firms that bring products or services to market (Lambert, Stock and Ellram) [11].

- A supply chain consists of all stages involved, directly or indirectly, in fulfilling a customer request. The supply chain not only includes the manufacturer and suppliers, but also transporters, warehouses, retailers, and customers themselves (Chopra and Meindl) [7].
- A supply chain is a network of facilities and distribution options that performs the functions of procurement of

materials, transformation of these materials into intermediate and finished products and the distribution of these finished products to customers [12].

Therefore, a supply chain can be explained as the things we do to achieve the results by influencing the behavior of the supply chain. The system coordination of the old business roles and the strategies across these business roles across supply chain and within a company is called Supply chain management. The purposes of getting improved and long-term individual's performances and companies can be achieved through supply chain—the process of coordination of products, inventory, location, and transportation among all participants in a supply chain to attain the best combination of efficiency and responsiveness for the market.

There is a difference between the concept of supply chain management and the traditional concept of operation management. Operation management typically refers to activities that happen within the boundaries of an organization. Supply chains refer to networks of companies that work together and coordinate their actions to deliver a product to market. Also, traditional operations emphasized more on activities such as procurement, maintenance, distribution, and inventory management. Supply chain management acknowledges traditional operations management and involves activities such as new product development, marketing, customer service and finance. In the broad view to fulfill of supply chain parameters, these novel additional activities have become part of part of this chain to enhance efficacy of work and fulfill customer requirements.

In the view of parameters of supply chain management, organizations and supply chain is viewed as single entity. It gives a systematic approach to handle effectively various activities which are required to coordinate different products and services together. This system approach promotes the best fit framework in which overly complex business requirements can be handled effectively by taking care of different requirements of different supply chains. The proper collaboration and supplier relationship is the success mantra for a successful and sustainable supply chain. As per discussed by Brammer and Walker, the most frequent occurring factor for Sustainable Supply Chain Management is the quality and depth of relationship between suppliers and the organizations [4]. According to Pagell and Wu, the best practice and a crucial component of Sustainable Supply Chain Management is cooperation among various suppliers [17]. A description of sustainable supply chain management has been shown in the Figure 9.1.

Various parameters which will affect a supply chain management and make it more sustainable are—Managerial approaches for SSM,

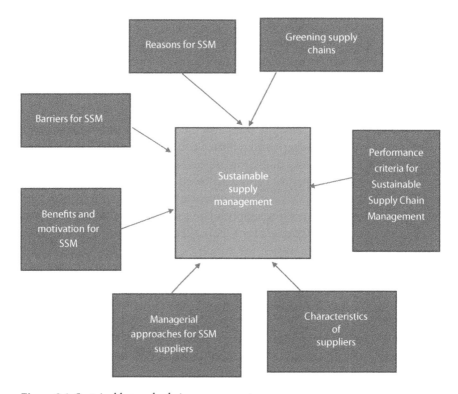

Figure 9.1 Sustainable supply chain management.

Characteristics of suppliers, Performance criteria for SSM, Benefits and motivation factors for SSM, barriers for SSM, Greening and enhance quality of supply chains and other reasons for SSM. Simpson and Power discussed that to execute the business processes; collaboration within the members of Supply chain is an essential step [21].

Some supplier development initiatives are innovative environmental design, joint waste minimization approaches, development of eco-friendly technologies, collaboration efforts for recyclable products and minimization of hazardous waste. Chen and Paulrai proposed that all the concepts which were used in the conventional SCM theory are being now used as prerogative practices in Sustainable Supply Chain Management theory [6]. Authors have also highlighted the difference between the traditional supply management and the necessity of partnerships in the modern day Researchers have conducted a case study analysis on a bag manufacturing company and found that applying reverse logistics or recycling techniques in the entire SC process can result in minimizing the product lead-time and supplier collaboration can boost sales and production efficiency.

In contrast to power-based compliance partnerships, the trust among the supply chain actors is mandatory. Blome have concluded that effective SSCM implementation can be attained from strong form of partnership and collaboration [3]. Nevertheless, in relationship management, compliance is also understood as negatively associated approach.

As per Zhu *et al.*, practices which are mentioned in management literature for extending sustainability to suppliers, supplier development initiatives can be developed to aim at increasing performance of the suppliers [30]. Examples of such initiatives are:

- Evaluation of suppliers,
- Collaboration among suppliers
- Training of supplier.

To make a successful implementation of Sustainable Supply Chain Management, suppliers have to become more socially and environmentally accountable. To evaluate the depth of collaborative relationships has already been identified by many researchers so far but still a wide scope is there to analyze SSCM. There is very less research has been done so far that can evaluate the collaborations such as imbalances in supplies. A major role has played by sustainable procuring in all around success of company and it should be extended to all the stakeholders instead incorporated within the organization. In the management literature, the best considered way is collaboration among true suppliers; however, its applicability is difficult. The most count of research has considered for larger corporations where suppliers are the medium and small enterprises (SME). Hence, to attain true collaboration of large and small companies, sustainable practices are necessities [14].

For a large business enterprise, the concept of sustainability is quite understanding and broad in terms of supply chain management. In a dynamic business environment, SSCM consist of perspectives based on integration of environmental, economic, and social aspects in the supply chain. For the value of propositions to the customers, supply chain profitability and successful implementation of SSC practices, collaboration between all its stakeholders along with optimal utilization of resources, funds, and information's.

Winter and Knemeyer discussed that the researchers in the field should identify the research opportunities and should drive into literature periodically. Various perspectives of SSCM like economic, social, governance, environmental and performance measurements should be more focused in the current research on SSCM. Current researches have also focused on empirical and quantitative modeling approaches for SSCM. Parameters have been identified which inhibits and enable the SSC practices for large organizations. More numbers of researches are required to be examined to attain the scope of triple bottom line in a supply chain context and enhance the social perspectives. The modeling approaches need to do across industries and in a more realistic uncertain decision environment to fully understand and integrate the SSCM practices across industry [27].

9.2   Blockchain Technology

A decentralized, open distributed ledger, is a software mechanism and can record all transactions efficiently and in a permanent way (KariKorpela, Jukka Hallikas) [9, 10]. It offers supports for transactions and trusted assets without any interference of central server and central trust to make the value exchanges among all partners of a supply chain management.

Trent McConaghy and Rodolphe Marques discoursed that to reduce cost of production, greater operations systems, and reveal new opportunities of business at a worldwide level is possible with the help of distributed ledgers, immutable cryptographic records and blockchain-enabled smart contracts [24]. Blockchain is the public ledger or database of records of all digital activities that participants have been shared. Crosby *et al.* described that majority of participants give their consents for each transaction in the digital ledger and consensus is guaranteed for each transaction. Each kind of fund which is stored will be verified on its network in a Blockchain technology.

Pilkington, explored that blockchain which does not associate with any organization and control of network is distributed among all its participants is called public Blockchain. For verification of each transaction, miners execute the process of verification for which they use specially designed devices or computers. These miners get their reward in digital form; it may be a predefined Bitcoin or any other cryptocurrency. Blockchain can be literally explained as a chain of blocks and these blocks represents an ordered data held at each step [19]. As shown in Figure 9.2, Blockchain can digitally connect different parties to work together.

Each block represents data which is stored in the form of digital signature (amount, date, time). This data reveals the information about a transaction and each block is different from another block of chain in the form of information stored. A unique code called "hash" has been assigned to the information stored in a block. We can also imagine a blockchain as a ledger—because that is essentially how most blockchains function. Each block of data represents some new transaction on the ledger, whether that means a contract or a sale or whatever else uses a ledger for. A blockchain is a record of transactions. The people or companies using Blockchain can

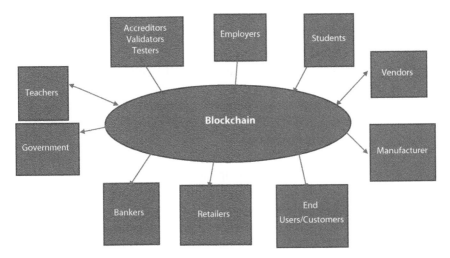

Figure 9.2 Example of Applications of Blockchain.

verify and make these transactions. These are important concepts about Blockchain technology. The complexity of the calculations increases with the increase in the mining capability to maintain the time needed to write data the specified block of text remains constant.

Blockchain is a protocol rather a single technology. This is a method of executing required things and recording any transaction. Ownership of Blockchain can be relocated to another party unlike the Internet in which data is being shared. There are many reasons to make Blockchain a desirable technology. In case where different currency exchange groups are dealing together, Blockchain can eradicate the requirements of reconcile dividing dividers. It also removes the role of central authority; their payment cost will also be eliminated, and accuracy of ledger can be maintained by the distribution among all users. All the transactions can be accessed and monitored by any participants in a computer only allowing for transparency and blockchain to be 'self-monitoring'.

In general, the salient features and benefits of Blockchain Technology are as follows:

(i)   Transparency: The data transparency has been maintained as a blockchain employs the notion of distributed agreement; entire history of activities can be read by all its users making the process completely transparent.

(ii) Traceability: History of information can be effectively and efficiently be accessed by using time stamped records.

(iii) Security: Data security is significantly strengthening in a distributed ledger because of the difficulty of staging a cyber attack.

(iv) Efficiency: Disintermediation can be attained as there is no requirement of centralized database. Processing time and cost is also reduced significantly because of no requirement of a trustworthy intermediary, like a bank, for database maintenance.

(v) Confidentiality: This is one of the aspects which is a matter of concern as each participant on the network can view every activity therefore confidentiality of data is difficult to manage. Though transparency and security are maintained in a blockchain's decentralized ledger, but confidentiality is not maintained. As a result, advanced cryptography and pseudonymous addresses are being used to save the data of users and their privacy in a BCT.

(vi) Immutability: In BCT, cost of auditing is also substantially reduced in view of integrity of its data, as once an activity or transaction is authenticated by a blockchain system, it can no longer be amended or reversed.

(vii) Increased Innovation: The innovations to decentralized architecture will provide new opportunities abound to create specialized, new uses. The smart shipper can be tapped and help in profit generation.

(viii) Customer Engagement: A better delivery timeline can be built by using Blockchain database by which the tracking of production and shipment is more convenient for the retailers. A deeper loyalty and client rapport can be developed by this kind of data sharing and a new level of transparency can be attained.

These features can be summarized in refer to two crucial aspects on transparency and removal of unnecessary parties. Therefore, decisions made on BCT adoption are imperative to ensuring business success.

9.3   Blockchain Technology in Supply Chain Management

We have discussed thoroughly in earlier sections about concepts of supply chain management and fundamentals of Blockchain. Now we can discuss how Blockchain are being used in Supply chain. The blockchain is tremendously scalable and efficient as it is decentralized. It is more secure and transparent as all the blocks are related with each other and the transactions are executed across all the nodes. Hence, the blockchain can be used to improve the transparency and efficiency of supply chains and all the activities from warehouse till delivery is influenced by this technology. For effective management of supply chain, series of built in commands are used in Blockchain technology. There is no conflict in the chain as all the chain entities have same ledger regarding the transactions. Blockchain records cannot be deleted which is crucial factor for maintaining supply chain transparency.

Ahmed Farahin his paper discussed that are emerging technology of Blockchain in the form of Bitcoin, has added a novel way of managing supply chain. This method has been relied upon on the success of this supply chain process from the perspective of Bitcoin, BCT has gradually operated on a range of purposes, either private or public and increased the satisfaction and confidence of customers. This paper highlights the oppurtunities of new digital world and challenges ahead of this modern technology. This study intends to examine the current theoretical and research framework of Blockchain technology in a rational. Empirical research aims to identify the measurable effect of materiality on a particular problem of credit risk modeling under the broader blockchain paradigm. To incorporate the fact that effect of BCT has measured and within the realm of technology which has significant impacted the growth of companies. The economic problems can also be highlighted due to use of digital ledger and explaining financial distress as well [1].

Nordgren et al. in their paper established that Blockchain technology is widely known for the emergence of Bitcoin in 2009 and has since received a lot of hype as a technology to disrupt the financial services industry. After Brexit, the UK border problems were possibly resolved by using Blockchain technology. There are few questions which are associated with functionality of blockchain though blockchain developers promise to provide security and speed of transactions.

A Blockchain technology can be called as internet of our time or a disruptive technology. Blockchain technology has revamp the accounting and financial field. The potential of Blockchain technology can be enhanced by resolving issues and criticism about Blockchain technology that needs to be associated [15].

Kiwillinski discussed that BCT is crucial to the value of supply chain management. The information provided by blocks of Blockchain is more reliable and transparent. Trading is only possible with the consent of all participants. With the help of network, transaction can be transparent across groups, safe and easily formatted [9]. The amalgamation of Blockchain with supply chain management has the following benefits:

- The fast and efficient Online transactions
- Smartphone Apps can be used for accounts renewal.
- Virtual data recognition systems
- The entire process is allowed to change.

Babich and Hilary described that the applications of BCT and SCM are still very less and very few cases can be observed [3]. BCT is fully utilized in the Finance sector only. The core values of SCM and BCT in Finance is the base of differences in their applicability. Information security is the core value of financial applications whereas; core value for application of SCM is system traceability transparency.

Typically, following three aspects could be adopted for Blockchain technology in SCM

- Smart Contracts
- Dis-intermediation
- Information asymmetries.

We shall expand on the features that will motivate our modeling assumptions. The paperwork processing (e.g. transactions, customs clearance, transportation, quality inspection) will be removed because of transparency feature of BCT which will significantly improve the efficiency of business. In this view, we can say that supplier's cost can be reduced by adoption of BCT. Smart contract is one of the well-known applications of BCT. When the predefined terms and conditions are met then smart contracts will be automatically enforced and verified each supplier.

One potential Smart Contract application is in the arts. For an example we can discuss music industry, artists and songwriters can get their royalty automatically in real time with the help of smart contract between two parties. Accordingly, high quality supply and production can be enhanced considering smart contract. Information asymmetry issues can be focused by functionality of BCT. The quality of information concerning service or product is typically asymmetric between consumers and seller that is monitored and certified by a third party which is best possible solution.

Giannakas discussed that taking another example of organic food with regard to the attribute credence, customers will not be able to differentiate between conventional foods and organic foods. In addition, the production cost of conventional foods is significantly lesser than that of organic foods. As consumers will pay for any kind of food without knowing about type of food, this can lead to loss to suppliers of organic food and there will be no incentive for such suppliers. Eventually the market of organic food would fail to grow. In this scenario, only a third party which may label certified (e.g. USDA & FDA) can stimulate the organic food market by providing necessary information to the consumers is the only solution for this problem [14].

Rousseau and Vranken report consumers are more interested in products which are produced in environmentally, socially and eco-healthy and friendly way. A report says that consumers were ready to pay 25% price premium for some quality products even with no provision of information. Blockchain technology helps in generating information about suppliers and help consumers in ensuring the information about quality products [20]. The price premium can reach to maximum if the actual information about environmental health effects of quality production can transparently reach consumers. Greater transparency is possible through Blockchain than traditional conveyors. This is preferable if misuse of property and corruption is at stake. For example, Block based assets can be utilized in providing utility funds; and even the last recipient who is getting subsidy are identified. At present, transactions between companies result in a type of 'quadruple entry book', in which each company automatically enters a double entry, and in theory two input sets are equal in value. This model can be significantly modified by blockchain.

The internal walls of any supply chain or any company can be removed by making direct entries on the blockchains, all transactions can be recorded authentically, truthfully to each party by using bookkeeping. The supply chain becomes more viable by elements of Blockchain. When a circulated data of a supply chain undergoes various transitions, transactions of the blockchain are made secure and immutable. Same goal can be achieved by satisfying different complex requirements. A mechanism to increase the mutability and ensures the transaction confidentiality to be endorsed, that prevents or blocks any malicious party participating in the supply chain from tampering or illegally modifying the payment and invoice information.

Hence in the case of supply chain, immutability and confidentiality of transactions must be protected by a mechanism. Blockchain technology provides a feasible solution to manage security problems by improving the product transparency and integrity.

The factors which affect supply chain with the amalgamation of Blockchain Technology are summarized as follows:

- Performance: The procedures and actions in a supply chain are more prone to frauds and human errors which reduce the performance. In a Blockchain-enabled system, all the activities are shown as electronic transactions. Therefore, execution becomes faster and performance will be improved.
- Scalability: A decentralized and well-networked database improves the scalability in the Blockchain by facilitating the involved entities and improves connection. Thus, all supply chain data is stored in a ledger and peer network established which recedes any single point of failure.
- Consensus: Blockchain ensures the immutability of data by using this mechanism throughout the ledger. It maintains nodes of network to keep and update information about all submitted transactions .The timestamp of the order received, and the amount transacted is maintained in the transaction.
- Location: The attributes and functionalities of Blockchain technology are independent of the user's geo-location. Hence the span of supply chain which is enabled by blockchain can be larger across the globe which allows the participants to provide services and products across the globe and carry out their business.
- Privacy: Privacy of users in the Blockchain maintained in the digital ledgers which encompasses immutable information. Pseudo Nymity is offered by public blockchain in which any user can work together through a new address and without disclosing their real identity with the ledger.
- Cost: Cryptocurrency technology helps in reducing the cost drastically in a Blockchain technology-enabled supply chain system. Cryptocurrency enhances the speed of transaction processing. Digital transactions improve the efficiency and make the workflow faster.

9.4   Elements of Blockchain That Affects Supply Chain

As we have discussed so far that in a supply chain, the very step is extraction of natural resources (raw materials) and to deliver to the next stage products are pre-processed, by the vendors and suppliers. Manufacturing is the next stage when ready to sell product take place from raw materials. After this, ready products are ready with distributors and they will further distribute constructed goods further to intermediaries' like retailers and wholesalers.

An active inventory has been maintained by the distributors before getting connected with the suppliers. Subsequently, the product is not being selling to public directly by the wholesalers but to other retailers instead, whereas the retailers dispose the purchased products to end users. Lastly, the consumers are the ones who purchase or receive goods or services for personal needs or use and not for business purposes of resale or trade. In the whole process of supply chain lots of transaction get generated and transferred to next phase of a standard supply chain.

Figure 9.3 depicts the combining blockchain technology with supply chain functionalities, and transaction take place at each step. Each transaction is conceptually, related to different actors of a supply chain which interacts under a blockchain network. Each participant submits transactions on the blockchain network in a specific way, depending on the completed activity. In the raw materials step, the suppliers that pre-process the natural resources are submitting transactions on the ledger concerning that initial process. These transactions include tags such as raw material name, quantity, quality,

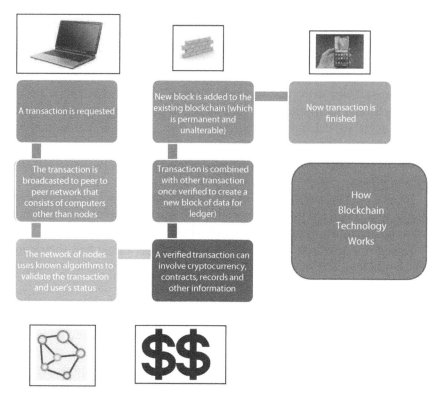

Figure 9.3 Transaction management in blockchain enabled supply chain.

origin geo-location, and others. The moment the raw materials are starting their journey to manufacturer, the appropriate transactions are submitted.

Steps/algorithm to implement a model for blockchain enabled supply chain

> Step 1: Identify the economic, driving and reliability elements for integrating the blockchain in to supply chain.
> Step 2: Identify the technical, operational, and organizational aspects.
> Step 3: Identify the resistance factors and cultural barriers for entrenching blockchain into supply chain.
> Step 4: Design a framework and authenticate the same to encompass blockchain enabled supply chain management process.

At any point of time, each member of network party can verify important details about their product is made from and the specific raw material. Similarly, the manufacturer has a continuous interaction with the help of blockchain and the Logistics next chain participant. Conceptually, this is the way by which different actors of a supply can interact under a blockchain network. Each party can submit transaction in a specific way on the blockchain network. In the same way; tags are identified at each step of transactions in a supply chain and proceed to execution of another step. New transactions with new tags information such as field experience of manufacturers, names, etc. are submitted after each step completion till the products are delivered to distributors. This process is represented by blockchain transactions that display important data tags, such as the merchant and customer address, exchange amount, product raw material quality, and others.

Finally, the final product will be received by the end user by a submitted transaction (included with appropriate tags) and verify every aspect of tag from the beginning of journey of supply chain of a product [28].

Table 9.1 summarizes the different supply chain actors and their current limitations and how blockchain technology adoption affected supply chain.

Supply chain is currently a vast Supply chain, in which different parties coordinates together. Many of the supplied products pass through multiple parties, unlike traditional networks of OEMs (original equipment manufacturer) and suppliers. Product life cycle has been reduced; operations and dynamic ability of supply chain have increased. The corporations are still required to update their traditional supply chain management by enabling

Table 9.1 Supply Chain actors, current limitations faced and blockchain impact.

Supply chain actor	Current limitations	Blockchain impact
Producer/Raw material	The origin and quality metrics of products is not proven to be transparent and global	End consumer has been benefitted by increased trust to know value chain and track the production raw material
Manufacturer	Capability to monitor product till final stage is limited. Ability of assessing quality measures is also limited.	Networks between raw material suppliers and distributors have been strengthening due to shared information system.
Distributor	Poor collaboration capabilities of Custom tracking systems Absence of trust and certification issues	Proof-of-conditions certifications and location is available due to all information registered in the ledger
Wholesaler	Absence of certification and trust of the products' path.	Capability to verify the transformation/ transportation conditions and origin of the goods.
Retailers	Lack of trust and certification of the products' path	Each individual product between the wholesaler and the end consumer is trackable. Capability to manage successfully return of faulty products
Consumer/End user	Limited trust in compliance of origin of product with respect to quality and fulfillment of specified and standardized product	Transparent and complete view on the whole journey of products from raw material to last procured products.

it with blockchain and integrating the potential of blockchain in their processes, thereby expand their business horizon to global levels.

In a new business applications, main applications of Blockchain that will result from this technology are Crowd funding, Smart contracts, Governance, sharing economy, Supply chain auditing, File storage, Prediction markets, Internet of Things (IoT) Neighborhood Micro grids, KYC (know your customer), AML (Anti-money laundering), Identity management, financial institutions audit trails, Digital identity, Tokenization, Stock trading and Land title registration and Faster transaction through Blockchain enables:

a) Administering payments immediately between parties with no intervention of third-party,
b) Ledger updation automatically
c) Simultaneously execution of transactions at both ends.

Companies which are implementing blockchain-enabled SCM are as follows:

- Secure Capital—Clearer settlement terms through blockchain verification
- TBSx3—Preventing fake products and improving transparency
- Fr8 Network—Enhanced data tracking for the supply chain
- British Airways—Using blockchain to resolve conflicting flight data
- Walmart—Giving employees visibility on where food comes from.

Piscini discussed that to enhance partnership along with the supply chain, operational efficiency can substantially be improved by having a Smart Contract and disintermediation. More research is required to enhance the scalability and expansion of a network, its compatibility and the integration of multiple blockchains should also be explored [18].

The underlying rationale is that once a company decides to disclose more product information to its potential suppliers, it is more likely to find a better supplier that can offer a more preferable yield rate, reflecting a reliable supply along with high quality. The traceability glinted by Blockchain technology's "proof of work" concept overcomes the information asymmetry issue among the participants along the supply chain. Considering, blockchain-savvy (or, broadly tech-savvy) consumers, we assume that the random demand can be boosted by BCT adoption—the greater the degree of adoption, the greater the demand, in the stochastic sense.

The information asymmetry can be solved by embraced BCT tool. Many studies have shown that information accessibility and truthfulness are two main forces to create a thriving authority goods market. In this sense, we recognize that BCT can operate as the safest solutions for disclosing data throughout the supply chain while at the same period certifying its validity. Zott shed light on how the supply chain actors help in designing a blockchain-enabled supply chain. At the first level of individual firms, the business model is often examined but a comprehensive framework for thinking can also be used as part of a systemic change because innovations in technology leads to industrial and structural changes [29].

Tsujimoto examined the term "platforms" and "ecosystems" with the concept of business model. Among partners of supply chain, the ecosystem construct should be clearly examined to report the interdependencies and interconnectedness. With the help of technology enablers e.g. government agencies &technology service providers supply chain actors become strengthen to beat competitors. The concept of platform tends to be treated as a subsystem of a business ecosystem [25].

The disruptive impact of blockchain technology requires supply chain actors to rethink many aspects of their business models as well as the governance issue. Teece also proposed some points on a business model. The architecture of the value creation, capture mechanism, delivery mechanism should also be employed for a successful BCT enabled supply chain. In the existing supply chain management, first step is to identify the 'pain' points. An effort for the consortium and optimal amount of time is to be deploying for Blockchain technology via an iterative process and then take decision about the entry point. The usage of technology and focus lies around the model of cryptocurrency called as Bitcoin, therefore in the next section, we are discussing basic concepts of Bitcoin [26].

9.4.1 Bitcoin

The boom of cryptocurrency has been brought attention towards Blockchain. The most prominent type of the cryptocurrency is bitcoin which is the primary character of Blockchain and introduced the consensus mechanism and financial services intermediaries which helped in enhancing trust. However, this perspective should not be limited only into its monetary properties. Nowadays, Blockchain techniques are impacting society in all domains and attracting people due to essential value of Blockchain: Trustable, Decentralized, collectively maintain, open source database and Reliable and applications of Blockchain are expanding in all segments of life. People under the pseudonym Satoshi Nakamoto created an online coin called Bitcoin. Submitting their white paperback in late 2008 and introducing the first code in early 2009, Nakamoto made bitcoin an electronic currency that could be sent to peers without the need for a central bank or other authority to use and modify a ledger, much less how it used virtual currency. Soon Bitcoin became the most effective way for financial transactions and Bitcoin proposal resolved many issues of conventional or other accounting methods [2, 22].

The engine that used the bitcoin ledger was named blockchain, which is the term now used to refer to all the bad ledger technology being distributed. The big and original blockchain was that which continues to generate in transaction of Bitcoin. Some work for a few hundred 'altcoins'—some of the same money projects have different rules—and different systems like Ethereum or Ripple. In global record systems, a potentially disruptive and low-tech technology called Bitcoin has attracted investors of financial sectors due to its few unique and simple features. Bitcoin works to pay miners—which creates a compelling legwork for sending new transactions—with newly created bitcoins [13].

Blockchain applied the mechanism which was initially made for Bitcoin. To control inflation, shipping difficulties were also automatically adjusted. Miners are motivated to generate new jobs rather switching to different smaller groups and reward was deployed to the oldest existing chain. But a challenge of ineffectiveness of new updates for a bitcoin client was there until all the participants agree to install them. Following are some reasons for attracting more users of Bitcoin:

- The low cost of payers
- Since inception of currency—accounting has been growing steadily
- In comparison to traditional bank, the system is more restricted.

Bitcoin does not have 'Know Your Client' or identity requirements—anyone with an internet connection can join and start receiving and sending bitcoins. While this makes the system cheaper and more accessible, it has made and appealed to criminals in much the same way as paper money, the Silk Road 'black net' marketplace that made extensive use of bitcoin before being shut down by the FBI in October 2013. Bitcoin does not have issues related to international borders because being an internet based currency. Bitcoin does not get affected by location of different parties. Many Blockchain projects are considering raising funds including payments applications internationally central banks issued as Ripple.

9.5 Challenges in Implementation of Blockchain-Enabled Supply Chain

Although blockchain technology can revolutionize supply chain, offer many services and can evaluate automated, cost efficient and more reliable systems, there are some drawbacks to using this technology in supply chain [23]

a) Blockchain technology is highly dependent on the Internet. So poor infrastructure can play spoil sport. And a high level of cyber security is a must.

b) Accounting and auditing are highly subject to legislation. Therefore, to ensure the full benefits of blockchain accounting, proper regulations should also be made. The process must be enabled so that any change in regulation is immediately adopted.

c) Blockchain capacity: To have a tight network, we need many tracks. The problem is that each of these traces must be based on the blockchain.

d) Another challenge is that supply chain actors need to identify an area where value could be co-created and benefits co-shared/captured by multiple players. Different consortium members tend to have different priorities and sometime conflicting goals due to the nature of their businesses and the relative 'location' in a supply chain network (O'Byrne) [16].

9.6   Conclusion

We can say that blockchain in current scenario can be considered an infant technology. It was assumed that this technology will work on the basic principles of Bitcoin cryptocurrency but later few measures are added to its design to enhance its global visibility. Thus, continuous activities were done by algorithm researchers, cryptographers, and the computer scientist to evolve Blockchain gradually. This technology is not being utilized for digital payments, but this basic technology has potential to alter almost all major activities of supply chain. Important aspects such as reliability, financial differentiation, flexibility, and cyber-technology which are essentials parameters of supply chain are applicable in current conceptual framework.

However, social impact is being met in a more encouraging way apart from technological challenges of Blockchain. More innovation is required in terms of impact of BCT on supply chain performance and its design. We just cannot consider a normal firm that deals from its suppliers and sell products to tech-savvy customers for the assessment of success of BCT in supply chain. But we should analyze adoption of this technology for up-stream supply and down-stream customers as well. Any company looks for maximizing total profit by jointly managing— Ordering and production design, Blockchain design and dynamic pricing and selling.

This can be included that deployment of BCT can help companies in lowering selling price, reduce order quantities and minimized the levels of target-inventory. Few special types of experience goods and credence goods got benefited by adopting BCT but others (search goods) may not prove beneficial. Considering the lifecycle of a typical experience good, we recommend the adoption of BCT as early as possible, and that it is adopted both to a higher degree and at an earlier stage.

This early adoption generates more understanding on adoption of BCT to serve well for SCM. With certain modifications, our framework and solution ideas can also apply to other settings, especially when adopting a new technology for SCM, such as cloud computing, IoT, AI, etc. BCT provides a disruptive and state-of-the-art business solution in a variety of contexts within supply chain management, especially for those serving potential tech-savvy consumers. Although we have endeavored to consider the major features of BCT, there are some other compelling factors that need to be considered to enrich the research. As one potential future research project, blockchain technology could significantly shorten the lead times of transactions, as well as at the same time speed up both information processing times and paperwork processing. From a financial perspective, cash flow could become faster or even immediate by leveraging cryptocurrency ecosystems throughout its supply chain network. In this case, it will be of interest to study the impact of BCT on process expedition. In the future, blockchain solutions from different companies, or even industries, will be able to communicate and share digital assets with each other seamlessly.

In summary, a blockchain can transform supply chains, industries, and ecosystems. Interestingly, even organizations, like banks and governments, who would seem to be losing out, can see opportunities to use blockchain to streamline their own businesses. Of course, an in-depth transformation of supply chains will not happen instantly. However, supply chains can already start using a blockchain for small portions of their operations. Smart Contracts can help eliminate the costly delays and waste that is currently experienced due to the manual handling of paperwork. After that, the door is then open to a smarter, faster, more secure supply chain from one end to the other

References

1. Ahmed Farah, N.A., Blockchain Technology: Classification, Opportunities, and Challenges. *Int. Res. J. Eng. Technol.*, 05, 05, 3423–3426, 2018.
2. Ganeshan, R. and Harrison, T.P., *An Introduction to Supply Chain Management*, published at Sementic Publishing House, London. http://silmaril.smeal.psu.edu/supply_chain_intro.html, 1995.
3. Blome, C., Paulraj, A., Schuetz, K., Supply chain collaboration and sustainability: A profile deviation analysis. *Int. J. Oper. Prod. Manag.*, 34, 5, 639–663, 2014.
4. Brammer, S. and Walker, H., Sustainable procurement in the public sector: An international comparative study. *Int. J. Oper. Prod. Manag.*, 31, 4, 452–476, 2011.
5. Babich, V. and Hilary, G., Distributed ledgers and operations: What operations management researchers should know about blockchain technology? *Manuf. Serv. Oper. Manag.*, 12, 1–32, 2018.
6. Chen, I.J. and Paulraj, A., Towards a theory of supply chain management: The constructs and measurements. *J. Oper. Manage.*, 22, 2, 119–150, 2004.
7. Chopra, and Meindl, Essentials of Supply Chain Management: Strategy, Planning and Operations, in: *Supply Chain Management: Strategy, Planning and Operations*, Prentice-Hall, Upper Saddle River, NJ, 2001.
8. Haber, S. and Stornetta, W., How to time-stamp a digital document. *J. Cryptol.*, 3, 2, 99–111, 1991.
9. Melnychenko, O. Application of artificial intelligence in control systems of economic activity. *Virtual Economics*, 2, (3), 30–40, 2019.
10. Kari, K., Jukka, H., Tomi, D., Digital supply chain transformation toward blockchain integration, in: *Proceedings of the 50th Hawaii International Conference on System Sciences*, 2017.
11. Lambert, Stock, Ellram, *Fundamentals of Logistics Management*, Irwin/McGraw-Hill, Boston, MA, 1998.
12. Mentzer, J.T., De Witt, W., Keebler, J.S., Min, S., Nix, N.W., Smith, C.D., Zacharia, Z.G., Defining Supply Chain Management. *J. Bus. Logist.*, 22, 2, 18, 2001.
13. Miguel, C. and Barbara, L., Practical Byzantine fault tolerance, in: *OSDI, 99*, pp. 173–186, 1999.

14. McCluskey, J., A game theoretic approach to organic foods: An analysis of asymmetric information and policy. *Agric. Resour. Econ. Rev.*, 29, 1, 1–9, 2000.
15. Nordgren, A., Weckstrom, E., Martikainen, M., Lehner, O.M., Blockchain in the Fields of Finance and Accounting: A Disruptive Technology or an Overhyped Phenomenon. *Oxford J. Finance Risk Perspect.*, 47, 47–58, 2018.
16. O'byrne, R. Supply Chains and Blockchain Part 2 – Making It Work. Available online   https://www.logisticsbureau.com/supply-chains-blockchain-part-2-making-it-work/, 27.03.2018.
17. Pagell, M. and Shevchenko, A., Why research in sustainable supply chain management should have no future. *J. Supply Chain Manag.*, 50, 1, 44–55, 2014.
18. Piscini, E., Dalal, D., Mapgaonkar, D. & Santhana, P. Blockchain to blockchains: Broad adoption and integration enter the realm of the possible: Tech Trends 2018. Abgerufen von https://www2.deloitte.com/insights/us/en/focus/tech-trends/2018/blockchain-integrationsmart-contracts.html, 2017.
19. Pilkington, M., Blockchain technology: Principles and applications, in: *Res. Handbook Digital Transformations*, p. 225, 2016.
20. Rousseau, S. and Vranken, L., Green market expansion by reducing information asymmetries: Evidence for labelled organic food products. *Food Policy*, 40, 31–43, 2013.
21. Simpson, D. and Samson, D., Developing strategies for green supply chain management. *Decision Line*, 39, 4, 12–15, 2008.
22. Nakamoto, S. *Bitcoin: A Peer-to-Peer Electronic Cash System*. Available at https://bitcoin.org/bitcoin.pdf, 2008.
23. *The Future of Blockchain: Applications and Implications of Distributed Ledger Technology* (n.d.), Chartered Accountants, Australia–New Zealand, 2017.
24. McConaghy, T., Marques, R., Müller, A., De Jonghe, D., McConaghy, T., McMullen, G., Henderson, R., Bellemare, S., Granzotto, A., *BigchainDB: A scalable blockchain database,* White paper, BigChainDB, ascribe GmbH, Berlin, Germany, 2016.
25. Tsujimoto, M., Kajikawa, Y., Tomita, J., Matsumoto, Y., A review of the ecosystem concept—Towards coherent ecosystem design. *Technol. Forecasting Social Change*, 136, 49–58, 2018.
26. Teece, J., Business models, business strategy and innovation. *Long Range Plann.*, 43, 2–3, 172–194, 2010.
27. Winter, M. and Knemeyer, A.M., Exploring the integration of sustainability and supply chain management: Current state and opportunities for future inquiry. *Int. J. Phys. Distr. Logist. Manag.*, 43, 1, 18–38, 2013.
28. Woodside, J.M., Augustine, Jr. F.K., Giberson, W., Blockchain technology adoption status and strategies. *J. Int. Technol. Inf. Manag.*, 26, 2, 65–93, 2017.
29. Zott, C., Amit, R., Massa, L., The business model: Recent developments and future research. *J. Manage.*, 37, 4, 1019–1042, 2011.
30. Zhu, Q., Feng, Y., Choi, S., The role of customer relational governance in environmental and economic performance improvement through green supply chain management. *J. Cleaner Prod.*, 155, 46–53, 2017.

10

Security Concerns of Blockchain

Neha Jain* and Kamiya Chugh

K.L. Mehta Dayanand College for Women, Faridabad, India

Abstract

Blockchain is a chain stored in a public database which is made up of blocks that contains digital information. Despite the fact that faultfinders are challenging its durability, safety and stability, it has officially changed the way of life of numerous people due to its overwhelming impact on many applications. The blockchain emerged as a novel distributed consensus scheme that allows transactions, and any other data, to be securely stored and verified without the need of any centralized authority. Distributed trust and therefore security and privacy are at the core of the blockchain technologies, and have the potential to either make them a success or cause them to fail. Although the feature of blockchain technologies may bring us more reliable and convenient services, the security issues and challenges behind this innovative technique is also an important topic that we need to concern. In this chapter, we will try to present security threats to the blockchain because a hacker cannot modify the data on the blockchain because each user has a copy of the book and the data in the block is encrypted. This chapter also describes security attacks and their prevention for developing advanced blockchain systems.

Keywords: Blockchain, security issues in blockchain, scandals of blockchain, blockchain model challenges

10.1 Introduction: Security Concerns of Blockchain

Blockchain is a technology that stores, executes, and manages transactions. This is considered a breakthrough in cryptography and cyber security. It is the integration of technology into mathematics, cryptography, algorithms, financial models and more. Blockchain is the fastest growing trend. Blockchain are the easiest way to execute transactions because they

---

Corresponding author: jain_neha200@yahoo.com

S.S. Tyagi and Shaveta Bhatia (eds.) Blockchain for Business: How it Works and Creates Value, (201–230) © 2021 Scrivener Publishing LLC

use cryptocurrencies that are immune to forgery, do not require central authority and are protected by robust and complex encryption algorithms.

Blockchain can be described as the digital form of transaction, redistributed and sharable leader of all cryptocurrency transactions. Blockchain supports distributed databases, in which different computer systems can be created. Each and every computer on the network is referred to as a junction or a point, and each node on the network automatically receives an identical copy of the blockchain in the remote locations that it downloaded. We can also say that this is a public lead for all cryptocurrency transactions stored in a continuous order to help customers track transactions. Transaction details are distributed to all permanently engraved members of the block, each member owning several bitcoins.

They have a mechanism for proposing information in the form of transactions for each of the nodes in the network in addition to the database, and the consensus is that the network can consider the accepted version of the database. Considering the fact that some actors may be defective or malicious, these actors accept content recorded on the blockchain throughout the network. It can be accomplished by several methods. Proof-work, proof-of-stack and proof-of-authority are among the most popular consensus algorithms.

10.2   Cryptocurrencies Scenarios

Bitcoin is a prime example of blockchain based cryptocurrency; As a result, it can be hacked by attackers very easily. In fact, various attacks have already been disclosed, such as the latest Slovenian-based bitcoin [1] mining market Social Engineering in Neishash 13, which has stolen nearly 64 million bitcoins. There are other approaches also that are defined for security, such as the integrity of double spending (e.g., the same coin for two different customers). These issues should be properly addressed without reducing the confidentiality of companies involved in cryptocurrencies.

In general, any blockchain based cryptocurrency has two main factors that cause secrecy. As we can see that many cryptocurrencies cannot provide benami assets in which the two addresses are in the same wallet and belong to the same user. Therefore, unlinkability is not possible as the same user uses dissimilar addresses for the input. While, the public chain discloses all the data used for transaction, the coins that used for transaction is also discloses to all the users. If the user is considering Bitcoin, then these aspects are visible in the recent work, which guides strict security principles for future reference based on past actions.

The solution of this problem can be done by starting confidentiality; improving anonymity in these situations is to use mixing services. Mixing methods are mostly used to create new cryptocurrencies which includes secret assets. Some of the proposals are discussed below. In this direction, it is one of the first mixing policies based on accountability policy to highlight the use and theft of random mixing fees. Furthermore, this approach provides optimization of the mix network for bitcoins to perform indistinguishable features against active attackers. In addition, BlindCoin has expanded the MixcoinProtocol to improve privacy features. In particular, the authors proposed that the blind signature scheme be used to ensure that any user hidden to the mixing server has input/output address mapping. Another mixing mechanism has been proposed, which deals with coinjoin.

In this chapter, we will try to present security threats to the blockchain because a hacker cannot modify the data on the blockchain because each user has a copy of the book and the data in the block is encrypted. This chapter also describes security attacks and their prevention for developing advanced blockchain systems.

10.3   Privacy Challenges of Blockchain

10.3.1   Protection Problems in Blockchain

Blockchain is considered to provide security and privacy with sensitive personal information as users can create generated addresses instead of using real ones. However, some researchers have suggested that Blockchain may be compromised by excessive privacy as the information recorded in the ledger is not changed or deleted. They are made with a public key, also known as an asymmetric key with two keys: one is a private key and the public key. The transmitter uses a public key to send the data while the receiver uses the private key to extract the information. Since the ledger in Blockchain is public, it can provide a few security problems.

Concern for privacy on the blockchain is referred to as protecting the transaction and not leaking information i.e. it means maintaining privacy in digital transactions. Transfers to the blockchain do not agree with these privacy issues such as details can be disclosed without user awareness, data may be misused, etc. This issue is exacerbated by blockchain as the secret information in the ledger is unaffected when the participants reduces control rights and changes the details. That is the main purpose of Blockchain to control the use of data from hackers.

Privacy on the blockchain takes place in two main areas: Privacy and control. Privacy means protecting data from unauthorized access. This also accesses the integrity, anonymity, anonymity, insecurity and protection of communications while the Administration relies on the copyrights granted to the user to control and maintain their personal information. Blockchain can privacy controls will be used with PET [2] i.e. Extended Privacy that guarantees minimal disclosure of personal data.

Therefore, the Secure Models have expanded to Blockchain to empower users with autonomy. Blockchain has many privacy challenges. Some of these are:

1. Trading Communication—Since Blockchain uses a public key, it is difficult for a hacker to handle sensitive information. Blockchain being the public community can create new addresses independently and at any time when there is an issue, the Ledger continues renewal and tracks all transaction records. Although if blockchain token-based, the same user addresses can be linked as follows:
   - Transaction Entry More: In this transaction, the user addresses are unique i.e. addresses the same unique user generating the first problem is to find the link. This problem is solved by having a single address but different in all of the activities.
   - Transaction by: These supply users when using the same address as the public access to some of the goods changes. To improve privacy, the user must issue a new democratic discourse to a refund during the transactions.
   - Hazardous pumpkins services: A mixture of services in the center of the space inside may be used by actors to upgrade their secrecy mixing which is done by multiple providers. However, privacy may be a defined as a challenge because the service of strangers both input and output pairs; Hence, privacy depends on a genuine lawyer.
   - Payments Web: The identity of the user can be connected to who you really are. When the client makes a transaction with cryptocurrency, a service provider can connect the user's real minted by history. This may cause a problem to fight and pumpkins.
   - Blockchain P2P Network policy: Blockchain supports the database when the node network connections pairs on the Internet. This network makes users able to trace

the entire process of their addresses in the IP sent by the new. Privacy focused blockchains randomly generated, such as Monero, refer to the layer within the privacy of their clients and blockchain system P2P, which connects to another system such as Tor (onion routing) or I2P. Nevertheless, it is shown that using Tor as a secret-layer network [6] to connect to the various systems can cause a new attack for the users.

2. Private Keys Management & rescue: As blockchain uses the public and private key, the private key is very important in the transaction. Each is used to sign transactions in blockchain. Key management is playing a major role in blockchain. This should not be put at risk, as these are subject to torture attacks or steal user's private keys. This can cause a problem when the various Trojans and Malware might destroy the Ledger where the keys are kept and also access the encryption keys.

It is the responsibility of the user to protect his keys inside his device using a secret bag or outsource the management of the keys from a thief or a hacker that pretends to be an actor and may steal all the sensitive information. It can be solved as a security trust that you will not do badly keys.

To overcome from this problem, several solutions are proposed to prevent the loss of key, such as the preparation of the folder, and fund documents including confidential data which includes both private and public keys, or don't share the one time password to prevent the loss from hacker. One solution to have is the Super wallets, when the actor holds the ledger in a safe place, and a limited number of intelligent phones can be found at fund everyday use. This reduces damage to loss or theft.

3. Malicious Smart Contracts: These Contracts basically match the agreement between the parties. They perform duties without a lawyer or lawyers. Smart contracts are made by validating and validating all gaps while the ledger records the code, input and output. Smart contract operations can raise the risk. Many contracts are usually encrypted by bytecode through a real blockchain machine, e.g. Ethereum Virtual machine. Before making an agreement of a smart contract, the participant must validate that the code in the smart contract is similar to the bytecode that has been sent in the

transaction. This agreement contains analysis tools, such as the Open Source Tool, which helps to solve the risk of smart contracts as they are done. One example of an attack on privacy is conflict and betting a contract agreement as a smart contract. However, smart contracts can be implemented in an assured manufacturing platform, but are also subject to security issues.

4. Immovable Data and Chain Data Privacy: As we learned earlier, privacy on the blockchain is related to privacy and control. To guarantee privacy, the information in the transaction must be encrypted. To ensure control, access rights are up to the user to protect and save information. Personal data of any kind such as hidden data, hashes should not be stored on-chain. It should be completely anonymous, or stored in the database. Blockchain supports methods such as enabling erasure that can block data and ensure integrity. It also allows for the continued addition of hashlinked records and removal of records both at the same time.

5. Post-Quantum Computing Resistance: In future scenario of Quantum Computing, some proof-of-work algorithms and validations are at risk. Quantum algorithms such as Shor's, may in the future break the log of elliptic public-key cryptography (ECDSA) or the integer factorization (RSA) problem required to generate a signature, which is the basis of several basic crypto-protocols used in blockchains (e.g. in bitcoin). To minimize this problem, hashes should not be stored in a chain without a previous random process.

6. Crystal-Privacy Performance: Cryptography Technologies is required to ensure privacy on the blockchain. Software's like ZKP or ZK-SNARKS [3] need to be completely anonymous on the blockchain. These systems are less efficient as they require more time to calculate and require more convincing evidence. New NIZKPoKs system i.e. Evidence of Zero-non-Interactive inaccessible information ensures better performance while operating with the key symmetric mechanism.

7. Privacy–Usability: If the user is not technical, privacy may cause him or her to troubleshoot keys, configure and select attributes to follow the requirements of the organization. Therefore, terms/specifications and associated blockchain termination applications are required to facilitate blockchain/data validation/choosing validated blockchain claims and

managing DID documents and information, and generally, to address and manage actor's privacy.

8. Emphasizing Privacy in the Contact Program: Future IoT has benefited from blockchain. They can include anonymous support for mixers, validators and ID authentication support, mobile money transfer, testing and naming potentiality, smart contract support, and valid location requirements. This is similar to the disintegration and various uses of blockchain that are not usable, and, therefore, difficult to integrate between each other.

10.3.2   Privacy-Preserving Mechanisms Analysis

The previously described privacy-protection practices can be classified into 4 main areas according to their privacy-protection purpose. The four categories and methods can be summarized as follows:

a. Derive the secret-protection and key management of smart contracts using SMPC Technique [4].

b. Methods that use identity data anonymization, mixing (anonymous signature), ring signing (anonymous signature), commitment schemes, and homomorphic hiding (such as conversion to coin addresses) to hide a user's identity in ZKP.

c. Transaction Data are methods of protecting the privacy of the contents of blockchain transactions. These include methods of mixing (e.g. coins trading benami notes), differential confidentiality, ZKKPs, and homomorphichiding (hiding the transaction amount).

d. On-Chain Data Protection, which combines technologies aimed at protecting data through encryption systems including public key encryption, feature-based encrypted data and confidential data sharing. There are some privacy-protection services, such as ZKPs and homomorphic concealment, may be applied to obtain anonymity of unique data (e.g. payer, payer) and transaction information (e.g. traded coins) used.

10.3.3   Data Anonymization-Mixing

In order to anonymize email usage, many authors has introduced mixing methods. Since then, these technologies have been used to make various services anonymous to many users. The main process is to coordinate a large enough number of users, delay the grouping of all their messages, and then return them at the same time or in random order. With the compilation and delay of messages, there is no relationship between the message creation and the user action of the network traveling message. This technique is not the message of personally identifiable information (PII), but of the interaction of the message on the network.

In the blockchain, mixing techniques are used to hide the history of a particular token. In bitcoin, users can create public-key pair accounts for each transaction, instead of reusing previous transactions, but transaction history can link those previous addresses to new ones, and when using multiple input addresses, all are identical. The use of a mixing technique can make transaction history addresses arbitrary.

10.4   Decentralization in Blockchain

Decentralization is an important part of the Blockchain. It allows public chain, private chain and consortium chain. Public chain allows transactions for everyone, consortium chain allows users that have taken permission and private chain only allows one participant or dictator. Decentralization allows users to trust every blockchain providers by ensuring trust. However, this trust can create an issue. A decentralized system is similar to a distributed one in that it doesn't have any single point of failure. A fully decentralized system does not always linked with each single point to achieve one sole task. The Decision making is done by each part of the system or a node as a whole. Every node is connected to each other but they are not connected in terms of messaging and collaboration. With decentralization, it is truly each to its own.

However, decentralization autonomous organizations i.e. DAOs are the self-made rules running on an open-source protocol or a smart contract that can only be changed if majority of the founding members agrees. These rules are transparent to all the members which are written into the protocol or smart contract.

The cost of making DAO's protocol or smart contract is lower than that of traditional organizations as they don't need any managers, employees, or office buildings. It can be executed and operated by the Code carrying out by the members. If the rules are more centralized, the DAO will be better, while the less centralized DAO—it will look like non-traditional company.

The cost reduction and efficiency are the advantages of DAO than Traditional Organizations, Such benefits will be the equivalent of the machine automation that revolutionized the production of goods, except that it will be applied to the management of organizations. There are various possibilities in DAO that will use Machine-to-Machine interactions. A DAO managing autonomous vehicles (AV) collects all the payments from the customers, pay every road tolls and parking fees and also prepares the summary at the end. After having lots of advantages, DAO has potential challenges that can harm the system and may get access to the system as DAO still needs to work upon its creation, should avoid early stage problems and try to make easier operations rather than complex. The aim of DAO is to build a "collective intelligence" for the management of organizations, to improve the hierarchical structure of today's large organizations, thus encouraging innovation and deterring bureaucracy. Their goal is not to replace managers with smart contracts that will automate decision-making, but rather to free managers from repetitive decisions to be able to concentrate their efforts on innovation and high-level strategic decisions affecting the long-term future of the organization.

10.4.1 Role of Decentralization in Blockchain

As we know the domain name system (DNS) stores all the names or addresses of a user in a internet, it converts numerical IP addresses into easy-to-remember URLs. But this process is a centralized process which is vulnerable to surveillance and censorship. Google is one of the largest which operates DNS servers. Whenever you enter a website URL into your browser, it's sent to a DNS server for lookup. The internet service provider, or Google, stores the user's request including your IP address and the website you're visiting.

Some DNS might block some sites or links to prevent from malicious attacks. DNS server operator decides which site you should visit and which site you shouldn't.

Thus, in this situation, the centralized system can be exploited by the Governments and companies for censorship.

Blockchain works mostly on cryptocurrencies, these are the currencies that used for transaction in digital process. These are encrypted by specialized encryption algorithms. Namecoin is other cryptocurrency service that stores data on the blockchain to create an alternative DNS. Namecoin cryptocurrency uses bit domain instead of .com, .in or .net. The addresses can be stored in a blockchain so that everyone can access it. If encryption algorithms are not there, it might create a problem of DNS poisoning which changes the IP address of a URL, the user wish to visit. This is done by criminals or by the government to protect us from visiting some particular sites.

However, the blockchain is using both private and public encryption; it will not be possible for any fishing or poisoning to take place. It is the responsibility of the user to concern for privacy done in your computer which should not create any network logs of your DNS request.

10.4.2 Analysis of PoS and DPoS

The crypto-Pro (Proof of Work) puzzle solving process is shaping up. Therefore, Proof of Stake (PoS) [2] evidence is suggested to improve power consumption of computer. When working on a block, the miner needs to add the figure to the winning agreement to build the block, which corresponds to the value of the block. The deposit of the wrong participant will be taken to compensate for the misconduct. PoS blockchain's intermediate level depends on the distribution of the stake, instead of the highly configurable computer power. Stake forwarded authentication (DPoS) doesn't need everyone involved to make blocks directly. Instead, actors can provide a specific hole. DPoS reduces several miners in the agreement, on the other hand, it makes the stakeholder difficult to build the block directly, which contributes to the trust model. As Stake Proof has reduced the number of miners to build blocks, the rate of centralization will increase. For example, EOS allows twenty-one large organizations to build blocks, generating an N0 = 21 space that is more centralized than fully open blockchains using PoW or PoS.

10.4.3 Problems With Decentralization

The blockchain can break its network into various layers like physical layer, platform software, smart contracts and clients. This type of problems doesn't occur in blockchain but occurs in full stack of the ledger. Decentralizations problems can be summarized in different layers of shareable blockchain [5].

- Physical Nodes: The physical node of a layer is placed at the bottom of a P2P network of miners system. All the physical nodes related to shareable blockchain are basically not centralized. This assumption doesn't hold as ASIC miners and mining pools skew the mining power distribution.
- Platform Software: The platform software layer runs on top of physical nodes. It includes the implementation of the consensus algorithm and the smart contract runtime. Public blockchain's platform software is often developed, maintained, and open sourced by a community of contributors. The impact is in many folds: First, the governing and decision making is usually led by a "core" development community, leaders of which have significant influences on the

platform software development. Second, since the trust of the platform software is critical and economically rewarded, the development community, in many cases, has strong incentives to make the platform reliable. Third, the platform software layer needs to be supported by the mining network. For example, a new update of the platform software will not happen or will fork the blockchain if it is rejected by the mining network owners.

- Smart Contract: Smart contracts are the applications deployed on the blockchain platforms. The application logics are encoded in smart contract code. The execution of smart contracts is triggered by function calls from clients or other smart contracts. The result of execution is reflected in the state changes of blockchains (e.g. a change in user's account balance). As to be discussed in Section 4.3, the execution of smart contract is fully replicated and sequential.

- Client
  The client layer serves the end users of smart contracts. It takes user inputs and displays the end results to users. The client layer only needs to interact with the platform layer using standard APIs. It is completely open since anyone is free to implement their own client.

These problems can be explained as follows:

1. Skewed Mining Power
   Skewed Mining Power is the first problem in decentralized network which causes PoW (Proof of work). This problem also lies at the bottom of the physical nodes layer. Mining in the network is defined in two systems: First, encouraged by the surging price of cryptocurrencies, the mining power has been raised. Second, as the number of mining nodes increases, there will be increased profit with variations. Hence, mining is done to stabilize the profit.

   The skewed mining power [5] has been distributed highly all over. This shows that blockchain is secured and maintained by few distinct entities. The skewed mining power is less vulnerable to attacks, approx. 51% attacks occurred.

2. Scalability of Transaction Throughput
   The decentralized system causes various problems like, scalability of blockchain transaction throughput.

3. Scalability of Smart Contract Execution
   Blockchain also became an issue in scalability of smart contracts as the smart contract is executed in current decentralized blockchain systems which do not scale as well.
4. Fully Replicated and Single Threaded Execution
   The mining node is repeated in every execution of the smart contract in decentralized blockchain systems. This repetition causes problem to identify the original address. Moreover, the computation power is similar to a single node in the blockchain system. The smart contracts or agreements are single threaded which means only one command can be executed at a time. Thus, it is impossible to leverage parallelism within a single node as well. Hence, the computation power of the entire Bitcoin or Ethereum network, which consists of more than hundreds of thousands machines, is less than a modern mobile phone.
5. Sequential Programming Model
   The smart contracts are executed in parallel manner but there are situations in which the execution of a smart contract is carried out sequentially. It has global variables, such as balances, which stores the token balance of each account. Given the generality of the smart contract language (Solidity is Turing complete), it is challenging to scale up the execution of smart contracts as they are currently written

10.4.4 Decentralization Recovery Methods

There are three ways to overcome the problem of decentralization

   i.   Mining power should be more decentralized by design.
   ii. Other forms of trust should be considered, when possible, to replace decentralization.
   iii. Smart contract should be scaled to achieve a higher scalability in overall.

1. Decentralizing mining Power
   One key factor that leads to skewed mining power is the emergence of specialized mining hardware, especially ASICs. Specialized mining hardware has outperformed personal computers by orders of magnitude in terms of both mining power (number of hashes per second) and mining energy

efficiency (number of hashes per watt). In addition, specialized mining hardware is usually very expensive. As a result, they mostly end up in the hands of a small number of groups, such as owners of big mining farms and ASIC miner manufacturers. One possible approach to democratizing mining power is to design ASIC proof hashing algorithms for PoW.

2. Trust, not necessary decentralization

Decentralization is a means to democratize trust rather than the goal. There are other ways of ensuring trust. For example, verifiable computation and secured hardware allows clients to run code on untrusted platforms. In doing so, an untrusted platform generates verifiable proofs for clients to vet the correctness of computation. With verifiable computation, trusting the majority of system nodes does not need to be assumed any more. As another example, formal verification and certified programming allow programmers to provide a mathematical proof showing that a blockchain implementation meets its specification by construction. This could be used to eliminate the unintended behaviors in blockchain implementations.

3. Scaling Smart Contract Execution

To achieve scalable execution of smart contracts, it is time to rethink the design of both the programming model and the runtime. First, new programming primitives need to be introduced to make parallel execution of smart contracts possible. For example, many programming constructs, such as concurrent data structures, can be borrowed from extensive programming languages research in past decades. Second, the smart contract runtime needs to be redesigned to support parallel execution of smart contracts and at the same time still maintains a deterministic transaction order and keeps all the transactional guarantees. Many existing approaches in databases and systems should be revisited and adopted to smart contract runtime.

10.5 Legal and Regulatory Issues in Blockchain

Blockchain faces lots of legal & Regulatory issues. Legal issue may be either because of Jurisdiction, DAO, Contract enforceability and many more. Earlier in decentralized manner, database is regulated by a peer of networks and act as an agreement while in centralized manner, data is maintained by the servers which process information and validate the data. In a decentralized database is controlled by a protocol or a smart contract that doesn't need any third party to validate.

Decentralized environments can be responsible in terms of legal issues as who owns the network is difficult to determine in these networks and who is responsible for the problem. Therefore, it becomes difficult to determine who has implemented information, where and when, who jurisdiction should be applied, who commands the information and who is trustworthy for integrity or confidentiality.

10.5.1   Legal Value of Blockchain and its Problems

Blockchain was designed to enhance distributed database which supports trustless transactions and performs cryptocurrency. As we know, blockchains are valid, easy to record the data in a ledger which tells who owns the data and also demonstrate that the data has not been altered still it doesn't mean that the transactions based on blockchain and the registration done in blockchain should be done legally.

The status of the blockchain requires [7]:

1. Signatures—who did the transaction or who owns the data.
2. Timestamp—when the transaction was done.
3. Validations—who validate the transactions.
4. Documents—which documents are attached as a contract with a transaction.

    i.   In Europe, such issues are handled under Electronic Identification; Authentication & Trust services Regulation (EIDAS). It has 3 different levels of e-signatures—simple, advanced and qualified which make it more complex to hack the information. Blockchain must aim to achieve simple and advanced signatures technically but also aims to achieve higher standard for legal binding. It can be achieved by using TSPs (Trust service Providers).
       By this, we came to know that blockchain doesn't have any legal authority by them.

    ii. Territoriality—Transaction between the users is carried out through Bitcoin. They are not placed at any specific location. If someone wants to crack the place where they are stored, then with little bit of technical knowledge they can operate a code. Territoriality makes the task difficult to achieve legal responsibility. Each and every node in the network is controlled by legal requirements and maintained by a head in centralized way that is responsible for each distributed ledger. In Regulatory, it might act as an "anchor". In this; blockchains will raise thorny issues of territoriality. In networking, any damage or destruction requires a direct analysis approach. Several challenges proposed in territoriality aspects which concludes court jurisdiction in relation to torts and non-contractual disputes.

iii. Enforceability—Smart Contracts are easier way to sign and agreed upon the law but in case if any event dispute, how enforceable would a smart contract be in a court of law? So all disputes must be clear in dispute resolution process attached to them. It covers two main terminologies:

a. Pseudonymity/Anonymity—laws should be effective if they are enforced with actions or penalties against the law breakers. But it is difficult task to detect who breaks the law? The potential for Pseudonymity or anonymity can be used to create lawless zones for the benefit of criminals. The problem of using Private blockchain technology is ignoring legal and regulatory laws which should be mandatory from which all the actors can be easily identifiable while in case of public blockchain technology it is difficult to determine the users who violate the laws. They are not traceable. Moreover some users or actors uses effective tools but different platform for the transaction which provides true anonymity instead of bitcoin or Ethereum which are trustworthy platforms for the transaction but doesn't support anonymity. It seems that providing states with identification tools should be a minimum condition necessary for a state's ability to enforce the responsibility and thus to ensure the impact of the law on human behavior in the blockchain space.

b. Enforcement Access Points—Suppose if the information to be sent and transactions to be carried out on a blockchain are not directly accessible to law enforcement or regulators that does not make blockchains un-relatable as there are many number of "access points" that authorities could use to enforce rules.

iv. Liability—It refers to the state of being legally responsible for the smart contract signed by the participants. The primary goal for which such a responsibility is imposed is to motivate/steer the behavior of a person towards the direction desired by the legislators. Liability regulations also have a compensatory function: their purpose is to provide the injured person with the opportunity and source to obtain compensation for damages. Today, the rules for attributing responsibility vary greatly depending on (i) who, (ii) to whom, (iii) what for and (iv) on what kind of consequences/pain a person is liable. The main kinds of liability in law systems usually include: criminal responsibility, administrative responsibility, contractual liability and tort liability. Partially separately regulated is the liability of board members towards the company. Also, many specific regulations and laws provide for special regulations on liability issues.

   a. Tort liability (liability of network participants generally)—Tort law generally deals with Issues of civil wrongs where one person can be held liable for damages caused to another. It should be noted that the risk of failure to identify the person who caused the damage also exists in the real world. It is not related only to blockchains. Usually, the injured party does not have any influence on whether the damage is done by a person who is easily identifiable.

   In some situations, governments have therefore decided to protect the injured/damaged party by other means, not only by relying on enforcing liability. For example, banks are obliged to create a pool of funds to cover damages to their clients caused by bank insolvency. National health insurance systems cover the risk of personal injuries. Insurance companies are obliged to maintain an insurance fund which is liable to pay compensation to victims injured in road traffic accidents in cases when a driver has not been identified or has not been properly insured.

v. Data Protection—Protecting data in a transaction is difficult to maintain. In fully decentralised blockchains, it can be difficult to identify data controllers and processors as defined under GDPR, and hence enforce their obligations. This has to do with issues around jurisdiction and access points, among others, similar to those discussed above. Particularly in cases where it is difficult, or perhaps impossible, to identify a data controller, it can naturally be tricky to enforce the GDPR's requirements for the data controller.

Last but not least, blockchains can make it difficult to exercise some data subject rights as defined in the GDPR. This is most evident in the GDPR's well-known "right to be forgotten" provisions [7], as data that is recorded on a blockchain can generally not be altered or deleted. Other rights, however, can be problematic in a blockchain context too, including rights to the rectification of personal data, to know if one's data is being processed and—an issue with smart contracts—the right to be protected from decisions made only on the basis of automated data processing.

The existence of regulations such as the General Data Protection Regulation (GDPR), which empowers citizens' rights to improve, delete, or forget their data, may conflict with blockchain technology, because the chain must be immutable, persistent, and should not be thought of. Blockchain holes must follow these rules to assure the user that their privacy is protected.

The goal of GDPR is to prevent the collection (and processing) of personal data that is not reasonably necessary to achieve its intended purpose, privacy-designed and ensured by default. Blockchain must also satisfy various rights, such as the right to information, consent to receive rights, direct access to data, data correction, forgotten, portable data, and access to information on data breaches.

Article 5 of the GDPR defines 6 regulations regarding the processing of personal data, which comply with 6 principles:

1. Validity, fairness and transparency: Process, objectively and transparently related to data content. Transparency: Giving information about data processing to be done. Fair: Data processing should conform to what is described. Valid: The processing must conform to the tests described in the GDPR.
2. Objective Limitations: Personal data may only be obtained for "specified, explicit and valid purposes". Data cannot be

processed inconsistently with those goals without further permission.

3. Data Minimization: The data collected on an item is "necessary, appropriate and limited for the purposes for which they are processed".

4. Accuracy: Data must be "accurate and up to date where necessary; every reasonable action should be taken to ensure that inaccurate personal data is relevant to the purposes for which they are processed or corrected."

5. Storage restrictions: Personal data is "stored in a formwitch that allows for the detection of more data than is necessary for the purposes for which personal data is processed", that is, the data is no longer deleted as needed.

6. Integrity and Confidentiality: Protecting data is essential to ensure proper security, including personal data, including protection and protection against illegal processing and risk, destruction or damage, including the use of regulatory information or organizational measures.

10.6   Smart Contracts

The success of bitcoin proved that it is possible to create digital cash with the help of blockchain. Users share the data with each other easily by using computer programs that runs in a decentralized manner and not under the control of any single party. Blockchain technology was the first concept that handles general-purpose computing. Blockchain consist of computer code that can be run on various devices between one or more parties. These codes or programs are self-executing.

Smart contracts are pieces of code stored on the blockchain that will self-execute once deployed, thus leveraging the trust and security of the blockchain network.

Smart Contracts doesn't mean it is a contract or agreement between two parties. They can be used for tokenization, used to code and automate business processes which are shared among multiple parties at the same time. Therefore, it enhances the performance of business processes and services. Smart contracts are efficient, transparent and run automatically between the parties that agreed to have an agreement based on terms and conditions which make its difficult or impossible for the opponent party to quit or back out for the proposal.

Smart Contracts can be categorized into two main points.

- Smart Legal Contracts
- Smart Contracts with Legal Implications.

1. Smart Legal Contracts—This is the smart contract or agreement that is shared between two or multiple parties which represents a legal contract consist of issues between them.

Issues in Smart Legal Contracts [2]

i. Formal Requirements
   This is a simple issue which states whether a smart legal contract meets formal requirements that are given by a law for a legally binding agreement.

ii. Signing Requirements
   This issue states that whether a legal binding contract has the proof of "who" signed the agreement and how this signature has been carried out. This problem mainly arises in Off-Chain process, where organizations have already designated people with signature authority. Smart contracts should be signed with these people and in a digital way.

iii. Immutability of Smart Contracts
   Smart contracts must be automated as more automated the smart contract is—less will be the Legal issues. Smart Contracts are considered as "tamper-proof' agreements which means no one will be able to alter the data still having lots of problems. The conclusion is that the use of smart contracts does not resolve or eliminate the problem of breaches of contract, contractual liability and enforcement. The problem of the lack of available tools to easily identify actors on a blockchain-based network therefore arises again.

iv. Smart Contract Audit/Quality Assurance
   It can become a serious issue if smart contract has a bug or flaw. If there is bug in an agreement that goes through the transaction process, it can be very harmful. It will be very difficult to change all the contract terms again. A smart contract might execute as written and yet still behave in ways not foreseen by its writers.

For this reason, smart contract "audits"—often complex, highly technical processes to check for the validity and viability of smart contract code—become important. That raises the question of whether such audits have to become requirements, or also need legal recognition of some kind to make a smart contract valid.

v. Legal status, effect & enforceability of Smart Contracts
The act of transacting, even if devoid of requiring any element of trust, must result in an enforceable change over rights attaching to or deriving from the asset concerned, whether this is a token or is represented by a token.

2. Smart Contracts with Legal Implications—which are artefacts/constructs based on smart technology that clearly have legal implications. The smart contract legal implications can be depicted in 3 ways

i.   Smart Contracts represents assets in Digital Form
ii. Smart Contracts representing DAO's
iii. Smart Contracts acting as autonomous agents.

10.7   Scandals of Blockchain

A blockchain is most simply a digital ledger bundling transactions together in 'blocks' that, when linked together, sequentially form what are meant to be immutable 'chains'. No one user can alter the record of transactions distributed across the wider network of geographically dispersed users.

The ability to verify, record and broadcast digital transactions has however continually been positioned by both supporters and detractors of the technology as offering important pathways for re-legitimating finance in the wake of the 2008 crisis. The initial and still most prominent manifestation of these technologies, Bitcoin, was explicitly deemed by developers and promoters to herald a less volatile, less fraudulent and less speculative financial order. While cryptocurrencies now numbering in the thousands have thus far failed to fulfil such expectations, the appeal of their underlying technology has not only endured but also catalyzed a wide array of blockchain applications that continue to raise hopes for re-legitimating finance.

That the use of this type of more centralized 'permissioned' or 'private' blockchains has grown across the wider financial sector is indicative of the extent to which this set of technologies has become socially accepted within the financial sector. However, our interest here concerns less the legitimacy of the technology itself than its contributions to the wider social legitimacy of finance. We therefore limit our focus to the more decentralized, bottom-up applications of blockchains undertaken since the mysterious appearance of the Nakamoto [8] white paper, which outlined design plans for its initial application to Bitcoin in 2008 (Nakamoto, 2008).

1. Moral economy, responsibility and legitimacy in scandalous times

   Legitimation involves a set of processes through which narrow sets of socio-economic.

   Practices come to be seen as contributing to the good of a wider community. The work of positioning financial practices within broader social goals can be traced, understood and measured in several ways.

   The concept of moral economy presupposes that the economic activities of production and consumption, as well as those of exchange and investment, are always normatively grounded in specific understandings of how agents treat and behave toward one another. The moral economy concept explains this as the product of a specific and ultimately contestable "inter-subjective consensus concerning appropriate economic goals, principles, values and activities" (Baker, 2018: 294). Foregrounding 'moral economies' therefore highlights the hegemony of a particular set of moralities at any one point in time, while also underlining the crucial role of human agents in working to shift normalized assumptions about how things should be.

   In terms of post-2008 global finance, the concept of moral economy directs our attention to how the values underpinning methods of exchange, credit allocation and investment remain entangled in an "on-going interactive process, in which normative claims and their systemic vision are advanced, accepted, rejected or modified".

   Working with 'moral economies' provides for a more nuanced understanding of such dichotomies, drawing attention to continuities as well as changes in dominant standards regarding how people should act towards one another in particular times and places. As Whyte and Wiegratz (2016: 5) have argued, this means avoiding the temptation to view moral economy as automatically referring to pro-social practice.

Moral economy therefore provides a more nuanced understanding of the moral shifts and continuities in actually existing political economies. On the one hand, it spotlights a growing concern for collective responsibility in post-2008 finance. Discussion among financial professionals since the crisis has widely emphasized issues relating to equality, stability, justice and fairness beyond simple profit making.

2. Second and related benefit of harnessing the moral economy concept is that while change is possible, dominant standards of how to act and behave towards one another are difficult to fully uproot. Change in a prevailing moral economy often entails more of a blending or mixing of competing visions of how to treat or act towards one another. Moral economies rarely swing from 'purely' hyper-individualistic to 'purely' hyper-collectivist (or vice versa).

Episodes of scandal reveal moral transgressions beyond narrow communities, granting unique insight into the ongoing quarrels among competing moralities underpinning financial practices precisely because they involve explicit articulations of normative expectations and incoherencies. As processes, scandals involve activists, journalists, whistle blowers and other actors exercising agency by more widely publicizing internal transgressions of dominant standards of behavior. As instruments, scandals advance certain material interests (such as those of agents able to sell advertising), as well as particular ideologies that can either challenge or reinforce existing social norms. Scandals, however, typically provoke responses that reinforce the status quo and assure us of the wider morality of a particular practice or social order" (Johnson, 2017: 704). Scandals can thereby reinforce the kind of hyper-individualism long dominant in finance through their tendency to "individualize and isolate transgression (Johnson, 2017: 704). Individualizing blame is pervasive in scandals where responsibility is asserted through 'strongplots' and archetypical stories geared towards identifying villains responsible for wrongdoing (Czarniawska, 2011). Scandals tend to shift attention away from questions of collective or systemic responsibility and change, while simultaneously focusing attention onto individual failings and blame.

10.7.1   Blockchain Technologies as Stumbling Blocks to Financial Legitimacy

Swartz (2018) has positioned Bitcoin alongside mutualistic self-help and cooperatives' visions of human society [4], in which 'everyone does their part' to ensure privacy and the integrity of the overall network. These goals are enabled by the open source nature of the computer protocols underlying Bitcoin and other blockchain experiments, developed in communities of programmers who maintain the underlying coding. Nigel Dodd (2018) similarly associates Bitcoin with a diverse set of social movements pursuing a shared goal of establishing universal world money.

In a second instance of scandalization, wider interest in Bitcoin became increasingly fixated on the individuals responsible for major swings in its US dollar exchange rate. The price of Bitcoin in the leading international exchanges peaked at $1,242 in late 2013, only to drop by half over the following three months.

The broader scandalization of Bitcoin through its association with individual legal Transgressions did little to help shift the dominance of the moral economy underpinning the legitimacy of finance. In their tendency "to command the public imaginary", the continual 'crypto-scandals' surrounding Bitcoin highlighted individual actions and wrongdoings over the technology's implicitly collectivist efforts to address some of the wider structural problems afflicting global finance as well as other social issues, like drug use. Widespread focus on the individuals responsible for the design, exchange rate volatility and use of Bitcoin in illicit markets provided little in the way of an acknowledgement of how blockchain technology could make a positive contribution to the fragile legitimacy of a sector characterized by speculation, fraud and other pathologies growing in both intensity and frequency since the 1970s.

10.8   Is Blockchain the Rise of Trustless Trust?

Blockchain Example

There was speculation that blockchain would disrupt the situation currently a large number of industries, from finance to digital ownership and medical R&D in tracking and tax collection. It doesn't matter of the degree of mental disturbance that may or may not occur play out, blockchain is certainly posing new questions for policy makers and administrators. So much for the way the Internet has opened up dozens of questions on how to manage transactions on the web, the new blockchain structure introduces the uninstalled a place for legal scholars and directors. Blockchain is important and may be renewable because Blockchain provides identity building trust. At the time confidence in institutions and authority figures is waning, a new system of trust is much needed.

"Trust in all four institutions—business, government, NGOs, and the media-doing right is rejected more in 2017."

Traditionally, trust has focused on any central authority an image that supports the rule of law, though, the credibility has been established through peer interaction in peer relationships where the trust system exists based on shared values. Blockchain creates a new build for trust, shared. Trust is not imposed on anyone a character in the system, but, rather, placed in the system as a whole. Blockchain technology makes it possible to rely on trust that everyone in the program shares the same information; me it comes from the same computer that will fit every other time. By moving a trust agency in a program that can be legally certified, you need to trust any single person. Therefore the system of "Reliable trust."

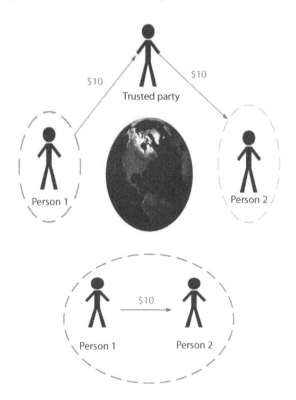

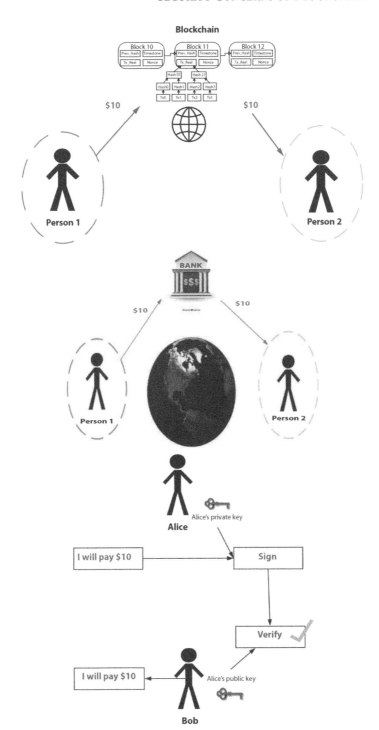

10.8.1   Why Do We Need a System of Trust?

The benefit of using blockchain is to rely on a Central authority number. This is the primary motivation for establishing Bitcoin. Bitcoin founding developers wanted a way out to distribute currency independently of any government structure. In the absence of a theoretical reason to oppose Centralized governance structure, here are some examples: This centralized control is not enough—for example, when the application needs a working environment a venue, usually for competitive reasons. The less obvious reason is to have an unreliable trust system required when the current system is fraught with inefficiencies Avoidance by having a universal consensus. Anytime there multiple parties that keep their own records of transactions, In case of a syndicated loan you have 10 major Banks are contributing to the multi-billion dollar major exchange there overhead, duplication, delay, as well as tremendous cost The risk of error. Blockchain's distributed ledger technology, in this case, offer a cheap, effective alternative.

Once upon a time with the blockchain established, digital infrastructure creates opportunities for automation across enterprises and industries. Because everything is on a common platform, and everyone involved can Enjoy the same level of visibility and transparency Blockchain is Not Decentralized or Trustless

Three modes of classification are described: Construction, political and psychological.

In terms of properties, the argument goes; you can ask two questions to determine if the network is managed:

- How many basic devices power the network?
- Are they geographically dispersed or concentrated in one area?

However, when we look at the major technology players such as FAANGs (Facebook, Apple, Amazon, Netflix, and Google), they have many servers widely distributed for the use of their billions of users.

Everywhere in the world keeps the same copy of blockchain, and holds everything. When a new task is created, changes are repeated across the network, reverberating everywhere. Blockchain is duplicated, not separate.

The following argument is that blockchain is politically limited depending on your answers to these questions:

- How many individuals/groups are involved in decision making?
- What does the division of power look like?

- What type of instrument is used to measure the influence of each participant?
- Are there ways to be reproduced in the system?

However, few figures can put the issue of political separation into perspective. In another, "97% of Bitcoin is owned by 4% of investors." In addition, Bitcoin is attacked almost entirely by mining pools:

Also, the way cryptocurrencies are exchanged is almost the same as the central exchange. Ultimately, key developers have central control over the future of the network.

The final argument for blockchain's decentralization is that you have rational reasons. For example, neither the CEO nor the board of directors gains control of the network. There are no entries, physical address, or bank accounts. While it is true that blockchain, as a technology and not a company, does not require these things, there are still structures involved with powerful people, such as key developers, mining pools, and "whale" investors with large wallets.

Ultimately, blockchain is not integrated into the traditional network, but it is far from expandable. And when we have to rely on key developers for all the future of technology, loyal users and investors to avoid falsifying applications, and relying on mining pools to secure transactions, it's not really reliable.

P.S. If blockchain was unreliable and fragmented, how important would it be? No one on the blockchain bubble has ever heard of foreign exchange.

Dapps (Decentralized Application) is available with standard browsers like Google Chrome anyway, and the front end may still work. Most people never look for smart contracts (let alone know what that means).

At the end of the day, you need a better reason to use blockchain than say "we split X."

10.9   Blockchain Model Challenges

You need to address these issues in order to run a successful business.

Blockchain technology is becoming more and more popular these days. The blockchain technology originally created by Satoshi Nakamoto for the popular digital currency bitcoin has now been developed to be more useful and valuable to tech users.

Despite the expansion of blockchain, not all businesses are open to the concept of blockchain. With a decentralized system that does not monitor the standard body; many still have doubts about how safe this new technology is.

If you really want to integrate blockchain into your business, here are five challenges blockchain entrepreneurs [9] must overcome in order to have a successful business.

1. Creating a new business model: The term "business model" refers to the overall structure of the organization to create a profitable business that includes the company's goals, objectives and detailed plans. Some business models are about creating a profitable product and selling it to interested customers. Ordering products from wholesalers, implementing inventory guidelines, creating an online catalog, processing orders, shipping domestically or internationally is more difficult. Most companies use a combination of different business models to ensure a successful business.

    Traditional business models have no blockchain and very few modern business models have their own set of rules. Due to the ever-changing constraints on blockchain technology, you always need to adjust your business model or create something new to suit the legitimacy. Unfortunately, this can be difficult, especially for a startup company that does not have the manpower or funding. If you want to avoid all the obstacles and legal implications that may arise in the future, it is best to create a new business model from scratch. This means rethinking all aspects of the business model, especially your channels, revenue streams, key sources and cost structure.

2. Integrating Blockchain: Startups have difficulty integrating blockchain into their existing businesses. Blockchain needs special attention, which is why business owners need to be creative with their innovations. Business owners who plan to integrate blockchain into their systems should know about the blockchain themselves and avoid or avoid any potential problems along the way.

3. Finding talent: People in the company are not just business owners; they must be knowledgeable about the blockchain. Employees also need to learn something about the blockchain.

    Unfortunately, despite the growing acknowledgement of such technology, it is difficult to find talented and knowledgeable people on the blockchain. Before implementing blockchain fully in the organization, employees need additional training and guidance, especially blockchain fundamentals such as crypto economics and cryptographic mathematics.

4. Get proper funding: Blockchain based businesses are very difficult to obtain financing due to their nature. Because of all the risks associated with blockchain, investors usually think twice before investing in these startups.

   To receive funding, blockchain entrepreneurs must seek out investors, especially those in the industry, who are open to blockchain. Another option is to look for a reliable connection that can introduce your company to investors and explain why your company is a good investment. Your target investor may be another person or company that has already invested in you and is well connected and profitable. The more successful your connection, the better chance you have of getting finance.

5. Misrepresentation of business: Many blockchain entrepreneurs have trouble assessing correctly. When you first get out; it is only natural that you are optimistic about the future returns of your company.

   The problem arises when your equity profits do not match the expectations of your investors. This can result in investors losing their money or losing trust in your business. To avoid this, be sure to properly calculate your future profit before giving an estimate of your company's value.

   If you want to use blockchain technology in your business, remember to prepare well in advance to overcome these challenges successfully. Blockchain may be a good new technology, but it can easily find its place in your new purpose.

References

1. Gupta, N., Security and Privacy Issues of BlockChain Technology, in: *Advanced Applications of BlockChain Technology*, pp. 207–226, Springer, 2019.
2. Amin, Md. R., A survey of Smart Contracts: Security and Challenges. *Int. J. Netw. Secur.*, 29, 05, 3, 2020.

3. Joshi, A.P., Han, M., Wang, Y., A Survey on Security and Privacy issues of BlockChain Technology, American Institute of Mathematical Sciences. Volume 1, Number 2, pp. 121–147, 2018.

4. Li, X., Jiang, P., Chen, T., Luo, X., Wen, Q., A survey on the security of blockchain systems. *Future Gener. Comput. Syst.,* arXiv:1802.06993 [cs.CR], 2017.

5. Zyskind, G., Nathan, O. *et al.,* Decentralizing privacy: Using blockchain to protect personal data, in: *Security and Privacy Workshops (SPW), 2015,* IEEE, pp. 180–184, Google Scholar, 2015.

6. Al-Saqaf, W. and Seidler, N., Blockchain technology for social impact: Opportunities and challenges ahead. *J. Cyber Policy,* 2, 3, 2017. 2. Peters, G.W. and Panayi, E., Understanding modern banking ledgers through blockchain technologies: Future of transaction processing and smart contracts on the internet of money, in: *Banking beyond banks and money,* Springer, 2016.

7. Sáez, M., Blockchain-Enabled Platforms: Challenges and Recommendations. *Int. J. Interact. Multimed. Artif. Intell.,* 6, 73, 2020.

8. Chu, S. and Wang, S., *The Curses of BlockChain Decentralization,* 2018.

9. Makridakis, S. and Christodoulou, K., BlockChain—Current Challenges and Future Prospects/Applications. 11. 258. *Future Internet,* 2019.

11

Acceptance and Adoption of Blockchain Technology: An Examination of the Security & Privacy Challenges

Amandeep Dhaliwal* and Sahil Malik

FMS, Manav Rachna Institute of Research & Studies, Faridabad, India

Abstract

Blockchain is one of the most prominent technologies of the present day along with Robotics & AI. It is assumed that blockchain capabilities can bring in great alteration to the world economies, businesses, and societies in general all over the world. The hype around it makes it seem to be a perfect technology but the reality is quite different. The truth is that blockchain as a technology is still immature and is developing as we discuss it. Therefore numerous issues exist in adoption of blockchain like privacy, decentralization, regulatory and business model challenges which need to be addressed before embracing blockchain as a foundational technology for businesses. This chapter explores the prevalent security and privacy challenges associated with blockchain in detail and the negative implications of these challenges. Lastly it suggests certain Blockchain applications which support the acceptance and adoption of blockchain technology.

Keywords: Blockchain, bitcoin, security, privacy, de-anonymization

11.1 Introduction

Blockchain technology is a radical innovation in field of information technology. Originally it was invented in 2009 as the backbone technology for Bitcoin [1]. But since then, with the advancement of blockchain technology, it has found application from just the crypto-currencies to a vast number of areas such as healthcare, agriculture, Internet of Things (IoT), SCM and others.

Corresponding author: amandeep.fms@mriu.edu.in

S.S. Tyagi and Shaveta Bhatia (eds.) Blockchain for Business: How it Works and Creates Value, (231–250) © 2021 Scrivener Publishing LLC

A Blockchain is defined as "a distributed database of records or public ledger of all transactions or digital events that have been executed and shared among participating parties" [2]. Each and every transaction is stored in the distributed ledger and must be verified by consensus of a majority of the participants in the system. This verified information can then never be erased [2]. Bitcoin, the digital currency introduced by Satoshi Nakamoto in 2009, is the most popular example of use of blockchain technology [3]. Bitcoins, based on public cryptology, are the first decentralized peer-to-peer digital currency which has no central server or principal authority to mint and supervise the currency [4].

In case of cryptocurrencies the blockchain formulates the basic underlying infrastructure that supports to carry out the financial transactions in a distributed decentralized way needing no intermediaries. Blockchain has led to development of robust ecosystem of not just Bitcoin [5] but also other altcoins such as Litecoin [6], Ethereum [7], Zero cash [8] and Monero [9]. An estimate of 2018 claims that [10], the market value of Bitcoin is over $112 billion while that of Ethereum is over $47 billion. It further states that more than 60,000 blockchain transactions are carried out per hour worldwide.

Though blockchain is most prominently used for cryptocurrency but at present it is finding uses in all the applications which work on decentralized platform. For example in case of Internet of Things (IoT) which works on peer to peer topology and various devices which are Internet enabled. Therefore, using the blockchain in IoT devices, all the connected devices can be easily automated and data can be synchronized much faster [11,12]. Similarly in case of Supply chain management systems, blockchain can augment the transparency of system and makes the tracking of ownership easier [13,14]. Blockchain further supports the identity management system and the public key infrastructure as discussed in Refs. [15–17].

Although blockchain is proving to be a powerful technology which has the potential to change the future of business transaction but it does have its dark side which consists of security and privacy issues of this technology and cannot be ignored. These issues can lead to huge losses for the parties involved. For example in a blockchain based supply chain management (SCM) system if the communication or information is not protected, it can lead to leaking of trade secrets which can be very harmful to suppliers. Even in other application based scenarios any financial or non financial information leaks can have drastic impact therefore it is very important to understand the various security and privacy issues which entail Blockchain technology. This study in depth deals with systematic evaluation of various security and privacy challenges and the potential application of Blockchain solutions in various domains.

11.1.1   Research Methodology

For identifying the various security and privacy challenges, an extant literature review was undertaken. Since Blockchain is a new technology hence the research papers post 2000 were targeted with more focus on research articles of last ten years. The databases like Scopus, Ebsco, Proquest, and Google Scholar were used to search for the papers. The search began with the initial keyword "Blockchain" to understand the wider concept which was later fine tuned to "Blockchain security", "Blockchain Privacy", "Blockchain issues", "Blockchain application" among others. In total 102 abstracts were downloaded based on the relevance to the subject matter which after further analysis were shortlisted to 61 full papers which were downloaded for further study. Based on the analysis of literature, the challenges of blockchain as well as the applications of Blockchain technology are presented in the next section.

11.1.2   Analysis

Blockchain has numerous advantages therefore; it is finding application in so many different areas and domains. In future too it is expected to grow and receive greater adoption but it does not have a perfect model but rather has challenges and issues especially in areas of security and privacy. Some of these security and privacy issues identified from literature are discussed below.

11.2   Security Issues of Blockchain

11.2.1   The Majority Attack (51% Attacks)

Though only one blockchain should exist as it's a sequential connection of the blocks generated, but if two different peers at same time are able to mine the answer for generating the block, then two latest blocks can be generated and blockchain can be divided into two. Therefore if more and more peers work together in order to become mining pools they would have more computing power. Once they hold 51% computing power it becomes a very serious security issue [18,19]. So if an attacker has 51% mining capability, they can dictate the Nonce value and hence the authority over blocks which can lead to falsified transactions [20]. They can easily decide which blocks are permissible and further modify transactional data within blocks. They can cause double spending attack [21,22] or stop the verification of transaction or even mine any available block [23]. In present day such mining pools are increasingly trying to dominate the blockchain thus this risk has become an issue. An example of such an attack was by GHash, a leading mining pool, which for a short time controlled the mining power exceeding the 50% threshold which forced the Bitcoin community to make large scale adjustments to deal with the risk and affected its market price [24,25].

11.2.2 The Fork Problems

Blockchain works on its decentralized nature which means that all participating nodes agree to common rules about blocks. This complete consensus among the network participants or the nodes means verified data leading to single blockchain which is deemed correct by everyone. But in certain situation like when new software is published or change in protocol is made, all parties may not agree to it or are not in consensus thus leading to alternative chains or fork situation [23]. This had a very wide range impact. Thus when a new protocol change or software upgrade is made it leads to two kinds of nodes in the blockchain—the New Nodes and the Old Nodes. Based on the interactions between the old and the new nodes two kinds of forks can occur

1. Hard Fork
2. Soft Fork.

11.2.2.1 Hard Fork

A hard fork means that though as per a rule change a systems starts working as per new rules and new nodes but the old nodes are still working as per old rules hence all such old nodes will see the blocks produced according to the new rules as invalid. The old nodes are not in agreement with the new nodes' mining therefore the one chain gets divided into two chains [23]. Though new nodes have stronger computing power than the old nodes but even then the old nodes which do not upgrade will continue working as usual on a completely different chain which they thinks is right, thus the ordinary chain will fork into two chains. It can be a huge risk again as two chains are created. The solution is the upgrading of all the nodes hence all nodes in the network are requested to upgrade to the new agreement. Therefore, in case of Hard forks where if no consensus is made, it can split the community into two entirely dissimilar blockchains which is risky for the blockchain users [26].

11.2.2.2 Soft Fork

In case of soft fork, though the protocol has changed to the new one, new nodes do not accept or approve the block by old nodes but they are backward compatible. The old nodes do not realize the rule changes and continues to accept blocks created by newer nodes which follow the new rule set [23]. Thus old nodes accepting the blocks from new nodes will end up building on top of blocks from new nodes and which will keep on working on the same chain as result only one chain is create though they do not fully understand or validate the new system. The risk is that soft fork does not make the old nodes aware that the fundamental principle of verification by every node is invalidated as the consensus rule has changed [23,24].

11.2.3 Scale of Blockchain

With the increasing advent of blockchain technology, it is being used in more and more applications right from IoT to healthcare to agriculture. Thus with the growing blockchain, the data is also becoming massive. Thus computing of data, loading and storing of data is becoming more difficult. It takes a lot of time to synchronize data so managing the entire systems in real time is getting difficult for the clients [23,27]. Though a newer version of Simplified Payment Verification might be a solution to this issue.

11.2.4 Time Confirmation of Blockchain Data—Double-Spend Attack/Race Attack

In comparison to traditional online payment system such as credit card which would take 2 or 3 days to confirm the transaction the blockchain based transactions like in case of Bitcoins it takes only about 20–45 min for transaction verification. Some data scientists even find this a slow rate and not good enough as it leaves window open for the double-spend attack and race attack

The double-spend attack takes place when same coin is spent twice [21]. When a Bitcoin transaction takes place, the transaction is confirmed after a while, only when the block has a depth of 5 or 6 in which the transaction is stored hence it can on average take 20 to 40 min [28]. Since the confirmation time is dependent on many factors there can be large variance in the range of timing for confirmation. In certain speedy payment situations, the traders do not wait for confirmation to come in; therefore in such cases the malicious attackers can fraudently spend the money twice.

Race attacks are also carried out in such similar situations. In this fraud the scammer carries out a transaction directly with the merchant, who promptly accepts it. The scammer then misusing the lag in the confirmation carries out contradictory transactions of transferring the same coins to himself on the network. In such a scenario, the probability of second transaction getting confirmed is high and hence the merchant ends up being cheated. In case of Finney [29] attack which is a more refined version of double spend is carried out using help of a miner. Thus faster time confirmation is required to protect against these attacks.

11.2.5 Current Regulations Problems

The blockchain technology has not received a whole hearted acceptance from the government and regulatory bodies. The basic premise of blockchain based on decentralization can be contrary to the regulators and governments need for control. Especially the case of Bitcoin bubble burst has made the government wary and cautious about this technology as Bitcoin was outside the purview of Central banks and the overall economic policy [23]. The regulatory bodies still have to research this new technology, understand and formulate new policies around it otherwise it will have risk on the market.

11.2.6 Scalability and Storage Capacity

Scalability and the current storage capacity are an important challenge in blockchain. In blockchain technology the chain of blocks is continuously growing. For example in case of Bitcoin it grows 1 MB per block every 10 min and the copies of the chain are stored only with the full nodes - those nodes which can fully validate the blocks and the transactions which are there in the network [26]. As the chain size grows the nodes needs additional storage space and hence it decreases the capacity of the system. Also the huge chains negatively impact the performance, increasing the synchronization time for new users. In blockchain network, nodes are supposed to authenticate each transaction of each block based on consensus protocol for Transaction validation. Further, the transaction confirmation time is dependent upon the computational power which is modulated by the number of transactions in a block and the time between blocks [23]. Therefore the consensus protocol directly influences the scalability of blockchain networks.

11.2.7   DOS Attack/Sybil Attack/Eclipse Attack/Bugs

DoS Attacks: In this cyber attack, the harmful attacker tries to crash network resource, website or make machine inaccessible to the genuine users by flooding the internet based host with non genuine requests and crashing the system and disrupting hosts services [30]. In P2P networks anonymity is used for hiding of IP addresses but a DoS attack might "disconnect a TOR node from the blockchain network" and reveal the identity [30].

Sybil Attacks: It is similar to DoS attack but in this case the malicious attacker creates a numerous fake identities so as to have an undue influence over a P2P network and sabotages the reputation system of it. Sybil attacks also can lead to de-anonymization in the blockchain, therefore increasing the probability of revealing the real identities of users [30].

Eclipse Attacks: In case of eclipse attack [31], the malicious attackers alters the view of the network to a node by controlling its connections, and segregating it from the rest of the network.

Bugs: The bugs in the Bitcoin software can be very hazardous. Though Bitcoin software is quite effective and reliable but even it has issue of software malfunctions or bugs. The two famous bugs' incidents CVE-2010-5139 in 2010 and the bug at time of up gradation from BerkeleyDB to LevelDB Bitcoin version created a furore leading to two different blockchains for 6 hrs. Thus software bugs threaten the security of Bitcoin transactions [32].

11.2.8   Legal Issues

In case of Bitcoins there is no central authority or minting authority to control or regulate it. Hence no censorship of any kind exists for Bitcoins. Though advantageous it is dangerous as well. Bitcoins involve huge volatility risks. The users of Bitcoin are often charged of using Bitcoins for illegal activities and financial frauds. Thus the blockchain technology has apparently given rise to illegal trade which again has legal repercussions [26].

Though many governments are developing new laws [33] for regulating the virtual currencies but at present the situation is unclear and uncertain. In some countries it is even made illegal [34].

11.2.9   Security of Wallets

The Bitcoin address are encrypted using public key encryption wherein the message or the hash value is encrypted using recipients public key and can only be decrypted using the associated private key of the recipient. Therefore, in case of Bitcoin the locked script of a Bitcoin transaction can be unlocked using the correct associated private key. The information regarding the private key required for unlocking script is stored in the Bitcoin wallet [20]. Thus, in case the wallet key is lost, then the Bitcoins are lost as there is no mechanism to still be able to use the coins or recover the information.

Therefore, to create a loss, the Bitcoin wallets are often targeted through hacking [35]. An estimate claims that in this way 30% of coins are lost every year [26].

11.2.10   The Increased Computing Power

The computing power of quantum computing computers is a threat to virtual currencies as they can infiltrate the security of digital signatures [23,26]. Similarly, as the technology is rapidly progressing, numerous new bugs, new threats, and security issues are being discovered. Since the blockchain data is immutable, these threats can easily compromise public blockchains with encrypted data.

11.3   Privacy Challenges of Bitcoin

One of the very important features of Blockchain is transparency. Therefore each transaction starting from the first block can be checked, audited, traced and verified. Each Blockchain transaction "consists of the ID of the previous transaction, the addresses of its participants, trade values, time-stamp and signature of its sender" [26]. Since the blockchain network of decentralized nature, therefore data mining can easily be used to track the transaction flow to reveal the users' physical identities. The apparent transparency of the system becomes a privacy threat especially in case of Bitcoins [3].

11.3.1   De-Anonymization

In Bitcoin to some extent there is form of unlink-ability with user's identity as there is no direct connection between the individuals and the Bitcoin wallets. The mechanism of Bitcoin allows users to always create pseudonyms and use multiple wallets when users join the Bitcoin system. But due to the public transparency of blockchain, the malicious attackers can actively hack and listen to network for information or perform a static analysis of the blockchain to reveal the identity or unmask the users. This is called de-anonymization [36]. This can be a serious threat for not only virtual currencies but also for the other applications based on public blockchain technology, which need higher privacy as they deal with sensitive data. Some of the common methods of de-anonymization are as follows:

11.3.1.1   *Network Analysis*

The Blockchain is established on the decentralized principle and the P2P network architecture which means that nodes when broadcasting transactions might leak its IP address. Thus with network analysis of this leakage, the Bitcoin addresses can be mapped to IP addresses and unmasking of the identity of users. Koshy *et al.* [37] studied the pattern of network analysis and identified three anomalous relay patterns a) multi-relayer & non-rerelayed transaction b) single-relayer transactions and c) multi-relayer & rerelayed transactions which can be used to reveal the identity. Similarly, Reid and Harrigan [38] found that "publicly available information from the Bitcoin faucets can be used for network analysis".

11.3.1.2   *Address Clustering*

The fundamental features of Bitcoin transaction can be used by the attackers to cluster and link addresses which are used by the same user: For example in the following situations:

a) "All the inputs in a transaction are normally signed by the sender, hence in one transaction it may be that all the addresses of inputs are controlled by the same user" [3].
b) The change address (where the price difference between what user intends to pay and the actual output price is received) which is created by wallet and the input address signify the same user [39].

c) "The transactions that do not contain an origin-destination pair signify the origin of a transaction list and the only destination address signifies the miner or a mining pool" [40].

d) Sometime to make the transaction confirmation process fast some additional markers such as identification information or certificates are used to leverage existing trust relationships [41].

Based on the above information the attackers can separate the network addresses into different clusters. Then using sophisticated data collection technology it can be discovered easily which addresses match with the same user thus revealing their identity. Though it's not easy to carry out but researchers [38,42] have utilized the above given information for analysing address clustering issues.

11.3.1.3   *Transaction Finger Printing*

Androulaki *et al.* [43] in his study found that using the cluster analysis on transaction fingerprinting which is based on extra consideration to transaction's user-related features and transaction behaviour such as "hour of day (HOD), time of hour (TOH), time of day (TOD), coin flow (CF) and input/output balance (IOB) and Random time-interval (RTI)," the probability of de-anonymize an individual user is easily achievable. In his experimental study of university students using only Bitcoins for their daily transaction, he could unmask approx. 40% of user identities even though students were adopting a new address for every transaction.

11.3.2   Transaction Pattern Exposure

Other than the personal identification, all the other transaction related information is shared across the public network. This information can be collected and used for creating statistical distributions to reveal the new patterns regarding the Blockchain applications and later be misused for influence. This can be done in two ways as given below.

11.3.2.1   *Transaction Graph Analysis*

This analysis is carried out to discover some transaction patterns like daily exchange rate or daily turnover rate etc. over a period of time. Ron and Shamir [44] in case of Bitcoins could easily identify in the transaction graph of Bitcoin network—all the largest transactions and the four characteristic transaction patterns. Therefore this can be real threat as the graph analysis reveals the user's financial history which along with the de-anonymization methods can prove to be very risky.

11.3.2.2   Autonomous System-Level Deployment Analysis

This is used to gain information about the structure, size and distribution of the core network of Bitcoin so as to maliciously impact the Bitcoin's ecosystem, its resilience and vitality. In this technique the Bitcoin network is crawled wherein the clients are targeted for collecting "their lists of other peer's IP addresses" to gain overall information about the Bitcoin networks size and distribution. In a study of Bitcoin system's size and distribution, Feld *et al.* [45] found that 900 AS contained just one single node while more than 30% of all nodes belong to 10 AS.

11.4   Blockchain Application-Based Solutions

Blockchain application-based solutions may be available in different domains like Healthcare, Bitcoins, IoT, Smart cities, etc. However, some selected domain has been chosen where the chapter delves upon in the following section.

11.4.1   Bitcoins

Bitcoin-NG [46] has created a Blockchain protocol on the lines of bitcoin's trust model. This Blockchain protocol is Byzantine fault tolerant which has improved the scalability limitations of trust model and the consensus latency of the bitcoin. Technically, lite coin [47] is identical to Bitcoin with improved confirmation times and storage efficiency. It is because Litecoin minimizes the time required to generate Block validating the work script which is a function of a memory intensive password-based key derivation function.

Ghost [48] with the help of making modification in its rule of chain selection increases the scalability of bitcoin. There are off chain solutions which are likely to increase the bandwidth by performing the transactions off the chain but there is a risk of losing data. There are challenges associated with the other proposals in the bitcoin protocol with the reduction in propagation delay [49] leads to keeping the security of the network on stake [50].

Instead of going for changing Blockchain scalability, Big Chain DB [51] has worked to fuse Blockchain with shared databases offered by big data. The attempt is to merge characteristics of shared databases like high throughput and low latency with the static and non- symmetric Blockchain system. Apart from it, IPFS inter-planetary file system [52] is advanced version of Blockchain protocol which acts like a warehouse to save and store shared files to configure P2P file distribution system enabling web becoming more convenient and safe to use. IPFS makes web more efficient and simultaneously maintaining the originality for each file.

11.4.2   IoT

Following are some Blockchain applications providing solutions in the domain of IoT. Although use of Blockchain in IoT is a recent phenomenon and there has been a series of benefits that can be thought of in IoT using Blockchain technology like providing secured data environment that ensures data protection in the form of providing authenticity and reliability of the data. Blockchain also channelizes data identification, authentification and authorisation through certain mechanism without the interference from central authorities.

11.4.2.1   MyBit

In an attempt to build an ecosystem, MyBit [53] plans a delivery model where group of people owns IoT assets and shares between them the revenues collected. It's an open investment opportunity where in the investor by default receives their shares of profits as and when their owned IoT assists are put to use. This is done through an automatic process executed by ethereum smart contracts. The platforms on which all transactions are executed is continuously updated, maintained and controlled by a central smart contract. Platforms are required to be installed and establishes link between different asset types and IoT devices.

11.4.3   Aero Token

Blockchain technology in aviation intelligence has been designed by Aero Token [54] which gives facility of real time navigation done through low altitude commercial drones. Blockchain enables drones sorties and navigation by authorising access over shared airspace to create a new market place of tomorrow. It's a win–win situation for property owners where they share their airspace to drone service providers for an access fees. This mechanism is developed using Ethereum smart contracts.

11.4.4   The Chain of Things

MARU is the application assigned by the chain of things [55] for the creation of Blockchain enabled IoT research lab. This solution is a combination of Blockchain and IoT hardware. Blockchain helps with 3 features—it gives identification, easy working, and security. The Chain of things offer 3 services or solutions—chain of security, chain of solar, and chain of shipping which works in different field. The security to IoT via Blockchain is delivered through chain of security. The production of solar energy by the connection of solar panels with the Blockchain is assured by The Chain of Solar and Chain of Shipping enhances safety in shipping and logistics industry.

11.4.5   The Modum

The Modum [56] in order to better the processes in supply chain, offers Blockchain which intends to enable database integrity for products in physical form by assessing environmental conditions. Modum has been designed in such a way that it is compatible to work on different platforms. In the field of medicine, Ethereum Blockchain has put to use for the distribution of the medical products. There is a smart contract in Ethereum that checks data collected by inbuilt sensors or the change in ownership of the goods every single time, the contract then gives the feedback that products have been able to fulfil customer's demands.

11.4.6   Twin of Things

Twin of Things developed by Riddle and Code works in the field of day to day objects [57] by providing secured ownership. It is a Blockchain enabled solution combined with encryption to produce an electronic name to be given to all physical objects. Blockchain technology established the secure medium of interaction and transaction between devices. The device in the Blockchain framework becomes its nodes with a crypto chip which is found to be a sticky NFC tag that can't be removed. This crypto chip is given the identity while doing a Blockchain transaction by an android application. This chip is used to interact with other devices in the system after its validation.

11.4.7   The Blockchain of Things

The Blockchain of Things [58] works in the field of integration of IoT for industrial purposes by providing a secured and open communication platform. In order to ensure rapidity in Bitcoin Blockchain integration, Catenis has been proposed which is a web service layer with end-to-end encryption. It is also compatible to use Catenis with other Blockchain like Ethereum and Hyperledger [59].

11.4.8   Blockchain Solutions: Cloud Computing

In the cloud computing environment, the disclosure of user data can lead to psychological and financial damages which are mostly due to leakage of sensitive users information [20]. The main concern to study in cloud computing environment is the security, confidentiality and integrity of storage and dissemination of the data as the privacy protection and anonymity is still a critical issue. The concept of Blockchain technology offers the anonymity which in case of cloud computing can not only provide a convenient but also a strongly secured service to the users. The use of secure electronic wallets is a solution to the security issues. In Blockchain, electronic wallets are used for transactions but they are not deleted properly it can lead to user information leakage [60].

Therefore to solve this issue a solution that can install and delete the electronic wallet securely should be implemented [4]. Further, the secure electronic wallets can also help in preventing the double spend attacks. Though mostly wallets are saved on computers but with the advent of mobile technology it is very important to ensure the security of these wallets on mobile devices as well. Just like in computers the transaction confirmation over the mobiles should only be done when both the accuracy of a time stamp generated and the integrity of the transaction through a mobile device are correct [61].

The blockchain technology tries to hide and prevent personal information of the cloud computing user from leaking by removing the electronic wallets completely. The blockchain therefore can use secure wallets which are installed, used and removed securely by sending the finished message. Thus, the blockchain solution improves the security by "providing residual information protection since it encrypts the data using a public key and verifies the complete removal of the electronic wallet" [4].

11.5   Conclusion and Future Work

Disruptive technologies always create a storm, which settles down when more and more people accept it. Blockchain is such a disruptive technology which no doubt has become a hot debatable issue in recent years but this technology is here to stay. The benefits of this technology are being realized overtime and therefore it is slowly gaining acceptance and applications in so many domains.

Blockchain is being adopted but at the same time yet being in infancy stage there is no adequate guarantee of it being perfect. It is therefore very imperative to understand the security issues or privacy issue and stay cautious as these can lead to loss for its users. This study has identified and presented an evaluation of the various common security challenges such 51% attack, Denial of Services, Sybil Attack, etc. along with the techniques adopted by malicious attackers for de-anonymization to provide a complete overview of these challenges. Based on the evaluation of these challenges further domain wise solutions are presented which can help in mitigating the negative issues that can crop up. Though the technology itself is improving with new technique's being developed which are more mature and stable on application side.

For future work one of the critical aspects is to frame the legal rules around this technology. The governments globally need to develop corresponding laws for this technology, as more and more enterprises are and would be embracing the Blockchain technology. Another aspect is the market preparation for this technology so as to prevent any negative impact to current system. Further the research efforts should be made in area of finding solutions for improving the security and privacy aspects of Blockchain. Emphasis should also be given to scalability and storage capacity solutions required for this technology. Beyond the all technical aspects of Blockchain, in case of cryptocurrencies the volatility risk is one of the critical aspects which is exploited by many people to take undue advantage of the scarce understanding of this phenomenon. Therefore, volatility issues need more research. Lastly, the Blockchain, the technology of future needs further research about its application in form of case studies in various domains and areas in which it can be adopted so as to understand its nuances and its repercussions.

References

1. Swan, M., Blockchain: *Blueprint for a new economy*, O'Reilly Media, Inc, Sebastopol, CA, 2020 Jan 24.

2. Stanciu, A., Blockchain based distributed control system for edge computing, in: *2017 21st International Conference on Control Systems and Computer Science (CSCS)*, IEEE, pp. 667–671, 2017 May 29.

3. Nakamoto, S., *Bitcoin A. A peer-to-peer electronic cash system*, Bitcoin, URL: https://bitcoin. Org/bitcoin.pdf, 2008.

4. Decker, C. and Wattenhofer, R., Information propagation in the bitcoin network, in: *IEEE P2P 2013 Proceedings*, IEEE, pp. 1–10, 2020 Dec 9.

5. Bitcoin Core, cited 2020 Apr29, Available from: https://bitcoin.org/en/bitcoin-core/.

6. *Open source P2P digital currency* [Internet], Litecoin, [cited 2020Apr29], Available from: https://litecoin.org/.

7. *Home*, ethereum.org, [cited 2020Apr28], Available from: https://ethereum.org.

8. *Zerocash* [Internet], Zerocash-玩币族, [cited 2020Apr27], Available from: https://www.wanbizu.com/p/1663.html.

9. *The Monero Project* [Internet], getmonero.org, The Monero Project, [cited 2020Apr29], Available from: https://www.getmonero.org/the-monero-project/.

10. *Bitcoin (BTC) statistics—Price, Blocks Count, Difficulty, Hashrate, Value* [Internet], BitInfoCharts, [cited 2020Apr29], Available from: https://bitinfocharts.com/bitcoin/.

11. Huh, S., Cho, S., Kim, S., Managing IoT devices using blockchain platform, in: *2017 19th International Conference on Advanced Communication Technology (ICACT)*, IEEE, pp. 464–467, 2017 Feb 19.

12. Conoscenti, M., Vetro, A., De Martin, J.C., Blockchain for the Internet of Things: A systematic literature review, in: *2016 IEEE/ACS 13th International Conference of Computer Systems and Applications (AICCSA)*, IEEE, pp. 1–6, 2016 Nov 29.

13. Kim, H.M. and Laskowski, M., Toward an ontology-driven blockchain design for supply-chain provenance. *Intell. Syst. Account. Finance Manag.*, 25, 1, 18–27, 2018 Jan.

14. Abeyratne, S.A. and Monfared, R.P., Blockchain ready manufacturing supply chain using distributed ledger. *Int. J. Res. Eng. Technol.*, 9, 5, 9, 1, 2016 Sep.

15. Ali, M., Nelson, J., Shea, R., Freedman, M.J., Blockstack: A global naming and storage system secured by blockchains, in: *2016 {USENIX} Annual Technical Conference ({USENIX}{ATC} 16)*, pp. 181–194, 2016.

16. A. Ebrahimi, Identity management service using a blockchain providing certifying transactions between devices, US Patent 9,722,790, Aug. 1, 2017.

17. Qin, B., *et al.* Cecoin: A decentralized PKI mitigating MitM attacks. *Future Gener. Comput. Syst.*, 107, 805–815, 2020.

18. Courtois, N.T. and Bahack, L., On subversive miner strategies and block withholding attack in bitcoin digital currency CoRR, vol. abs/1402.1718, 2014.

19. Eyal, I. and Sirer, E.G., Majority is not enough: Bitcoin mining is vulnerable, in: *International Conference on Financial Cryptography and Data Security*, Springer, Berlin, Heidelberg, pp. 436–454, 2014 Mar 3.

20. Park, J.H. and Park, J.H., Blockchain security in cloud computing: Use cases, challenges, and solutions. *Symmetry*, 9, 8, 164, 2017.
21. Karame, G., Androulaki, E., Capkun, S., Two Bitcoins at the Price of One? Double-Spending Attacks on Fast Payments in Bitcoin. *IACR Cryptol. ePrint Archive*, 2012, 248, 1–17, 2012 Oct 16.
22. Rosenfeld, M., Analysis of hashrate-based double spending, CoRR, vol. abs/1402.2009, 2014.
23. Lin, I.C. and Liao, T.C., A survey of blockchain security issues and challenges. *IJ Netw. Secur.*, 19, 5, 653–9, 2017.
24. Bozic, N., Pujolle, G., Secci, S., A tutorial on blockchain and applications to secure network control-planes, in: *2016 3rd Smart Cloud Networks & Systems (SCNS)*, 2016 Dec 19, IEEE, pp. 1–8.
25. Bradbury, D., The problem with Bitcoin. *Comput. Fraud Secur.*, 1, 2013, 11, 5–8, 2013.
26. Reyna, A., Martín, C., Chen, J., Soler, E., Díaz, M., On blockchain and its integration with IoT. Challenges and opportunities. *Future Gener. Comput. Syst.*, 1, 88, 173–90, 2018.
27. Karame, G., On the security and scalability of bitcoin's blockchain, in: *Proceedings of the 2016 ACM SIGSAC Conference on Computer and Communications Security*, 2016 Oct 24, pp. 1861–1862.
28. *Avg-confirmation-time* [Internet], Blockchain.com, [cited 2020Mar23], Available from: https://www.blockchain.com/charts/avg-confirmation-time.
29. Becky, M.H. and Finney, H., *All about cryptocurrency* [Internet], BitcoinWiki, BitcoinWiki, 2019, [cited 2020Apr29], Available from: https://en.bitcoinwiki.org/wiki/Hal_Finney.
30. Bissias, G., Levine, B.N., Ozisik, A.P., Andresen, G., An analysis of attacks on blockchain consensus, arXiv preprint arXiv:1610.07985, 2016 Oct 25.
31. Heilman, E., Kendler, A., Zohar, A., Goldberg, S., Eclipse attacks on bitcoin's peer-to-peer network, in: *24th {USENIX} Security Symposium ({USENIX} Security 15)*, pp. 129–144.
32. Eyal, I. and Sirer, E.G., Majority is not enough: Bitcoin mining is vulnerable, in: *International Conference on Financial Cryptography and Data Security*, 2014 Mar 3, Springer, Berlin, Heidelberg, pp. 436–454.
33. Langouet, N. and Langouet, N., *Is Bitcoin Legal?* [Internet], Vanilla Crypto, [cited 2020 Mar 2], Available from: https://vanillacrypto.com/is-bitcoin-legal/.
34. Wilkes, T., *Regulatory fears hammer bitcoin below $10,000, half its peak* [Internet], Reuters, Thomson Reuters, 2018, [cited 2020Feb28], Available from: https://www.reuters.com/article/uk-global-bitcoin-idUSKBN1F60CG.
35. Bamert, T., Decker, C., Wattenhofer, R., Welten, S., Bluewallet: The secure bitcoin wallet, in: *International Workshop on Security and Trust Management*, 2014 Sep 10, Springer, Cham, pp. 65–80.
36. Feng, Q., He, D., Zeadally, S., Khan, M.K., Kumar, N., A survey on privacy protection in blockchain system. *J. Netw. Comput. Appl.*, 15, 126, 45–58, 2019 Jan.

37. Koshy, P., Koshy, D., McDaniel, P., An analysis of anonymity in bitcoin using p2p network traffic, in: *International Conference on Financial Cryptography and Data Security*, 2014 Mar 3, Springer, Berlin, Heidelberg, pp. 469–485.

38. Reid, F. and Harrigan, M., An analysis of anonymity in the bitcoin system, in: *Security and Privacy in Social Networks*, pp. 197–223, Springer, New York, NY, 2013.

39. Becky, M.H., *Change, All about cryptocurrency* [Internet], BitcoinWiki. BitcoinWiki, 2019, [cited 2020Apr2], Available from: https://en.bitcoinwiki. org/wiki/Change.

40. Vornberger, J., Marker addresses: Adding identification information to Bitcoin transactions to leverage existing trust relationships. *INFORMATIK 2012*, 2012.

41. Vandervort, D., Challenges and opportunities associated with a bitcoin-based transaction rating system, in: *International Conference on Financial Cryptography and Data Security*, 2014 Mar 3, Springer, Berlin, Heidelberg, pp. 33–42.

42. Liao, K., Zhao, Z., Doupé, A., Ahn, G.J., Behind closed doors: Measurement and analysis of CryptoLocker ransoms in Bitcoin, in: *2016 APWG Symposium on Electronic Crime Research (eCrime)*, 2016 Jun 1, IEEE, pp. 1–13.

43. Androulaki, E., Karame, G.O., Roeschlin, M., Scherer, T., Capkun, S., Evaluating user privacy in bitcoin, in: *International Conference on Financial Cryptography and Data Security*, 2013 Apr 1, Springer, Berlin, Heidelberg, pp. 34–51.

44. Ron, D. and Shamir, A., Quantitative analysis of the full bitcoin transaction graph, in: *International Conference on Financial Cryptography and Data Security*, 2013 Apr 1, Springer, Berlin, Heidelberg, pp. 6–24.

45. Feld, S. and Werner, M., Analyzing the Deployment of Bitcoin's P2P Network under an AS-level Perspective. *Proc. Comput. Sci.*, 32, 1121–1126, 2014.

46. Eyal, I., Gencer, A.E., Sirer, E.G., Van Renesse, R., Bitcoin-NG: A scalable blockchain protocol, in: *13th USENIX Symposium on Networked Systems Design and Implementation (NSDI 16)*, Santa Clara, CA, USA, pp. 45–59, 2016.

47. Martindale, J., *Bitcoin vs. Litecoin: How does a popular altcoin match up to the original?*, Digital Trends, 2018, https://www.digitaltrends.com/computing/ litecoin-vs-bitcoin/(accessed April 30, 2020).

48. Sompolinsky, Y. and Zohar, A., Accelerating Bitcoin's Transaction Processing, Fast Money Grows on Trees, Not Chains. *IACR Cryptol. ePrint Archive*, 2013, 881, 2013.

49. Decker, C. and Wattenhofer, R., A fast and scalable payment network with bitcoin duplex micropayment channels, in: *Symposium on Self-Stabilizing Systems*, Springer, Edmonton, AB, Canada, pp. 3–18, 2015.

50. Stathakopoulou, C., Decker, C., Wattenhofer, R., A faster Bitcoin network, in: *Tech. rep.*, ETH, Zurich, Semester Thesis, 2015 Jan 21.

51. BigchainDB: The blockchain database, cited 2020Apr30, Available from: https://www.bigchaindb.com/whitepaper/bigchaindb-whitepaper.pdf

52. Labs, P., *IPFS Powers the Distributed Web* [Internet], IPFS, [cited 2020Apr30], Available from: https://ipfs.io.

53. *MyBit* [Internet], MyBit, cited 2020Apr30, Available from: https://www.mybit.io/tokensale.

54. Aerotoken (AET), *Price, MarketCap, Charts and Fundamentals Info* [Internet], BeInCrypto, cited 2020Apr30, Available from: https://beincrypto.com/price/aerotoken/.

55. Lombardo, H., *Smart IoT Singapore—How Blockchain can Change the Future of IoT* [Internet], Chain of Things, Chain of Things, 2017, [cited 2020Apr30], Available from: https://www.chainofthings.com/news/smartiotsingapore.

56. Chronicled Launches Digital Supply Chain Platform with ... [Internet], [cited 2020Apr30], Available from: https://www.prnewswire.com/news-releases/chronicled-launches-digital-supply-chain-platform-with-secure-smart-phone-enabled-temperature-loggers-300454592.html.

57. AWS about Modum [Internet], From Finished Product to Consumer, 2019. [cited 2020Apr30], Available from: https://modum.io/news/aws-about-modum.

58. News & Events 2016–2018. Riddle&Code, The Blockchain Interface Company, [cited 2020Apr30], Available from: https://www.riddleandcode.com/news-events-archive.

59. *Blockchain of Things* [Internet], [cited 2020Apr30], Available from: https://blockchainofthings.com/.

60. Murphy, E.V., Murphy, M.M., Seitzinger, M.V., *Bitcoin: questions, answers, and analysis of legal issues*, Library of Congress, Congressional Research Service, Washington D.C., 2015.

61. Haber, S. and Stornetta, W.S., How to time-stamp a digital document, in: *Conference on the Theory and Application of Cryptography*, Springer, Berlin, Heidelberg, pp. 437–455, 1990.

12

Deficiencies in Blockchain Technology and Potential Augmentation in Cyber Security

Eshan Bajal[1†], Madhulika Bhatia[1*], Lata Nautiyal[2], and Madhurima Hooda[1]

[1]*Amity School of Engineering Technology, Noida, India*
[2]*University of Bristol, Bristol, UK*

Abstract

There are many user cases and actors who play a role in the transactions that are automated and activities involved. These activities are changed securely by many users in the network. The changes and updations are logged when we implement. Blockchain is a shared database providing a token manager to keep track of logs generated by nay data transaction. There are lot of security concerns related to blockchain technology. But on the other hand it represents a greater cybersecurity threat than old technologies-like database. Users have same level of risk when they use blockchain. In this chapter the major concerns to security related to blockchain is discussed as well as issues and facts that reveal that blockchain inviting new challenges or edging off risk of security. This chapter aims at privacy challenges as well decentralization challenges related to blockchain technology. There are issues with business models as well as regulatory concerns. There are scandals and perception of end user will also be contended. The other side which shows that really Blockchain is trust-worthy or inviting new challenges for system architect as well database administrators.

Keywords: Anonymization, BDoS, moopay, sandboxing, content delivery network

Corresponding author: madhulikabhatia@gmail.com
[†]*Corresponding author*: eshanbajal@gmail.com

S.S. Tyagi and Shaveta Bhatia (eds.) Blockchain for Business: How it Works and Creates Value, (251–294) © 2021 Scrivener Publishing LLC

12.1   Introduction

Blockchain is gaining popularity whether due to genuine interest or as a hot keywords that is in trend which everyone tries to know something about. Its cornerstone is the DLT (Distributed Ledger Technology) [1] which uses a decentralized public Ledger that is used while interacting in a strictly peer-to-peer network adhering to a protocol and protected by cryptography. Due to the nature of decentralization, that is the absence on a central governing body and transactions and data that are not verified and owned by one single entity as they are in typical systems but rather, the validity of transactions are confirmed by any node or computer that has access to the network. This transparency of the ledger is one of the reasons blockchains rise to fame as it is theoretically impervious to tampering. However, this technology also has its fair share of privacy issue, from its fundamental functioning to external agents such as DDoS attacks and security breach of the independent nodes. The shared ledger also means any malicious change or modification will become permanent and immutable. We discuss some of the common issues faced in the real world with regards to the use of blockchain networks.

12.2   Security Issues in Blockchain Technology

We can consider many issues when it comes to security starting from the anonymity of the end user, the general stability of the decentralized network, the core concept of being trustless to the knee jerk reaction of the governing bodies in response to scandals and scams particularly in cryptocurrency, a product of this technology that is the most well-known. But one thing that is constant is that we are absolutely in the dark when it comes to knowing what companies or service providers do with our data once they get it. Due to these, customers and users are reluctant to give their information to the service providers on the web, but they need this to create user access. This creates a helpless scenario where the users have no choice but to give their data and pray that is not being misused or sold to third parties.

Cyber security is a big issue particularly in this day and age where the rapid change in technology makes a huge portion of the general population unaware of the risks to their online security or the ways to secure them against it. The rise of Big Data and Machine learning have made is possible to comb thorough the data of millions of users and archive it for a variety of uses [2].

Blockchain technology was thought to be the next step in security and bring about a renaissance [3] in the cyber security domain due to a variety of reasons that will be discussed. However, the reality is a bit grimmer. As with any new technology there arise a number of problems associated with it, along with unforeseen repercussions due to the use of such a unique technology. We shall discuss the many security issues Blockchain faces in the following sections.

12.3   Privacy Challenges

Privacy is the capability of a single person or a group to seclude themselves or data therefore expressing them discerningly. Privacy in blockchain means being able to perform transactions without leaking identification information. At the same time, privacy allows a user to remain compliant by discerningly divulging themselves without showcasing their activity to the entire network. In practicality the blockchain network is highly vulnerable to privacy leaks [4] due to the visibility of the discrete user's public key and IP trace.

- A recent study [5] shows that a person's cryptocurrency transaction can indeed leave traces that can be traced back to their IP addresses even if they are using a firewall or similar protective services.

This is possible because the nodes can be uniquely identified by the client and this data can be used to trace its origin. One way to circumvent this problem would be to use a custom allocated dynamic IP address range or use the TOR network [6]. However, this is improbable as IPs providers usually assign a static IP address and the admins can simply block the connection to the client from the tor network. A research done at the University of Luxembourg [7] shows in details the different methods used to deanonymize clients in a P2P network and they find that their attacks have an 11 to 60% success rate of deanonymizing the client. The study also concluded that the most important factor was the number of connections to the victim's entry node.

- The rise of smartphones has also seen a surge in deployment of apps that use these smartphones as nodes on the network (mainly for mining purposes). The use of mobile platforms as a member of the network also poses a problem of unrestricted data collection that reflect a wealth of detail about their families, political and religious views, association to an organization, location etc.

Europe's data protection legislations have done a great deal of work on 'the right to be forgotten' [8].

It states, "The data subject shall have the right to obtain from the controller the erasure of personal data concerning him or her without undue delay and the controller shall have the obligation to erase personal data without undue delay". The data added to the ledger when a member/node is working is part of it is permanently added to the network. In case of a public blockchain this means that the information is publicly visible as long as the blockchain is online or has a functional node. This raise concerns as it goes against everything the legislatures have done to secure privacy of the common individual. The sharing of medical history, legal information and financial data via private blockchain also raises similar concerns to potential leak in the future as the data cannot be destroyed.

Two main methods have been proposed to improve the privacy of the nodes in the blockchain.

Two main methods have been proposed to improve the privacy of the nodes in the blockchain [9] as shown in Figure 12.1.

1. Mixing
   The real IP of the user is not completely anonymous but actually pseudo anonymous. Making multiple transactions from the same address increases the likelihood of being tracked or identified. Mixing is a service that takes input from multiple sources and provides multiple output sources acting as an intermediate. If person X makes a transaction with person Z through person Y, then Y takes in input from multiple inputs m1, m2, m3 and has multiple outputs o1, o2, o3, etc. This makes it harder to track the transaction between

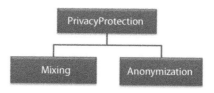

Figure 12.1 Types of privacy protection.

person X and person Z. However, this requires us to trust the intermediate to not sell our information or outright steal it. There are solutions to it, for example Coinjoin [10] employs a central mixing server to shuffle output addresses to prevent theft.

2. Anonymization

Zero-knowledge proof is used in Zerocoin [11]. Miners do not have to validate a transaction with digital signature but to validate coins belong to a list of valid coins. The origin of a payment is not linked with the transaction itself to prevent graphical analysis. The destination address and the amount however are visible. Zerocash was proposed to address this problem. In Zerocash, zero-knowledge Succinct Non-interactive Arguments of Knowledge (zk-SNARKs) [12] is leveraged. The real value of the coins and the value possessed by a user are kept confidential.

12.3.1   BGP Hijacking Attack

BGP is an IP protocol defining how the packets are sent to the destination. By manipulating the BPG traffic an attacker can intercept the blockchain network. It typically requires the network operator to be compromised first leading to the hackers controlling the operator. Thereafter both network and node attacks can be performed. The attacker can effectively divide the blockchain network and slow its message propagation speed. By redirecting miners to the attacker's own pool, he can steal the victim's cryptocurrency. It was estimated that $82,000 was stolen for unsuspecting victims over a period of two months using this exploit. The network administrators do not have a reliable way to track down such attacks and instead rely on system surveillance that detect rogue activity, for example BGP-Mon. The recovery is manual and requires a lot of manual reconfiguration to undo the hijacking [13].

12.3.2   BDoS (Blockchain Denial of Service)

Classis DoS attacks are almost useless against blockchain and can be extremely expensive to try [14]. The hash wars between Bitcoin SV and Bitcoin ABC in late 2018 are proof of its limited success. This is where Blockchain Denial of Service (BDOS) comes in. The inherent properties of the protocol by Nakamoto [15] and the other modified versions built from it are all exposed to cheaper forms of DoS attacks.

The peer discovery protocol has a mechanism which prevents multiple retransmissions of the same addresses. That means for each connection it has; a node maintains a history of addresses which were sent over this connection. This history is emptied once every 24 h and more importantly does not limit the number of elements it holds. If one floods this with fake addresses, then they can increase the response delay at the user's end and prevent it from connecting to new blocks [16]. In a controlled trial a container was sent fake addresses at 30,000 per second. It was found that the time after which the user would be unable to access new nodes due to the response delay generated was just 45 min.

12.3.3   Forcing Other Miners to Stop Mining

A different approach is to generate and publish only the header of a block and provide proof for it [17]. This would convince the honest miner that the best course of action is to stop mining. This happens because given a header, a rational miner has three possible actions: (1) to extend the main chain, ignoring the header, (2) To extend the block header (SPV mine), or (3) To stop mining, neither expending power nor winning rewards. If the miner follows option 1 and extends the main chain, finding and broadcasting a new block, the attacking miner uses his relatively high connectivity (as in selfish mining) and propagates the full block corresponding to the header BA. This causes a race between two groups of miners, those that hear of the attacker's block data first and those that hear of the rational miner's block first. Therefore, if original profitability in the "no attack" setting isn't too high, in both cases, the attacker can ensure that the honest miner ends up losing money. So, the BDoS attacker's threat means that the honest miner is better off giving up and just not mining, i.e., going with option 3. First, the attack will succeed if the hash rate of the attacker is sufficiently large. Second, it will succeed if the hash rate of miner is small enough. Finally, it will succeed if miner i wasn't making much profit in the first place.

12.4   Decentralization Challenges

Merriam-Webster defines Decentralization as "the process by which the activities of an organization, particularly those regarding planning and decision making, are distributed or delegated away from a central, authoritative location or group."

Decentralization is the backbone of blockchain that removes the presence of a central regulatory authority and instead makes the entire network function in a strictly P2P manner as shown in Figure 12.2. In other words, unlike a distributed system, the nodes are connected to other nodes only. This is a great evolution as the drawbacks of a central node such as delay and congestion could be seen as early as 1970 in the star network topology on local computer groups. In general terms, we recognize that a network is decentralized when the control of the network is shared among a subset of the network's nodes. The node is a member on the network and can be a system anywhere in the world. The active nodes are capable of intercommunication amongst themselves. Now let us talk about the problems of decentralization.

- A consensus on which node should be the current leader does not solve the problem of trust. The current leader must be trusted. It must do the job of verifying and assembling blocks in a fair manner. Thus, the leader in current leader-based consensus protocols is required to provide some credentials: proof of work, proof of stake, proof of capacity or proof of unique identification [18], etc.
- Rewards gained for the work of authenticating and assembling blocks, create an incentive for nodes to compete for the rewards. This incentive tends to create a special class of nodes. For example, Bitcoin started as a network of peers where every node could verify transactions and compete for

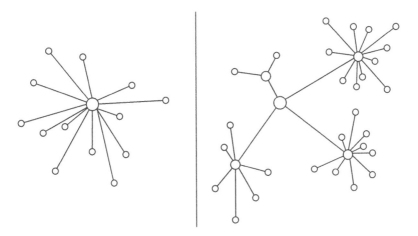

Figure 12.2 (a) Centralized and (b) decentralized systems represented by nodes and edges.

a reward. Today it is a two-class network (miners and users) and is controlled by large pools of owners.

- When the assembly of a block is left to one node, one of the major requirements of consensus theory is invalidated: the agreement is not based on a majority consensus about what information will be stored on the blockchain. The only agreement reached is the method for choosing a leader node.

- A bottleneck is introduced when the node that created the next block has to broadcast the information to all the other nodes. The impact of the bottleneck depends on the speed at which the node that found the key value sends data. If they are too slow another node will take the credit.

- The process is inefficient; large blocks of data are more subject to transmission errors and re-transmissions of maximum size packets.

- Redundancy is very high. Each transaction included in a block has already been received by every node separately, when the transaction was initially issued. A secondary effect is a huge increase in storage and bandwidth requirements [18] (something quite difficult in places with poor infrastructure).

- The system becomes open to majority takeover attacks (51% Attack): An attacker or a group of attackers who have more than 50% computational power on the network can take control breaking the three core concepts as shown in Figure 12.3 and prevent miners from completing blocks,

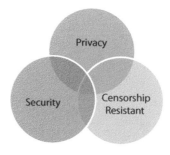

Figure 12.3 The three aspects of decentralization.

reverse transactions and force double spending of coins [19,20].

- Scaling is difficult as has been demonstrated before [21] due to limitations of the number of transactions that can be executed per second.
- Rise of ASICs, special hardware specifically designed for mining that outperforms personal computers in an order of magnitudes in terms of both computation and energy efficiency has resulted in a skewed mining pool with a small group having a lot if the mining power [22, 23].
- Lack of focus, the independent decision making at all the levels creates a lot of ambiguity and confusion about the principle of the system. The centralized body in a centralized system employs qualified personal to make decisions for the system that might not benefit the individual personally, but benefits the system as a whole. In decentralized systems the process of governance is often slow and gets drawn out due to mundane reasons.
- The improvement in security and transparency comes at the cost of reduced speed [24]. The consensus or rather the process of reaching consensus amongst the nodes can be a very time-consuming task depending on the complexity and the number of nodes.
- Decentralization by definition removes the central authority and accountability. If a network goes offline or the network undergoes a hard fork as in the case of Ethereum [17], some users would be forced to suffer losses with no way to address their grievances. The owners or network administrators cannot be held responsible the same way one can hold a hospital or bank responsible for some faults.
- Cost of running and maintaining all the nodes will always be greater than the total cost of running a centralized system. The nodes which are usually personal computers are not as energy efficient as servers designed for the purpose.
- High bandwidth, every node is updated when a new block is mined and every block also has the transactions history of all the blocks from the genesis block. This requires a significant amount of bandwidth of around 3 GB per day and the total size of the blockchain history on a node can be upwards of 50 GB [18].

12.5   Regulatory Challenges

While blockchain enables bitcoin users to hold, send, and receive money online, these distributed ledgers do more, including clearing and settlement of digital asset trading and distributed computing without having the need for central intermediaries. As blockchains mature and disrupt how data is conceived and stored, there could arise unintended consequences prompting regulatory authorities to mull over the need for intervention.

The distributed ledger is an asset database that is shared across a network. This can comprise of anything from electronic, financial, legal or physical. The changes made are also reflected in almost real time. In regions such as EU where the interest rates are negative, this would provide a better and more transparent alternative than the current cash-based systems.

Legal code is extrinsic and can be physically enforced if a breach is detected forcing compliance of the offending parties. In contrast, the digital code is intrinsic meaning that the code can detect a breach and report an error, but that is all it can do. There is no automatic regulatory or corrective action taken unless such provisions have been arranged for while writing the code. Also, this digital code adheres to the set rules even if it generates unforeseen and undesired aftermath [25].

Subsequently, for blockchain innovation as utilized in bitcoins and soon numerous different applications, consistence costs are lower since members need just to utilize consistent client packages. Despite this, the fact remains that where implementation costs are concerned these could be questionable as the clients of the framework need to accept the expense of noteworthy computational assets particularly where the most well-known disseminated record frameworks are concerned. When it comes to blockchain technologies like bitcoin which is based on anti-institutional beliefs, it struggles to form a cohesive governance mechanism.

A research done by BBVA showed the various regulatory challenges blockchain needs to overcome to be viable in the industry.

As the shared distributed ledger has no physical location, the legal liability is almost non-existent to a specific group, should something go wrong. This is in conjugation to the conflict of the legal regulations of different territories [26]. Following this same reasoning, liability also represents a concern, as there may be no party ultimately responsible for the functioning of distributed ledgers and the information contained therein. The legal framework cannot be fully prepared for the undesired or unforeseen outcome even with rigorous compliance to the existing rules.

Cryptocurrency which is supposed to be a virtual counterpart to cash i.e. it can be used for transaction without the verification of a central regulatory agency, lack a proper law for its use in many countries [26]. For example, some governments have, or have threatened to, make cryptocurrencies illegal in their territories. Bitcoin is only entirely unrestricted in 110 countries and is outright banned in Algeria, Morocco, Ecuador, Iran, Pakistan, and more [27]. In Bangladesh, police have reportedly arrested Bitcoin owners. The looming threat of uncertainty will not be resolved unless the governing authorities can propose proper rules and guidelines for the use of such a technology.

Many experts now firmly believe that the extraordinary cryptocurrency boom of late 2017 was the direct result of collusion between exchanges. Specifically, a small group of crypto-owners with huge holdings allegedly used the shady dollar-pegged Tether to artificially inflate the price. The University of Texas found that just 87 of the largest Bitcoin purchases made with Tether between March 2017 and 2018 accounted for 50% of all Bitcoin's compound gains over the same period [28].

- The immutable ledger is in direct conflict with the Right to be forgotten—which is granted by the European regulation to protect private data. At present the only possible recourse is to change its policy to right to prohibit the use to said data by third parties.
- Legal framework regarding the legal validity of documents stored in blockchains as evidence of possession or existence (Laws to verify the truth of the documentation pushed onto the chain such as ownership, incurring extra cost for another layer of verification and making a part of transition redundant).
- The openness and anonymity also contradict and conflicts with anti-money laundering (AML) and know your customer (KYC) regulations [29, 30].

Blockchain uses (smart) legal contract for enforcing the rules of the network as well as a normal contract. As far as jurisdictional issues are concerned, there is not only the issue of whether the distributed ledger itself has a specific location, but also the issue of signatories to the contract being subject to different laws under their respective jurisdictions. Regarding liabilities, numerous parties are involved in smart contracts: not only the parties to the contract, but also the creator of the same (usually some kind of encoder) and the custodian of the contract (ideally there would be no need for the latter party). This makes the enforceability of the contract difficult due to the different jurisdictions the parts may be in as well as the lack of proper laws to define what makes a smart contract enforceable in a court of law like its physical counterpart.

12.5.1　Principles to Follow While Regulating

As blockchain is still developing, it is malleable and will change as it expands and grows into new domains. This means that the law also needs to change as the old paradigm will no longer suffice to deal with its intricacies. The key priority that the lawmakers and stakeholders need to realize is to tailor such regulations in a manner that fit the interests of both the parties. The regulators won't be able to do alone and need vital input from the industrialists and experts to address their fears and concerns. Only through a complex collaborative effort will we be able to develop a set of regulation that is satisfactory to the vast majority. The following principles should be considered before taking and regulatory actions

The objective of regulation is to give a sense of certainty to the experts, industrialists and entrepreneurs about the legal aspects so that they find it easier to identify things that are legal from those that are not. Hence, we must consider the views and objectives of the ones who are regulated. With legal ambiguity, entrepreneurs would be hesitant to work on a new subject if they fear, they could face prosecution in the future due to a change of laws. When online payment was introduced in digital marketplace, people were hesitant to give their credit card details [31]. But with time and proper regulations being put into place, it has become accepted in all households across the globe. Uncertainties create many problems such as legal compliance for the small firms, increased costs of litigation and law-making that will require many amendments down the road.

12.5.1.1　Flexible to Legal Innovation

Blockchain is still a relatively new technology and prone to changes. Regulators should be aware that it can be used for both good and selfish intensions. So regulatory strategies must take accountability for the public policies and their implications on the general populous. Instead of being hostile towards the industry for mishaps the authorities should put value in innovation itself: innovation that is considered to benefit the public. Such development should be encouraged and the regulations should make necessary provisions for such growth and experimentation. Their role is to protect the people and that should not change to authoritarian control due development of the technology in a certain direction that might not conform with their views. We have seen that the premature implementation of laws as a knee jerk response to a negative event or public uproar leads to potential pitfalls in the future [32]. Blockchain is a technology and a business aspect and thus needs specialized frameworks to draft its regulations that will govern it.

The legal scenario is constantly changing with the changes in the society and the views of its people. Blockchain will also inevitably force certain aspects of the law to change to incorporate, which should be taken as a sign of progress. Experience has also shown that it is better to use a combination of legal and technical code to overcome the limitations of the traditional top down legislative approach. Technological innovation also ensures a continuous interaction between stockholders while respecting the public policy. Co-regulatory approaches can be taken where a "the regulatory regime is made up of a complex interaction of general legislation and a self-regulatory body" [33]. This is also a representation of the workings of blockchain ecosystem. With the increasing number of fields blockchain is predicted to influence a polycentric co-regulation will bring the participants in one platform where the regulations can be discussed. The wisdom of the group will offer insight where the capabilities of an individual fail. The risk of implementing inadequate or potentially controversial policies gets reduced drastically.

12.5.1.2   Experimentation Should be Encouraged

New information on blockchain is still hard to come by as the technology is relatively new. We find two major reasons for this, firstly the technology in itself is not sufficiently developed to get reliable results and test them to understand more about how it functions. Secondly, there are very few experts in this field and the people involved are mostly self-taught without professional guidance. They may not be familiar with all the intricate workings of the technology. This will slowly go away with time when they get more time and experience with the technology.

Regulators should make this a key feature in their approach and promote such methods at the same time giving legal clarity to the participants. The technology mainly benefits the innovators but the benefits are not only limited there. The regulators themselves might reap huge benefits in the future from the implications of this technology. A number of approaches are described to enforce regulations without disrupting the growth. They can for example rely on small scale projects and run blockchain. The problems that are discovered would help in gaining insight into the potentials aspects we need to keep in mind while dealing with the technology. A further option is the use of the 28th regime used in context of the EU. A 28th regime is an optional legal framework that does not replace the current existing framework, but rather works with it as additional laws should they be needed for enforcement. The private firms would get the choice of relying on either framework for their businesses and the legal system would not need to go through a major up haul. This would be easier in the EU where one can facilitate transactions across borders without any change to the existing legal system. An extra benefit is that the laws act as a test case and provide useful data for further research.

12.5.1.3   Focus on the Immediate Implications

Regulators should focus on the system where blockchain is being used instead of the technology itself. Like the internet, cloud storage, personal computers, etc., any disruptive technology is not inherently bad. It occupies a morally and legally neutral gray area. The outcome depends on the end user using this to pursue their own agenda. People have been known to use it to set up shady website that offers illegal services and also to pay off other criminals with untraceable cryptocurrency. These activities are already illegal and laws exist to deal with such infringements and punish the offender accordingly. We can easily modify these laws to suit the needs of regulating crime using blockchain and its products. FinTech is a brilliant example of a positive use of this technology [34] and companies such as BitPesa [35] have made a difference by improving the lives of other people. We tend to generalize and classify these as good or bad, but in real world nothing is necessarily black or white, it is what we make of it. There is no way to stop the expansion of a blockchain except to enforce control at the protocol level or to shut down the internet itself. Regulatory authorities should refrain from doing such actions until the scene becomes a little clearer.

12.5.1.4   Regulators Should Engage in a Transnational Conversation

In an ideal world, a global blockchain would be regulated by a global regulatory body. If such cooperation is not achieved, rules will be fragmented, cooperation will find it difficult to work with each other to solve the many illicit activities based off of blockchain, and innovators face a blow by having to come to terms with the intricacies of manifold regulatory frameworks. Yet, everyone knows that this is a fool's dream and none of these are very realistic option. Short of such a radical option, more realistic methods that are capable of pursuing the same goals should be encouraged.

This includes transnational cooperation and dialogue, including on questions of experience sharing as well as technological and data interoperability. In the United States, many of the states are realizing the benefits of cross-jurisdictional cooperation on this matter. The American Uniform Law Commission has recently passed a model act to regulate digital cryptocurrencies. The European Commission is trying to shepherd such efforts as part of its internal market competence [36, 37].

12.5.2 Regulatory Strategies

The next section deals with the five types of regulatory strategies that have been implemented or are being considered to regulate blockchain. Each approach has its own merit and demerit along with their distinguishing features. But the main goal is to see the divergent approaches taken to so that we can formulate an even better strategy in the future.

12.5.2.1 Wait-and-See

The most primitive approach is similar to the ad hoc build and fix approach of developing small-scale software. The main aim of the regulators is to educate and not regulate. They keep monitoring the technology. New rules are added as new aspects unfold and develop. This allows everyone to observe the technology through its initial phases of development and make explicit guidelines later as the need arises as elucidated in Figure 12.4.

This approach has been very widely used for dealing with a new technology that is in its infancy. The European Commission also follows this ideology of the wait-and-see approach, most prominently on its economic platforms. They actively monitor the progress and organize workshops and fund pilot projects. While it may seem like they are just passively observing, a lot of data is collected and analyzed about it. The results of this analysis can in turn provide valuable information like providing an alternative approach of finding potential loopholes in the existing framework. We would also understand why further experimentation is needed

Figure 12.4 Steps of wait-and-see approach.

to gather more data or to switch to a different approach to implement it more efficiently. If hard rules are implemented now, they would require to be audited very soon to overcome newly discovered shortcomings.

We first need to decide if our existing legal frameworks are indeed sufficient to deal with the potential problems that might arise during the wait-and-see approach. The U.S Internal Revenue Service classified bitcoin as property instead of currency. Thus, the laws for regulating is follow those same laws that apply to your house. On the flip side, the context of tokens is not determined and the lack of certainty of the laws make growth in the entrepreneur market slows down. Workarounds are being researched to circumvent such shortcomings.

12.5.2.2   Imposing Narrowing and Broadening Guidance

The regulators start off by issuing informal guidelines based on the initial information they possess. These guidelines are narrowed or broadened as new information is available. The major drawback is that these guidelines are not properly drafted laws and thus are quite difficult to enforce in court. In fact, most of these guidelines would not hold any value in court. Influential groups can apply pressure on the regulators and force new laws to suit their needs. This is done in a variety of ways like lobbying, slander, litigation techniques or even false advertisements.

12.5.2.3   Sandboxing

Sandboxing as shown is Figure 12.5, is a fairly new approach which allows the regulators to observe, as well as legal certainty for the players in the domain.

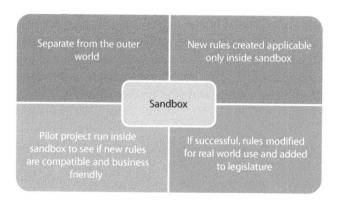

Figure 12.5 Different features of sandboxing.

"A regulatory sandbox can be defined as a set of rules that allows innovators to test their product or business model in an environment that temporarily exempts them from following some or all legal requirements in place. In exchange, these actors are often obliged to operate their business model in a restricted manner, for instance through a controlled number of clients or risk exposure, and under close regulatory supervision."

This technique is considerate of the needs of both the regulators and the regulated. The lawmakers do not have to deal with uncertain outcomes and the innovators can experiment with newer approaches without fearing to getting in trouble. FinTech sector is the best example of when technological change brings about regulatory change as well. This technique was first used in FinTech services itself in the U.K. in 2016 [38]. The British framework allowed the in a differently regulated environment for a defined period of time. This approach was later taken by other firms like Swiss Financial Markets Supervisory Authority, etc.

Sandbox has its own set of advantages and disadvantages that need to be addressed separately. Sandbox acts as a Black box and creates conflict with transparency. The rules of a sandbox are also not very friendly to the businesses. For example, what about consumers that used a certain service before the firm entered into the sandbox thinking their relations would be covered by the generally applicable regime but then no longer are? There are some further limitations such as the restriction to a single jurisdiction, making global transaction almost impossible. The advantage is that it offers some time for the regulators to observe the different aspects of the technology while offering legal counsel when needed.

12.5.2.4   Issue a New Legislation

Regardless of the still starting of the innovation's improvement, various locales have just made the stride of sanctioning new enactment. While this shows the benefits of depicting the locale as a dynamic, blockchain-accommodating setting to pull in blockchain development, it likewise bears the danger of being untimely. Such authoritative excitement may without a doubt demonstrate to have negative outcomes in the long haul as the innovation keeps on advancing, which may bring about a requirement for administrative correction in the near future. Besides as Walch has noticed, the wording encompassing blockchains stays agitated, which may likewise prompt confusions in connection to the use of such administrative structures [39]. Various instances of said approach can be pinpointed. In March 2017, Arizona gave state enactment that qualifies marks verified through blockchains and shrewd agreements as electronic marks. Russia has made a legitimate system to sanction ICOs. Vermont has thought about enactment to make blockchain records allowable proof in courts. Then again, France has approved obligation put together crowd funding recorded with respect to blockchain.

In the long term the many nuances become more of a headache that the regulators do not want to deal with. They get burdened and pass laws that curb the innovation and enforce laws they know would not be effective. Legislator actions should not be premature but they should not be too late to avoid ambiguity. Legislators work becomes easies as time passes and people adopt standard set of terminologies and principles. The International Standards Organization (ISO) has already begun working on setting standard terminologies making things easier in the future [40].

12.5.2.5   Use Blockchain in Regulation

The process of regulation can implement blockchain itself to optimize the process. They would get a bigger opportunity to understand the technology by using it for them. A few occurrences of such an initiative can be seen in some parts of the world. Ukraine hopes to acknowledge the issues of transparency and accountability by partnering with Bit Fury and putting the government data on a blockchain [41]. Georgia is experimenting with using ledgers for registering the deeds to lands [42]. Estonia uses blockchain to enhance the healthcare industry [43]. Singapore has launched its Smart Nation project for inter-bank transactions. Dubai is trying to use blockchain to connect an entire city [44, 45].

The benefits of these projects are multi-fold. The pilot projects give hands on experience which will influence regulatory approaches. Secondly, it creates a platform for the different factors such as the government and the innovators to discuss policies and future potential. Thirdly, existing governments sees the potential to render the process more streamlined. Others approaches have been suggested such as a voted regulatory system for the blockchain, Blockchain as a Service (BaaS) and consensus by regulation. These are novel ideas and more research and analysis is required to understand the feasibility of such unique approaches.

This was the overview of the current regulatory scenario in the blockchain industry. Each approach has their distinct merit and demerit and none of them are perfect. The Internet is supposed to be free for all, but ISP regulations exist; similarly blockchain might be resistant to censorship but it will still come under the regulatory hammer. Further research and newer innovations might bring about some drastic change in this environment that could change the existing models and approaches.

12.6   Business Model Challenges

The term "business model" refers to the company's overall structure in creating a profitable business, which includes the company's purpose, goals and detailed plans. Some companies use a simple model to sell a particular set of products to an existing customer base while others use more complex model starting from manufacturing all the way to international shipping. Traditional businesses don't have the need or the provision to implement blockchain in their current environment. We highlight some of the problems faced in the industry.

- Creating a new model for business
  The average business does not have a provision for blockchain and very few models have the flexibility to accommodate it. The start-ups have the shorter straw when it comes to overhauling their entire business to remain compliant to the ever-changing rules of blockchain. To avoid all the hassle the best way is to redesign a new business model from scratch that will require rethinking revenue streams, resources and mode of operation.
- The Process of Integration itself
  The proposal to implement is not enough as the next requirement would be talented people who can work on blockchain. Special care is required for the integration of blockchain and as such requires the business owners to have a good degree of knowledge about it, to avoid potential problems in the future.
- Finding the Experts and Engineers
  This is very difficult to find as it is a new technology and a single blockchain engineer can cost the company over 70,000 dollars annually; new start-up would also face a lot of trouble finding willing investors as many people are not yet open to the use of blockchain. Additionally, we must consider the cost to train and mentor these new employees to integrate them into the company.
- Lack of Funding
  Investors shy away from any blockchain based company due to its uncertainty in future stability and ROI. Entrepreneurs can overestimate profits; problem begins when your estimated profits don't match the expectations of your investors. This can lead to investors pulling out their funding or losing

their trust in your business. A study showed that the distributed characteristics of blockchain cannot be applied without up hauling the financial services. This is very risky and investors do not fund such endeavours for obvious reasons. A survey by the Tech Republic involving over 500 people across the industry showed that the average proposed ROI was 24% but the actual projects only saw returns as low as 10% [46]. The delivery and efficiency of the approach is difficult to measure and leaves room for such gross overestimates.

- Stakeholder buy-in
  It is required to move any project to production. But in case of blockchain it has been proven to be vastly more difficult and challenging. Production value also requires teamwork with other members outside the organization. This dependency on outside agencies can have conflicts with the stakeholders.

- Uncertainty
  Although blockchain is not in its infancy anymore, it is far from mature and stable. Many are sceptical about the promises of blockchain and whether is could be sustainable due to scalability issues. It is very much possible that this technology would be abandoned by the big tech players leaving the smaller players with a defunct technology. Another possibility is being replaced by a different and better form of technology with different but more manageable drawbacks that could overshadow blockchain completely. Commercial application also requires the acceptance of blockchain by the masses, which in general are not going to be comfortable with the complexities or knowledge needed to operate it.

- Network management
  The next challenge is the coordination between the business teams. Owing to the structure of the application the nodes would need to interact with other nodes outside the company. These nodes are hosted by other companies or independent third parties. The IT team would have to manage the different permissions, protocols and privacy controls such a system would require, a great take in and of it. Manual deployment would also take a long time making it mandatory to use automation requiring its own set of experts. The chances of errors while defining control access and rights also increase. Multiple protocols are present in

the market today such as the Hyper ledger Sawtooth and as more protocols are introduced the complexity of managing their interaction increases [47]. The final issue in this field is monitoring and benchmarking, which are severely limited due to the absence of lower level data. Autonomy is limited which is good for the public but detrimental to the company trying to use it for business.

- Lack of Readymade database schemas
  In the current system the credentials are managed by HTTPS or similar security layers like SSL on the server side without any human intervention. But in blockchain human labour would be required as each issue would have to be specifically solved [48]. Blockchain also comes with trade-offs as mentioned before, like speed and governance factors. The five major factors would be speed, decentralized trust, censorship resistance, openness and transactional cost. If one of them gets compromised, the others will also be compromised.
- Reliability and Robustness
  The errors of other frameworks proved that some flaws remain in the blockchain architecture especially in role specific privatization of data. Backward secrecy control are difficult of incorporate when the newer participants cannot see the transactions that have taken before them joining the network. Blockchain also does not follow standardised firewall regulations and companies cannot guarantee their compliance in the future [49]. There are no definitive hardware or software rules that are followed in this case. Lastly, platform interoperability is still a challenge for the industry with daunting tasks of consensus amongst the machines and humans on protocols and standards.

Blockchain will no doubt bring a massive change, creating new markets and making some obsolete, but it lies in the hands of players who can leverage such a technology while affording its massive resource requirements.

12.7   Scandals and Public Perception

The conception of a new technology brings with it a group of people who try to make a profit off of it by unethical means. In blockchain, particularly in cryptocurrency such as bitcoin, there have been many incidents that have desecrated the public opinion. This alters their perception as something that is unstable and prone to theft among the technologically illiterate. In this section we discuss the major scandals that hit blockchain. Most of these will include the theft of cryptocurrencies in some form as they are the most prominent use of this technology. Bitcoin was the first cryptocurrency and thus will have the most cases associated with it. Other cryptocurrencies such as Ethereum, NiceHash, LitCoin, etc. also have their fair share of controversies. as summerised by Figure 12.6.

- Mt Gox
  The first and one of the largest known cases in scams and scandals is the infamous Mt Gox which controlled 70% of bitcoin during its time in power. Sadly it fell victim to numerous attacks; hacks and internal theft which made them lose over 150,000 bitcoins over a period of 4 years. Finally, Homeland security got involved and things went downhill until it filed for bankruptcy in 2014. Amidst the confusion the manager of Mt Gox Mark Karpelès, stole 1 million dollars for himself. A couple of days later Mt. Gox filed for bankruptcy protection in Tokyo, reporting that it had liabilities of about 6.5 billion yen ($64 million at the time), and 3.84 billion yen in assets. According to sources, the company had lost close to 750,000 of its customers' bitcoins, and around 100,000 of its own bitcoins, the equivalent of 7% of all bitcoins, which at that time were worth about $473 million. Such acts cause irreversible damage to the reputation to a company and by extension the products aka cryptocurrencies [50–53].
- Moopay
  Moopay, the company behind Moolah and the MintPay exchange filed for bankruptcy in late 2014. The main twist to

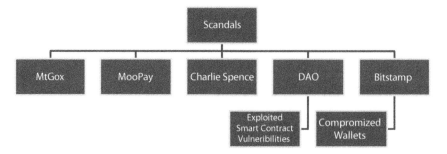

Figure 12.6 Scandals related to Blockchain.

the normal story was that the CEO Alex Green was actually a long time online scammer named Ryan Kennedy. He claimed as Alex, that the company had run out of funds and had to cease functioning while in reality he stole $2 million from them in bitcoins. When his actions were caught he showed little remorse citing that he had to create the identity as he "fucked up on a catastrophic level". He was later arrested in 2016 after the SEC were investigating him for a long time and sentenced to 11 years in prison on charges related to violence.

- Online Black-market
  A main concern is the use of cryptocurrency to purchase illegal substances and services from your home and be anonymous while doing it. The Silk Road was an entire online black market that could be accessed only via the Tor network with properly setup connection. It became a marketplace for trade of all things that are illegal that used bitcoins exclusively.

  a. The founder of Silk RoadRoss Ulbricht along with others has been arrested by the FBI for illegal money laundering schemes. Ross a ledged that he was a scrape goat set up by Mark Karpeles of Mt Gox who was the real owner of the website. The FBI charged him with money laundering, narcotic trafficking and attempting to kill six people. In 2015 the FBI seized over 140,000 BTC from him and the court sentenced him to five concurrent sentences including two life sentences without the possibility of parole. This has most certainly created smaller illegal trafficking websites that are still out there [54, 55].

  b. Shrem was the co-founder of BitInstant, the bitcoin exchange and the investment company Intellisys Capital. His downfall begun with his arrest at JFK airport returning from Amsterdam charged for "engaging in a scheme to sell over $1 million in Bitcoins to users of "Silk Road". Shrem later took a plea deal and got charged with adding and abetting unlicensed money transmission [56]. He served two years in prison and got out in 2017 to join the blockchain wallet Jaxx as a director.

  c. Chinese officials made multiple arrest related to running a Ponzi scheme with bitcoin promising up to 600% returns. One such example is the now defunct bitcoin exchange MyCoin, which was based in Hong Kong and shut down by local authorities in February 2015. A series of investigations by the Hong Kong Commercial Crime Bureau (CCB) revealed that relative investors may have lost up to $400 million. The scheme asked investors to invest at least 400,000 Hong Kong Dollars for 90 bitcoins. The funds were to be put in a My Coin account for the period of a few months, while MyCoin promised them a return of 150%. Several arrests were made but it is unclear how much of the defrauded funds have or will be returned to the victims.

d. The European bitcoin exchange Bitstamp had some of its wallets compromised on 4th January 2015, and lost 19000 BTC, around $5 million at that time. It was speculated that 6 employees were subjected to phishing attacks in the weeks prior to the breach. Shortly after they also reported a massive DDoS attack though no data or money was stolen. This introduced many new security measures in all the big companies in this industry.

- DAO (Decentralized Autonomous Organization)
DAO a decentralized Autonomous organization that ran encoded smart contracts based on Ethereum was subject to a heist of massive consequences [57]. The ether was converted into DAO tokens which were given to holders. It was supposed to form "a form of venture capital vehicle that would invest in projects in the sharing economy". It went as far as to collect 150 million in funding to build a finical institution resembling modern democracy. However due to human error the hackers transferred a third of its funds in their accounts. These funds could not be transferred back due to the immutable nature and the highly quinquennial decision of a hard fork was taken. The community split into Ethereum and Ethereum Classic with the former reversing the transactions of the hackers and the latter going with the unmodified blockchain. Thus, two different cryptocurrencies emerged from the divergence.

On 5th April, 2017 a message was posted by bitcoin developer Gregory Maxwell who pointed out how an ASCIBOOST technology could be exploited to gain mining advantages. The estimated payoff from this was estimated at $110,000 per year. The company behind this technology, Bitmain came under fire although they denied all allegations.

The portrayal or cryptocurrency is a bit grim in the current situation. The public perception is painted by such events many of which go unreported and many which are suppressed. Reading such bleak news about this technology will most certainly make people sceptical and cautious about this technology. Many people do not understand the working behind such events and go with the view of the reporters. A positive public perception is very important. If people like an idea it gets a lot of attention, as a result draws investors and government agencies to part take in it. With the initial funding in place the companies can start to make products that directly benefit the consumers. This makes it grow and solidifies it as a part of the industry. More avenues open up for research work and its consequent development. But the reverse is also true and the lack of proper backing wrecks the initial phase.

> Back in July, 2019 wired.com published an article titled 'There's No Good Reason to Trust Blockchain Technology' which is biased and focuses mainly on bitcoins.

They are not alone and many others publish similar articles in wake of scandals. The main problem is that such articles are more easily available to the common man and who now associate blockchain with scams only [58]. This generates a negative public perception which is very detrimental to any developing technology a can kill it in its infancy. However not all hope is lost, many improvements have been made to improve the security of blockchain and everyday many people strive to make this a technology without faults. A system created in early 2017 used bitcoin technology to tighten security and defend people against identity theft.

> A HSBC survey found that around 59% of the population are still absolutely unaware about blockchain and 80% of those who know about it don't understand it or know how it works.

> A news report on Bitcoin.com claimed that nearly $4.5 billion has been spent in Bitcoin wagers in online casinos.

In PwC's 2018 survey of 600 executives from 15 territories, 84% have some level of involvement in it, perhaps more out of fear of missing out. A survey by Deloitte found that 53% of companies have placed blockchain as one of their top five priorities, a 10% increase from last year and 47% see a ROI in less than 3 years. The survey also says that 77% companies believe they would lose competitive edge if they do not adapt to blockchain technologies.

One of the major problems for creating the bad press might be the absence of advertisement of the progress made or challenges overcome, to counter the negativity spread by scams and scandals. For example, Power Ledger is an Australian company enabling peer-to-peer energy trading [59]. Their vision is to create a world of free control of the energy eco system that can be produced and offered when needed. A huge number of articles can be found online about the real world use of blockchain but most of these are in developmental phase or not well publicized. Some examples include Guard time (health record security), REMME (alternative to login and password using SSL stored in blockchain), Bank Hapoalim (collaboration of Israeli bank with Microsoft for managing guarantees), Maersk (streamlined marine insurance solution) [60] etc.

When it comes to public perception it has been observed that there are mainly two schools of thoughts elucidated in Figure 12.7. The first group thinks that blockchain is a revolutionary and disruptive technology. They creates hype around it and making everyone rush to get into it. A recent survey found blockchain to be the most overrated word in the 2018. It is little surprising considering many companies tested blockchain with very little to show for it. The survey suggests that companies did this as a marketing strategy to get free attention from the media. McKinsey & Co. found that the vast majority of such pilot projects and proofs of concept were still stuck in "developmental phase" or were on the verge of being shut down. They also trumped about the freedom of blockchains and how governments won't be able to regulate it. The second group consists of individuals who believe that this technology is another gimmick that will fade and fade into oblivion. They put is as a local hype like the Google glasses which will ultimately fail due to lack of public support. Bill Barhydt the CEO of Abra, believes that blockchain will not amount to anything in the near future. Some have pointed out that despite bold claims and over $130 billion in crowd funding nothing tangible was seen till 2018 and the adoptions after that have merely added blockchain to solve problems they themselves created.

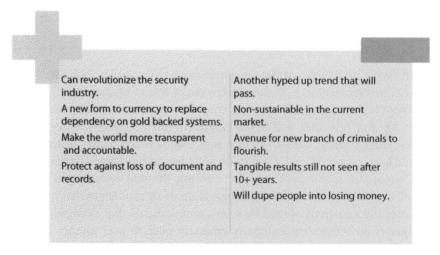

Can revolutionize the security industry.	Another hyped up trend that will pass.
A new form to currency to replace dependency on gold backed systems.	Non-sustainable in the current market.
Make the world more transparent and accountable.	Avenue for new branch of criminals to flourish.
Protect against loss of document and records.	Tangible results still not seen after 10+ years.
	Will dupe people into losing money.

Figure 12.7 The two different public perception on Blockchain.

Both groups are correct in their assumptions. A new technology can be a wide spread success (e.g. the mouse with a scroll wheel) or it can die out. But as an individual it is very important to not make a bias decision. Instead one should read the facts and make their own judgement.

12.8   Why Blockchain is Trustless

Trustless does not mean the lack of trust, but rather the lack of need to place trust in third party organisations and agents. Although somehow the word "trust less" has been associated closely to trust rather than the lack of it. In this section we discuss the various factors that make this system trust less and also put that claim to the test. It is seen that in basic cash transaction one person hands over a physical object (cash) to the recipient. The authenticity of the note can be verified and the person cannot give the same object to two different persons.

In most modern payment system, the participants are the parties involved in the transaction and a hidden intermediary such as the bank or a payment gateway. We place our trust in the bank to deduce the amount from our account and add it to the respective account of the recipient. Using blockchain technology we eliminate the third party and employ the nodes to verify by a process known as mining. Wikipedia defines mining as 'the process of adding transaction records to Bitcoin's public ledger of past transactions'. Each block also needs to send proof of work which is to attach the history of past messages and spend some time trying to find the hash (fixed for the network).If one miner were to change a block, he would have to change all blocks that come before it or be removed due to inconsistency. This costs computational power which is not possible in the fixed time frame it is given for the work. Thus, the traditional methods of tampering with information are not possible in blockchain. Blockchain minimises trust and distributes it evenly among all nodes in the network [61].

- No one is given special privileges, not even the administrators; this eliminates the problems associated with central organizations such as transaction tax, human and database errors, data leaks and theft by the organization itself.

It is not a hundred percent trustless in the sense that we place our trust in blockchain instead of the central authority. However, the blockchain is the collection of all the members who are its nodes and cannot abuse its power, much like a single person does not have a lot of power in a democracy. For example, if one purchased a product from an e-retailer they place their trust in a lot of people they do not know. They trust the website, the e-retail business itself, the software, the database to store the order correctly, even the delivery guy who can misplace the package but report that it was delivered. When using blockchain these problems are circumvented because the database, the order information, the order status cannot be changed for personal use. The entire process needs little human intervention except for "hard forks" to directly change protocols, the management of cryptocurrency exchanges, the emission of ICOs, and investor recourse.

In spite of all this there have been multiple papers over the years that have supported the claims that blockchain is indeed trustless. For example, Forogolu and Tsilidou emphatically state the point that "the whole thing about blockchain-based architectures is that they allow trustless transactional activity," [62], and Kiviat makes the bold assertion that "trustless means that—for the first time in history—exchanges for value over a computer network can be verified, monitored, and enforced without the presence of a trusted third party or central institution," [63]. Madisetti explain that "peers do not need a trusted intermediary for interacting with each other," since a "blockchain network is not controlled by a central authority and all the transactions are verified and validated by a consensus among the peers" due to which "the peers do not need to trust each other" [64].

Multiple features conglomerate together to make this possible as discussed. A few are common knowledge and expected of every technology while others are revolutionary and disruptive in the way they can change the flow of the future.

12.8.1   Trust Mechanism

All nodes must perform some computational work to be considered eligible for a mining reward. The way this works is, when a transaction or modification is made in the blockchain the miners work (spend computational and electrical energy) to find a hash for the transaction. When a hash is found the modification is considered validated and added to the growing chain. The work done is called proof-of-work which is a piece of data that is hard to produce but easy to validate. It is done by brute force methods which involve a lot of trial and errors which makes. The pool of miners that finds the next hash gets rewarded with cryptocurrencies providing them incentives to keep working. As all miner need to provide a proof-of-work it is impossible to cheat this system. Other alternatives have been proposed such as proof-of-stake (having a certain value in crypt currencies), proof-of-identity and even a M2M based proof-of-trust.

12.8.2 Anonymity

In this day of growing concern about how and why our data is being used, people live in fear of their data being stolen and used for malicious activities. An alternative to the current system of central agencies to enforce it are needed. Blockchain provides a refreshing alternative to this arcane system. The users who are part of the blockchain are relatively more secured than their centralized counterparts. Although the origin can be traced, the purpose of the transactions is almost impossible to find. The data works with the public and private keys which can be stored offline in USB drives. To overcome what little issue remains, newer models are being developed and tested.

12.8.3 Use in Digital Wallets

This links with the previous context of anonymity. Blockchain has been around since 2004 but made its debut in 2008 due to the works of Satoshi Nakamoto who launched the first cryptocurrency Bitcoin. Bitcoin or other cryptocurrencies do not need to tell the details of the transaction to the banks. If person A transfers 0.0000023 BTC to company C, we do not now the purpose of the transaction or the services used [65]. The transaction fee for cryptocurrencies is a fraction of what normal financial institutes charge. In fact, in some country's workers can be paid in cryptocurrencies and they would be exempt from paying taxes due to the classification of cryptocurrencies.

12.8.4 Forgery Resistance

A problem that has plagued digital financial institute for decades was the double spending problem. Basically, the same funds could be used to purchase two different products. The tangible equivalent is the scams where the same property is sold to multiple clients without them knowing about each other. This problem was first solved by blockchain due to its unique feature of consensus acknowledgement. Counterfeit currencies can be created and put into circulation which is not possible to identify unless one specially looks for the minor defects that they will possess but cryptocurrencies cannot be forged [66] and will be automatically checked by the network when used. Till date no report exists of creating or using fake cryptocurrencies.

12.9   Use of Blockchain in Cybersecurity

With the increase in personal data and the data gathered from our internet activities, the demand to get access this data has also increased. It is estimated that a persons annual browsing data is worth a little more than $210 when sold to target advertising firms or similar corporations. Data is an universal currency. So it is no surprise that people would device new ways to steal or track this data. Cybersecurity is a vast field and comprises of active and pro-active protection against attacks,damage and theft of information and identity. The advent of blockchain gives us new angles to improve and strenthen the curent cybersecurity model by argumenting it with elements of blockchain.

It is not surprising that such a vast field is constantly growing and keeps needing more and more innovation to stay ahead of cybercriminals. Since 2016 the number of cyber attacks per day have increased more than 300%. When Uber was hacked the records of 57 million customers was leaked [67] while a breach in Friend Finders security compromised 412 million accounts [68]. No technology is safe,what is safe today can be compromised tomorrow. Even the Tech giants like Amazon and Facebook are not immune although their chances of getting compromised are very low. Even Apple product that were thought to be "unhackable" are getting attacked [69]. In 2018 alone macbooks were targeted by 49,000 types of new malwares. Cyber security threats are not limited to only computers, databases; IoT devices like camera, smart TV, wifi enabled printers, house appliances connected to virtual assistants can all get compromised by cyber attacks. The IoT in particular with the rise of smart autonomous devices with little to no security provides a freeway for hackers into a persons private data. The ever evolving nature of technology along with its deeper penetration in all asects of our lives makes it quite the challenge to keep up with the security aspects of it.

While new technologies are being developed in the cyber security industry, blockchain has emerged as a new and potentially revolutionary technology to change the cybersecurity scene. The different features of blockchain like immutability, concensus mechanism, digital contracts, bit notary gives us new and more effective tools to meet the current needs of the cyber security industry. We will discuss the various fields shown in Figure 12.8 that are the most prone to cyber attacks and discuss how

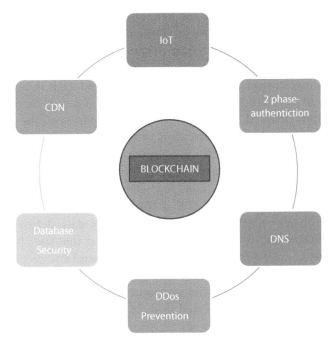

Figure 12.8 The different uses of Blockchain in Cybersecurity.

comlementing it with blockchain would provide inreased security and privacy at a economically and commercially viable level.

12.9.1 Blockchain Database

Traditional databases have been around for over 2 decades now. Many new technologies have been developed to increase security from endpoint encryption to data modification via special tokens. We even see the rise of databases being provided as a cloud service for corporate use. But the problems that plagued them from the early days of its life still remain. The databases is vulnerable to physical calamities and damages that could not have been prevented. A survey also found that around 40 to 55% to attacks on databases occur from within and by employees with admin access and privileges [70]. A paper published in 2019 demonstrated how we can create a decentralized database that supports both sql and non-sql based commands. Users are identified by unique public keys and their transactions are signed by this public key. A master table stores the index of the recent transactions and the associated data store entries. This enables a fast synchronisation and validation. The unsynchronized parts are quickly synchronized by the other members. The users can choose to be a node only concerned with its own transactions or provide resources for computing other transactions. The integrity of data is checked by a consensus mechanism and the operation is rolled back if consensus is not reached. This process can be completed in a few seconds and the user promptly updated about the status of his transaction. The consensus mechanism is based upon correctness, convergence and agreement [71]. The main aim of the consensus is to reach an agreed data store state in as little time as possible. This is done keeping a threshold for byzantine consensus errors.

A different approach is to keep a traditional database and connect it to a multi-tier enterprise application. All the data defined and the user operations are defined in an immutable log that uses blockchain technology. User applications would be able to send and receive data to and from the network nodes. The user query would be stored in a local database in a node close to the user and when consensus is reached, the transaction would be updated to the main database. In case a node fails the user could be seamlessly transferred to another node making it a zero-time recovery system. The faulty node can be repaired and put back in the pool.

As the data is present on nodes, a blockchain based database can also implement recovery nodes which are special nodes at remote locations which hold a copy of the database. In case of a disaster, the main database can be restored to the state of these recovery nodes without permanent loss of data. This would also be economically more feasible than maintaining an offshore backup in the form of a data center. The immutability brings the inherent feature of auditability to the system. In case of a traditional database, user A performs a CRUD operation for users B and C on table E. With the addition of the blockchain layer the operation is recorded as a blockchain transaction and the transaction with the corresponding access is signed and sent to concerned peers. Once the consensus is reached the network finalizes and included it in the data store. If User C requests a select query on table T and sends it to node N, it identifies the user from the signature of the query. If the user C has permission to perform the operation, the node executed the query and returns the result to user C. Using these approaches, we get a little more latency but it provides a better security and also protection from insider attacks.

With the advance of technology and the introduction of faster internet connectivity we may see newer methods of securing the database and perhaps even the local data security may be enhanced with blockchain.

12.9.2 DNS Security

The domain name service is used to mainly resolve host names in common language to their corresponding IP addresses. It provides some important services such as protection from bot-based spam, sharing the load during unusual traffic and provides privacy by masking the actual namespace of the organization. Blockchain based DNS such as the DNS Chain give the required softwares to replace the X.509 public key structure and provides MITM proof of authentication [72]. Considering case of Zooko's Triangle theory we see that this approach will have all the three properties. The current DNS is controlled exclusively by the system administrator and they are free to change it as they please. In the blockchain based method, all nodes would have equal privilege and priority. Only the owners could change existing names and structures with their private keys.

Concerning security, we see obvious benefits to this approach. Even with all the enhancements of DNSSEC, the traditional DNS has vulnerabilities in its protocol that make it vulnerable to DoS and DDoS attacks. In the newer approach the domain is stored locally on all the nodes. This eliminates the need of the server to deal with the protocols for encoding and decoding the DNS address. All the lookups are performed locally and the DDoS attacks cannot impact the performance. This technique also makes the data of the protocol immutable thereby reducing the damage a server or protocol attack can do. Additionally, it offers greater security to the clients protecting them from eavesdropping and others similar attacks.

Another approach is to create a combined Single Key (CSK) which is a modified version of the PKI [72, 73]. These systems allow the X.509 certificates to be added to a public blockchain and when a CSR is accepted the certificate is also broadcasted on the blockchain network. The network can then verify the certificate and reach a consensus on its authenticity. The changes propagate through the network faster than the CLR system. Additionally, the system is always updated about the status of the certificates used in the network.

12.9.3 IoT Security

In the recent times IoT is coming out of its infancy and has started making its presence known in most households. This has been in many forms from smart speakers, Smart TVs, automatic doorbells, Smart security sensors and many more that share a vast amount of sensitive data amongst each other to achieve home automation. The list is endless and with the big tech companies making investments it will only grow and reach an estimated $20 million in the next decade. Many of these devices are lightweight with low power overhead [74]. So, they make an appealing target for various cyber-attacks. These devices do not have the energy overhead to implement computationally and energy intensive encryption protocols. Moreover, most of the widely used security system is highly centralized and hence not suited for a distributed system like IoT. If any device such as a smart door lock were to get hacked, the hacker would then get access to all the connected devices including our phones via the layers of the IoT. Most of the non-security devices in home automation like Alexa-enabled coffee makers do not have proper security and provide a lucrative opportunity for hackers to use it as an entry point into the home network. While applying blockchain there are two major ways for implementing it to secure the entire ecosystem.

The first is by using a local private blockchain connected to a smart miner in the home of each user. The blockchain headers would enforce policies that would define the access to the information. Each transaction would be stored in a block and the blocks would have additional parameters to uniquely identify the type of transaction along with the devices involved. The miner authorizes, authenticates, and audits transactions. In addition, the miner is involved in generating genesis transactions, changing the transactions structure, distributing and updating keys and cluster management. The miner collects all transactions into a block and appends the full block to the Blockchain. Additional capacity is managed in the form of local storage connected to the miner. The smart devices can communicate directly with each other or with devices on other networks. The miner would use the policies as a guideline to generate a shared key that the user can use to access and control the devices in his home. The devices would be able to send messages among themselves as long as the key is valid. When the key is no longer required the miner can simply send a control message to all the devices revoking their access. The devices can request a new key from the miner which decides if it should be granted by rules set by the user. It also maintains a log of all the devices that requested for the shard key and the list of transactions that took place which immutable and safe from tampering [75, 76].

The second method is to store the access control in a distributed blockchain and implement smart contract between the nodes. In this method we do not use the IoT devices as part of the blockchain and instead use a management hub that makes the request on behalf of the IoT devices. Entities called 'managers' interact with the smart contract to define the access control policies of the devices and individual users. The IoT devices are registered under the managers and a device can come under multiple managers.

Especial node called the agent used to deploy the smart contract which becomes the owner during the lifecycle of the access control. Management hub which are high-performance devices would be connected between the node and the Iota device acting as a mediator. This could use both a private or public blockchain to validate the transactions. The rest of the structure is similar to the standard IoT ecosystem. Both these approaches make the system resilient to DoS attacks while not compromising on performance. They also provide general security, maintain permanent logs and remove the problem of a single point of failure.

In case of IoT on a large scale like an intercity service, the devices are capable of intelligently managing the resources like power, gas, mobility and environmental resources similar to the system by Anderson [77]. A multi-layer Blockchain is integrated into the mainframe of the city namely the physical, application, database and service layers. In such cases the main security comes from pseudo anonymization, so that the identity of the producer or consumer can only be revealed by the joint treatment of data without precluding that merging data from multiple sources leads to identification. Personal data would no longer be identifiable without the use of additional attributes [78]. This approach splits the data into chunks and distributes it among several IoT devices. Thus, only the owner can rebuild the data. If a service requests access the owner can choose to share the public key via a pre-defined access list.

Blockchain can also be leveraged to provide an alternative to a database-backed structure which is useful in application such as supply chains. When coupled with the sensory data from IoT devices the system is capable of monitoring the supply and handling procedures. The key factor is from blockchains in the inherent multi-party nature of communication between devices. Sensory readings from the IoT devices offer more real-time information and provide a greater level of trust and transparency. Two of the most common sensors currently used in pilot projects are the TTI (time and temperature sensor) and the GPS sensor along with the RFID chips for quality control. The industry has shown considerable it rests in this application go traceable supply chains with more transparency and immutable records. Walmart and IBM have started working on proprietary technology; however, the specifics are not available to the public as of now. Authors in this field have proposed many real-world applications of supply chain such as:

- Blockchain based Agri-food supply chain [79].
- Blockchain based wine traceability system to track the production and purchase of wine to maintain authenticity [80].

- Using blockchain to store the ownership and manufacturing information coupled with RFID tags to prevent counterfeit products from reaching sellers.
- Permissioned blockchain controlled by a consortium of government and regulatory bodies to ensure food providence.

12.9.4   DDoS Prevention

Distributed Denial of Service attacks are nothing new; they have been around for a long time. There have been multiple attempts but none have been able to provide a long-term secure solution to this problem. The main weakness of all which makes security difficult is the DNS which is a partially centralized system mapping system names (IP) to domains. At the moment blockchain is the only technology that offers a solution to this problem [81] which is why big companies like Sound Cloud, Facebook, and Twitter are looking into ways to implement blockchain into their security network. By making the entire server decentralized, the network request is sent to one of the millions of nodes present all over the world. If a hacker tries to overload, he server by flooding it with requests, the network would simply send the extra requests to other nodes. In this architecture a single node will never get overwhelmed and the network will always have additional nodes to deal with excessive traffic. An additional benefit is that a simple program can be used for maintenance of the nodes; this would reduce manpower costs and be much simpler than redirecting traffic and taking a server offline for maintenance [82].

We have talked about how IoT can benefit from blockchain. It is imperative to know about the DDoS attack in the IoT network. In IoT, a hacker can hack multiple devices and inject them with malicious codes indoctrinating them into the botnet to act as a node the sends request during the DDoS attack. In the paper (DDoS Botnet Prevention using Blockchain in Software Defined Internet of Things) the author proposed a security system involving three modules: SecPoliMod (SecurityPolicy Module), ConMod (controller) and LogMod (Log Module) to prevent the IoT device from becoming a part of the botnet [82]. These modules work together at different internet layers to block suspicious traffic and use special "colored coins" to ultimately prevent innocent IoT devices from becoming a soldier in the DDoS attack.

12.9.5   CDN (Content Delivery Network)

Content Delivery Network is a network of multiple systems containing the same set of data to increase delivery speed, provide higher bandwidth and reduce dependency. Currently the BitTorrent protocol is implemented in certain circles to provide similar service. However even with the hash verification, BitTorrent protocol surfers from the Byzantine Consensus problem where the systems on the CDN could have different data values due to uncontrollable factors or network errors. Also, it is possible to fake a hash and send incorrect pieces to corrupt data to cause data corruption. This system also provides primitive security against IP tracing and hacking. We have an opportunity to improve this system by implementing blockchain into it [83]. The immutable nature would prevent anyone from sending corrupt data packets and the transactions can be logged to validate transfer of data. As the system is already set up the implementation would be relatively easy while benefiting from the increased bandwidth of the network. We can improve security and provide a more streamlined service to the average user without him bothering about the minute intricacies. This new system could also help wash off the stigma of piracy associated with torrenting applications.

12.9.6   SMS Authentication

Authentication is the act of determining the legitimacy of a user's identity mainly to give him access or service. Authentication also validates this identity generally by the use of digital certificates or matching passwords. Two factor authentications use a combination of a password and a second unique identification method which must be present in conjugation to be considered valid. Two phase authentications using one-time password (OTP) has been implemented in India for a long time. We are seeing other countries starting to implement similar technique to provide better protection against cybercrimes. Generally, in 2 factor authentication a one-time password is generated after the user has entered their password and requested for a service. This password generally consisting of 6 digits is sent to the user's registered mobile number via SMS. However, attackers have found ways to bypass this system and gain access to the users account without their permission. A framework based on blockchain could be used to add better security and make the authentication process more secure. A study by Jesudoss and Subramaniam concluded there were 11 possible ways an attacker could get the password [84]. Other independent studies have shown that the authentication model of Dropbox, Twitter can be compromised by exploiting certain vulnerabilities. On the other hand, the attacker can simply intercept the OTP or capture the session cookies to regenerate the OTP. In the event that the user loses their phone, the attacker can convince the carrier that they are the original owner and get access to all calls and SMS received on the phone. This is a fatal weakness and many services now request the users to use alternative form of authentication to bypass this problem.

There are some approaches that have been implemented by researchers with limited success. One approach is to use a pseudo random function to generate the OTP [85] and send it to the user in the form of a smart contract. The root value is used to generate multiple values which is finally used for authentication. While this makes it impossible to tamper with the OTP, a MITM attack can still get access to the OTP. The second approach is making the user a member and uses a membership function to generate the OTP. This is similar to the previous approach in the way that third party attack cannot be performed. However, this method also sends the OTP as plain text making it vulnerable to interception and phishing attacks. The last approach makes the user a wallet node in the blockchain. The web application asks the user to send a contract to the Ethereum blockchain and waits for a set period of time. Ethereum checks the integrity of the user's transaction with the web application an validates it. In case of a valid request the Ethereum 2FA contracts generates the OTP [86] and encrypts it with the user's public key before sending it to him. Ethereum also computes the hash value of the OTP and conveys it to the website. The user decrypts and computes the hash from the OTP he receives and sends it to the web application. If both the hashes are found to be equal then the service is granted to the user. By using the public key to encrypt the OTP we make it impossible for any attacker to use it. Even when the attacker gets the encrypted OTP, it would be impossible for them to decrypt the values by brute force before the request time out closes the transaction.

References

1. Maull, R., Godsiff, P., Mulligan, C., Brown, A., Kewell, B., Distributed ledger technology: Applications and implications. *Strateg. Chang.*, 26, 5, 481–489, 2017.
2. Sagiroglu, S. and Sinanc, D., Big data: A review, in: *International conference on collaboration technologies and systems (CTS)*, IEEE, pp. 42–47, 2013.
3. Kollmann, T., Hensellek, S., de Cruppe, K., Sirges, A., Toward a renaissance of cooperatives fostered by Blockchain on electronic marketplaces: A theory-driven case study approach. *Electron. Mark.*, 30, 2, 1–12, 2019.
4. Joshi, A.P., Han, M., Wang, Y., A survey on security and privacy issues of blockchain technology. *Math. Found. Comput.*, 1, 2, 121–147, 2018.

5. Henry, R., Herzberg, A., Kate, A., Blockchain access privacy: Challenges and directions. *IEEE Secur. Priv.*, 16, 4, 38–45, 2018.

6. Dingledine, R., Mathewson, N., Syverson, P.F., Tor: The second-generation onion router, in: *Usenix Security Symposium (USENIX '04)*, 2004.

7. Biryukov, A., Khovratovich, D., Pustogarov, I., Deanonymisation of clients in Bitcoin P2P network, in: *Proceedings of the 2014 ACM SIGSAC Conference on Computer and Communications Security*, pp. 15–29, 2014.

8. Rosen, J., The right to be forgotten. *Stan. L. Rev. Online*, 64, 88, 2011.

9. Feng, Q., He, D., Zeadally, S., Khan, M.K., Kumar, N., A survey on privacy protection in blockchain system. *J. Netw. Comput. Appl.*, 126, 45–58, 2019.

10. Maurer, F.K., Neudecker, T., Florian, M., Anonymous CoinJoin transactions with arbitrary values, in: *2017 IEEE Trustcom/BigDataSE/ICESS*, 2017, August, IEEE, pp. 522–529.

11. Sasson, E.B., Chiesa, A., Garman, C., Green, M., Miers, I., Tromer, E., Virza, M., Zerocash: Decentralized anonymous payments from bitcoin, in: *IEEE Symposium on Security and Privacy*, IEEE, pp. 459–474, 2014.

12. Sasson, E.B., Chiesa, A., Garman, C., Green, M., Miers, I., Tromer, E., Virza, M., Zerocash: Decentralized anonymous payments from bitcoin, in: *Security and Privacy (SP), 2014 IEEE Symposium on*, IEEE, pp. 459–474, 2014.

13. Apostolaki, M., Zohar, A., Vanbever, L., Hijacking bitcoin: Routing attacks on cryptocurrencies, in: *2017 IEEE Symposium on Security and Privacy (SP)*, 2017, May, IEEE, pp. 375–392.

14. Rodrigues, B., Bocek, T., Lareida, A., Hausheer, D., Rafati, S., Stiller, B., A blockchain-based architecture for collaborative DDoS mitigation with smart contracts, in: *IFIP International Conference on Autonomous Infrastructure, Management and Security*, 2017, July, Springer, Cham, pp. 16–29.

15. Nakamoto, S., Bitcoin: A Peer-to-Peer Electronic Cash System, https://bitcoin.org/bitcoin.pdf, 2018.

16. Mirkin, M., Ji, Y., Pang, J., Klages-Mundt, A., Eyal, I., Jules, A., Blockchain Denial of Service. in: *Cryptography and Security*, v.3, arXiv preprint arXiv:912.07497 1, 2019.

17. Lin, I.C. and Liao, T.C., A survey of blockchain security issues and challenges. *IJ Netw. Secur.*, 19, 5, 653–659, 2017.

18. Hoy, M.B., An introduction to the blockchain and its implications for libraries and medicine. *Med. Ref. Serv. Q.*, 36, 3, 273–279, 2017.

19. Sayeed, S. and Marco-Gisbert, H., On the Effectiveness of Blockchain against Cryptocurrency Attacks. *Proceedings of the UBICOMM*, 2018.

20. Chohan, U.W., The double spending problem and cryptocurrencies, *CBRI Working Papers: Notes on the 21st Century*. SSRN, p. 2, 2019.

21. Chauhan, A., Malviya, O.P., Verma, M., Mor, T.S., Blockchain and scalability, in: *IEEE International Conference on Software Quality, Reliability and Security Companion (QRS-C)*, IEEE, pp. 122–128, 2018.

22. Dev, J.A., Bitcoin mining acceleration and performance quantification, in: *IEEE 27th Canadian Conference on Electrical and Computer Engineering (CCECE)*, IEEE, pp. 1–6, 2014.
23. Chu, S. and Wang, S., The curses of blockchain decentralization, *arXiv preprint arXiv:1810.02937*, 3, 2018.
24. Kiayias, A. and Panagiotakos, G., Speed-Security Tradeoffs in Blockchain Protocols. *IACR Cryptol. ePrint Archive*, 2015, 1019, 2015.
25. Finck, M., Blockchains: Regulating the Unknown. *Ger. Law J.*, 19, 4, 665–692, 2018.
26. Jacquez, T., *Cryptocurrency the new money laundering problem for banking, law enforcement, and the legal system*, ProQuest Dissertations Publishing (Doctoral dissertation, Utica College, 10251759, pp. 5–9, 2016.
27. Di Giuda, M., Countries where the cryptocurrencies are banned: Busted for Bitcoin, htps:www.Bitnewstoday.com., 2018.
28. McCrank, J. and Irrera, A., *Cryptocurrency tether used to boost bitcoin prices*, Forthcoming, The Routledge Handbook of FinTech (Routledge, UK), pp. 4, 2018.
29. Gill, M. and Taylor, G., Preventing money laundering or obstructing business? financial companies' perspectives on know your customer procedures. *Br. J. Criminol.*, 44, 4, 582–594, 2004.
30. Ma, Z., Jiang, M., Gao, H., Wang, Z., Blockchain for digital rights management. *Future Gener. Comput. Syst.*, 89, 746–764, 2018.
31. Abd Aziz, N.N. and Abd Wahid, N., Why Consumers are Hesitant to Shop Online: The Major Concerns towards Online Shopping. *Int. J. Acad. Res. Bus. Soc. Sci.*, 8, 9, 8, 2018.
32. Thomas, Z., Bitcoin regulation: the latest developments assessed, in: *International Financial Law Review*, Euromoney Institutional Investor PLC, 2013.
33. Marsden, C.T., Internet co-regulation and constitutionalism: Towards European judicial review. *Int. Rev. Law Comput. Tech.*, 26, 2–3, 211–228, 2012.
34. Kursh, S.R. and Gold, N.A., Adding fintech and blockchain to your curriculum. *Bus. Educ. Innovation J.*, 8, 2, 6–12, 2016.
35. Njuguna, M.E., *Adoption of Bitcoin in Kenya*, A Case Study Of BitPesa, p. 22, 2014.
36. Reddy, A., Coinsensus: The Need for Uniform National Virtual Currency Regulations. *Dickinson L. Rev.*, 123, 251, 2018.
37. Miseviciute, J., Blockchain and virtual currency regulation in the EU. *J. Invest. Compliance*, 2018.
38. FinTech Regulatory Sandbox, Monetary Authority of Singapore, http://www.mas.gov.sg/Singapore-FinancialCentre/Smart-Financial-Centre/FinTech-Regulatory-Sandbox.aspx, p. 6, 2018.
39. Walch, A., The path of the blockchain lexicon (and the law). *Rev. Banking & Fin. L.*, 36, 713, 2016.
40. Gramoli, V. and Staples, M., Blockchain Standard: Can We Reach Consensus? *IEEE Commun. Stand. Mag.*, 2, 3, 16–21, 2018.

41. Chavez-Dreyfuss, G., Ukraine Launches Big Blockchain Deal with Tech Firm Bitfury, in: *Reuters*, https://www.reuters.com/article/us-ukraine-bitfury-blockchain-idUSKBN17F0N2, 2017.

42. Jonathan Keane, E., *Sweden Moves to Next Stage with Blockchain Land Registry*, COINDESK, https://www.coindesk.com/sweden-moves-next-stage-blockchain-land-registry/, 2017.

43. Jonathon Marshall, E., *Estonia Prescribes Blockchain for Healthcare Data Security*, PWC BLOGS, http://pwc.blogs.com/health_matters/2017/03/estonia-prescribes-blockchain-for-healthcare-data-security.html, 23, 2, 2017.

44. Lohade, N., Dubai Aims to be a City Built on Blockchain. *Wall St. J.*, https://www.wsj.com/articles/dubai-aims-to-be-a-city-built-on-blockchain-1493086080, 2017.

45. Finck, M., Blockchains: Regulating the Unknown in *German Law Journal*, vol 19, 4, pp. 665–692, 2018.

46. WolkoffWachsman, Melanie, What do you think about blockchain?,https://www.techrepublic. com/article/what-do-you-think-about-blockchain-tell-us-in-a-quick-survey/, 1, 2019.

47. Olson, K., Bowman, M., Mitchell, J., Amundson, S., Middleton, D., Montgomery, C., *Sawtooth: An Introduction*, The Linux Foundation, Jan., 2018.

48. Lesavre, L., Varin, P., Mell, P., Davidson, M., Shook, J., A taxonomic approach to understanding emerging blockchain identity management systems, *arXiv preprint arXiv:1908.00929*, 2019.

49. Ahluwalia, S., Mahto, R.V., Guerrero, M., Blockchain technology and startup financing: A transaction cost economics perspective. *Technol. Forecasting Social Change*, 151, 119854, 2015.

50. Chen, W., Wu, J., Zheng, Z., Chen, C., Zhou, Y., Market manipulation of bitcoin: Evidence from mining the Mt. Gox transaction network, in: *IEEE INFOCOM 2019-IEEE Conference on Computer Communications*, IEEE, pp. 964–972, 2019.

51. Feder, A., Gandal, N., Hamrick, J.T., Moore, T., The impact of DDoS and other security shocks on Bitcoin currency exchanges: Evidence from Mt. Gox. *J. Cybersecur.*, 3, 2, 137–144, 2017.

52. Steele, S. and Morishita, T., Lessons from Mt Gox: practical considerations for a virtual currency insolvency, in: *Research Handbook on Asian Financial Law*, Edward Elgar Publishing, 2020.

53. Bohannon, J., *The bitcoin busts*, 2016. https://science.sciencemag.org/content/351/6278/1144.

54. Christin, N., Traveling the Silk Road: A measurement analysis of a large anonymous online marketplace, in: *Proceedings of the 22nd international conference on World Wide Web*, pp. 213–224, 2013.

55. Huang, A., Reaching within silk road: The need for a new subpoena power that targets illegal bitcoin transactions. *BCL Rev.*, 56, 2093, 2015.

56. Roy, J., BitInstant CEO Charlie Shrem Arrested for Alleged Money Laundering, TIME, 2014. https://time.com/1892/bitinstant-ceo-charlie-shrem-arrested-for-alleged-money-laundering

57. FalKon, S., The Story of the DAOŁŁIts History and Consequences, (accessed April, 2018), https://medium.com/swlh/the-story-of-the-daoits-history-and-consequences-71e6a8a551ee, 2017.

58. Vasek, M. and Moore, T., There's no free lunch, even using Bitcoin: Tracking the popularity and profits of virtual currency scams, in: *International conference on financial cryptography and data security*, 2015, January, Springer, Berlin, Heidelberg, pp. 44–61.

59. Ledger, P., *Power Ledger white paper*, Power Ledger Pty Ltd, Australia, White paper, 8, 2017.

60. Katona, Z. and Sarvary, M., Maersk line: B2B social media—It's communication, not marketing. *Calif. Manage. Rev.*, 56, 3, 142–156, 2014.

61. Zheng, Z., Xie, S., Dai, H., Chen, X., Wang, H., An Overview of Blockchain Technology: Architecture, Consensus, and Future Trends. *Proceedings—IEEE 6th International Congress on Big Data, BigData Congress 2017*, June, pp. 557–564, 2017.

62. Foroglou, G. and Tsilidou, A.L., Further applications of the blockchain, in: *12th Student Conference on Managerial Science and Technology*, 2015.

63. Kiviat, T.I., Beyond bitcoin: Issues in regulating blockchain transactions. *Duke L.J.*, 65, 569, 2015.

64. Bahga, A. and Madisetti, V.K., Blockchain platform for industrial internet of things. *J. Softw. Eng. Appl.*, 9, 10, 533–546, 2016.

65. Kaushal, P.K., Bagga, A., Sobti, R., Evolution of bitcoin and security risk in bitcoin wallets, in: *2017 International Conference on Computer, Communications and Electronics (Comptelix)*, IEEE, pp. 172–177, 2017.

66. Li, Y.N., Feng, X., Xie, J., Feng, H., Guan, Z., Wu, Q., A decentralized and secure blockchain platform for open fair data trading. *Concurr. Comp.: Pract. E.*, e5578, 32, 7, 2019.

67. Tagliaferro, J., *Why Everyone is Still Getting Hacked*, 2017. http://www.cs.tufts.edu/comp/116/archive/fall2017

68. Walters, R., *Cyber attacks on US companies in 2014*, The Heritage Foundation, vol. 4289, pp. 1–5, 2014.

69. Whittaker, Z., Malicious websites were used to secretly hack into iPhones for years, says Google, https://techcrunch.com/2019/08/29/google-iphone-secretly-hacked/, 2019.

70. Liu, L., De Vel, O., Han, Q.L., Zhang, J., Xiang, Y., Detecting and preventing cyber insider threats: A survey. *IEEE Commun. Surv. Tut.*, 20, 2, 1397–1417.s, 2018.

71. Gaetani, E., Aniello, L., Baldoni, R., Lombardi, F., Margheri, A., Sassone, V., Blockchain-based database to ensure data integrity in cloud computing environments, *Italian Conference on Cybersecurity 2017*, 10, 2017.

72. Karaarslan, E. and Adiguzel, E., Blockchain based dns and pki solutions. *IEEE Commun. Stand. Mag.*, 2, 3, 52–57, 2018.

73. Liu, J., Li, B., Chen, L., Hou, M., Xiang, F., Wang, P., A data storage method based on blockchain for decentralization DNS, in: *IEEE Third International Conference on Data Science in Cyberspace (DSC)*, IEEE, pp. 189–196, 2018.

74. Bekara, C., Security issues and challenges for the IoT-based smart grid. *FNC/ MobiSPC*, pp. 532–537, 2014.
75. Dorri, A., Kanhere, S.S., Jurdak, R., Gauravaram, P., Blockchain for IoT security and privacy: The case study of a smart home. *IEEE International Conference on Pervasive Computing and Communications Workshops (PerCom workshops)*, IEEE, pp. 618–623, 2017.
76. Samaniego, M. and Deters, R., Blockchain as a Service for IoT. *IEEE International Conference on Internet of Things (iThings) and IEEE Green Computing and Communications (GreenCom) and IEEE Cyber, Physical and Social Computing (CPSCom) and IEEE Smart Data (SmartData)*, IEEE, pp. 433–436, 2016.
77. Andersen, M.P., Kolb, J., Chen, K., Fierro, G., Culler, D.E., Popa, R.A., *Wave: A decentralized authorization system for IoT via blockchain smart contracts*, Tech. Rep. UCB/EECS-2017-234, EECS Department, University of California, Berkeley, 2017.
78. Biswas, K. and Muthukkumarasamy, V., Securing smart cities using blockchain technology. *Proc. IEEE 14th Int. Conf. Smart City*, Dec. 2016, pp. 1392–1393.
79. Fu, H., Zhao, C., Cheng, C., Ma, H., Blockchain-based agri-food supply chain management: case study in China. *Int. Food Agribusiness Manag. Rev.*, 1–14, 2020.
80. Biswas, K., Muthukkumarasamy, V., Tan, W.L., Blockchain based wine supply chain traceability system. *Future Technologies Conference (RTC)*, 5, 2017.
81. Javaid, U., Siang, A.K., Aman, M.N., Sikdar, B., Mitigating IoT device based DDoS attacks using blockchain. *Proceedings of the 1st Workshop on Cryptocurrencies and Blockchains for Distributed Systems*, pp. 71–76, 2018.
82. Shafi, Q. and Basit, A., DDoS Botnet prevention using blockchain in software defined Internet of Things. *16th International Bhurban Conference on Applied Sciences and Technology (IBCAST)*, IEEE, pp. 624–628, 2019.
83. Ak, E. and Canberk, B., BCDN: A proof of concept model for blockchain-aided CDN orchestration and routing. *Comput. Networks*, 161, 162–171, 2019.
84. Jesudoss, A. and Subramaniam, N., A survey on authentication attacks and countermeasures in a distributed environment. *Indian J. Comput. Sci. Eng. (IJCSE)*, 5, 2, 71–77, 2014.
85. Eldefrawy, M.H., Alghathbar, K., Khan, M.K., OTP-based two-factor authentication using mobile phones, in: *2011 Eighth International Conference on Information Technology: New Generations*, IEEE, pp. 327–331, 2011.
86. Alharbi, E. and Alghazzawi, Two Factor Authentication Framework Using OTP-SMS Based on Blockchain. *Trans. Mach. Learn. Artif. Intell.*, 7, 3, 17–27, 2019.

13

Internet of Things and Blockchain

Priyanka Sharma

Manav Rachna International Institute of Research & Studies, Faridabad, India

Abstract

The idea of the Internet of Things (IoT) is fascinating and energizing, however the most testing part of IoT is the safe condition that associates all the structure squares of IoT-engineering. The blockchain is a database that keeps up constant information records. It is dispersed normally, implying that the ace PC isn't liable for the whole arrangement. Rather, the taking an interest hubs have a chain duplicate. It is continually developing—information records are just remembered for arrangement. Blockchain innovation is a lost connects to settling protection issues and depending on the Internet of Things. Blockchain modernization might be the silver covering for the IoT business. It may be utilized well to follow billions of connected gadgets that empower exchange management and correspondence between gadgets that permit significant investment funds for IoT mechanical engineers. This problematic methodology stays away from dissatisfaction, building a progressively amicable organic method for working gadgets. This part depicts the historical backdrop of IoT, genuine examinations utilizing IoT gadgets in the present and future world, different kinds of sensors and actuators, mix of blockchain and IoT, edge registering and blockchain are isolated into 6 areas.

Keywords: IoT gateway, voice controller, contextual analyses, august smart lock, kuri mobile robot

Email: priyanka.fca@mriu.edu.in

S.S. Tyagi and Shaveta Bhatia (eds.) *Blockchain for Business: How it Works and Creates Value*, (295–336) © 2021 Scrivener Publishing LLC

13.1   History of 'Internet of Things'

KEVIN ASHTON
(Father of IoT)

IoT is a 16-year old concept carrying a fundamental idea of related gadgets which has been around since the mid-70s. Consequently, the idea was designated "implanted Internet" or "incorporated registering." The first name of "Web of Things" was utilized by Kevin Ashton in 1999 during his vocation at Procter and Gamble. Ashton, who works in acquisition, encouraged senior administration to concentrate on one more enlivening innovation called Radio Frequency Identification (RFID [46]). The Internet was new in 1999 and as it was legitimate, he called his show "The Internet of Things".

Kevin Ashton accepts that Radio Frequency Identification (RFID) is first required on the Internet of Things. He inferred that all gadgets were "labels" that PCs could discover, download and dispatch. Somewhat, stamping is accomplished through methods, for example, computerized perception, code, and QR code. One of the conspicuous advantages of the Internet of Things is sell off control. In spite of the fact that Kevin has pulled in the consideration of some P&G administrators, the Internet of Things name has not gotten a lot of consideration in the following decade.

The IoT started reaching its height in 2010 [23]. Subtleties have been discharged that the Google Street View administration creates 360 photographs, it also spares big information from the WiFi arrange.

In Figure 13.1 y-axis depict the level of expectations by the world in July 2019 and the coming years, x-axis showing the time, for example the

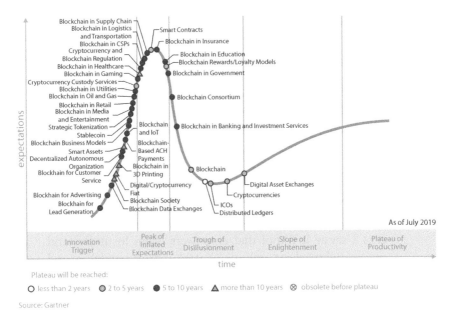

Figure 13.1 Hype cycle for emerging technologies, 2019.

dark blue dot shows that in 5 to 10 years Blockchain for customer service is expected [10]. In 2019, Gartner, the market research firm that launched the "booming promotional-tech cycle", released a new feature, "Blockchain and IoT" from its list.

Technologically-oriented magazines such as Forbes, Fast Company and Wired have started using IoT as their terminology to explain this phenomenon. In simple terms, any device which is connected to the Internet is the Internet of Things.

This incorporates anything from portable to support configuration to fly motors. Medical gadgets, like, heart checking or establishment of bio-chip transponders on livestock can transmit data over the system. It has a huge Internet arrange associated by systems and gadgets. A ring, entryway handle, associated with your advanced mobile phone gives a genuine case of the most recent growth to the Internet of Things. At the point when the doorbell rang, a boisterous voice came up and it permitted you to see somebody and converse with them.

The Internet of Things showcase reached a critical stage in January 2014 when Google Nest declared its obtaining of 23.2 billion. The chart beneath shows that the appearance "Web of Things" rises above every single other idea of notoriety. This diagram shows the developing interest for IoT gadgets later on.

13.2   IoT Devices

IoT gadgets incorporate remote sensors, programming, activators and PC hardware. It is associated with an Internet-empowered item, which permits programmed information move between articles or people without human intercession. Its motivation is to work for individuals who originate from home, industry or business. Figure 13.2 y-axis shows the number of connected devices in billions and x-axis shows the years wise statistics of internet connected devices.

Figure 13.3 shows all the things connected to internet. Like smart homes which have internet connectivity, medical data such as heartbeat which again is being captured by smart watch which is an IoT device and so on.

1. Google Home Voice Controller

   It is a savvy IoT tool that empowers client to understand media, lights, alerts, volume control, indoor regulators and numerous different capacities with their voice.

   Highlights

   a) Google empowers the client to tune in to home media.
   b) Client controls the TV and the speakers.
   c) Can handle time and alert.
   d) It can remotely control volume and home light.
   e) This causes the client to design their day and complete things consequently.

2. Amazon Echo Plus Voice Controller

   It is a famous and trusted IoT device. It can play melodies, make calls, set clocks, inquire questions, check the climate,

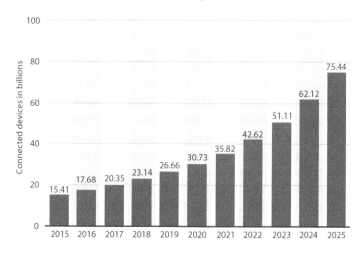

Figure 13.2 Market of IoT by 2025.

Figure 13.3 Futuristic IoT devices.

shopping records also, and oversee land and numerous different things.

Highlights

    a) Headphones Amazon Echo can play melodies by associating with outside speakers or earphones.

    b) Ability to send calls and messages by means of voice order.

    c) Amazon Echo has 6–7 receivers, great specialized highlights and commotion scratch-off. It can hear your voice every which way, in any event, when playing melodies.

    d) It has capacity of controlling custom brilliant apparatuses, including lights, attachments and that's only the tip of the iceberg.

3. Amazon Dash Button

    It is essentially a gadget associated with an Internet Entry and guarantees clients don't lose important family unit things, for example, Soda pops, nourishments, clinical and individual consideration, kids and recreational Creatures. The client must be an individual from Amazon Prime.

Highlights

    a) This permits the client to arrange items rapidly and doesn't need to remember the message and it additionally causes the client to decrease the item search time required.

b) The Amazon Dash button empowers the client to arrange from referred to brands, for example, Bounty, Tide, Cottonley, Glade, Chlorax.

c) It doesn't acknowledge the new request until the pre-request is finished until the client permits different requests.

d) It is a solid IoT item intended to make client life simpler.

4. August Doorbell Cam

It is an IoT gadget that lets you respond your entryway from anyplace or from a distant area. Checking your entryways routinely and in any event, finishing changes in your entrance.

Highlights

a) Doorbell can pair with all August shrewd locks permits guests' simple access to your home in your nonappearance.

b) HD gives clear, full-shading HD video even around evening time.

c) It will consistently open your entryway and snap the minutes paving the way to the dynamic notice.

d) Free 24 Free Video Recordings.

e) The process accompanies a quick establishment process.

5. August Smart Lock

This smart Lock has demonstrated as dependable IoT security Hardware. Permit the client to work their entryways from any location. This causes the shopper to get the criminals in your home far from the family.

Highlights

a) Entering permits the client to think about each and every individual who enters and enters your home.

b) It gives boundless advanced keys and there is no dread of the key being taken.

c) Provides reports on whether your entryway is appropriately shut.

d) It has a pleasant open auto highlight and naturally opens when the client moves toward the entryway.

e) Installation is simple and perfect with most standard chamber.

6. Kuri Mobile Robot

It is a home robot and is well known household robot. Planned explicitly for amusement, Kuri speaks with clients and has every day housekeeping meetings.

Highlights

a) Kuri has an intelligent sensor and a HD camera.

b) Includes Gest pregnancy mechanics and receivers.

c) The heart is the light of the heart and the speaker.

d) The show map incorporates coordinated sensors for show and drive frameworks.

7. Belkin WeMo Smart Light Switch

It encourages the client to deal with their home lights utilizing your voice on your cell phone or divider. These coordinated switches interfaces through your home's Wi-Fi system to provide distant access to lights—no participation or center point required.

Highlights

a) It accompanies cut on cuts and required spaces.

b) Easy to turn on/off, press anyplace to flip.

c) WiFi markers and night lights are accessible.

d) WiFi start abilities are accessible.

e) Installation. It is exceptionally quick with simple establishment.

8. Footbot Air Quality Monitor

Foot Boat is a solid IoT gadget that assists with estimating ecological contamination and improves air quality in homes, workplaces and indoor open spaces. This typically brings about an ideal outcome.

Highlights

a) It Clears air contamination.

b) It maintains accessible moistness and temperature.

c) A much needed refresher grows more concentration and vitality.

d) Ending backing to expand client's lifetime.

e) A quick and simple establishment process.

9. Flow Air Pollution Monitor

Stream air contamination is an astounding development in the IoT advertises. The Air Quality Tracker and its application show all the outcomes on a guide that tells the client that air quality is poor and grimy.

Highlights

a) The client educates the client concerning air quality.

b) The body accompanies a hardened steel body.

c) Functional is a utilitarian touch to its body.

d) R has great RGB LEDs.

e) User has an extraordinary client manage and simple establishment.

10. Nest Smoke Alarm

It is an extremely helpful IoT instrument. It lets your cell phone think, impart and alert you of any undesirable crises in your home. It tests itself.

Highlights
   a) The client can deal with this alert via telephone without extra equipment.
   b) And establishment is simple and can be arrangement with an iPhone, iPad or Android gadget.
   c) The item structure looks extraordinary.
   d) It contains shading blends like green, yellow, red to speak with the client relying upon the conditions.

13.3   Sensors and Actuators

IoT isn't only a procedure—however a blend of various profound situated strategies. IoT gadgets incorporate processors, sensors, activators, and handsets.

The sensor must store the data it gathers and act carefully to acquire valuable data from it. The sensor can be a phone which can quantify till it gives contribution about its current status (inside + climate). Actuator is a gadget utilized for environmental change, for example, air temperature control.

Working With IoT Frameworks
   I. Sensor and Actuator
   II. Communication
   III.Individuals and procedures

   I. Sensors and actuators—It give the world an advanced sensor framework. Area information incorporates GPS sensors that utilization the camera and amplifier, practically everyone's eyes and ears, just as body parts running from temperature changes to pulses to pressure changes. Figure 13.4 gives a case of utilizing different sensors and PCs
   II. Communication—Data collected by the sensors is digital and it is transmitted to networks. Below is a diagram showing the various methods used in the connection?
   III. People and processes—IoT devices are used to facilitate people following a specific process. So they play a very important role. These network inputs are able to be integrated in two way systems which combine information, community and systems for good verdict.

Figure 13.5 shows different ways in which people can connect to internet like through MAN, LAN, or through wifi etc. There are numerous

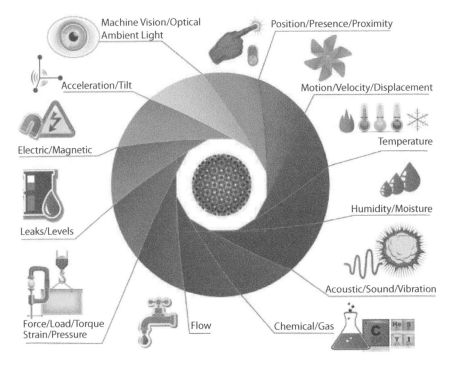

Figure 13.4 Examples where sensors and actuators are used (source: https://s3.amazonaws. com/postscapes/IoT-Harbor-Postscapes-Infographic.pdf).

difficulties with information assortment, the board, correspondence and information handling. Figure 13.6 shows IoT devices require Individuals and Procedures in which they can communicate like through mobile apps connectivity can established similarly through remote monitoring a connection can be established between individuals. These IoT gadgets gather a lot of data and need to figure out what information is fitting for their circumstance, procedure or store and the degree of correspondence required. Capacity, pre-preparing and information handling should be possible at a remote server or system edge. Figure 13.7 shows a case of how information streams from sensors to actuators.

Sensors, activators, process servers, and correspondence systems structure the fundamental foundation of the IoT system. Now and again, middleware requires some innovation. Middleware is programming that connects the working framework or database and applications, particularly over the system. Middleware can be utilized to interface and deal with all private IoT gadgets.

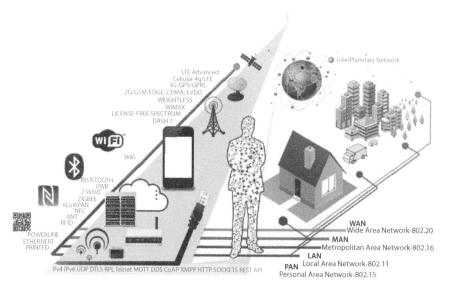

Figure 13.5 Ways of connecting through web for data sharing.

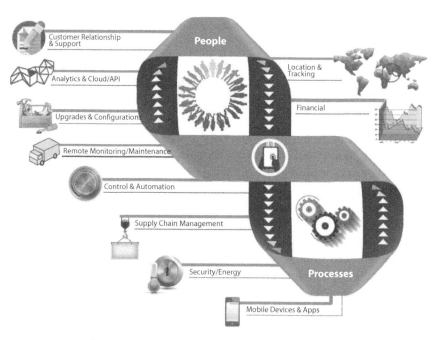

Figure 13.6 People and processes.

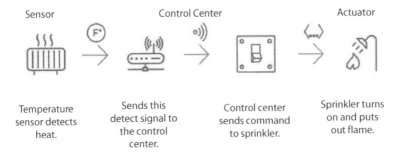

Sensor   Control Center   Actuator

| Temperature sensor detects heat. | Sends this detect signal to the control center. | Control center sends command to sprinkler. | Sprinkler turns on and puts out flame. |

Figure 13.7 Sensor to actuator flow.

Construction of the IoT-System

There is certifiably not a solitary agreement on IoT engineering, which is generally acknowledged. Various scientists have proposed various layers. The accompanying figure shows the various layers of the specialists proposed, some calling it three-advance and some more, and now called five layers in a day.

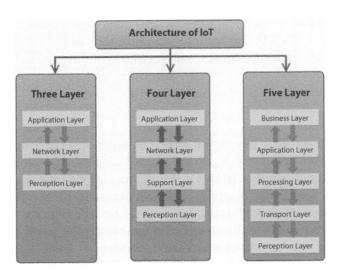

Figure 13.8 Architecture of IoT systems.

The most essential structure is the three-dimensional structure [32]. Figure 13.8 shows that popularly there are three types of architecture for IoT. Three-layer, Four-layer and Five-layer architectures. One layer comprises of remote sensors and finders. The subsequent layer incorporates the sensor information joining framework and simple to-advanced information trade. In Layer 3, data is given or used to improve the framework [32].

Layer 1: A Layer of Mindfulness
Sensors gather information from the earth and convert it into valuable information. The IoT part is quickly developing into mechanical camera frameworks, water level enhancements, home voice controllers, air quality sensors, child observing hardware and the sky is the limit from there. These instruments gather client information including login time, rate and use hours, area insights, etc. Since these gadgets make torrential slide of information, it is essential to process a few information rapidly, i.e., time-delicate information—hazard discovery, quick accident measurements, abrupt terminations, etc.

Layer 2: Network
The information gathered by sensors or activators is crude. This information must be gathered and changed over into computerized radio for use by different clients. To do this information handling, it is critical to utilize an information procurement framework (DAS or DAQ). Information assortment is a sign examining process that estimates true states of being and changes over examples from advanced numerical reproduction to PC reenactment. The DAS sensor interfaces with the system, associates with the yield, and performs simple to-advanced transformation. Web Gateway gets incorporated computerized information and steering over Wi-Fi, wired LAN or the Internet in consistent Phase 3 procedures.

Layer 3: Display
This layer is applied to give explicit application administrations to the client. At the point when information is gathered, cleaned and tried, data can be added to the server for investigation and use in new items and administrations.

Three-dimensional blueprint characterizes state of the Internet of Things, however research is regularly lacking for study since it centers on the positive parts of the Internet of Things. Mainly the layers can be put together in three categories which are as follows:

(i) Transmission layer transmits from tangible layer to tactile layer and systems like RFID, NFC etc.
(ii) The middleware layer stores, investigates and form enormous volumes of data from the transport division. It gives diverse application benefits [8] in the subordinate layers. It uses much advancement like information, disseminated computing and big information modules.

(iii) The business layer covers the whole structure, together with plans of action, applications and advantages, and buyer security. The above structure is the fundamental structure of the establishment. Shrewd IoT is another kind of engineering dependent on cloud administrations for doors.

13.4   Cloud and Haze-Based Engineering

In certain elements of the layer, information preparing is for the most part disguised by PCs in the cloud. Such a haze of cloud organization puts the cloud at the middle, the applications at the top and the insight arrange at the base [32]. Distributed computing [7] is protected on the grounds that it gives extraordinary adaptability and heartiness. Engineers can offer their own stockpiling instruments, programming apparatuses, information mining, AI devices and cloud-based representation devices.

As of late, there has been another advancement of framework design, to be specific mist registering [27–29], in which sensors is information handling and examination. The arrangement of haze [30] gives a particular pathway as appeared in Figure 13.9, which incorporates checking, stacking, stockpiling and assurance among first and last layers. Advancement layer empowers separating, preparing and examination of sensor data. Security layer empowers interpretation and assures information honesty and privacy. Checking and streamlining happens at the edge of the system prior to information sent to the cloud. Five-layered design is ordinarily utilized for reference in IoT.

Various Types of Sensors

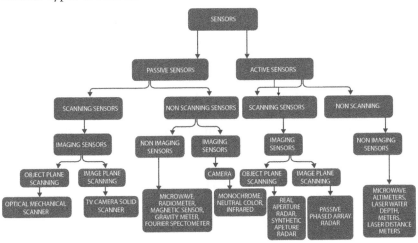

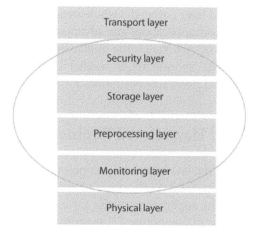

Figure 13.9 Haze architecture for smart IoT gateway.

Figure: Broad categories of sensors.

All IoT frameworks must have at least one sensors to gather information from the earth, person. IoT sensors are littler in size, more affordable, and utilize substantially less force. They can be decreased by highlights, for example, battery limit and development ease. Below I have explained different types of sensors used in present era.

   I. Versatile-Based Cell Sensors

It has versatile, forward looking and changed sensors. With the expanding ubiquity of cell phones in the populace, scientists are keen on creating shrewd IoT arrangements utilizing cell phones because of interior sensors [33, 34]. Different sensors stand apart inside current cell phones.

(1) The accelerometer controls the speed and quickening of the cell phone. It generally gauges three parts of the cell phone's development. There are a few kinds of accelerometers [35]. On a mechanical accelerometer, we have a quake sensor in the lodging, which is associated with the lodging by a spring by tow. Information models caught by the accelerometer can be utilized to decide the client's physical action, for example, running, strolling and biking.

(2) Accurate telephone direction is acquired from the whirligi g. Strength is estimated utilizing variable change when the seismic weight is uprooted.

(3) Cameras and receivers are the most remarkable sensors since they catch visual and sound data, which can be broke down and prepared to acquire an assortment of substance data.

(4) The zoomagometer distinguishes the attractive field. It very well may be utilized as advancement in applications to identify the nearest metal.

(5) GPS (Global Positioning System) phone [31], which is significant data for savvy applications. This position is acquired utilizing the trinity standard [36]. Separation is estimated with at least three satellites (or convenient A-GPS portable towers) and the connections are secured.

(6) Light sensor gets most extreme accessible light. It tends to be utilized to set the screen brilliance and different applications where a particular move must be made dependent on the light power accessible like lights in the room can be controlled.

(7) Proximity Sensor utilizes Infrared (IR) LED [25] that discharges radiation. In view of the time distinction, we can figure the separation. For instance, we can utilize it to distinguish that the telephone is near the face when talking.

Different cell phones, for example, the Samsung S4, incorporate a thermometer, gauge and dampness sensor to quantify temperature, environmental weight and mugginess. The application likewise works with speedy questions to tell understudies about their sentiments. This data is helpful for evaluating feelings of anxiety, public activity, conduct, and understudies' trying practices.

Another application made by McClernan and Chaudhry [37] is that content-related data is utilized, for example, the nearness, area, and related exercises of the client's smoker. Sensors give data identified with client development, position, visual pictures and surrounding sounds. Outline Smartphone sensors are utilized for an assortment of human practices (see Ref. [38]) and to improve human health.

II. Therapeutic Sensors

The Internet of Things is extremely helpful for social insurance applications. We can utilize sensors, which can quantify and screen different clinical boundaries in the human body [39]. These projects can screen understanding wellbeing while in or out of the clinic. Afterward, they can give continuous criticism to the specialist, family members or patient. McGrath and Scaniel [40] depict in detail the different ideas that the body wears to screen human wellbeing. Figure 13.10 smart watches and fitness tracker which contain sensors is a very good example of IoT device.

Figure 13.11 is showing a futuristic IoT gadget which can be embedded in skin. There are many detecting gadgets accessible available. They are furnished with clinical sensors that can quantify different boundaries, for example, pulse, beat rate, circulatory strain, internal heat level, and respiratory

Figure 13.10 Smart watches and fitness trackers (source: https://www.pebble.com/).

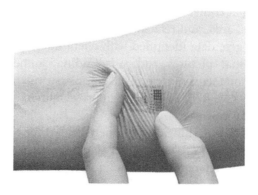

Figure 13.11 Embedded skin patches (source: MC10 electronics).

rate and glucose levels [41]. The ensemble incorporates shrewd watches, scarves, monitor clasps and savvy garments.

Another epic IoT gadget is to screen skin cuts that are promising. Watchman lines resemble tattoos. They are anything but difficult to pull and utilize and exceptionally economical. These Patients can wear these dots foe some days so that significant wellbeing boundaries can be consistently observed [42]. These stains can be applied like any tattoo to the skin as appeared in Figure 13.5.

For instance, the pulse relies upon the specific circumstance. On the off chance that it is, we can't break the unpredictable heartbeat. In this manner, we have to consolidate information from various sensors for legitimate compliance. Figure 13.12 shows an IoT gadget which is called a Brain sensing headband with embedded neuro sensors.

III. Neural Sensors

It is conceivable to comprehend the signals in the mind, give a condition of the cerebrum, and train us for better consideration and core interest. This is known as neuro feedback [43].

Innovation used to contemplate mind signals called EEG (Electroencephalography). The neurons in the mind impart by electronic means and make an electronic field that can be estimated as of the exterior relying upon the waves. The cerebrum effect can be isolated into alpha, beta, gamma,

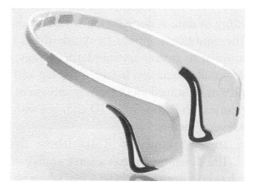

Figure 13.12 Brain sensing headband with embedded neuro sensors (source: http://www.choosemuse.com).

theta, and delta waves relying on the recurrence. The neuro feedback may be procured continuously and can be utilized to prepare the mind to center, focus on things better, oversee pressure, and have a superior mental life.

IV. Common and Ecological Sensors

Common sensors are utilized to catch boundaries at the interface, for example, temperature, moistness, pressure, water contamination and air contamination. Temperature and weight boundaries may be projected with a gauge. Quality of air may be estimated by sensors that identify the nearness of significant components noticeable all around (see Shekhar *et al.* [44]).

Substance sensors are utilized to identify synthetic and organic materials. These sensors have a location component and a transducer. E-nasal and e-language are strategies used to see synthetic compounds dependent on smell and taste, individually [45]. There is an assortment of substance sensors in the e-nose and e-tongue, which are perfect with test acknowledgment programming. Sensors inside the nose of the nose and tongue produce complex information, which would then be able to be examined by design acknowledgment to decide the reason.

These sensors can be utilized to screen contamination levels in shrewd urban areas, [1] and to screen quality of food in savvy kitchens, eatables examination and horticultural items during the acquisition procedure.

V. Radio Frequency ID Identification (RFID)

It is an analytic method where the RFID tag (little radio wire chip) conveys the information that is perused by the RFID. Transmitting of data is done by tag which sends it by radio waves. The equivalent applies to standardized tag innovation. Dissimilar to customary standardized tags, this doesn't require a visual association between the tag and the understudy, and can be stayed away from in any event, when performing duties. The scope of RFID changes with size. It can go up to several meters.

There are two kinds of RFID labels: dynamic and detached. The dynamic tag has a force source and the dormant tag has no force source. Detached labels attract vitality to the electromagnetic waves delivered by the peruser and are in this way less expensive and longer [47, 48].

RFID innovation is utilized in a wide assortment of utilizations, including gracefully chain the executives, get to control, verification, and item following. RFID is added to the item to follow the tag, and the peruser needs to record its quality as the article goes through it. Along these lines, object development can be followed and RFID goes about as an internet searcher for shrewd items.

Chips which are small in size are put in the front of the vehicle. At the point when the vehicle arrives at the barrel of the understudy, it peruses the marker information and decides if it is an approved vehicle. RFID cards are given to people, recognized by the RFID pursuer, and given access in like manner

Kinds of Actuators

I. Pressure Driven Actuator

The pressure driven actuator comprises of a chamber or channel that utilizes water driven capacity to perform mechanical activity. Mechanical development is influenced by line, revolution, or swaying. A water-driven actuator creates a lot of vitality, since the liquid is for all intents and purposes compressible. The recovery of this technique is its restricted speed.

II. Pneumatic Actuator

Pneumatic actuators permit more ca pacity to be produced by little weight changes. A pneumatic actuator changes over vacuum or packed aviation based armed forces into high weight in vertical or rotational movement. Air power is required with the fundamental motor control, since it can react immediately when beginning and halting, so there is no compelling reason to store the force source when put away in activity. Valves for the most part utilize this power to move wind stream layers to influence valve stream.

III. Electric Actuator

The circuit repairman can give power/torque to enactment from multiple points of view. Electronic hardware is utilized to drive the motor that changes over the electric engine to engine torque. Another alternative is the electro-water powered actuator, where the electric engine is consistently on the main edge, yet it additionally gives a light to the utilization of the pressure driven Samuel, which is utilized to move initiation capacity to diesel motors/hydrodynamics Machines.

IV. Turned and Minimized Polymer or Overly Wound Polymer Actuator

This actuator is a coordinated polymer that can be changed over into electrical vitality. [Expert] The TCP master resembles a battling spring. TCP activators are generally made of silver-covered nylon. TCP activator can likewise be produced using other electrical coat, for example, gold. The TCP actuator must be stacked to keep the muscles flexible.

V. Warm or Attractive Actuator

Actuators can be separated by utilizing warm or attractive powers in strong state materials utilized in business applications. Warm work can be incited by warmth or warmth by the Joule impact and is minimized, lightweight, conservative and high quality. Activators utilize molded memory, for example, shape-memory combinations (SMAs) or attractive shape-memory amalgams (MSMAs).

VI. Mechanical Actuators

A mechanical machine attempts to make movement by turning a particular kind of movement, for example, a rotational movement, into another sort of line movement. The impact of these actuators relies upon the blend of apparatuses and rails or auxiliary components, for example, pulleys and chains.

VII. Delicate 3D Actuators

Embellishment, freestyle solidifying and veil lithography. In any case, these procedures require a more extended time span to accomplish hand-held devices, post-preparing/get together and development on the grasp. To stay away from the across the board and tedious parts of momentum development forms, analysts have discovered a proper creation strategy for the fruitful combination of delicate activators. In this manner, concentrated delicate tissue frameworks that can be actualized in one stage through quick prototyping methods, for example, 3D printing are utilized to lessen the hole between the structure and usage of delicate activators, making the procedure quicker, more affordable and simpler.

For instance, we may consider a keen home framework that has numerous sensors and activators. Activators are utilized for cautions or alerts and they additionally control the temperature of the home (through the indoor regulator). A case of round dissemination is utilized to control/lock entryways, turn on/off light/other electronic gadgets, and be controlled remotely.

Subsequent to covering practically a wide range of sensors and actuators, it will be fascinating to perceive how these sensors and actuators are utilized when coordinating IoT with blockchain.

13.5 Blockchain and IoT

Blockchain is a greater arrangement than the Internet. Join blockchain and IoT and you have two incredible arrangements on the Internet that require the each other for some reasons. Blockchain is structured as the reason for applications including exchanges and interchanges. This may incorporate shrewd agreements (savvy customer contracts are consequently produced when a particular rule is reached, for instance contingent upon item or ecological conditions) or other a

A. Engineering can be divided into six unique segments:
1. Wireless Sensor Networks: A remote sensor arrange is a correspondence organize that permits confined interchanges to applications with low force and light prerequisites. Likewise, IoT gadgets having a place with the remote sensor organize are restricted in their ability for reconciliation, memory, and/or power accessibility. One of the prerequisites of the engineering is that all gadgets should be remarkably distinguished in the blockchain arrange. Open key generators can give a reasonable answer for a difficult that produces huge quantities of irregular numbers that are satisfactory. Ordinarily, utilizing existing IoT cryptographic innovation would consequently make an open key for all gadgets. Along these lines, implementing encryption will guarantee various identifiers. Actually, current IoT correspondence standards, for example, CoAP [12] as of now bolster secure channels through DTLS [13].
2. Managers: An administrator is the substance liable for dealing with the entrance control consents for a lot of IoT gadgets. As a rule, administrators are viewed as lightweight

noses in our framework. Lightweights don't store blockchain data or secure blockchain exchanges as diggers do. Thus, discouraged gadgets can become directors in our framework without speaking to a snag to their Hardware boycott. What's more, executives utilizing this strategy don't should be continually associated with the blockchain arrange, which assists with decreasing their Hardware assets. Any association can be enlisted as a chief. Nonetheless, gadgets enrolled as IoT gadgets must be enlisted under the administrator's control. Moreover, all IoT gadgets enrolled in the framework must be at any rate one enlisted director. In addition, nobody would have the option to deal with the apparatus. An enrolled IoT gadget can be possessed by various chiefs simultaneously. After enlistment of the IoT administration under the administration of a supervisor, executives can determine certain entrance control consents.

3. Agent Node: The specialist is a blockchain-explicit property engineer answerable for the main portion of a keen agreement in our framework. The specialist claims the shrewd agreement during the lifetime of the entrance control framework. When a keen agreement has been gotten on the blockchain organize, the specialist hub gets a location showing the shrewd agreement inside the blockchain arrange. So as to connect with a savvy contract, all hubs in the blockchain organize need to realize that keen agreement address.

4. Smart Agreement: The entrance control framework is administered by the capacities characterized in one savvy contract. This savvy contract is one of a kind and can't be expelled from the framework. In this manner, all exercises permitted in the entrance the executive's framework are characterized in the savvy contract and are activated by blockchain exchanges. When the exchange is started through the exchange, diggers will keep the subtleties of the exchange accessible around the world. The keen agreement and its activ ity are likewise accessible around the world. Furthermore, it ought to be noticed that directors are the main associations with the capacity to counsel a brilliant agreement to characterize new approaches in the framework.

5. Blockchain Network: A blockchain system can be a private square or it very well may be an open blockchain box. Private blockchains are those that can be perused by

anybody however are composed distinctly by a private area. The diggers in the system help keep the system secure and stable by permitting exchanges and putting away duplicates of the blockchain. Hubs can utilize the blockchain interface to store and access worldwide access control strategy for explicit gadgets. This data is completely usable and is carefully designed.

6. Hub Management: IoT gadgets are not part of the blockchain organize because of seriously handicapped issue as far as CPU, memory and battery. That impediment limits IoT gadgets to being a piece of a blockchain arrange. Being a piece of a blockchain organize implies keeping a duplicate of your blockchain and track of system occasions. In spite of the fact that there are lightweight arrangements that don't store all blockchain data set up and depend on different hubs [14], those basic arrangements despite everything beat most of IoT gadgets. Accordingly, in design it is desirable over utilize a hub called the executives center point. An administration place is a method of deciphering data inserted in CoAP messages by IoT gadgets into JSON-RPC messages comprehended by the blockchain hub. The administration place is legitimately associated with the blockchain hub, for instance, a gap. Numerous sensor systems can be associated with a center point control hub for systems administration destinations and different center point the executives locales can be associated with the equivalent blockchain hub. IoT gadgets will have the option to demand get to data from the square utilizing the administration center point. Center administration areas can't be necessary gadgets. Such gadgets require superior to have the option to process numerous applications all the while from IoT gadgets. In the least complex situation where verification isn't required, any IoT gadget will have the option to associate with any control point straightforwardly and get to the blockchain arrange. In any case, as a rule get to control is required. In such a case, IoT gadgets will have the option to interface with explicit administration centers. After the IoT gadget is introduced on the framework, the area administrator for that device should advise the particular authoritative center hub about the validation of that thing.

IoT is an alluring advancement program that offers boundless advantages, yet there are numerous downsides to the current IoT engineering. The table presents a correlation among blockchain and IoT. It has boundless advantages and receiving an IoT-empowered methodology can take care of numerous issues particularly security. Table 13.1 shows the difference between the two technologies Blockchain and IoT on the basis of various parameters mentioned.

The divided, free, and trusting blockchain capacities make it a suitable alternative for the establishment of IoT arrangements. IoT security is about something other than ensuring touchy information. Also, blockchain innovation is viewed as the best answer for explaining protection and trust issues in IoT. It very well may be utilized to follow millions of gadgets, to authorize exchange and correspondence among gadgets which takes into deliberation critical reserve finances for industry engineers [18].

In IoT organize; blockchain can store a predictable record of savvy gadgets. This component empowers programmed activity of keen gadgets without the need of brought together specialists [19]. Along these lines, blockchain will open a progression of IoT conditions that were troublesome, or even difficult to execute without them. One of the energizing capacities

Table 13.1 Difference between blockchain and IoT.

Basis	Blockchain	IoT
Organization formation	Not centralized	Centralized
Resources	Resources are consumed to the fullest	Resource restricted
Latency	Block Mining is time consuming	Demands low latency
Scalability	large networks scale poorly.	contains large number of devices
Bandwidth	High bandwidth consumption	IoT devices have limited bandwidth and resources
Security	Has better security	Security is one of the biggest challenges of IoT.
Privacy	Ensures the privacy of participating nodes	Lack of privacy

of blockchain is the capacity to control a record with exact, dependable cut-off points on all exchanges that happen on a system.

Advantages of Blockchain and IoT

1. Open: All members can see all the exercises and all the squares as every member has their own content. The substance of that action is secured by the private key of the member [16], so despite the fact that all members can see it, they are ensured. IoT is an amazing framework where every single associated gadget can share information together and simultaneously secure clients' protection.

2. Grouping of positions: Most members must tie down an exchange to endorse it and supplement it with a circulated record. No single authority can affirm an exchange or set explicit guidelines for the exchange. Enormous numbers of trust passages are there since the majority of the system members need to agree for the exchange [21].

3. Steadiness: Each area has its own duplicate of the record containing everything that is done on the system. Irrespective of one hub being confined, the blockchain will be kept by other hubs also [22]. Duplicacy of information at every point in the IoT will upgrade data sharing prerequisites.

4. Security: Blockchain can possibly give a protected system over questionable gatherings that are required in IoT for different gadgets and huge articles [11].

5. Speed: Blockchain exchanges are dispersed over the system in minutes and will be prepared whenever for the duration of the day [15].

6. Cost investment funds: Existing planning are increasingly expensive because of great foundation and support costs related with unified growth, vast homesteads, and transmit communications hardware.

7. Inaction: Having a reliable record is one of the key advantages of blockchain modernization. Adjustments in the conveyance in group must be confirmed by the recurrence of areas. As a result, the swap over can't be altered successfully [12]. Trustworthy record for IoT information will build security and protection which are the greatest difficulties for this innovation and for every single new innovation.

8. Secrecy: Purchasers and dealers utilize mysterious and exceptional location numbers that keep their character hidden.

The component has been usually censured as it is expanding the utilization of digital forms of money in unlawful online markets. Although, it may be viewed as a preferred position when utilized for different motives, for example, constituent self-governing foundations [13, 19].

There is no uncertainty that incorporating blockchain will have numerous rewards. Blockchain modernization is definitely not a total model with its blemishes and problems, these problems are stated below:

1. Scale: Scalability issues on the blockchain can prompt, indistinct over the ultimate fortune of digital currency. Scale of blockchain is weakening as the quantity of hubs in the system increases. Basic issue is as IoT systems are depend upon to contain an enormous number of hubs [21].

2. Vitality: Efficiency and frameworks contain various types of gadgets with all in all different figuring abilities, not all will have the option to utilize similar calculations at the necessary speed [14, 20].

3. Capacity: Primary advantages of blockchain are requirement of focal server to store exchanges and the IDs of gadgets, though the record has to be place away on the hubs themselves [24]. The disseminated record will increment in size as time passes by and the expanding number of areas.

4. Absence of abilities: Innovation in blockchain is new. Hardly any persons have good amount of information and abilities about blockchain, banking in particular. In some foundations, there is a lack of understanding of blockchain functions [6].

5. Legitimate and Collaboration: ability to interface various persons from a variety of nations without needing a lawful code, a main aspect for designers and specialist co-ops. The test will be an important edge to receiving blockchain for some organizations and applications [26].

6. Naming and Acquisition: Blockchain innovation isn't intended for IoT, suggesting that hubs were not planned to be available to one another on the organization. The form is a Bitcoin [9] application anywhere the IP locations of other "senders" are inserted inside the Bitcoin client and are utilized by destinations to make a system topography. In IoT

edge registering comes in the picture which has been examined beneath.

13.6 Edge Computing

Expansion of IoT and across the board infiltration of remote system, amount of edge gadgets and created information has developed quickly. According to International Data Corporation (IDC) [5], universal information will land at 200 zettabytes (ZB), and 80% of IoT information will be equipped at the system edge by 2025. There is another estimate by DC which states 150 billion gadgets will be associated all about by 2025. For these circumstances, information mode based on cloud isn't productive enough to deal with edge-created data. Transfers all the information is made by a unified model to the cloud server farm through the system and sends its gigantic capacity to take care of PC issues and keep funds, which provide administrations through cloud to produce financial advantages though, the usual distributed computing has a few defects.

1. Latency: Applications in IoT condition have greater constant pre requisites. In a dispersed representation, application sends information to a server farm and takes input, which builds the foundation. For example, fast vehicles require fraction of second to reaction time.
2. Bandwidth: Moving a lot of information conveyed by edge gadgets to the cloud progressively will be very beneficial for transmission of information. For instance, excess of information is being delivered by Boeing 787; somewhat the transferring speed among the plane and the satellite is deficient to help continuous arrangement [2].
3. Availability: As most Internet administrations are conveyed to the cloud, access through organization is a usual activity now days. For instance, mobiles acquainted with voice-managements, Siri, baffled if the management is unapproachable. The only way conduct a major test for cloud specialist co-ops to keep the guarantee of 24 × 7.
4. Power: Data focuses utilize a great deal of strength. According to Sverdlik [1], server commenced vitality exploitation in the US which stated an increase of 4% by 2020.

5. Security and Privacy: Information on planning a huge number of homes is firmly connected to client lives. For instance, installed cameras at homes send out video information from house to cloud will expand the danger of getting to clients' personal information. Following the accomplishment of the General Data Protection Regulation (GDPR) [4], protection of information and issues has got consecutively significant for distributed computing organizations.

These difficulties have moved to peak, needing the handling of data in business. Since 2014 quick improvement was taking place with the point of decreasing current expenses and capacity of broadcasting, taking toward the foremost limitation of cloud server, convenience expanded and confirming of data security. Figure 13.13 shows a three layered view of how cloud is also connected to edge computing [3], first layer contain the cloud services and data centres, second layer contain edge or process and third layer contains the IoT devices.

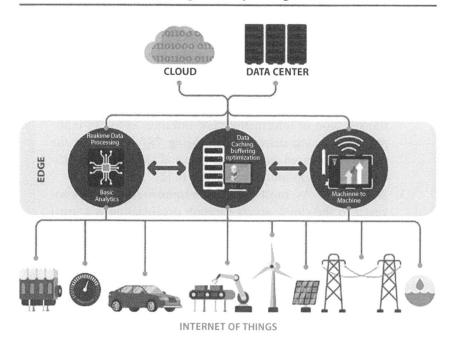

Figure 13.13 Relationship of cloud computing and IoT (source: https://innovationatwork. ieee.org/real-life-edge-computing-use-cases/).

A. Edge Computing Basics

1. Interpretation: Edge PC is another worldview where edge infor-mation administrations are on the net, moving toward the rise of IoT. Registering edge leads to the empowering innovations for the advantage of cloud management for IoT services.

   The edge of the Internet is a good concept. For instance self-driving and human services are at a bigger competence. It is good for contravention, organizing and dispersal bandwidth keen sensor data from gadget.

2. Functions: The Edge PC has two communicates: one from gadget to cloud (upstream) and the other from cloud to gadget (downstream). Gadgets are considered to be data makers. Edge readies the personal computer does the data piling, funds, makes ready, just as disseminating solicita-tions and interpretation administrations from cloud to cli-ent. Functionality of edge is to satisfy the need properly like safety, firm quality and safety insurance.

3. Three-Tier Edge Computer Model: By breaking down the particular states of a PC structure, a three level model: cloud, edge and IoT. The basic level is the IoT, drones, sensors, and home gadgets and the modern Internet. Diverse association conventions are used to interface the IoT with the next stage, the edge. For instance, edge with a flexible height by way of 4G, sensors at home can converse all the way through the home port with the help of Wi-Fi. Consideration of IoT and edges will in general have lower power utilization attributes and shorter separations, whereas detachments between edge and cloud have higher yield and important pace. Ethernet and 5G are the preferential associated choices among edge and cloud. Figure 13.14 shows a three-tier edge computing model where the tree tires are IoT, edge and cloud.

4. Edge Versus Cloud: Edge processing and distributed comput-ing are not connections that were supplement both. The fame of amazing gadgets and the fast improvement of present day virtualization and cloud innovation have carried PC pressure to the edge, enlightening the concept of distributed comput-ing. Edge needs registering authority and unusual help for the distributed computing, and it requires a PC model to process huge data. A good amount of information is geared up at the edge of the association, though it's not stacked into the cloud, which load on the transmission capacity organize and the

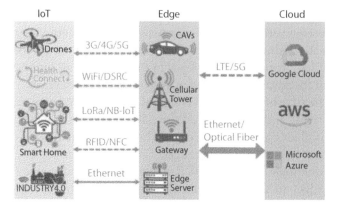

Figure 13.14 Three tier edge computing model.

force utilization of the server. Management of information by information creator doesn't require the responsiveness of the distributed computing place all the way through the business, which creates the foundation and to improve the administration's response abilities. Lastly PC stores the secret data of client's apprehensive gadgets instead of downloading them, controlling the threat of information exploitation and ensuring defense and protection.

13.7 Contextual Analyses

Blockchain empowers IoT gadgets to improve security and convey lucidity of thoughts. According to IDC, 25% of IoT shipments allowing blockchain-based arrangements by [17] 2020. Blockchain gives a different domain to IoT gadget and its application. Financial institutions, for instance Deutsche Bank, and HSBC who are using blockchain innovation.

IoT is bringing up many business chances to drive wonderful options. Nowadays gadgets are furnished with sensors, transferring the information to cloud. Combining these innovations can make the frameworks work better. Figure 13.15 name change to Blockchain Improving the Golden state food supply chain and logistics, the figure shows that by using Blockchain and IoT devices at shipping and transporting it can save lots and lots of time.

Here are a couple of genuine contextual analyses of Blockchain Enterprise's utilization of how incorporating IoT with Blockchain is putting a colossal effect on business examples of which explained below:

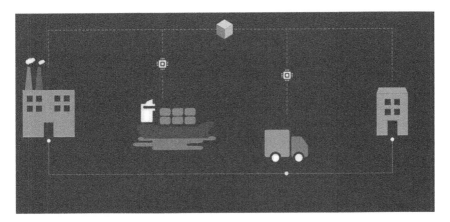

Figure 13.15 Golden state food disrupting supply chain and logistics.

1. Supply Chain and Logistics—The worldwide gracefully chain incorporates different associates like virtual provider and switches, etc., building it tough for beginning to end conveyance delays have been the supreme test.

   These way businesses are making IoT-empowered vehicles to follow travel all through the release process. Because of limitations on chain, IoT and Blockchain combined can help increased reliability. Sensor information is placed away on the blockchain.

   Brilliant State Foods (GSF) is a multidisciplinary provider, prominent for creating food items. Helping 150,000 cafés, GSF focuses on making and delivering the products to top notch items.

   GSF is working with IBM to improve business forms utilizing Blockchain and IoT. Confidential information on the blockchain guarantees that issues are tended to and detailed naturally before making severe problems. It is helping GSF to build a strange, secure and simple record, by diverse partners to improve responsibility and straightforwardness.

   A broad industry issue in the shipment of merchandise is the absence of correspondence that influences transporting era. Blockchain, by its ability to give shared information, is the simplest answer for the trouble. The thought is to maintain the communications sent to the Smart Log blockchain, track them using IoT, and make tasks using great agreements, in this way moving great demand and association to the business. Figure 13.16 shows the difference between smartlog (a Blockchain and IoT based platform) and previous logging system.

Six associations from four distinct nations are as of now dealing with the task. Here is an instance where IoT and blockchain shows that the numerous associations are joining to extend innovation.

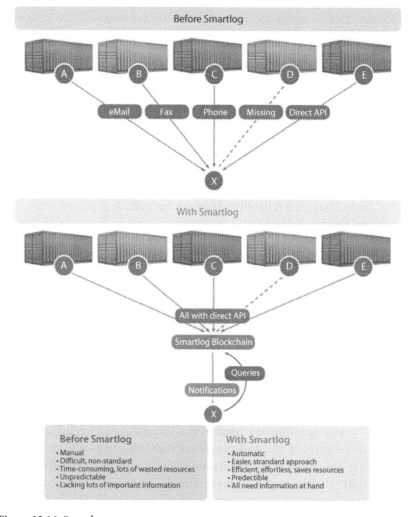

Figure 13.16 Smartlog.

1. Automotive Industry

   Figure 13.17 shows how smart parking can be introduced by using a Blockchain and IoT based platform Netobjex. Digitization is accessible nowadays as an important need. Automobile industry uses IoT-equipped sensors to grow vehicles. Connecting IoT-powered vehicles with an all-inclusive system permits numerous clients to trade significant data efficiently. The automobile industry is one of the vibrant instances of blockchain and IoT where incorporated innovation can upset the installment of automatic vehicles and automatic traffic control.

   NetObjex has indicated a shrewd arrangement utilizing IoT and blockchain. The amalgamation brings a way of finding parking space and stores installments utilizing crypto wallets. IoT sensors outline the expenditure, and charge happens rightfully of the crypto wallet.

2. Shrewd Homes

   Shrewd IoT-empowered gadgets assume a significant job in our lives. Blockchain and IoT creates house defense framework to be remotely overseen on a mobile phone. Integrated way of trading data made by IoT gadgets doesn't have security evaluations and information possession. Blockchain can lift smart level home by explaining security issues and evacuating the framework that has been introduced inside.

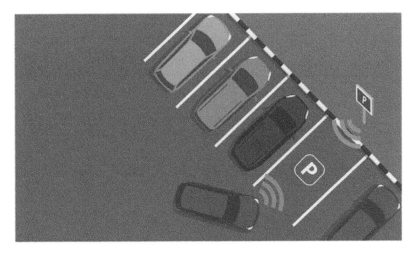

Figure 13.17 Reshaping of the automotive industry using NetObjex.

Telstra is attempting to improve the security of homes. Telstra, Australian media broadcast, and media association intend savvy home measures. Blockchain and biometric security have been measured to guarantee that nobody can bargain the data caught on shrewd gadgets.

Applications like face and voice recognition and biometric put away to assure security. After the information is placed on blockchain, it can't be modified and it is only shown to the ideal individual. Figure 13.18 shows how Transformation of Sharing Economy business is done by slock-it (a Blockchain based platform).

3. Financial Sharing

Financial sharing has become a generally acknowledged idea approximately throughout the world. To acquire more cash via flawlessly sharing assets blockchain can be helpful.

Airbnb is utilizing it directly with the help of IoT and Blockchain. Novelty of blockchain is used to share the highlights or capacities of IoT gadgets.

They intend to build up the Universal Sharing Network (USN) to make a safe online market for gadgets. USN is

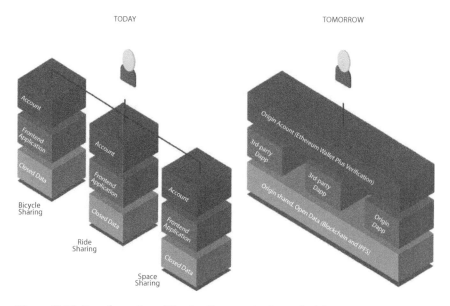

Figure 13.18 Transformation of Sharing Economy business-slock it.

providing everything on lease or shared or sold firmly with no responsibility of middle people.

Bright agreements make sure of the confidentiality of information and straightforwardness by controlling access to data.

4. Drug Store Sector

The account of fake meds in the field of medication is increasing every day. Concoction industry is in charge for manufacturing and delivering of drugs so following a total medication venture is hard. Blockchain innovation can help screen the conveyance of medications from their source to the objective.

Figure 13.19 shows how Mediledger has changed pharma industry by introducing Blockchain. Mediledger is one who is utilizing IoT and blockchain, expected to follow the reasonable distinction in professionally approved medications. The data put away on a dispersed record is usual, available for makers, wholesalers, and clientele engaged with the conversion line.

5. Horticulture

Growing various nourishments for an expanding populace while limiting regular impressions and guaranteeing lucidity over the flexibly chain is fundamental for high consumer loyalty.

Blockchain amalgamation with IoT can possibly reshape the food chain industry. With the help of IoT sensors on

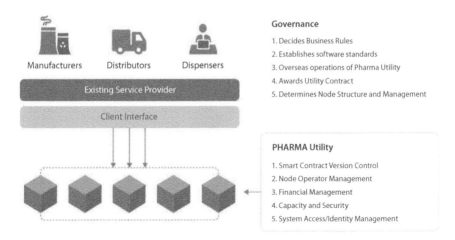

Figure 13.19 Game changer of pharmacy industry—Mediledger.

homesteads which are sending their information straight-forwardly to blockers it can help improve the natural pecking order undeniably.

Figure 13.20 shows how Pavo has changed the outlook of thr agriculture industry by introducing Blockchain. Pavo uses IoT and blockchain that brings matchless truth. IoT collects information and cultivated equipment gadget is put away in squares. Additionally, the Pavo permits ranchers to shift crops through forward agreements that can keep ranchers from sitting tight for installment after reap.

6. Radiological dosimetry with the IoT Blockchain
   Clinitraq is a medicinal services organization at present building up a dosimeter utilizing the Net Objex IoT-Blockchain Platform. They identify the degree of radiation offered to it. Presently it may take 40–60 days to give results. Ultimate advantage to persons working in wellbeing or science as it dispenses with the danger of radiation.

7. Blockchain Biometrics
   Australian telecom organization Telstra utilizes blockchain combined with IoT to make its home safe and sound. Telstra is providing secure system by transferring biometrics or face recognition.

8. Improves proficiency via robotizing planning
   Van Dorp is a property the executive's organization (FC) that affirms 20,000 resources in Netherlands. The protection of air, lighting and warming frameworks is done by the organization. Time Series utilizes transformations of Artificial

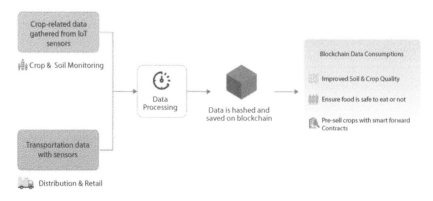

Figure 13.20 Transformation of agriculture—Pavo.

Intelligence and Mendix to provide undertaking the board planning.

IoT planners are presently ready to follow how various frameworks are moving all through their structure and inform Van Dorp expert is there. Time Series automated changing the planning option along with Van Dorp was there to fabricate the proficiency of altering by 30%.

9. Honey bee Foods on the IoT Blockchain
   The organization is at present taking a view at the utilization of blockchain. Costa will stamp vessels and fish to follow them by way of IoT. The association will perform assembling an application utilizing IoT and blockchain, for synchronization among fishers.

10. Blockchain and IoT to help the Palm Oil Industry
    Apical, one of Indonesia's biggest palm oil exporters believes that IoT and blockchain can improve the procedure of information securing corresponding to tree creation and interest in the palm oil industry. Organizations using IoT innovation quality and profitability of the industry can be achieved.

11. Blockchain and IoT to Eliminate Water Waste
    The measure of water it can introduce can reach up to a trillion liters of water per year. Aquai made water sensors that tracks how much water you use and consequently secures water holes. Aquai plans to accustom varied administrations related with water harm brought about by spills.

12. Use Blockchain and IoT to quantify stream contamination
    Water quality checking can be a costly and tedious process, Libelium and Airalab have come together to give a less costly solution. "Automaton on the Volga" is the suggestion that uses automation with IoT and blockchain, modernization to gather water contagion levels. This method collects water study of the Kuybyshev Reservoir on the Volga River and sends information to the Ethereum blockchain. Libelium water sensors and Airalab were used in combination that empowered Robonomics Platform.

Numerous ventures have started investigating potential IoT and Blockchain frameworks to improve proficiency and mechanization. In present scenario lot of attention is towards Security in IoT from both scholarly world and business associations.

13.8 Fate of Blockchain and IoT

IoT will assume a significant job in our general public for the coming era, in military and non-military concerns like Drones, etc. It's the nature of IoT framework like at the military, the potential IoT threat is in question and the development of the activity (s) must be programmed.

There is an absence of openly available IoT information and the inaccessibility of agent databases, required for its defense study. Incorporating investigation on to how blockchain can be utilized as a community oriented reason for ensuring other IoT and related frameworks (for example digital body frameworks).

References

1. *Here's How Much Energy All US Data Centers Consume*, Data Center Knowl., San Francisco, CA, USA, 2016.
2. Shi, W., Pallis, G., Xu, Z., Edge Computing [Scanning the Issue], in: *Proceedings of the IEEE*, vol. 107, no. 8, pp. 1474–1481, Aug. 2019.
3. Shi, W., Cao, J., Zhang, Q., Li, Y., Xu, L., Edge computing: vision and challenges. *Edge Things J.*, 3, 5, 637–646, Oct. 2016.
4. Voigt, P. and von dem Bussche, A., The EU general data protection regulation (GDPR), in: *A Practical Guide*, 1st ed., Springer, Cham, Switzerland, 2017.
5. Zwolenski, M. and Weatherill, L., The digital universe: Rich data and the increasing value of the Internet of Things. *Austral. J. Telecommun. Digit. Econ.*, 2, 3, 47, 2014.
6. Karafiloski, E., Blockchain Solutions for Big Data Challenges A Literature Review, in: *IEEE EUROCON 2017—17th International Conference on Smart Technologies*, no. July, pp. 6–8, 2017.
7. Stanciu, A., Blockchain based distributed control system for Edge Computing, in: *21st International Conference on Control Systems and Computer Science Blockchain*, pp. 667–671, 2017.
8. Banafa, A., IoT and Blockchain Convergence: Benefits and Challenges. *IEEE IoT Newsl.*, [Online]. Available: http://iot.ieee.org/newsletter/january-2017/iot-and-blockchain-convergence-benefits-and-challenges.html, 2017.
9. Ziegeldorf, J.H., Grossmann, F., Henze, M., Inden, N., Wehrle, K., CoinParty: Secure Multi-Party Mixing of Bitcoins, in: *Proceedings of the 5th ACM Conference on Data and Application Security and Privacy—CODASPY '15*, no. August, pp. 75–86, 2015.
10. Jentzsch, C., *Decentralized Autonomous Organization to Automate Governance*, white Pap, pp. 1–30, 2016.

11. Dorri, A., Kanhere, S.S., Jurdak, R., Blockchain in internet of things: Challenges and Solutions, arXiv1608.05187 [cs], no. August, 2016.

12. Stallings, W., The Internet of Things: Network and Security Architecture. *Internet Protoc. J.*, 18, 4, 2–24, 2015.

13. Torkaman, A. and Seyyedi, M.A., Analyzing IoT Reference Architecture Models. *Int. J. Comput. Sci. Softw. Eng.*, 2016.

14. Cisco, *The Internet of Things Reference Model*, White Pap, pp. 1–12, 2014.

15. Kshetri, N., *Can blockchain Strengthen the Internet of Things?*, pp. 68–72, IEEE Computer Society, no. August, 2017. https://ieeexplore.ieee.org/document/8012302.

16. Ahram, T., Sargolzaei, A., Sargolzaei, S., Daniels, J., Amaba, B., Blockchain technology innovations. *2017 IEEE Technol. Eng. Manag. Conf.*, no. 2016, pp. 137–141, 2017.

17. Daza, V., Di Pietro, R., Klimek, I., Signorini, M., CONNECT: CONtextual NamE disCovery for blockchain-based services in the IoT. *IEEE Int. Conf. Commun.*, 2017.

18. Atlam, H.F., Alenezi, A., Walters, R.J., Wills, G.B., Daniel, J., Developing an adaptive Risk-based access control model for the Internet of Things, in: *2017 IEEE International Conference on Internet of Things (iThings) and IEEE Green Computing and Communications (GreenCom) and IEEE Cyber, Physical and Social Computing (CPSCom) and IEEE Smart Data (SmartData)*, no. June, pp. 655–661, 2017.

19. Atlam, H.F., Alenezi, A., Alharthi, A., Walters, R., Wills, G., Integration of cloud computing with Internet of Things: Challenges and open issues, in: *2017 IEEE International Conference on Internet of Things (iThings) and IEEE Green Computing and Communications (GreenCom) and IEEE Cyber, Physical and Social Computing (CPSCom) and IEEE Smart Data (SmartData)*, no. June, pp. 670–675, 2017.

20. Atlam, H.F., Alenezi, A., Hussein, R.K., Wills, G.B., Validation of an Adaptive Risk-based Access Control Model for the Internet of Things. *I.J. Comput. Netw. Inf. Secur.*, 10, January, 26–35, 2018.

21. Samaniego, M. and Deters, R., Blockchain as a Service for IoT. *2016 IEEE Int. Conf. Internet Things IEEE Green Comput. Commun. IEEE Cyber, Phys. Soc. Comput. IEEE Smart Data*, pp. 433–436, 2016.

22. Wang, Q., Zhu, X., Ni, Y., Gu, L., Zhu, H., Blockchain for the IoT and industrial IoT: A review, 10, 100081, June 2020. https://www.sciencedirect.com/science/journal/25426605/10/supp/C.

23. Christidis, K. and Member, G.S., Blockchains and Smart Contracts for the Internet of Things. *IEEE Access*, 4, 2292–2303, 2016.

24. Alenezi, A., Zulkipli, N.H.N., Atlam, H.F., Walters, R.J., Wills, G.B., The Impact of Cloud Forensic Readiness on Security, in: *Proceedings of the 7th International Conference on Cloud Computing and Services Science (CLOSER 2017)*, pp. 511–517, 2017.

25. Atlam, H.F., Attiya, G., El-Fishawy, N., Integration of Color and Texture Features in CBIR System. *Int. J. 48 Blockchain with Internet of Things: Benefits, Challenges, and Future Directions.*

26. Asatryan, D., 4 Challenges to Blockchain Adoption from Fidelity CEO, 2017.

27. Bonomi, F., Milito, R., Natarajan, P., Zhu, J., Fog computing: a platform for internet of things and analytics, in: *Big Data and Internet of Things: A Road Map for Smart Environments*, pp. 169–186, Springer, Berlin, Germany, 2014.

28. Bonomi, F., Milito, R., Zhu, J., Addepalli, S., Fog computing and its role in the internet of things, in: *Proceedings of the 1st ACM MCC Workshop on Mobile Cloud Computing*, pp. 13–16, 2012.

29. Stojmenovic, I. and Wen, S., The fog computing paradigm: scenarios and security issues, in: *Proceedings of the Federated Conference on Computer Science and Information Systems (FedCSIS '14)*, September 2014, IEEE, Warsaw, Poland, pp. 1–8.

30. Aazam, M. and Huh, E.-N., Fog computing and smart gateway based communication for cloud of things, in: *Proceedings of the 2nd IEEE International Conference on Future Internet of Things and Cloud (FiCloud '14)*, Barcelona, Spain, August 2014, pp. 464–470.

31. Schmidt, A. and Van Laerhoven, K., How to build smart appliances? *IEEE Pers. Commun.*, 8, 4, 66–71, 2001.

32. Gubbi, J., Buyya, R., Marusic, S., Palaniswami, M., Internet of Things (IoT): a vision, architectural elements, and future directions. *Future Gener. Comput. Syst.*, 29, 7, 1645–1660, 2013.

33. Lane, N.D., Miluzzo, E., Lu, H., Peebles, D., Choudhury, T., Campbell, A.T., A survey of mobile phone sensing. *IEEE Commun. Mag.*, 48, 9, 140–150, 2010.

34. Khan, W.Z., Xiang, Y., Aalsalem, M.Y., Arshad, Q., Mobile phone sensing systems: a survey. *IEEE Commun. Surv. Tut.*, 15, 1, 402–427, 2013.

35. Woodford. *Accelerometers*, 2020. http://www.explainthatstuff.com/accelerometers.html.

36. How Do Global Positioning Systems, or GPS, Work?, 2005, https://www.nasa.gov/audience/foreducators/topnav/materials/listbytype/How_Do_Global_Positioning_Systems.html#.VmxoY5Ph5z0.

37. McClernon, F.J. and Choudhury, R.R., I am your smartphone, and i know you are about to smoke: The application of mobile sensing and computing approaches to smoking research and treatment. *Nicotine Tob. Res.*, 15, 10, 1651–1654, 2013.

38. Pei, L., Guinness, R., Chen, R. *et al.*, Human behavior cognition using smartphone sensors. *Sensors*, 13, 2, 1402–1424, 2013.

39. Bui, N. and Zorzi, M., Health care applications: a solution based on the internet of things, in: *Proceedings of the 4th International Symposium on Applied Sciences in Biomedical and Communication Technologies (ISABEL '11)*, October 2011, ACM, Barcelona, Spain.

40. McGrath, M.J. and Scanaill, C.N., Body-worn, ambient, and consumer sensing for health applications, in: *Sensor Technologies*, pp. 181–216, Springer, 2013. https://link.springer.com/chapter/10.1007/978-1-4302-6014-1_9.
41. Pantelopoulos, A. and Bourbakis, N.G., A survey on wearable sensor-based systems for health monitoring and prognosis. *IEEE Trans. Syst. Man Cybern. Part C: Appl. Rev.*, 40, 1, 1–12, 2010.
42. Swan, M., Sensor mania! The internet of things, wearable computing, objective metrics, and the quantified self 2.0. *J. Sens. Actuator Netw.*, 1, 3, 217–253, 2012.
43. Gruzelier, J.H., EEG-neurofeedback for optimising performance. I: A review of cognitive and affective outcome in healthy participants. *Neurosci. Biobehav. Rev.*, 44, 124–141, 2014.
44. Sekhar, P.K., Brosha, E.L., Mukundan, R., Garzon, F.H., Chemical sensors for environmental monitoring and homeland security. *Electrochem. Soc. Interface*, 19, 4, 35–40, 2010.
45. Bhattacharyya, N. and Bandhopadhyay, R., Electronic nose and electronic tongue, in: *Nondestructive Evaluation of Food Quality*, pp. 73–100, Springer, Berlin, Germany, 2010.
46. Manna, S., Bhunia, S.S., Mukherjee, N., Vehicular pollution monitoring using IoT, in: *International Conference on Recent Advances and Innovations in Engineering, ICRAIE 2014*, ind, May 2014. https://ieeexplore.ieee.org/document/6909157.
47. Want, R., An introduction to RFID technology. *IEEE Pervasive Comput.*, 5, 1, 25–33, 2006.
48. Zhu, X., Mukhopadhyay, S.K., Kurata, H., A review of RFID technology and its managerial applications in different industries. *J. Eng. Tech. Manage.*, 29, 1, 152–167, 2012. https://doi.org/10.1016/j.jengtecman.2011.09.011.

14

Blockchain Applications

Boby Singh*, Rohit Pahwa†, Hari Om Tanwar‡ and Nikita Gupta§

MRIIRS, Faridabad, India

Abstract

A blockchain is an open record to which everybody approaches except without a central authority having control. It is an empowering innovation for people and organizations to work together with trust and straightforwardness. A standout among the other known better uses of blockchains is cryptographic monetary forms, for example, Bitcoin and others; however numerous different applications are conceivable. In this chapter, we will be discussing about the specific qualities every particular application in detail.

Keywords: Blockchain application, blockchain administration, blockchain in big data, digital verification, blockchain health, blockchain science, blockchain learning, blockchain government

14.1 Introduction to Blockchain

Blockchain which was originally Blockchain, is nothing but a collection of blocks connected to one another using cryptography holding up a hash value with contains all the necessary details, like the timestamp and the information about the transaction itself. It sure needs a data structure to design up that organization of data, so the data structure which is used to store the data is a tree, and Merkle tree to be specific. Also, it's easy to connect all the blocks to one another using a tree (Figure 14.1).

Corresponding author: bobbysingh147963@gmail.com
† *Corresponding author:* rohitpahwa2017@gmail.com
‡ *Corresponding author:* hariom274.hot@gmail.com
§ *Corresponding author:* nikkiguptahewo16@gmail.com

S.S. Tyagi and Shaveta Bhatia (eds.) Blockchain for Business: How it Works and Creates Value, (337–360) © 2021 Scrivener Publishing LLC

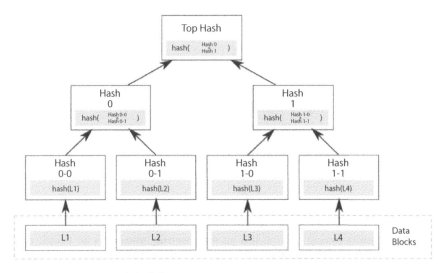

Figure 14.1 Diagram of Blockchain.

Blockchain in Administration

An important function of Government is to manage different types of information about individuals, organization, asset and many more. To manage different types of information the government recruits various people to handle these records that include birth and death dates or information about marital status, business licensing, property transfers, or criminal activity. Manage and use this information can be complicated for the government. Some records exist in the paper form and someone who wants to change the information in official paper, for this citizen has to appear in the front of a government regulator. Because the regulator has to protect the data against unauthorized user. A blockchain-based digital government can protect data from hacker and also it helps to reduce fraud simultaneously it helps to increase trust and accountability with the help of blockchain technology, government, individual, businesses share resources over a distributed ledger using cryptography. A blockchain-based government has the potential to solve legacy issues. Blockchain technology extends way beyond Bitcoin.

Blockchain's ease of use, immediate scalability as well as it is using every area of life. Let's look at how public administration can benefit from blockchain technology.

Blockchain provides a private, enterprises chain specifically for government. The main objective of this technology to assign different level of access only to the authorized user as well as it ensures independent validation of transaction and operation that establish full security.

14.1.1 Uses of Blockchain in Administration

a. Data sharing: If the government wants to share data between organizations of different countries, they can easily share it through decentralized technique. In the case of decentralized, information is stored on the various systems where all the systems are connected to each other, so that, government can access the information securely. It is a very fast and efficient technique. On the other hand, centralized data is stored on single server or system. So, it is a very arduous task for the government to save the information from hacker .It is very exorbitant and inefficient technique.

b. Verified Ownership: Blockchain ensures security only authorized dealer can deal. This deal becomes more valuable when you are dealing with property rights that are often transferred. This situation can be highlighted by giving an example: someone who wants to sell water or mineral rights to investors. This technology will determine who will own the exact rights. In this case, a person who has official rights can take legal decision and judgment.

c. Bookkeeping: Blockchain helps to track each fraction of bitcoin. Blockchain helps to maintain the privacy of the owner through cryptocurrency. Nowadays Blockchain is integrated with accounting which allows local authority, as well as big organization, where employer can track each individual purchases and invoices. When each invoice is verified by blockchain you don't send the duplicate invoice. This technology is used to determine the exact information. Blockchain helps to clear the payments instantly rather than recipient have to wait a few days for the payment to clear. Blockchain has implemented across the entire accounting department as well as it supports real-time accounting of expenditures and incomes.

d. Improved Trust: Whether it is a passport, driving license or any document can be faked. Blockchain helps to improve government-generated documents. There will be no need for wasting human time and energy to figure out such types of data and document. Blockchain technology verifies such types of document in a few second.

e.   Asset Management: We can implement all the assets in the digital form with the help of blockchain. Blockchain prevents people from selling a city-owned asset for personal profit and also take care of all the assets of the country. Apart from that, we can use blockchain in a real-world application such as we can track all the government-owned real estate, simultaneously it helps to determine how much futile building and piece of land is available in the city or country. If blockchain is adopted worldwide, very soon it would solve the problem of unemployment. Even most of the countries have adopted this technology such as Australia, Canada, USA and many more. Furthermore, blockchain is gradually starting to be implemented in bookkeeping to speed up accounting, payment processing and it also enables money transparency.

f.   Smart Regulation: Blockchain allows various agencies to create and design legal documents and regulation so that it can monitor all the verified and authorized users.

g.   Identity Management: Blockchain technology allows government regulator and citizen to register their identities, assets, all the legal document on the blockchain so that government people and normal citizen can use this electronic information in upcoming future.

14.2   Blockchain in Big Data Predictive Task Automation

Let's suppose the government has huge volumes of data and the government wants to analyze such types of data for security and validation purposes this process is known as data analytics. Huge data provide the opportunity to examine large and uncover hidden pattern, unknown correlation, and customer preference. Normally Big data contain information in various forms such as a mix of structured, semi-structured, and unstructured. Basically the government gathers this information through a survey, phone calls, personal interaction, social media and many more resources. Apart from that, these types of data which is created and designed by the organization is fruitful for authority. Nowadays, the internet is a good source of information.

Any technological advancement has its own challenges and limitations. If we talk about some major challenges of data science include inaccessible data, privacy issues and enormous information. The control of such type of issues is one area where blockchain plays an essential role. Blockchain ensures the security and privacy of data. The objective of blockchain is focused on validating data while data science involves making a prediction from a large amount of data.

14.2.1 How Can Blockchain Help Big Data?

Blockchain has brought a new way of managing and operating with data. In the case of blockchain all data should be brought together but a decentralized manner where data may be analyzed with each individual device. Blockchain integrates with other advanced technologies such as cloud computing, Artificial intelligence and Internet of Things (IoT).

14.2.2 Blockchain Use Cases in Big Data

a. Data Integrity: Data recorded on the blockchain are trustworthy because they must have gone through a verification which ensures its quality. The activities that take place on the blockchain network can be traced. Blockchain technology is used to verify the physical document which was encoding with digital signature.

b. Preventing Malicious Activities: Blockchain helps to prevent various malicious activities because it uses various algorithms to verify transaction so it is impossible for a single attacker to attack an entire network. If an attacker tries to attack on data can easily be identified and expunged from the network. Because the data is distributed, it makes it impossible for the single attacker to generate enough computational power to change the validation criteria and allow unwanted data in the system. If someone who wants to change the blockchain criteria, for this majority of the node has to come together. Majority power will make a new consensus, so it is not possible for a single attacker to attack the entire network.

c. Making Prediction: Blockchain data, just like other types of data, can be analyzed to reveal various information and this information is used to predict various future outcomes. What is more, blockchain provides structured data gathered from individuals or individual devices. In predictive analysis, we use a large set of data to determine the accurate outcome of a social event like customer preferences, customer lifetime value, dynamic price as it relates to businesses. Most of the time, investors use this technology to get the right data analysis. Due to the distributed nature of blockchain, huge computational process helps data scientists' in the smaller organization to predict analysis tasks.

d.   Real-time Data Analysis: Blockchain plays a vital role in the financial and payment system. The purpose of developing blockchain is for real-time cross border transaction. Nowadays, several bankers and fintech innovators are exploring blockchain, because it works very efficiently as compared to other technologies as well as it settles the various geographical barriers. On the other hand, the Organization that requires real-time analysis of data on a large scale can use blockchain technology. With blockchain, banker and financial organization can observe changes in data in real-time making it possible to make a quick decision, as well as it helps to track the abnormal activities.

e.   Manage Data Sharing: Blockchain provides facility storing of different types of data. A project team member who is working on the same data does not need to repeat the data analysis task which has been carried by some other team member. Also, a blockchain platform can help scientists to monitor their work, so that they can reach on conclusion.

14.3   Digital Identity Verification

Before starting with DIV (Digital Identity Verification), let us try to understand *what Digital identity is?* As you already know that in this world, every individual can be identified using many different assets like passport number and government issued IDs.

Similarly, digital identity is knowledge about an entity that is used by computer systems to represent an external agent that can be a person, agency, application or device defining identity as a "collection of entity-related attributes." The details found in a digital identity make it possible to determine and authentication of a user who is communicating with a web-based business system without the participation of the user.

Traditional Methods of Identity Managing Records
Previously, these identity records are maintained in unified physical form within the organizations where these strategies are open and always on the risk of getting breached, fraud and extortion, which is not safe when we are talking in terms of security.

Major challenges facing in traditional methods of identifications are:

a. Usability
b. Privacy
c. Globalization.

14.3.1 Why Digital Identity Matters?

Digital Identity guarantees precision while speeding up the client on-boarding process and forestalling Anti Money Laundering (AML) and false exercises while financial transaction. Advanced personality Management plans to institutionalize and streamline resident administrations gave by countries. Thus, a solid computerized personality stage can help convey numerous administrations, contacting our lives in different ways.

Some of the examples are mentioned below:

a. The National Digital Identity (NDI) framework, a piece of the Smart Nation activity in Singapore, which when finished is required to assist residents with access to e-taxpayer supported organizations all the more safely.
b. In India, more than 1 billion Indians today have an Aadhaar ID, a computerized character that is getting connected to all the social plans and has changed the manner in which appropriations are being paid out to monetarily more fragile areas of society.
c. Smart cards were given as ahead of schedule as 2014 in Nigeria, improving security and open administrations in the nation.
d. Kenya went with the same pattern with an advanced ID that has additionally decreased social violations.

14.3.2 Blockchain (Definition and its Features)

The introduction of Blockchain technology has created an opportunity to convert the relationship between human beings and their organizations which are set up and maintained. Blockchain technology can supply secure

solutions through integrating trust in the network itself. As for digital identification management, Blockchain enables identification owners to have
sovereignty of their identification and identity primarily based personal
records, control access to their information & enables identification proprietors to proportion minimum amount of records while making sure
integrity and trust.

A blockchain can be best explained as a time-stamped series of
immutable information that is managed by a cluster of computers and isn't
owned by means of any single entity. Every of those blocks of records (i.e.
Block) are secured and certain to every different using cryptographic standards (i.e. Chain).

The cause why anyone is so excited about the blockchain is for its following three capabilities:

    a. Decentralization: Not one of the statistics in the blockchain
       is owned by way of one centralized entity. All of the nodes
       in the blockchain's community hold the information.
    b. Immutability: As soon as a fact has been entered within the
       blockchain, it can't be tampered with. This happens because
       of cryptographic hash features.
    c. Transparency: All of the nodes of the community can
       see all of the information that has been entered into the
       blockchain.

The 3 Important Issues That Blockchain Will Resolve
What are the 3 important troubles plaguing the digital identification area
which the blockchain can resolve?

    a. Digital devices shouldn't be easy to replicate.
    b. Virtual files should be tamper proof.
    c. Digital approaches ought to be tamper evidence.

14.3.3   Why do we Need Blockchain in Digital Identity?

Blockchain can be used to evacuate the current problems facing in the field
of Digital Identity which are:

    a. Impassability—According to a survey, more than half of the
       population in this world does not have their identity proof,
       where most of them are poor people. Where the process of
       identification's paperwork is quite complex, not accessible

and lack of knowledge are the main obstacles due to which billions of people are left out of this identification system. One cannot perform a task without a proper proof or verification of their identity.

b. Insecure Data—Today, 80% of the world's population identities are stored in centralized database of government, inspite of having many different strategies of cyber security and there are many user accounts that attract the hackers.

c. Identity Theft—In this current society, it is very easy to create fake identities because of the fragility between offline & digital identities that play a role in growing evil like "Fake News or Viral" which is not healthy for the democracy.

14.3.4 How Does a Blockchain Work?

The gadgets where information is stored, the "pages" of this ledger, are blocks. Each block contains hashed records. A hash is a function widely utilized in cryptography. It's a mathematical algorithm that transforms a bit of information into a string of alphanumeric values: the "hash" or "hash price". If the identical statistics is introduced in the center, it'll usually deliver the same hash in the output. If there's even the slightest trade in the input facts, the output hash can be extensively one-of-a-kind (this is called the avalanche impact). Avoiding any correlation among hashes, it's a "one way characteristic" because the usage of the hash price within the output to locate what changed into the information in the center is extremely tough.

14.3.5 Why is a Blockchain Secure?

What makes blockchain relaxed is the truth that each block wherein information is recorded cannot be modified retroactively without the consensus of the general public of the community. Which means that for a piece of information to be modified, all of the blocks created after it might have to be changed and 51% of the network might need to agree on that exchange. Seeing that blocks are being created each moment, changing those and the blocks previous it till accomplishing the only we intended to alternate, could require great computing power. Blockchain is created to provide the solution of the double-spend trouble of digital currency and to behave as a ledger, a registry, of the transactions of Bitcoin. Everybody that transacts Bitcoin acts as a node within the network, registering a transaction on the Bitcoin blockchain. This makes it decentralized, as no important authority is needed and everybody within the community can write on the ledger, and permits for consensus inside the network without a want of a middle-man. The more human beings are in the community, the greater difficulty it is for majority collusion so that it will subvert the veracity of the records on the blockchain. With a public, immutable, registry, managed with the aid of collaboration and collective altruism, these virtual end customers ought to easily affirm transactions and be confident that the finances were being transferred handiest once and not digitally copied infinitely.

14.3.6   What's Blockchain Identification Management?

Identity management can contains all the processes and technology inside a company that are used to perceive, authenticate and authorize a person to get right of entry to offerings or structures in that said agency or different related ones. The trouble with contemporary identification control structures Identity has a hassle. If it's paper-based totally, which includes delivery certificate sitting idly in a basement of a city corridor, it's a challenge to loss, theft of fraud. A virtual identity reduces the extent of paperwork and will increase the speed of approaches within firms by way of taking into consideration extra interoperability among departments and other establishments. However if this virtual identity is saved on a centralized server, it turns into a hotspot for hackers.

Blockchain is considered as a key of advancement in the period of digitalization, wherein everything is either computerized or has a computerized portrayal, and associated. Blockchain's inventive innovation have the capability of carrying straightforwardness and trust to computerized biological system, by doling out everything an advanced character, conveying the capacity as opposed to concentrating, and robotizing the procedures with brilliant agreements. Consequently, the idea of "decentralized computerized personality" is a significant part and maybe the beginning stage of how a Blockchain is organized.

In Blockchain, resource proprietors are identified by deviated cryptographic. Blockchain based personality arrangements use the idea of Hitler kilter cryptography, so as to relegate advanced character to things. A few parts of Blockchain make the innovation reasonable for and making sure about personality the board:

    a. Blockchain record is changeless and straightforward (in view of authorizations), and changelessness and straightforwardness are principal for personality the board.

    b. Blockchain is impervious to single purpose of disappointment and disavowal of administration assaults.

   c. Blockchain gives an efficient execution of open key cryptography and hashing, which:

   d. Can be stretched out for advanced personality possession.

   e. Helps to ensure the authentication of the user.

   f. Can be used for outsider confirmation of records.

   g. Helps encouraging authorization based record imparting to shrewd agreements.

   h. Blockchain disposes of or diminishes restraining infrastructure in personality the board, as it isn't constrained by a focal position, which likewise empowers character and record mix in worldwide scale.

   i. Blockchain bolsters motivators by means of cryptographic forms of money, which can be used for specific undertakings, for example, giving impetuses to the members to information sharing.

Beginning from undeniable guidelines of protection including the use of a complicated password to deploying modern technology which includes Biometrics, Gadget getting to know and robot manner Automation, more than one technique are being evaluated for virtual identity safety. Powerful though they are, while carried out on a Centralized digital identification control machine, those answers prove costly and sometimes not as effective. One of the main drawbacks of any such centralized machine is that which manipulate the statistics stays with one entity. Tampering with and the lack of records is simple, with identity taking time. Estimates peg identification of information breaches to seven months. And, that is wherein blockchain answers are increasingly more being explored, given their inherent traits of engendering and transparency and consumer manage, all key elements for digital identification control.

14.3.7 Advantages

Advantages that act as the main pillars of a blockchain primarily based answer for digital identity are:

   a. Trust—In blockchain-based totally structures, the metadata used for communications is maintained within the dispensed ledger. The authenticity of the information is demonstrated thru multiple nodes, through a consensus mechanism. This decentralization is useful within the context of virtual Identities, especially while national Identifiers are used throughout more than one company.

b. Safety—Blockchain technology has been designed to preserve records in an encrypted and immutable way, and secured thru cryptography, thereby, preserving the identity blanketed and traceable. Furthermore, blockchain primarily based structures removes the vulnerability associated with password safety.

c. Integrity—The gain of this form of identity device over conventional ones is the capacity to keep each identification across all of the nodes in the network. Though the information is shipped across peer-to-peer networks, its miles continuously reconciled and kept updated. Additionally, the blockchain network does not have a unmarried factor of failure, making it hard for hackers to break the integrity of the facts set.

d. Simplicity—A blockchain framework simplifies the process for every stakeholder involved:

e. Identification Issuers—Automation of the issuance of digital identity reduces time and guide interventions.

f. Identification Verifiers—Consumer on boarding and records verification is simpler and price powerful.

g. Identity Proprietors—Blockchain actions far from centralized statistics management, giving users manipulate over their identity. It is also viable for customers to create their own identification information for social media/fee transactions. That is called a "Self Sovereign virtual identity".

h. Privacy—Regulators internationally are clamoring for Privacy of citizen's personal and touchy facts. Blockchain encryption combined with the virtual signature guarantees "privacy with the aid of layout" through pseudonymization. Affixing the virtual signature to all transactions completed via the user makes it foolproof as nicely.

14.4 Blockchain Government

Government of any country is a very essential part and also plays an important role in it. Having blockchain in the government sector is a beneficial step for the citizens of that country. Because blockchain helps in removing a lot of drawbacks or loop holes in the working of the government sector.

This blockchain system in this sector can make government processes easy and smooth.

14.4.1 Decentralized Government Services

Decentralized government services means there is no central headquarters of any kind of the services provided by the government. This system also helps in increasing trust in the people for the government by make them participating in their process, by giving them the authority to see, verify and check the data. Decentralized can also called as kind of distributed network everywhere or distributed ledger technology which means every participant in the blockchain is having its own copy of the data, this make the government process transparent and also helps in increasing trust in the people. And there is a one more property of blockchain is that it is immutable means the data cannot be changed. For example while registering our land it should be very beneficial and can be helpful in reducing or solving many land disputes. These features transparency, immutability, etc. of blockchain helps in minimizing frauds and corruptions in many government services. As we all heard of much news of many scams in the government organizations.

Blockchain in the public sector makes it very difficult to hack; the reason is that it uses cryptographic hash functions, data encryption and its distributed ledger technology. As this data belongs to the government and public so, this makes their data very secure and increase accountability. Blockchain also good for the removal of black market or black money in to the government as there is no middle man in between you and the service, you doesn't have to pay extra money to the middle man in between for the service that is already yours. Say for example you are taking loan from a bank and all your papers are clear, you can get the loan easily, but the middle man came into the picture and ask you a cut from that loan. But in some cases both the parties are involved in this kind of practice which basically a loss for the government.

As it is necessary for everyone, it is kind of peer to peer network in which there is no disturbance in between. Blockchain is a kind of chain of blocks each block is having data and address of its previous block, which helps in traversing all previous blocks or transactions. Blockchain also helps in identity management, as it plays an important role in having or providing these services. This means the person doesn't have to show his identity to every organization separately, the person have to show his identity to only one organization which is acceptable to every other organization.

And as a result of these features of blockchain it ultimately reduces the cost per service for the government which further people gets the benefit of the service at a much cheaper cost. Blockchain also makes a great impact on saving time and labor on the services provided by the government. Blockchain makes it easier for the government to manage their services more efficiently and more helpful for the people use that services easily and without any fear of theft, fraud, etc.

14.4.2   Liquid Democracy and Random Sample Election

Blockchain plays a vital role in liquid democracy and also a great part in random sample election. Politics has an essential duty in the government for governing the people and the process should be clean and transparent which can only be done by blockchain. As we all knew the image regarding to the politics in our country is not good which indirectly means that there is a flaw in our current system that has to be changed. By using blockchain in politics helps in increase in the involvement of the general public into the system which is very important because government is of the people for the people and by the people. Most of the people after election feel insured regarding their vote that what happen to the vote is it at the correct destination or might somebody change or some kind of fixing in that election. There has to be an efficient system that have the potential to keep the vote with full security and transparency so that the people are assure that their vote is at right place.

Blockchain in the election system of our country provides huge benefits to the people and to the government also. After applying this system then there is no need of recounting of votes as this is happening with full transparency and full security, which as a result in saving a lot of time and money of the government because they doesn't have to recount the votes. This leads to the increase in the trust of the people into the procedure or system of the government which is a great benefit for them that their people believe in their governance. This system increases the value of votes of the people and their involvement in the making of government. This system is helps in making an unique identity for having a fair election as this system is very difficult to hack or crack if somebody changes a block in the chain it has to change all the block in that chain which impossible.

People can see all the schemes provided by the government in this system because of the distributed ledger technology. This is also very beneficial in reducing corruption and black money. This system helps government in categorizing people according to their income, purpose of work and many other factors which through which the government provides them different schemes which of their benefits and it also help in collecting taxes from the people of different groups. In this system people can also keep the record of the money that the government took from them in the form of taxes, that where the money is gone and in which sectors the government is spending that money which is basically the right of the people to that what happen to their money.

This system increases the control of the public on the government. Government is answerable to the public regarding their work if they find any kind of misuse of their money or any kind of the actions taken by them. This system helps government in making appropriate schemes, rule, decision to take, and many other factors that a leader of the party should do for the people as they chose him the leader. This system is basically distributed trust among the people this leads to a better future of the people by having a fair and efficient governance for them that all the decisions are made by the all the people. This system helps in reducing poverty in the country and helps in improving agriculture which is a huge part in our country and it provides 16% to the GDP by providing them proper schemes provided by the government, proper identity and proper support in their agriculture.

14.5   Blockchain Science

14.5.1   FoldingCoin

So there is a pervasive or widespread research already commenced to look out for a serious concern related to medical issues like counterfeit folding of protein in some people's body. So The Stanford University makes sure that the analysts get all the data which is to be needed for the study of the same. An institution by the name of FoldingHome (FAH) was set up and this is where the role of FoldingCoin comes into play.

See the interesting part here is, anyone from all over the world can be a part of this Institution FoldingHome by simply handing-out or granting to run The Stanford's medical research department and you will be rewarded with an estimated amount of the cryptocurrency FLDC (FoldingCoin).

Features of FoldingCoin

a. Typical Hardware: FoldingCoin unlike the other cryptocurrency uses a typing hardware which is easily available and simply accessible, so it makes it pretty easy to mine a coin like this one.

b. Secured: FoldingCoin is extremely secure with these advanced set of protocols, this gets rid of the risk of attack on the system.

c. World-Wide Spread: FoldingCoin is widely spread in the whole world just after the Bitcoin. The reason of this wide-spread is the security of the FoldingCoin and also everyone is aware of the fact that rewards provided is also good.

So all of these factors self-facilitate to help grow the community involved in the cryptocurrency FoldingCoin. FoldingCoin has its own wallet which is a very safe platform for the means of collecting and storing of FLDC coins. Anyone interested can find it on the official website. Other means to collect and store the FLDC coins can be the hardware wallets, or some other wallets available in the market if found authentic or even convincing.

14.5.2   GridCoin (GRC)

GridCoin was developed and evolved in 2013, by Rob Halford. The GridCoin is ensured with a technique names as Proof-of-Stake (PoS) in which the nodes gets to earn an interest rate of 1.5% annually. In this technique, there is a special algorithm designed which manages to cover a large population over the distributed network of the cryptocurrency blockchain. In this sort of a technique, the next person to attain a block or a node is selected by some means of random selection over some factors like the wealth, age, etc.

Features

a. Innovation: GridCoin turned out to be one of the most innovative and also very practical when it comes to analyze all the applications of the blockchain yet. It accomplishes a new goal in the area of cryptocurrency and blockchain. GridCoin is considered to be a very efficient component of this technology, as it explores immense computational function into a blockchain network to a great degree by its contribution to various extensive and critical projects of science via the BOINC (Berkeley Open Infrastructure for Network Computing).

b. Efficiency: GridCoin efficiently adopts PoS structure and maintains security of the blockchain because of the fact that it causes no harm to the energy reserves and completely safe to acknowledge.

14.5.3   Global Public Health

Blockchain technology can be proven to widen the health care system because of its main characteristic which is the sharing of data or sensitive information in an enormously secure manner. Not just in a healthcare system, but in any department it's remarkably important to secure the data. You cannot accept to compromise your data at any cost. This is the reason why Blockchain Technology has been so widely accepted in all the sectors of the world.

The main purpose of Blockchain Technology in health management domain is to secure the disease surveillance, medical records, insurance billing and many more things. No wonder the technology is already applied to many hospitals and other health sectors of the society. This technology is said to be so favorable that it can actually up rise and transform the health databases and improvise the access to prescription databases, scan reports, surveillance systems, archives of images and medical reports universally.

This technology can prevent a lot of damage to happen, during a pandemic. It can reduce a lot of time and efforts when there are some national health issues striking. So, because of the presence of this technology, the data can be distributed safely among the network rather than being dependent on it in the time of need. In such serious issues, the time factor make a big difference, so the time saved by using this technology for medical reporting and data analyzing can be put to good use.

Blockchain along with the Artificial Intelligence (AI) can be used in quadrate treatments, personalize medicines and recommend the health by providing the patient's hereditary factors, medical history and some other extraneous factors.

A few advantages and disadvantages of adopting the technology of blockchain in the Global Health Security are listed below:
Advantages:

    a. It has certainly upgraded the security of the classified data and dependable conservation against the exposure of the sensitive data like identities, transaction details, transaction passwords, etc.

    b. It has raised the efficiency

    c. Reduced the charges

    d. Although the main objective of implementing this technology is to secure the sensitive information, but also, this technology help and enhances the access of the information broadly.

    e. This technology makes network robust that means, you no more need to be dependent on any particular system, the network is decentralized while using the blockchain, reducing the dependency for a single computer or a database.

Disadvantages:

    a. A disadvantage to opt this technology is, this technology has not flourished completely, so you might feel challenges for new technical issues popping out.

    b. Although the distributed network mechanism of this technology is a perk, but it also can be a risk factor to compromise the data or information.

    c. The cost efficiency is however yet to be proven.

14.5.4   Bitcoin Genomics

Blockchain is a technology which is widely decentralized and a fixed or a constant database. This database can be shared among all the member of the network securely. This kind of a technology for first introduced in the help of maintaining a public ledger in the famous decentralized cryptocurrency, Bitcoin. For this technology to wide spread all over the world in different institutions and organizations there are mainly three factors which is the reason to make this happen. First and foremost is the tendency of the decentralization, no one system or entity can control the whole network. The second is the stability, no past record or the transaction details added to the node can be changed or altered afterwards. The third is the security of the data; the data is highly secured by encoding it using advanced cryptographic methods. All the above mentioned factors help Bitcoin to be immensely authentic and convincing to adopt as to store the sensitive information.

Now among all the factors, Decentralization of the data in the network is considered to be as most favorable one in the technology of Blockchain at places where there is an essential need of a third party or a mediator such as financial agreements and joint resolutions. Such agreements have an implicit demand of including a third party to reach out for a conclusion. So, there is always a concern for the middleman to be biased to any of the party, therefore blockchain resolves this complication as you don't need any middleman or any kind of a mediator in any sort of agreements.

Essentially all the applications of Blockchain resemble two interconnected processes known as Mining and Transaction. Mining is forming new blocks or nodes that are interconnected to each other in a tree structure and Transaction is the data present in the blocks which can be the record of exchanging assets among the users. The characteristics of Bitcoin and Blockchain Technology makes it useful to store data in research centers, hospitals, health management systems and other administrations.

14.6   Blockchain Health

Healthcare is one of the biggest and important industries of the world. This is a very sensitive industry because it deals with trillions of money every year. And the situation of life and death makes it more important for us. Any kind of limitations or disadvantages lead to a lot damage in this sector sometime which you cannot make it correct. This property of this sector makes it unique from every other sector.

14.6.1   Health Coin

Health coin is a kind of crypto currency like bitcoin. It can be purchase by using real money through online. It can change a lot of things such as it also helps in making transactions from one country to another at a large scale also. Health coin is so popular because it uses the principles of blockchains. This makes the health coin revolutionary as it is able to solve many big problems in the health sector regarding to quality of the health care provided, security of transactions, and amount of transaction and all the previous records of the transactions that has happened in the past. Health coin also provides us various features or services that we can buy using them such as insurance, health checkups from a reputed hospital and many other health benefits. As we can say that health coins are the future of health sector because in many ways such as in terms of money it is the largest in the world, it is government free P2P network and we can pay directly with the health coins.

14.6.2   EMR on Blockchain

EMR stands for electronic medical record which is basically a record of patient's medication and his medical history. Each patient is having its own EMR and there are millions of patients so we can assume that's how big this data base is as it is a digital store in some place. This increases in the risk of hacking the data, which is a major drawback of health care sector. Except this, it is a very efficient way of keeping the record of the patient and it is easier for the patient to his track of the medical records and medication time.

After adding EMR on blockchain, it removes all the disadvantages in the EMR only and also adds some other efficient features to it. The decentralize property of blockchain makes it more efficient to use from any system and to multiple hospitals also for better prescription of various expertise. EMR stores on blockchain makes it very difficult to hack due to decentralization of data and cryptographic hash functions use to encrypt this data which very necessary now days because recently many cases coming up of stealing of this data at a great amount. Blockchain also helps in reducing a lot of efforts by not creating the record again and again, once the record is created it can be use multiple times and also into every other hospital. This made it very easier for patients and as well as for doctors also to check their patients through EMR on blockchain.

Patients doesn't have to stand in long queue in order to wait for their turn to get the doctor's prescription for the disease he is suffering sometime patient can die due to late prescription this kind of things only happens in our country because of the too much crowd in the hospitals this made difficult for the patient to get to the doctor in time. What if the patient is suffering from some kind of disease such as corona virus, in that case the person can spread this disease to a lot of people in that hospital while standing in the queue. These kinds of careless things can make a very dangerous situation in that hospital and which allows you to know how to control these kinds of situations which can be very difficult for anyone.

By EMR on blockchain the patient can take online appointment from the required doctor, this can save a lot of time for the patient and doctor as well. The patient can take online appointment by just giving its medical record to the doctor on the online portal, as result doctor can give the appointment or can give the proper medication as per the requirement. What if the doctor is not aware of these kinds of diseases such as corona virus in that case the doctor will be going to suffer from these diseases. To avoid this and the previous kind of situation EMR on blockchain would be very helpful as this will give the doctors an idea of the diseases which are new in the world and what are their symptoms and precautions to take as per the diseases. EMR on blockchain can also help in further research of the diseases which will be helpful worldwide.

14.6.3 Bit Coin Health Notary

Notary means to verify or to authorize from a specialized authority in that particular field. Health notary now a days is very helpful and it is necessary also as we see crime rate increasing day by day. It is necessary also because if we will not authorize from the right authority there would be bad outcomes related to health issues. What if we will authorize it from some local authority as a result our patient will suffer ultimately because they are unskilled or not properly trained to do this kind of work.

Bit coin health notary works on the principle of blockchain which is very beneficial for everyone; it can be patient or may be doctor. Having the property of blockchain makes it very reliable to use. Because of having security like blockchain it is using in multiple field and many other government health organizations and also in other sectors as well. The immutability property of blockchain also very useful in this nobody can change the data of the notary, what if somebody changes the data in that notary then all the number of patients going to be suffer who are related to that notary.

14.7   Blockchain Learning

14.7.1   Bitcoin MOOCs

MOOCs (Massive Open Online Courses) are available to learn everything about the upcoming growing and thriving concept which is the Cryptocurrency and Blockchain. Blockchain is ought to be well-suited for the data and information which are meant to be highly secured, like the transaction details. So this is the need of the world in the days to come, with the massive load of data booming every single day in multiples. So even if you feel a bit interested in possessing knowledge about the upcoming trend, Cryptocurrency and Blockchain, Online courses are available to get a hands-on the new technology. Accomplish good knowledge and you can actually contribute or make a difference in the community. What's new is, you will find this technology really interesting and you will be more eager to know more about it, as it gets even more interesting when you actually use it in your real life problems. You can learn about its varying cryptos like Bitcoin, FoldingCoin, LearnCoin, GridCoin, LiteCoin and many more. You can get a complete knowledge as well as on the practical aspect and get a good kick start to a new career.

14.7.2   Smart Contract Literacy

A Smart Contract is likewise a contract but rather digital and Smart, and by Smart it means it consists of set of rules and protocols which aids the identification, verification and imposes the negotiation to hike the conduct of the contract. Smart Contracts made a reasonable transaction to be made without even the incorporation of a third party.

The Blockchain Technology is glorious for its network to be distributed, so it is easy for all the parties to access it and therefore ends the wish of a mediator. It is also helpful in plenty other ways like it saves a lot of time and it is highly secure. Another great aspect of smart contracts is that it reduces the rivalry or the conflict between the parties as everything is now out in the open among all the parties.

A Smart Contract assists you commerce shares, money, property or anything that is of some value in a very fast, efficient and a transparent way. Also, there is no middleman, so the charge for the services of a middleman is also excluded in the trade.

Smart Contracts can be used in many areas like Management, Government, Automobile, Real Estate, and Healthcare. Here are some Features of Smart Contracts:

a. Secure: The Contract or the document is encrypted using Cryptography. So the documents are safe, only the person with the key to it can access the document or else it takes a very skilled hacker to access the document and decrypt it.

b. Accurate: These Contracts are found to be immensely accurate.

c. Trustworthy: Your Contract is shared among the network, only to people or the parties involved in the contract. No other people can access the contract from outside the network.

d. Autonomous: As clearly there is no involvement of a mediator or a third party, so this contract is entirely your driven rather shaped by someone else. So there is a zero chance of a contract which is biased to any party, it is always favorable to both the parties as it is made by the consent of both the parties.

e. Backup: If someday you lost the access to your document, you can always get the record of the same from the friend in the same network.

f. Speed: Smart Contracts are designed with algorithms to meet an end to the requirements of both the parties, so it extensively saves a lot of time of both the parties.

g. Saving: As Smart Contracts makes an end to the need of a middleman, it saves the money for both the parties that could be the charges of the service of the middleman.

14.7.3 LearnCoin

LearnCoin is the Educational Practice of the Cryptocurrencies. In the recent time, flourishing Cryptocurrencies like Bitcoin and LiteCoin have drawn quite attention to this technology. Now most people want to invest and develop the technology of Cryptocurrency. Also it is now more likely to develop your own cryptocurrency due to the open source nature of these two cryptocurrencies. Due to the availability of previous written source code, for just a small fee, you can actually be able to build your own cryptocurrency. But these services might not provide you some functionality or key features of the cryptocurrency already in use. So these codes will not provide you the key insights to the main functions but the source code is easily available.

References

1. Rosic, A., Smart Contracts: The Blockchain Technology That Will Replace Lawyers, available at https://blockgeeks.com/guides/smart-contracts/.
2. Singhal, A. et al., What is FoldingCoin (FLDC), available at https://coinswitch.co/info/foldingcoin/what-is-foldingcoin.
3. Alkan, C. et al., Realizing the potential of blockchain technologies in genomics, available at https://www.ncbi.nlm.nih.gov/pmc/articles/PMC6120626/, 2018.
4. Singhal, A. et al., What is GridCoin (GRC), available at https://coinswitch.co/info/gridcoin/what-is-gridcoin.com.
5. Berryhill, J., Bourgery, T., Hanson, A. et al., Guide to Blockchain technology and its use in the public sector, available at https://www.oecd.org/fr/gov/administration-innovante/oecd-guide-to-blockchain-technology-and-its-use-in-the-public-sector.htm, 2018.
6. UseBitcoinsInfo, How Public Administration can benefit from Blockchain Technology, available at https://usebitcoins.info/index.php/news/7642-how-public-administration-can-benefit-from-blockchain-technology.
7. Sarikaya, S., How Blockchain Will Disrupt Data Science: 5 Blockchain Use Cases in Big Data, available at https://towardsdatascience.com/how-blockchain-will-disrupt-data-science-5-blockchain-use-cases-in-big-data-e2e254e3e0ab, 2019.
8. Sharma, A., How Blockchain and Big Data Complement Each Other, available at https://hackernoon.com/how-blockchain-and-big-data-complement-each-other-92a1b9f8b38d, 2019.
9. Lubin, J., Blockchain in Government and the Public Sector, available at https://consensys.net/blockchain-use-cases/government-and-the-public-sector/.
10. Shashank, A., 5 Benefits of Using Blockchain Technology in Healthcare, available at https://hitconsultant.net/blockchain-technology-in-healthcare-benefits/#.XpVMMevivlU, 2018.

11. Anwar, H., Blockchain for Digital Identity: The Decentralized and Self-Sovereign Identity (SSI), available at https://101blockchains.com/digital-identity/, 2019.

12. Tykn, B.V., Identity Management with Blockchain: The Definitive Guide, available at https://tykn.tech/identity-management-blockchain/, 2020.

13. Lubin, J., Blockchain in Digital Identity, available at https://consensys.net/blockchain-use-cases/digital-identity/.

14. Reiff, N., Blockchain Explained, available at https://www.investopedia.com/terms/b/blockchain.asp, 2020.

15. Swan, M., Blockchain: Blueprint for a New Economy, available at https://books.google.co.in/books?id=RHJmBgAAQBAJ&pg=PA37&lpg=PA37&dq=Digital+art+blockchain+attestation+services&source/#v=onepage&q=Digital%20art%20blockchain%20attestation%20services&f=false, 2015.

15

Advance Concepts of Blockchain

Raj Kumar

Manav Rachna International Institute of Research & Studies, Faridabad, India

Abstract

The blockchain technology is going to revolutionize the world in the near future. It will become a household name in times to come. The blockchain technology can be used for wide range of services such as making secure online transactions, creating digital identifications, improving efficiency of supply chain, and can be used to create data backup which can't be mutated. It can be utilized by hospitals for maintaining patient records. The blockchain technology provides much needed privacy for patient data. The crime control agencies can use blockchain technology for tracking ownership of weapons. The future applications of blockchain technology are numerous and it is very difficult to explain it in a single chapter. However, the topics such as community supercomputing, blockchain geonomics, blockchain learning, community coin, monetary and non-monetary currencies, some prominent alternate coins, demurrage currencies have been discussed in detail.

Keywords: Blockchain, bitcoin, supercomputing, genomics, non-monetary currencies

15.1 Community Supercomputing

Community supercomputing is a novel concept and blockchain is the underlying technology which helps to make it possible. The world population is 7.8 billion plus and the number of connected devices is 22 billion plus worldwide. This number is bound to grow exponentially with the rise of new technology like Internet of Things (IoT) where all the devices will be converted into smart and communicating devices. The community supercomputing wants to take advantage of the hardware devices which are used by people for their personal works. An average resident uses computing resources for only few

Email: Rajkumar.fca@mriu.edu.in

S.S. Tyagi and Shaveta Bhatia (eds.) *Blockchain for Business: How it Works and Creates Value*, (361–372) © 2021 Scrivener Publishing LLC

hours in an entire day and for major part of the day the computing power of a computing device is either underutilized or unutilized. In supercomputing, the members of the community pool their hardware resources using block-chain technology and create supercomputing. Here the usage of community resources will be based on payment basis. If an individual shares his comput-ing resources with other members of the community, the computing power user has to pay the money to the hardware service provider and vice-versa. This concept may become as a source of passive income for community mem-bers. As seen in Figure 15.1 x-axis and y-axis denotes the length and breadth of any typical city. The connected thin lines depict interconnected com-puter. The multi-color filled circles depict blockchain-based supercomputers by using the hardware of connected computers of the community.

The community supercomputing platform can help in enhancing the speed and simultaneously lower the cost of computing. This platform can act as a great booster for graphics rendering, scientific research, machine learning and scientific research. This feat can be achieved by using household computers (Figure 15.2).

- Bitcoin for Contagious disease relief

The blockchain technology can enable us in controlling pandemic. Whenever, any person is infected by the contagious disease, that person acts as a spreader and other people are infected by him. Once it is identi-fied that an individual is having symptoms of the communicable disease, it becomes vital to trace the contacts of that person. A person may infect others during interaction with others at various places such as office, park, neighborhood, etc. The block chain makes use of distributed ledgers which can be used to respond faster during health crisis.

Surveillance of contagious disease and the infected can be the key in controlling the spread of disease. The inherent feature of blockchain technology helps to avoid hacking of disease related data. Duplicity of

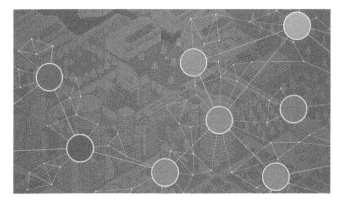

Figure 15.1 Community Super Computing (Courtesy of Getty Images).

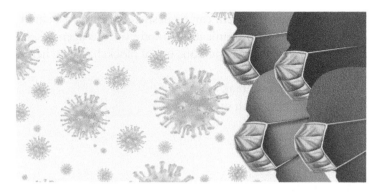

Figure 15.2 Contagious disease and humans.

data can also be avoided using blockchain. The disease related records created by blockchain are immutable, decentralized, deterministic, data integrity and resilient to attacks. The workgroups involved in contagious disease control belong to various independent departments such as hospitals, pathology laboratories, police, municipality, disaster management, etc. The blockchain infrastructure can play a key role in providing coordinated efforts and thus it will eventually help in controlling the epidemic (Figure 15.3).

Preparedness for future epidemic can be of paramount importance. Keeping in mind the past experiences of Spanish Flu, Ebola, Zica, and

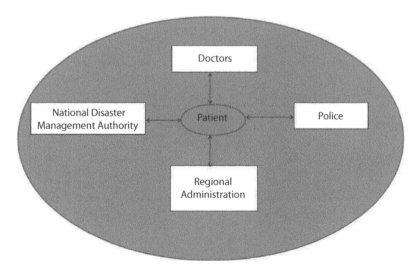

Figure 15.3 Block chain provides a seamless secured information exchange between various stake-holders for controlling contagious disease (Source: Self).

COVID19 virus; a robust system can be designed using blockchain which may help to reduce the communication among various agencies. Hence it can be summarized that the meticulous use of blockchain can help us in:

- Prevention of outbreak
- Early detection of an outbreak
- Faster response
- Effective surveillance.

15.2   Blockchain Genomics

Genomics deals with the information of DNA of an individual. The more accurate information about the DNA can be helpful in better identification of disease at an early stage and it will be helpful in treatment of many diseases. Several diseases which are genetic in nature can be controlled. However, a large amount of data needs to be processed in genome sequencing. Few years back, the cost of genome sequencing was pretty high. However, the advancement in computing has opened new avenues in this area. The block chain technology is giving path-breaking solutions in this domain.

The genome sequencing (Figure 15.4) is of high importance. Since block chain is a digital public ledger and the processing is done on distributed

Figure 15.4 Genome sequencing.

computers. The security of genome data carries risk. The genome sequencing is a computing intensive process. The traditional data storage servers act as a single source of data storage and distribution. If the server fails then the data cannot be used. The distributed computing provides decentralisation of data.

The genome sequencing using blockchain can facilitate the large scale uses in controlling the chronic disease prediction, development of new vaccinations. A large number of companies are involved in lot of research in this area. Since this technology is still in infancy stage and a lot of issues related to storage, transmission and managing such big data imposes a challenge. This technological advancement can be a boon for all the stakeholders such as patients, insurance companies and medical institutions.

A lot of challenges still need to be answered such as unclear ownership of genome sequencing data. Since, the blockchain is a distributed public ledger, so the computing will be done using more than one computer. Since, all the computers are working at a peer level such issue need require further deliberations. Earlier the data was stored by an authorised organisation but if the genome related data is stored on any such central repository, there is risk of data being used without the permission of an individual.

But the traceability and verifiability feature can help in tracing of data. This traceability can be done with the help of timestamp technology. Traceability helps to verify an item's history and location by using identification documents.

15.3   Blockchain Learning

Bitcoin MOOCs and Smart Contract Literacy

In today's era, the technology based learning is very widely accepted by students, teachers and other stake-holders such as parents (Figure 15.5). The use of blockchain will infuse more transparency into the learning landscape. The immutable ledger technology help in tracing what kind of transactions have taken place between the student and the teacher. This will force the student community to be more alert and active. The teacher will also be more concern about teaching quality and pedagogy. The records will be created at every stage. Neither the teacher nor the student can lose any information. Every education system has third party assessment organisations for carrying out the quality audit. Since all the records are online, the quality audit will also be done smoothly.

The student, teacher and university will engage in digital contract about course outcome and programme outcome. Each party will be under obligation to carry out the expected role. There will be immediate benefit to the

Figure 15.5 Smart Learning (Courtesy: Manav Rachna).

learner. The university and teacher can incentivize the student for scoring good grades and for following all the instructions.

Educational records can be maintained in the form of tamper-proof ledgers for long term by making use of block chain technology. The transactions are verifiable and it is a permanent and perfect method of storing educational certificates. The documents are cryptographically signed and open standard for digital signature needs to be followed. The open standard of digital signature is helpful in globally verifiable documents.

Two leading organizations, MIT media lab and Learning Machine, have developed a software named BlockCerts. BlockCerts is using block chain as the underlying technology and is freely available for creating and sharing educational certificates which can be verified online for its authenticity. Another leading organization, SAP, has also introduced block chain based TrueRec software. It is a digital repository and based on Ethereum.

15.4   Community Coin

Community Coin may provide us with a very novel approach of democratizing currency. The community currency works as a peer-to-peer, trust-based currency among a related group. The community currency is limited to a particular geographical location. The peer-to-peer community based currency is not under the direct control of any central agency. The concept of digital currency will empower people to have their own currency and it can be used within the group (Figure 15.6).

The Community Coin empowers the members to transfer money among peer network. There is no limit on the amount to be transferred and no

Figure 15.6 Blockchain-based Bitcoin.

charges in the form of levy are involved. The transfer of funds is instant and the member can spend the currency once received.

Introduction of new community coin can be done with the help of Proof-of-Stake methods to carry out all transactions. The community coin can be used by anyone and the transaction will be recorded in the ledger. The same ledger can be used to check the authenticity of the transaction. The community coin involves the use of online wallet. The wallet has to be online to carry out transaction. Your power comes on the amount of community coins held by you and staking performed by you. The community coin is public in nature and uses open source code. The public and distributed nature of community currency makes it powerful and nobody has authority than anything else.

15.4.1 Monetary and Non-Monetary Currencies

A cryptocurrency is a type of digital asset that works by combining cryptography and digital signature for asset transfers. This combination can be used for peer-to-peer networking and decentralization. In certain scenarios either proof-of-work or proof-of-stake scheme is used to create and manage the currency. It permits electronic money systems to be decentralized. Bitcoin is most popular form of crypto-currency, a peer-to-peer electronic monetary system based on cryptography. The asset class which can be exchanged against cash is known as monetary currency. The monetary asset can be converted in cash, if there is a need. The amount of money lying in any bank account, fixed deposits in any bank and the cash in hand comes under monetary assets. Blockchain-based virtual currency is a type of unregulated digital currency that is only available in electronic form. It is stored and transacted only through designated software, mobile or computer applications, or through dedicated digital wallets, and the transactions occur over the internet through secure, dedicated networks. Virtual currency is considered to be a subset of the digital currency group, which also includes cryptocurrencies, which exist within the blockchain network.

Non-monetary assets comprised of those assets which do not have fixed exchange rate at which a deal can be carried out. The example of non-monetary assets includes the buildings, the physical facilities such as plant and warehouse, etc. In case of non-monetary assets, the rate of selling will depend on various external factors also such as demand in the market for that asset class, the general economy conditional of that particular geographical location. The investment in the share-market instruments such as equity, commodity, gold and silver also varies according to the trajectory of the market (Figures 15.7 and 15.8). The government advisories and the

Figure 15.7 Gold.

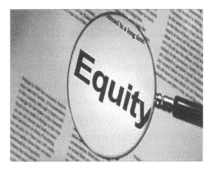

Figure 15.8 Company Shares.

changes in laws many times change the situation drastically. The government can control the above assets by appointing watchdog to ensure interest of the larger groups. Table 15.1 shows difference between monetary assets and non-monetary assets based on various parameters such as effect of demand and supply, cash value, how to liquidate the asset, etc.

15.4.2   Difference Between Monetary and Non-Monetary Assets

Table 15.1 Comparison of Monetary assets and Non-Monetary assets.

S. No.	Monetary Assets	Non-Monetary Assets
1.	Have specific value in cash	No fixed value and value will keep fluctuating over time
2.	Can be easily liquidated and converted to cash	Considered as illiquid
3.	Cash value remains constant	Changes as per time-value of money, this change is relative in nature
4.	Cash value does not change as per demand and supply	Changes according to demand and supply
5.	Comprises of bank balance and amount received from debtors	Property and plant comes under non-monetary assets

15.4.3   Currency Multiplicity

Like in existing economic system, majority of the countries have their own currency and that currency is valid in a certain geographical part of the word such as United States Dollar is used in US, British Pound is used in UK, Indian Rupee is used in India, etc. (Figure 15.9).

The concept of currency multiplicity is widely prevailing in blockchain based cryptocurrency. The cryptocurrency of today's time are known by various names such as bitcoin, litecoin and dogecoin. The blockchain based cryptocurrency are traceable and they can be monetized. The first blockchain based cryptocurrency was launched in 2009. However, with the passage of time, technology has taken a big leap in terms of hardware-development and software have also evolved a lot. This advancement has given rise to lot of new currencies. More than 6000 ALTCOINS (i.e. alternate coins or various variants of cryptocurrencies) exist as on this date and this number is increasing with passage of time.

Figure 15.9 Indian Currency and US Currency.

15.4.4   List of Some Prominent Alternate Coins is Given Below

a.   Ethereum (ETH)
b.   Bitcoin Diamond (BCD)
c.   Ripple (XRP)
d.   Litecoin (LTC)
e.   Tether (USDT)
f.   Bitcoin Cash (BCH)
g.   Libra (LIBRA)
h.   Bitcoin Private (BCP)
i.   Monero (XMR) ...
j.   EOS (EOS)
k.   Factom (FCT)
l.   Fusion (FSN)
m.   Safe Exchange Coin (SAFEX)
n.   Nexus (NXS)
o.   Nano (XRB)
p.   VeChain (VET)
q.   Verge (XVG), etc.

The cryptocurrency based ALTCOINS have revolutionized the world while keeping in mind the business perspective and the purpose of currency. A few concerns still need to be addressed to make it fool-proof and to enhance the confidence of the users. The risks involved are:

a.   There is no central authority. The currency is community and trust based. This very feature gives rise to risk.

b. The transactions in cryptocurrencies are irreversible, after confirmation. If some wrong transaction is done, it can't be reversed.

c. There is no third party for arbitration.

d. In certain part of the world, the cryptocurrencies are not legalized and the user will not be able to approach any authority in such countries.

All the users are recognized with the help of their digital codes. There is no physical identification like Social Security Number, etc. So this anonymity increases risk factor.

15.5   Demurrage Currencies

Demurrage is the cost incurred in owning or holding currency over a given period of time. It is also referred as a carrying cost of money. For commodity money such as gold, demurrage is the cost of storing and securing the gold. For paper currency, there is printing cost involved, it can take the form of a periodic tax, such as a stamp tax, on currency holdings. Demurrage is sometimes cited as economically advantageous, usually in the context of complementary currency systems.

However, the circulation and usage of blockchain based currency can drastically reduce the demurrage. Cryptocurrency don't have any printing cost like cash. Cryptocurrency don't have any storage and procuring cost like gold and silver. Hence, it can be summarised that implementing cyrptocurrency will increase the printing, transferring and storage cost of currency. It can be used with a great ease and will benefit the society in a big way.

Reading List

1. Walid, A. and Nicolas, S., Blockchain technology for social impact: Opportunities and challenges ahead. *Journal of cyber policy*, 2, 3, 338–354, 2017. Available: https://www.tandfonline.com/toc/rcyb20/2/3.

2. Supriya, T. and Vrushali, K., Blockchain and Its Applications—A Detailed Survey. *Int. J. Comput. Appl.*, 16, 6, 20–24, 2017. Available: https://www.ijcaonline.org/archives/volume180/number3/aras-2017-ijca-915994.pdf.

3. Ketki, R. and Sheetal, Y., Blockchain Technology in Cloud Computing: A Systematic Review. *Int. Res. J. Eng. Technol.*, 5, 4, 1918–1921, 2018. Available: https://www.irjet.net/archives/V5/i4/IRJETV5I4428.pdf.

4. Peters, G.W., Panayi, E., Chapelle, A., Trends in crypto-currencies and blockchain technologies: A monetary theory and regulation perspective, [Online] *SSRN Electronic Journal*, 2015, 1–25, 2015. Available: http://dx.doi.org/10.2139/ssrn.

5. Kosba, A., Miller, A., Shi, E., Wen, Z., Papamanthou, C., Hawk: The blockchain model of cryptography and privacy-preserving smart contracts, in: *Proceedings of IEEE Symposium on Security and Privacy (SP)*, San Jose, CA, USA, pp. 839–858, 2016.

6. Sharples, M. and Domingue, J., The blockchain and kudos: A distributed system for educational record, reputation and reward, in: *Proceedings of 11th European Conference on Technology Enhanced Learning (EC-TEL 2015)*, Lyon, France, pp. 490–496, 2015.

7. Tschorsch, F. and Scheuermann, B., Bitcoin and beyond: A technical survey on decentralized digital currencies. *IEEE Commun. Surv. Tut.*, 18, 3, 2084–2123, 2016.

Index

Printed and bound by CPI Group (UK) Ltd, Croydon, CR0 4YY

27/10/2024

14580467-0003